D1255660

This book places culture center-stage in the investigation of the transformation of Rome from Republic to Empire. It is the first book to attempt to understand the so-called Roman Revolution as a cultural phenomenon. Instead of regarding cultural changes as dependent on political developments, the essays consider literary, artistic, and political changes as manifestations of a basic transformation of Roman culture. In Part I the international group of contributors discusses the changes in the cultural systems under the topics of authority, gender and sexuality, status, and space in the city of Rome, and in Part II through specific texts and artifacts as they refract social, political, and economic changes. The essays draw on the latest methods in literary and cultural work to make a holistic approach to the Augustan Cultural Revolution.

The Roman Cultural Revolution

The Roman Cultural Revolution

Edited by

Thomas Habinek

Professor of Classics, University of Southern California

Alessandro Schiesaro

Professor of Latin, King's College London

CAMBRIDGE
UNIVERSITY PRESS

PUBLISHED BY THE PRESS SYNDICATE OF THE UNIVERSITY OF CAMBRIDGE
The Pitt Building, Trumpington Street, Cambridge CB2 1RP, United Kingdom

CAMBRIDGE UNIVERSITY PRESS
The Edinburgh Building, Cambridge CB2 2RU, United Kingdom
40 West 20th Street, New York, NY 10011–4211, USA
20 Stamford Road, Oakleigh, Melbourne 3166, Australia

First published 1997

Printed in the United Kingdom at the University Press, Cambridge

Typeset in Times 10/12pt, in QuarkXPress™ [GC]

A catalogue record for this book is available from the British Library

Library of Congress cataloguing in publication data

The Roman Cultural Revolution / edited by Thomas Habinek, Alessandro
  Schiesaro.
      p.   cm.
   Includes bibliographical references.
   ISBN 0 521 58092 7 (hardback)
      1. Rome – Civilization.   2. Rome – History – Augustus, 30 BCE–14 CE
   I. Habinek, Thomas N.   II. Schiesaro, Alessandro.
   DG279.R618   1997
   937′.07 – dc21
                                                      97–49925
                                                        CIP

ISBN 0 521 58092 7 hardback

Contents

Illustrations

Contributors

W. MARTIN BLOOMER is Assistant Professor of Classics at Stanford University. He is the author of *Valerius Maximus and the Rhetoric of the New Nobility* (Chapel Hill 1992) and *The Roman Literary Economy* (Philadelphia 1997).

FLORENCE DUPONT is author of numerous studies of Roman literature and society including *L'acteur-roi* (Paris 1985), *Le théâtre latin* (Paris 1988), and *Le citoyen romain sous la republique* (Paris 1994). She is Professeur at the Université de Nancy II and membre du Centre Louis Gernet.

ELAINE FANTHAM, Geiger Professor of Latin Literature at Princeton University, has written extensively on Latin literature and Roman cultural history. She is co-editor with Helene Foley and Natalie Kampen of *Women in the Classical World* (Oxford 1994) and author of *Lucan* Pharsalia *Book 2* (Cambridge Greek and Latin Texts 1992).

ANDREW FELDHERR teaches at Princeton University. He has just completed a book entitled *Spectacle and Society in Livy's History* (Berkeley 1998).

THOMAS HABINEK, Professor of Classics at the University of Southern California, is the author of *The Colometry of Latin Prose* (Berkeley 1985) and *The Politics of Latin Literature* (forthcoming, Princeton University Press). He was for many years chair of the editorial board of the journal *Classical Antiquity*.

PHILIP HARDIE is Lecturer in Classics at the University of Cambridge and a Fellow of New Hall. His recent publications include *The Epic Successors of Virgil: A Study in the Dynamics of a Tradition* (Cambridge 1993) and *Virgil* Aeneid *Book IX* (Cambridge Greek and Latin Classics 1994). He is currently working on Ovid and on a study of *Fama*.

BARBARA KELLUM, Associate Professor of Art History at Smith College, Northampton, Mass., studies the art and monuments of Augustan Rome. Her recent publications include "The Phallus as Signifier: The Forum of

Augustus and Rituals of Masculinity" in *Sexuality in Ancient Art*, edited by Natalie Kampen (New York 1995).

ELEANOR WINSOR LEACH is Professor of Classical Studies at Indiana University. She is the author of *Vergil's Eclogues: Landscapes of Experience* (Cornell University Press 1974) and *The Rhetoric of Space: Representations of Landscape in Republican and Augustan Rome* (Princeton 1988) as well as numerous articles in the fields of Roman literature and Roman painting. Her current projects include a book entitled *Roman Painting and Roman Society* and a biographical essay on the archaeologist Mary Hamilton Swindler.

ELLEN OLIENSIS is assistant professor of Classics at Yale University. Her first book on *Horace and the Rhetoric of Authority*, is forthcoming with Cambridge University Press.

ALESSANDRO SCHIESARO is Professor of Latin at King's College London. His extensive writings on didactic poetry and prose include *Simulacrum et imago: gli argomenti analogici nel* De rerum natura (Pisa 1990). He is currently completing a monograph on Seneca's *Thyestes*.

ANDREW WALLACE-HADRILL is Professor of Classics at the University of Reading and Director of the British School in Rome. He is the author of, among other works, *Suetonius: The Scholar and his Caesars* (New Haven 1984) and *Houses and Society in Pompeii and Herculaneum* (Princeton 1994).

Acknowledgments

We would like to express our gratitude to the individuals and institutions that made this volume possible. The Department of Classics at Princeton University, through its Magie Fund, and the Council for the Humanities, also at Princeton, were generous sponsors of the conference at which the essays contained here were orginally presented. The Department of Classics at the University of Southern California provided crucial resources for the preparation of the final version of the manuscript. Besides the contributors, the following individuals provided support and encouragement at various stages from the planning of the conference through the preparation of the final manuscript: Paul Alpers, Carlin Barton, Ted Champlin, Thomas Cole, Don Fowler, Mark Griffith, Natalie Kampen, André Lardinois, Georgia Nugent, Josh Ober, and Richard Saller. We are also grateful to the many faculty and students who attended the conference at Princeton, to Claire Campbell and Peter O'Neill for help with the bibliography, and to Pauline Hire of Cambridge University Press for her encouragement, patience, and good advice.

Introduction

Thomas Habinek and Alessandro Schiesaro

The transition from Republic to Principate at Rome has been described as a revolution at least since the publication of Mommsen's *History of Rome* in 1863. For Mommsen, Roman history from the time of the Gracchi onward consisted of a revolution in stages, one involving continual struggle between the senatorial aristocracy and other elements of the Roman elite and culminating in the dictatorship of Julius Caesar. In this century, Ronald Syme applied the term to a narrower period of time, the years 60 BCE to 14 CE, and placed special emphasis on the conflicts that followed the death of Julius Caesar and led to the institutionalization of the principate under Augustus. For Syme, this period of Roman history constituted a revolution because of the significance of the political changes that transpired and because of the violent means through which those changes were effected. In describing the revolutionary changes that transformed Roman society, Syme focused on changes in personnel within the Roman elite, especially the replacement of the old Roman aristocracy by new men of Italian origin.

From a Marxist standpoint, the Roman Revolution was nothing of the sort, since both before and after the rise of Julius and then Augustus Caesar, the Roman economy was still agrarian in orientation and dependent on slave labor. The idea that cultural change might qualify the period in question as a revolution would be anathema to traditional Marxism, as it would, interestingly enough, to a non-Marxist historian like Syme. For Marx, culture is part of the superstructure in a society, and thus dependent upon and secondary to changes in the economic base or infrastructure. Culture can reflect transformations in the base and may be used as a weapon in class struggle, but change in culture cannot in and of itself constitute revolution. While Syme's revolution bears only superficial resemblance to Marxist class struggle, Syme nonetheless shares the view of culture as secondary to more basic shifts in power, in his case, shifts in the personnel and structures of state authority. As he expressed it in *The Augustan Aristocracy*, Augustus and his allies had won the civil war and it was left to the educated class to "devise formulations of acceptance" (1986:441). In this respect, Syme's work makes assumptions about the secondary importance of literature and art comparable to those made by the many specialist scholars who have interpreted the politics of texts and artifacts exclusively in terms of their alleged preference for or against Augustanism.

The present collection of essays, as its title suggests, seeks to place culture front and center in the study of the Roman Revolution. Participants in the conference from which this volume was distilled were invited to consider the expression "The Roman Cultural Revolution" as referring either to the Roman Revolution as a cultural phenomenon or to the methodological changes in Roman studies required by a more holistic approach to culture. On both counts, the project runs contrary to still-prevailing tendencies in the study of ancient history, literature, and art which tend to isolate each from the other and to subordinate the latter two to a relatively narrow version of the former. In insisting on the centrality of culture, both as an explanatory phenomenon and as an analytical category, we hoped to foster within Roman studies something of the spirit of cross-disciplinary exchange that has become familiar in Renaissance studies since the advent of the new historicism and, more recently, in the study of archaic Greece, with the publication of major work explicitly identifying itself as "cultural poetics." While none of our contributors has been asked to take an oath of allegiance to a particular method or school of thought, it seems fair to say that all are committed to crossing the boundaries between culture and politics or culture and economics that have defined the limits of their respective sub-disciplines of classical studies. Culture here is regarded neither as superstructure, entirely dependent for its shape and direction on an economic base, nor as independent aesthetic activity, isolated from the cross-currents of the broader society. Rather culture is understood to consist of the sum total of practices and beliefs that differentiate one people from another. This concept, it should be noted, is closely akin to what the Romans called *mores*, as Andrew Wallace-Hadrill observes in his opening discussion of the Romans' own description of the end of the Republic as *mutatio morum*, that is to say, cultural revolution.

The essays in this collection have been divided into two sections on the basis of their rhetorical aims. Essays in the first section, entitled "Transformation of Cultural Systems," seek to replace the traditional narrative of the Roman revolution with one emphasizing cultural change; essays in the second section, "Texts and Contexts," examine specific instances of elite cultural production as they refract the social, political, and economic changes of the era. In the first section, the areas of change analyzed are authority, sexuality, and space. Authority is the broadest of the three categories and potentially encompasses the other two as well. As Stephen Greenblatt has noted in discussing "culture" as a term for literary study, culture, when used in the broad sense employed here, is both enabling and constraining: enabling in the sense that it makes possible the production of meaning within a given community, and constraining in that it defines limits beyond which a person, activity, or belief is marginalized or even excluded from the community in question. Wallace-Hadrill analyzes the reorganization of authority in the early Principate as it pertains to the management of time, tradition, language, and law; but as succeeding essays by Thomas Habinek and Florence Dupont indicate, other topics, such as sexual conduct and the use of space can be assimilated to his account as well. For Wallace-Hadrill, if a single definition of the Roman Revolution had to be assigned, it would consist of the reclamation by Julius and especially Augustus Caesar of the authority previously yielded by the Roman *nobiles* to experts and expert discourses. The early Caesars recognized the need for such expertise in the management of the Roman empire and successfully harnessed it to the aims of centralized state authority. Yet as Habinek and Dupont argue, the cultural revolution, that is to say the reorganization of authority, was not entirely a one-way street, since sectors of the population other than those immediately surrounding the emperor had a role in the remapping of the social and symbolic space of Roman culture. Habinek's focus is on the poets of the period, especially Ovid, as they express but also promulgate a transformed interpretation of the erotic to correspond to the material transformations of the era, while Dupont describes the gradual development of the institution of *recitatio* as the creative response of displaced aristocrats to the loss of political oratory as an arena for the acquisition of glory.

While the essays in Part One examine the process of cultural change as reconstructed from surviving texts and artifacts, essays in Part Two shift the focus and instead consider specific texts and artifacts as they refract aspects of the cultural transformations of the period. For the majority of the essays, the aspects of cultural change viewed through the lens of elite cultural productions correspond to those presented in Part One, namely authority, sexuality, and space. Thus Alessandro Schiesaro examines the protocols of knowledge advanced by Vergil in the *Georgics*, protocols that closely ally the georgic poet with the *princeps'* interpretation of the right relationship between technical expertise and the social good, while Barbara Kellum's essay on the gendering of Augustan monuments touches on issues raised by both Habinek and Dupont, and Eleanor Leach's study of Horace's representation of material Rome in his *Odes* considers both the expertise of the poet as a sub-category of authority as analyzed by Wallace-Hadrill and the city of Rome as a symbolic space with cultural significance comparable to that assigned by Dupont to the Roman forum.

At the same time, papers by Ellen Oliensis, Andrew Feldherr, and Martin Bloomer, which consist of local analyses of Horace's *Satires*, Livy's *Histories*, and Seneca the Elder's *Controversiae* and *Suasoriae* respectively, call attention to a further feature of the Cultural Revolution not addressed in Part One, namely the phenomenon of "status anxiety." In a society organized around overlapping and sometimes conflicting status hierarchies of gender, citizenship, wealth, lineage, and expertise, status anxiety is perhaps always present as at least a potential source of psychic and discursive disruption. During the years in question, however, the rigidification of Rome's status structure through the emperor's articulation of the *ordines*, together with the widening of the pool of potential players in the high-stakes game of power politics through expansion of the franchise, broadening of membership in the Senate, and emphasis on "all of Italy" as unifying symbol, seem to have generated acute outbreaks of an always-latent condition. The papers on status anxiety thus serve a double function of adding yet another item to the list of Roman *mores* transformed, or at least severely problematized, by the revolution and of exploring individual writers' use of literary production as a means of negotiating their own status in a period of both anxiety and opportunity.

Ellen Oliensis identifies Horace's status anxiety at least in part through silences in book two of his satires: silences that contrast sharply with the poet's personal assertiveness in book one. In so arguing, she calls attention to an important aspect of current strategies of reading, which require attention as much to what a linguistic structure avoids conveying as to what it articulates. In the interest of truth-in-advertising, it behooves us as editors to alert the reader to what our simple bipartite arrangement of essays in this collection obscures or erases, and that is the rather different strategies for integrating culture and society employed by our contributors and the correspondingly different assumptions about artistic and cultural autonomy implied by each.

At one end of the spectrum, perhaps the most deterministic interpreter is Habinek, whose paper takes its start from Milligan's characterization of sexuality as an "entirely responsive ideology." In Milligan's view, sexuality in the modern world is determined by broader economic and social conditions which it in turn helps to sustain. Habinek's argument, linking the emergence of sexuality in Roman culture to the development of Rome as a world-city follows a similar pattern of exposition, and his conclusion, that the refashioning of the sexual subject that took place between Catullus and Ovid offered psychic recompense for the dislocations of the revolution while preparing the way for the reproduction of the social order through the institutions of heterosexuality, privacy, and state-sanctioned pleasures, has a decidedly Althusserian ring to it. At the other end of the spectrum, Philip Hardie, in a paper on the fifteenth book of Ovid's *Metamorphoses*, comes close to claiming that it is Ovid, not Augustus, who invented the principate. As Hardie notes, the principate cannot be said to exist until power has been transmitted across time, to a second and additional generations. It is poetry in general, and specifically Ovid's poetry, with its ability to situate the history of Rome and of Augustus in an all-encompassing cosmic narrative, that serves as an ideological enabler of such a transition. As Hardie puts it, "Ovid's final triumph is to reverse the expected dependence of poet on *princeps* ... In an ineluctable collusion between artist and ruler we finally see the prince of poets foist on his master a poetics of principate." And yet despite the differences in outlook between Habinek and Hardie, each makes important gestures in the direction of the others' concerns: in Hardie's case the phrase "ineluctable collusion" signals an awareness of the poet's embeddedness in his social and political context, while Habinek's discussion of the invention of sexuality expressly acknowledges its ability to produce new knowledge about the human subject and new channels for the application of power.

Elaine Fantham and Martin Bloomer also argue from silences and omissions in the literary texts, and their discussions lead in alternative, although not necessarily incompatible directions as well. For Fantham, Propertius' silence about the new city of Rome seems to bespeak a lack of conviction on the part of the ostensibly patriotic poet of the fourth book of the elegies. In Bloomer's reading of the prefaces to Seneca's *Controversiae* and *Suasoriae*, silence about the past of republican oratory, specifically about Cicero, makes possible declamation's claim to cultural validity. Propertius' silence would thus seem to constitute a strategy of resistance, while Seneca's inclines decidedly in the direction of repression. The contrast between the two essays is not simply between a backward-looking Propertius and a forward-looking Seneca, but also between readings that assume in one case a degree of distance between the poet and his context and in the other an engagement of the writer with his context through his writing. Bloomer finds in Seneca's promotion of declamation and declaimers a concrete example of Duncan Kennedy's observation that "politics are thus inscribed in language-in-use as part of its meaning, and create their effects partly by their ability to conceal their presence" (1992:41). For Fantham the meaning of Propertius' poetry is to be constructed by reference to his *representation* of the city around him. For Bloomer the significance of Seneca the Elder's prose treatises consists in their *intervention* in their political and social context.

Finally an interesting contrast in conceptualizations of culture becomes apparent in the essays by Schiesaro and Kellum. Schiesaro carefully explains the ideological implications of his nuanced reading of the *Georgics* within the Roman traditions of didactic writing (specifically Lucretius and Cicero), yet for all that his Virgil appears much more enmeshed in literary than in cultural intertexts. Is Schiesaro's privileging of the literary/formalistic a necessary move in the interpretation of ancient literature or an evasion of the thorny cultural and political implications of his own argument? Kellum, on the other hand, sees the "meaning" of Augustan monuments as emerging not simply from their formal interrelationship with previous styles and types, but from their evocation of the human body, their use as sites for rituals of power and manhood, and the reactions they prompted in ancient and later observers. Is her more overtly political reading of the monuments made possible, even necessary by the fact that they were visible to a wider cross-section of the Roman population than the text of the *Georgics* seems likely to have been? Or has she implicitly accepted a more totalizing view of culture than have Schiesaro and some of the other contributors to the collection? And yet – to reverse the direction of implied critique – what are we to make of her repeated references to significative "play" in her discussion of the gendering of Augustan Rome? Does the playfulness of Augustan culture undermine or reinforce the structures of domination and exploitation? Is it the wickedly clever artist who creates an elaborate and scatological visual pun on the opening line of the *Aeneid*, or the poet Virgil himself, with his excrutiatingly nuanced negotiation of traditional vs. modern protocols of knowing, who stakes a more powerful claim to personal and political autonomy?

If in a broad sense the essays in this volume seek to revise Syme's privileging of politics over culture, they can also be differentiated from more recent studies that for all their emphasis on an integrated approach to culture, nonetheless treat it as derivative of and secondary to political power. For example, Paul Zanker, whose work *The Power of Images in Augustan Rome* has received well-deserved attention for its integration of art and literature and for its description of the system of visual arts that characterizes Augustan Rome, still describes art and poetry as "in the service of power." Indeed, his discussion of private life, taste, and "Mentalität" consists of one chapter surrounded by eight on public art and political propaganda. Karl Galinsky's *Augustan Culture* (Princeton 1996) – so recent that the contributors to this volume have not been able to take advantage of it – is in some ways more compatible with the approaches adopted here. He, like Wallace-Hadrill, uses "authority" as a unifying concept for understanding the transformation of Roman society during the age of Augustus. And like most of the contributors to this volume, his discussion of Latin literature of the period considers its role in the development and circulation of what he calls Augustan "ideas, ideals, and values." But in contrast to Wallace-Hadrill, who considers the ways in which broad prior changes in the nature and typology of authority prompted Augustus' reorganization of political structures, Galinsky focuses on Augustus' conceptualization of his own *auctoritas*. And in contrast to the various contributors to this volume who trace literature and art's involvement in the creation of new cultural practices, Galinsky reads them as manifestations of new ideals. In other words, where he relies on the traditional humanistic notion of culture as a set of products, we seek to make use of a social scientific framework in which culture is understood as a dynamic process consisting of various intersecting practices and discourses. Perhaps closest in spirit to the present collection is Claude

Nicolet's study, *Space, Geography, and Politics in the Early Roman Empire* which shows how a specific practice – governance across long distances – both shapes and is shaped by other practices and discourses, such as the triumph, cartography, ethnography, and administrative procedures. While the issues explored here differ (even the essays on space consider the space of the city as opposed to the space of the empire), the interpretation of culture as an ongoing negotiation of practical necessities, inherited forms, and competing interests underwrites both his work and our own.

To the question, was there a Roman Cultural Revolution, the essays in this collection answer a resounding yes. More than that, they contend that the revolution was itself a cultural phenomenon. The political changes that concerned Mommsen and Syme did not in and of themselves generate the cultural changes; rather they were expressions of the same transformation of structures of authority that manifested themselves in countless other aspects of Roman life. The revolution was felt not simply as a change of political institutions and procedures and the disappearance of a significant sector of the elite, important and painful as those developments were. It was also felt in the daily acquiescence in the authority of experts, in the structuring of time by a new calendar, in the new organization of erotic sensations, in the psychic and symbolic reorientation necessitated by the physical transformations of the city of Rome. The Roman Cultural Revolution was, as Fredric Jameson has said of all cultural revolution, a "moment of truth," – indeed more than that, a moment when the very procedures for determining and constructing truth underwent radical transformation. Who produced the revolution, how did different sectors and interests impose or negotiate new shares of power for themselves, what role did literary texts and visual images play, individually and collectively, in what Kennedy has called the "mobilisation of meaning" to the advantage of one sector or another: these are questions which the individual contributors address to differing degrees and from differing vantage points. Together, however, in their commitment to analysis that cuts across the usual divides between culture and politics, form and history, literature and society, they bear witness to a distinctive "moment of truth" in the continuing evolution of Roman studies.

I

The transformation of cultural systems

I   *Mutatio morum*: the idea of a cultural
    revolution

Andrew Wallace-Hadrill

Cultural revolution?

The title of this collection, *The Roman Cultural Revolution*, is a challenge,
and a double one. Even to speak, in a way that in the English language must
inevitably evoke Syme, but which has its context in a far broader debate, of
a "Roman Revolution," raises epistemological disquiets. The transformations
of the Roman world at the turn of the era keep odd company with those of
eighteenth-century America or France, let alone those of early twentieth-
century Russia. To add the word "cultural" gives an already controversial
expression a very particular spin, with inescapable shades of Mao's China. It
makes it the more urgent to grasp the nettle at the outset and ask what might
be at stake in talking about a Roman cultural revolution.

No doubt linguistic usage entitles us to speak quite blandly of a "Roman
Revolution," on analogy with the "Glorious Revolution" of 1688, in the sense
of an abrupt political caesura, without any overtones of a broader social revolution, let alone the implication of a class struggle, conceived in Marxist terms
or not.[1] From opposite angles, historians have repudiated the expression,
whether because they deny that Marxist class concept is applicable to Roman
society,[2] or because it seems perverse to call an oligarchic coup that shored
up the dominance of a landowning class anything other than a *rivoluzione
mancata*.[3]

There is a minimalist case that the ancients themselves had a well-articulated
concept of revolution, from Plato and Aristotle to Polybius, into which the
Roman civil wars, resulting in sharp changes in political structures, linked to
major redistributions of land and extensive judicial murders of the landowners,
surely fit.[4] More powerful is Mommsen's vision of the fall of the Republic,
from the Gracchi onwards, as a slow process of revolution which results not
in a pure autocracy, but one permanently tempered in theory and practice by

---

[1] So Brunt (1988), 9–10; but North (1989) for the case for avoiding the term. Heuss (1982) is
a useful roundup of opposing positions.
[2] So e.g. K. Christ in Heuss (1982), 16.   [3] So F. De Martino in Heuss (1982), 20–31.
[4] Heuss (1956).

revolution. It is a vision to which the representation of Mommsen's position as a straightforward law-bound constitutionalism does less than justice.[5]

But Syme's "Roman Revolution" is something more provocative. The title is a masterpiece of irony and paradox: its cutting wit is too easily lost in solemn theoretical discussion. Were we to follow a classic Aristotelian definition of *metabole* as the displacement of one constitution by another, there is no doubt that Augustus' replacement of what in Greek terms could be described as *demokratia* by *monarchia* should qualify as a major "revolution". But one central thrust of Syme's book is precisely to deny this revolution. Call the constitutions by what names one will, the political realities remain unchanged: "In all ages, whatever the form and name of government, be it monarchy, republic, or democracy, an oligarchy lurks beneath the façade" (Syme 1939: 7). Here then is the irony of the title: since the reality is merely that one oligarchy has replaced another, there is no revolution, only a coup. Yet this irony is overlaid with paradox: having denied one revolution (of a classical and un-Marxist type), Syme replaces it with another, far more reminiscent of class-struggle. "In the Revolution [note the use of the capital letter] the power of the old governing class [N.B.] was broken, its composition transformed. Italy and the non-political orders in society triumphed over Rome and the Roman aristocracy" (Syme 1939:8). Syme wishes to replace the stale discourse of constitutional change with a more radical one of social revolution, of the triumph of peripheries over the centre, of the doom of a nobility and the rise of new men and colonial elites, and his title has the effect of drawing attention to the paradox.

Not only is Syme's Revolution explicitly a social one; it is also implicitly a cultural one. Two chapters (XXIX, "The national programme", and XXX, "The organization of opinion") spell out the theme of the book's title more overtly than any other. The character of the social revolution envisaged is recapitulated forcibly:

It was not Rome alone but Italy, perhaps Italy more than Rome, that prevailed in the War of Actium. The Principate itself may, in a certain sense, be regarded as a triumph of Italy over Rome . . .
The Italian bourgeoisie had their sweet revenge when the New State was erected at the expense of the *nobiles*, as a result of their feuds and their follies.
That will not suffice to prove that the Princeps was merely a docile instrument in the hands of an uncompromising party of puritan nationalists. Augustus himself came of a municipal family. (p. 453)

Having characterised the opposition between the old regime and the new as one of class – Augustus is not only the leader of an Italian bourgeoisie,

---

[5] Mommsen (1887:II, 1133): "nicht bloß praktisch, sondern auch theoretisch eine durch die rechlich permanente Revolution temperirte Autokratie"; cf. Heuss (1973:65): "Das Kaisertum hat seine revoluzionären Wurzeln nie abzuschneiden gewuß . . . Im römischen Kaisertum war jedoch der Kaiser die Revolution selbst."

but himself a member of it, despite his birth on the Palatine and his Praetorian father, let alone his ties of blood and adoption to the patrician Julii – , Syme sets about constructing an "Italian" and "bourgeois" ideology and culture in contrast to that of the Roman nobility.

> The same men who had won the wars of the Revolution now controlled the destinies of the New State – but different "mores" needed to be professed and inculcated, if not adopted. It is not enough to acquire power and wealth: men wish to appear virtuous and to feel virtuous. (p. 440)

It is this new municipal puritanism, more significant in profession than in practice, that is seen to underlie the Augustan moral legislation, one supposedly at variance with the professions as much as the practice of the traditional aristocracy:

> The Roman aristocracy, avidly grasping the spoils of conquest, wealth, luxury and power, new tastes and new ideas, had discarded without repining the rugged ancestral virtues. (p. 453)

The next chapter recruits the writers and artists as moral spokesmen of the new dominant bourgoisie. There is no difficulty, of course, in seeing Livy or the Augustan poets as Italians, nor of underlining the importance of the theme of Italy in their works (the artists are rather harder to bring into this frame, since we know nothing of their origins, though Vitruvius, oddly enough, is used less than he might be as the voice of a *consuetudo Italica*).

   Syme's vision of a cultural revolution consisting in the displacement of a Roman aristocratic ideology by an Italian municipal one seems to me in several crucial respects flawed. We may leave aside the misleading use of the term "bourgeoisie", which smuggles in assumptions of a class with a different socio-economic base from that of the Roman landowning nobility which Syme surely never intended in earnest.[6] The assumption that "Italy", the national unity of which even today is undercut by a fierce sense of regional diversity, had already by Augustus' day achieved a cultural and ideological coherence in contrast to that of Rome, is premature. The process by which some measure of cultural homogeneity emerges in the cities of Italy is a complex one still much in need of study;[7] such unity as emerges can scarcely be explained except in the context of the dominating influence of Rome itself. A pre-existing "Italian" ideology should not be taken for granted. The contrasts of metropolitan aristocratic with Italian municipal morality are retrojections

---

[6] Syme (1939:457, n.2), repeating the expression "Italian bougeoisie" indicates by a reference to Rostovtzeff, albeit critical, the origin of this expression; but, e.g. at p.451, he makes clear that the economic base of the class he is speaking of was landed property. It is further enshrined in the title of the collection *Les bourgeoisies municipales italiennes*, which contains much discussion of relevance to the question.

[7] The valuable studies in Zanker (1976) now require a sequel.

from Tacitus and Pliny; the belief that the municipal new men did, and the Roman nobles did not, subscribe to *antiqua parsimonia*, is a sentimental reconstruction of the past.

The aim of this chapter, however, is not to pick holes in Syme, but to explore the idea of the cultural revolution. The important point to make is not that Syme's cultural revolution is as open to question as his social revolution, but that even for Syme a credible revolution must extend beyond the political and social sphere into questions of ideology and culture. What conditions would we expect to be fulfilled in order to speak of such a revolution? That there was marked and rapid cultural change throughout the period of the couple of centuries of the turn of the era, all would, I take it, agree. But if we want to call it a revolution, and to align it with the periodicity of political revolution, we will have to argue for some sort of overarching coherence: a transformation from one cultural *system* to another, in each of which the political component intermeshes intimately with the rest of culture. One is looking, in a word, with Foucault, for a sort of shift in discourses, from one way of knowing things (one "epistemological system") to another.

There are many grounds for scepticism. Too much change, it could be urged, occurs in this period, too disparate in nature to be lumped together except arbitrarily as a single revolution. Any attempt to construct great systemic shifts in the fashion of *The Order of Things* and even of *Discipline and Punish*, must provoke a certain scepticism in anyone reared on traditions of British empiricism.[8]

Nevertheless, the argument of this chapter is just that. It seeks to explore the possibility that the political and social revolutions of the first century BCE, such as they were, involved a parallel revolution in ways of knowing. I do not wish to assign causal priority to either side. It is no more helpful to suggest that cultural change *caused* social and political change than that it is merely a second-order reflection of more fundamental changes. It is more a matter of our understanding of how the pieces fit together. Just as the political changes implicit in Augustus' transformation of the republic can be seen in a different light when put, as by Syme, in the context of changes of the social composition of the ruling class, so both these transformations emerge in a different light when set in the context of changes in the cultural arena.

In the following pages, as a first step towards a picture of a cultural revolution, I shall start by looking at the Roman construction of the crisis of the late Republic as a moral one. If the Roman category of *mores* only partially

---

[8] Foucault (1970) and (1977). See e.g. Patricia O'Brien in Hunt (1989) for the central part of Foucault in contemporary cultural history; Cameron (1986) on the challenge to the ancient historian in using him.

overlaps with our category of culture, it offers at least a parallel for the attempt to encompass explanations of political crisis in a broader context. I shall then move my focus from morality to a rather different area, of shifting locations of authority. Authority is a better test of cultural revolution than power. That power is restructured and exercised in different ways under Augustus is obvious. What makes the Augustan restoration revolutionary is that it involves a fundamental relocation and redefinition of authority in Roman society. By focusing on authority, it may be possible to grasp something of the links between the refashioning of political authority on the one hand, and the refashioning of moral, social and cultural authority on the other, which together I see as constituting a cultural revolution.

Culture and mores

Not the least difficulty in the attempt to identify cultural revolution is the confusion both in definition and in theoretical underpinnings that surrounds the term "culture." For all the vogue for a "New Cultural History", and the homage paid to figures like Foucault and Geertz, the limits of "the cultural" remain obscure and contested.[9] Moreover, a difficulty for the historian studying past societies must be that this category is so clearly a modern one, closely associated with historically contingent conditions: the rise of the European nation state and the perceived role of "culture" in procuring unification, at least for the ruling class;[10] the nineteenth-century construction of class divisions, in which "culture" is at first constructed as a defining feature of the upper class, and then is appropriated for the counter-culture of a working class;[11] and the role of ethnography and social anthropology in plotting the societies of the Third World onto the cognitive map of the colonial and post-colonial West, so creating an alternative conception of culture to identify an alternative model of society.[12]

It may therefore help to start by asking what in Roman thought could conceivably correspond to our proposed construction of a "cultural revolution," not because one should or can only think about antiquity in its own conceptual framework, but because the ancients' own construction of their experience is

---

[9] For attempts to establish the arena of cultural history, see Hunt (1989); Dirks, Eley and Ortner (1994).

[10] On culture and nationalism, see e.g. Gellner (1983), Pounds (1994); valuable insights into the connection of the idea of *Kultur* with German national consciousness are offered by Elias (1978), 3–50.

[11] See esp. Williams (1958) and (1982). Classics in the appropriation of the term to "popular" or "working-class" culture include Hoggart (1957) and Thompson (1963).

[12] The new sense of "culture" as as whole way of life that defines a society goes back to Edwin Tylor; for awareness of the subjectivity of cultural anthropology, see e.g. Clifford and Marcus (1986), Geertz (1988), Boon (1982).

a primary object of our study. There is no single Roman notion equivalent to that of "culture." Even the Greek *paideia* only covers part of "culture" (it would by its very definition exclude the culture or *ēthē* of a barbarian tribe); and it in turn has no Roman equivalent. *Disciplina* (or *studia*) in the sense of literary education and learning, and *humanitas* (the combination of education and the humane behaviour of a civilized man) cover various aspects, but even the latter, which has the widest semantic field, has very different connotations.[13]

The implications of the lexical gulf between Greek and Latin are revealing. It is not just a matter of chance that no single Latin word for culture emerges, for *paideia* is a core value of Greek culture which defines "Hellenism" (*hellenismos*) in contrast to barbarism. *Humanitas* implicitly denies the Greek claim to a monopoly of good education and civilised behaviour. It also leaves adequate space for the core Roman concept of *mores*, and the construction of Roman *mores* as in fundamental opposition to mere Greek *paideia*.

In the preface to the *Tusculan Disputations*, Cicero declares the natural superiority of Roman culture to Greek.[14] There his demonstration depends on the distinction of what is natural and what is learned. In *mores* and *instituta vitae*, domestic and political, our ancestors, for Cicero, self-evidently did better – who can beat them for *gravitas, constantia, magnitudo animi* and so on? But these depend on *natura*. Only in *doctrina* were they beaten, and that is because they were not trying. (For the casual Roman concession of this inferiority, we can compare the example of metonymy of the *Ad Herennium*: Italy cannot be beaten in arms, nor Greece in learning.)[15] Learning emerges as a social phenomenon. The crucial element is social respect, *honor*: at those times and to that extent that any discipline has enjoyed respect at Rome, it has flourished, and the Greeks have been beaten.

Cicero's scheme sets up a distinction between aspects of culture that are conceived as external and internal. Literary pursuits are seen as "external", not naturally part of Roman life, even if they can be learned and passed on. Morals and ways of life are seen as internal, "natural", a part that is of the Roman character that is passed from generation to generation, almost genetically. What Cicero falls short of admitting is that the *mores* and social institutions in which Romans excel are products of the same structures of *honor*. His nature/culture antithesis sets *disciplina/paideia* against *mores* where we would put them together.

That means that the Roman picture of cultural change (in our terms) goes in two separate directions. The transformation of Roman structures of knowledge

---

[13] Ferrary (1988) 505–17 discusses the overlap (and lack of it) between the Greek terms *philhellēn* and *paideia* and the Latin *humanitas*.

[14] For a discussion, see Harder (1952).

[15] *Ad Her.* 4.43: *armis Italia non potest vinci nec Graecia disciplinis.*

through *paideia* passes with remarkably little comment, in spite of Cato's reported warnings of the dire effects of Greek literature. We have of course not only the *Brutus* but Suetonius' *Lives of the Learned* to document the advances in *doctrina*: all these stick to the party line that social respect, *honor*, is the crucial factor for the flourishing of a discipline at Rome. Doubtless, if we had Varro on the Nine Disciplines we would hear more along these lines.[16] But though the annexation of new disciplines adds provinces to the Roman intellectual empire, it is not perceived as changing its structure.

The transformation which concerns the Romans is that of *mores*. Though *mores* may be, to a Roman, nature not culture, they are subject to change. Emulation is the mechanism through which the *maiores* have transmitted their practices to the present, and it is the mechanism through which *mores* are corrupted. The leading men, *principes*, bear the heavy responsibility of setting a model to society: look back and you will see, "that the state always had the character of its leading men, and that whatever transformation of manners (*mutatio morum*) emerged among its leaders, the same followed in the people".[17] Just a few men who enjoy the benefit of social respect, *honore et gloria amplificati*, have the power to corrupt or correct the manners of the state. The derivation of the sentiment from Plato does not diminish its value as a statement of Roman perception of the possibility of cultural revolution.

I do not wish here to examine in detail the well-known passages of the historiographical tradition from Polybius to Sallust and Livy that associate political crisis in the late Republic with changing *mores*.[18] It would be hard now to take such passages at face value, not least because of our awareness of the rhetorical nature of accusations of immorality.[19] Let us here simply remind ourselves that the main, indeed the only, Roman theory of the fall of the Republic is, in our terms, a cultural one: of the corruption of *mores*. Politics is not conceived as an autonomous sphere, but as part of the fabric of ancestral ways that includes religion and daily life: already Polybius in his sixth book lays as much emphasis on the aristocratic funeral and religious control as on constitution and military arrangements in his account of what made Rome work. Augustus' solution is represented not as strictly political, but as the correction of *mores*. Too often when we think of Augustus as "moral reformer" we think of the marriage and adultery laws. But it is modern, not Roman, thought that restricts "morality" to the private sphere and separates it from "politics". All Augustus' reforms, the "political" ones too, are aimed at *mores*. And he would, of course, protest most vigorously at our notion of

---

[16] Cf. Rawson (1985), 117.

[17] *De legibus* 3.31: *qualescumque summi civitatis viri fuerint, talem civitatem fuisse; quaecumque mutatio morum in principibus exstiterit, eandem in populo secutam.*

[18] I know no satisfactory discussion of this tradition, but see e.g. Meier (1966), 301–6, Earl (1967), Lintott (1972).

[19] Edwards (1993), 9ff.

a cultural revolution. He was in the business of restoring ancestral *exempla*, supplemented by a few of his own.

What makes the theory of decline and restoration of *mores* significant in our pursuit of a "cultural revolution" is its power and adaptability as a totalising explanation. Not only does it assume that public and private life come wrapped up in one another, but it spills over the Ciceronian divide of *mores* and *doctrina*. Literary and artistic culture, that is to say, are subject to the same moral imperatives as politics. A key Augustan passage is the preface to the essay *On Ancient Orators* of Dionysius of Halicarnassus. We are offered a slow wasting and disappearance of true oratory from the death of Alexander, and the growth in its place of a shameless rhetoric, sprung from some Asian sewer, driving out the old Attic Muse from her inheritance like a tart pushing out a dutiful wife in the household of a playboy. But the decline is followed by a *metabole*. "Whether some god set it in train, or the revolution of nature itself recalled the old order, or human impulse guided multitudes to the same goal – whatever the cause, this generation has restored to the old, respectable rhetoric her just honour . . ." Atticism has displaced frigid, inflated, Asianism, and the Romans take credit for it. "The cause and beginning of this great change lies in Rome. The mistress of the world makes all other cities look to her. Her own men of power, who govern their country on the highest moral principles, are men of education and fine judgement. The discipline they impose has strengthened the wiser elements of the community . . ." and Dionysius predicts the extinction of Asianism.[20]

Not for nothing is this passage a cornerstone in Paul Zanker's theory of revolution in *Bildersprache*.[21] The metaphor of moral decline and restoration, once applied to rhetoric, can be conveniently reapplied to the visual arts. Zanker sees in Augustanism the expulsion of the whore of Hellenistic art, which in its pathos and exuberance sat so ill alongside traditional Roman morality, and the restoration of the good housewife of classicism, pure and unblemished (even in its depiction of scenes of copulation), and chiming with the priestly morality of post-Actium Augustus.

I do not suggest, however, that the route to an understanding of Roman cultural revolution lies in the appropriation of Roman moralising theory. Just as Cicero had emphasised that the contrast of Attic and Asianic oratory is facile and misleading, so the contrast of hellenising and classicising art seems to me a rhetorical tactic, which involves screening out a range of alternative moralising perceptions. We may take some comfort in being offered by the Romans a conceptual structure that allows itself to be employed so holistically, and which encourages the idea that politics, religion, family life, public and

---

[20] Dionysius of Halicarnassus, *On the Ancient Orators*, preface.
[21] Zanker (1988a), 239ff.; cf. Wallace-Hadrill (1989).

private morality, rhetoric and literary activity and the visual arts might all move together under some common transforming impulse. But it would make a poor basis for our own analysis.

Authority

To develop my own picture, I wish to shift from morality to authority. Asking whether the French and other revolutions have cultural origins, Roger Chartier leans on Lawrence Stone's analysis of the origins of the English seventeenth-century Revolution, and identifies transformations in five cultural and intellectual areas on which political change is premised: in religion, law, relations of court and country, mental attitudes and the growth of a frustrated intelligentsia.[22] I shall not attempt to do a Chartier and reapply these five areas to the Roman revolution. Instead I want to pick up on the idea of relocation of authority. In the English and French Revolutions, such relocations emerge as crucial: above all the relocation of religious authority brought about by Puritanism and Jansenism (independent moral judgement acquires primacy over the pronouncements of authority), and the collapse of the moral authority of the royal court, as it loses its role as aesthetic arbiter and trend-setter, and is pilloried instead for moral depravity.

It is not difficult to rethink the Roman Revolution as one of social authority – not least because of the explicit importance attached to the idea of *auctoritas* by the participants down to Augustus himself. The crisis of the Roman Republic is a crisis of authority through which the social system is constructed.[23] From the Gracchi onwards, and even before, we can observe the Roman ruling class setting about demolishing the authority on which its own dominance was based. I am not only thinking of the representation of the tribunates of the Gracchi and their successors as attacks on the *auctoritas senatus* (though this too is indicative).[24] I am also thinking of the demolition of *moral* authority that results from mutual onslaughts on morality and luxury.

As Catharine Edwards has well shown, we may regard accusations of immorality as a rhetorical strategy in a power struggle.[25] But the effect of the strategy is devastating. An elite that attributes its position to its superior *mores*, its trusteeship of ancestral values, and judges its success by its ability to inspire emulation, *imitatio*, fatally exposes its power when its monopoly of those values is questioned. Mutual accusations of luxury and immorality both reinforced the assumption that power was indeed founded in morality, and undermined the credibility of the power-holders in making good their claim.

The analogy of the French court is instructive: as long as Versailles with its elaborate rituals and etiquette is the focus of social life, it dictates French

---

[22] Chartier (1991), 169ff.   [23] Nippel (1984); North (1989) for a review of Brunt.
[24] E.g. Sallust, *Jugurtha* 42.   [25] Edwards (1993), 24ff.

fashion, and enables the king to maintain his own power by playing off rival social groupings against one another.[26] But with the retreat of the royal family into private life, the shift of authority in fashion to the salons of Paris, and the growing attacks on the luxury and depravity of the court, the moral authority of the palace is undermined (there is a lesson here for the contemporary British monarchy too). The picture of the ruling class of the late Republic as morally bankrupt cannot be brushed aside as a quaint (or even traditional) bit of Roman moralisation. To state that *mores* have collapsed is to state that moral authority has collapsed. Without moral authority, there can be no political authority.

Augustus' restoration of *mores* was the basis of his restructuring of authority in society. The attribution to the imperial court of the role of moral exemplar is a definition of its power. Here Zanker has rightly stressed the success of Augustus in offering his image as a moral paragon.[27] The accuracy with which the self-presentation of Romans at all social levels mirrored the imperial image, down to the hairstyle which is the chronological fall-back of imperial sculptural history, is testimony of Augustus' success is appropriating the traditional moral authority of the nobility. At the same time, the immorality of Julia threatened to subvert the whole authority of the palace. The re-emergence of accusations of immorality within the imperial household exposes not only the internal power struggles of the palace,[28] but the fragility of imperial authority. None of Augustus' successors lost that moral authority without forfeiting political power.

The relocation of authority is not restricted to this axis of politics and morality. The case for a Roman cultural revolution depends on observing its pervasiveness, to the extent that the cultural transformation which we call "Hellenisation" is inextricably bound up in the relocation. With all brevity, I shall pick out four examples of this process: tradition, law, time, and language. The common theme in each area is that what seems to us in retrospect an inevitable adoption of superior civilisation and rationality also involves a redefinition of authority: a collapse of the authority of the Republican ruling class, a shift in the control of knowledge from social leaders to academic experts; and an appropriation of that authority by Augustus.

Tradition

Tradition, we are beginning to appreciate, far from being something static and inert is subject to invention and reinvention. A distinction may be made between the customary practice of a "traditional" society and the paraded

---

[26] Chartier (1991), 178ff.; see also the classic analysis of Elias (1983).
[27] Zanker (1988a), 301ff.   [28] The line pursued by Syme (1984).

"traditions" of the modern world which lay claim to spurious ancestry in the mists of time; yet even the "customs" of African tribes may prove to be an accommodation to the mind of the colonial administrator.[29] Tradition, far from being the common ground of a cohesive society, is the focus of a power struggle: an instrument of dominance of old over young, insider over outsider, male over female.[30] Those who can carry their vision of "how we have always done things" have a powerful instrument of control over a society.

A leitmotif of the literature of the late Roman Republic is on the one hand the crucial importance of following tradition, the *mos maiorum*, if Rome is to survive and succeed, and on the other an awareness that tradition is slipping away, and needs to be painstakingly reconstructed, both at a theoretical level by rediscovery of what lost tradition was, and at a political level by its re-establishment and reimposition.[31] In this process, the antiquarian emerges as a key figure.[32] Think of Cicero's words of praise for Varro:

When we were like strangers abroad and lost in our own city, your books led us back home, so to speak, so that at last we were able to recognise who and where we were. You revealed the age of our native land, its divisions of time, the rules of sacrifice and priesthoods; discipline at home and at war; the location of regions and places; and the names, types, functions and causes of all matters divine and human. (*Academica Posteriora* 1.9)

The picture of Romans as peregrines in their own city stands on its head the traditional assumptions about the guardianship of cultural identity. It was precisely the function of the *nobiles*, men with ancestors, to know, imitate and transmit the *mores maiorum*. That is what Polybius or Sallust tell us so emphatically about Roman funerals.[33] Yet now the nobility emerge not as custodians of knowledge, but as traitors.

But by the negligence of the nobility the discipline of augury has been dropped, and the true practice of auspices is spurned, and only its appearance retained. And so most functions of the state, including warfare on which its safety depends, are administered without auspices ... By contrast, religion had such force for our ancestors, that some of them ritually veiled their heads and vowed their lives to the immortal gods for the republic. (*De natura deorum* 2.9–10)

The opening of the fifth book of the *Republic* extends this pessimistic vision. The idea that the greatness of Rome derives from its respect towards ancestral

---

[29] The classic study is the collection edited by E. Hobsbawm and T. Ranger, *The Invention of Tradition* (Cambridge 1983). On custom versus tradition, see Hobsbawm, 2; undercut by Ranger's account of African manipulation of custom, 252ff.

[30] E.g. T. Ranger in Hobsbawm and Ranger, *op.cit.*, 254–60.

[31] Much of the extensive Ciceronian and late Republican discussion of *mores maiorum* was gathered by a series of German dissertations in the thirties: Plumpe (1932), Rech (1936), Roloff (1937).

[32] Rawson (1985), 233ff., on antiquarianism.   [33] Polybius, 6.53; Sallust, *Jug.* 5–6.

custom is epitomised in the Ennian line, *Moribus antiquis res stat Romana virisque*. But now all is changed.

And so before living memory traditional custom by itself made men outstanding, and excellent men preserved the old ways and practices of their ancestors. But our age, having inherited the *res publica* like a masterpiece of painting that was already fading with age, has not only neglected to restore the old colours that were there, but has not even troubled to preserve its shape and outlines ... It is by our own faults, not by accident, that we keep the *res publica* in name only, and have long since lost its substance. (*De republica* 5.1–2)

Cicero, we should note, is not talking about the fall of the Republic as a political system, but about the collapse of a whole way of life, of a way of being Roman. Varro steps in where the nobles have failed.

He feared that the gods should perish, not by enemy invasion, but by the negligence of citizens, and he claimed that this was the doom from which he was rescuing them, and that it was a more useful service that things should be stored away and preserved in the memory of good men through books of this type, than when Metellus is said to have rescued the sacred objects of the Vestals from burning, or Aeneas to have saved the *penates* from the sack of Troy. (fr. 2A = Aug., *Civ.Dei* 6.2.48.)

Antiquarianism presented a frontal challenge to the authority on which the nobility based their claim to power. It was now the antiquarian, by his laborious study of obscurely worded documents, and displaying the credentials of Greek academic learning, who "knew" what the "real" Roman tradition was. The "memory of good men," as Varro put it, now started from books, not oral tradition. The noble priest and jurisprudent not only finds his authority subverted, but is subjected to contumely as the man who has betrayed his own ancestors.

The late Republic thus produces a dislocation of authority: social authority and academic learning pull in opposite directions. Augustus brings the two back into unison. He is not an antiquarian; but he reads, respects, employs, and exploits antiquarians. Verrius Flaccus teaches in his palace; Gaius Melissus would rather be an imperial freedman and Palatine librarian than claim his free birth.[34] The lowly social status of the academic makes it easier for Augustus to incorporate them within his own household; and in a massive and pervasive "restoration" of tradition defined by antiquarian learning, he associates his authority with theirs.

Law

Knowledge of the civil law was one specialised branch of knowledge of ancestral tradition, and one of extreme importance. At least as Cicero reconstructs the past, knowledge of law was implicit in the exercise of patronage. So

---

[34] Suetonius, *De grammaticis* 21.

the vision of the *patronus* offered by Crassus in the *De oratore* (3.133) is of a noble strolling in the forum, or sitting on his throne at home, offering advice indiscriminately on points of law, land management, and money. Legal knowledge is conceived as an obligation linked to social status: Mucius the Pontifex is said to have reproved the young Servius that ignorance of the civil law was base in a patrician, a noble and an advocate.[35] Yet the lifetime of the same Servius Sulpicius Rufus sees, according to Cicero, the collapse of this link:

Among the many excellent practices of our ancestors was the high respect they always accorded to knowledge and interpretation of the corpus of civil law. Until the present age of confusion (*hanc confusionem temporum*), the *principes* kept this profession exclusively in their hands; but now, with the collapse of every other grade of social distinction, the prestige of this science has been destroyed – and that in the lifetime of one (Servius) who equals any of his predecessors in social standing, and excels them all in science. (Cicero, *De officiis* 2.19.65)

The substantiation of Cicero's claim has taken not only Kunkel's classic study of the social origins of the Roman jurists, but a string of books by Bauman.[36] But what matters is not so much the social origins of the jurists as the location of legal knowledge and authority within the structures of Roman society.

Here Bruce Frier's brilliant essay on the *Rise of the Roman Jurists* makes the points relevant to my argument.[37] Frier looks at the emergence of juris-prudence as an autonomous profession. He outlines a shift from what he calls the "external" to the "internal" function of the jurists. The traditional external function of the jurisconsult lay in advising those who consulted him on precise points of law, an essentially casuistic skill, which led directly to the patronal power described in the *De oratore* (3. 133). The internal function developed as a consequence of the writing and teaching of Scaevola the Pontifex in the early first century. It lay in the development of a legal science, systematic and theoretical, which considered hypothetical problems, which categorised and gen-eralised. In Q Mucius, Frier sees "the father of Roman legal science and . . . the inventor of the legal profession".[38]

Frier offers a variety of explanations for this transformation – growth in citizen numbers, increase in commercial activity, and political instability[39] – which are clearly relevant at different levels, but which do not take into account the intellectual context of changes in *scientia*. In an earlier generation, Fritz Schulz, under the influence of Wilamowitz, had pointed to Hellenism and the impact of dialectical argument derived from Greek philosophy and

---

[35] Pomponius, *Dig.* 1.2.2.43, *turpe esse patricio et nobili et causas oranti ius in quo versaretur ignorare*; apparently derived from Servius' own account.

[36] Kunkel (1952); Bauman (1983, 1985, 1989).   [37] Frier (1985), esp. 139ff.

[38] Frier (1985), 171.   [39] Frier (1985), 273ff.

rhetoric: "Hellenism provided the mould of theory into which Romans poured their national life".[40] I do not wish to subscribe to a vision of Hellenism as a cultural wave driven by its own impetus which transforms Roman life.[41] But I do wish to draw attention to the way in which the nobles themselves, patricians and *pontifices* like Mucius Scaevola and Servius Sulpicius, redefine the authority of their own discipline. Using Greek learning to advance the *scientia* of which they were traditional custodians, they transform the knowledge they have inherited, putting it beyond the reach of any but experts. Servius published 180 volumes – who could now keep up? Authority in matters of civil law can no longer derive from the social position of the expert consulted: only his mastery of an intricate discipline will carry conviction.

Cicero's telling reaction is to see this as part of a pattern of "confusion". It is confused because the expectation still persists that social authority and possession of knowledge will coincide, as they do in Servius. But by the time we reach Augustus, expectations have been restructured. Augustus himself is no jurisconsult: yet he and his successors are the ultimate source of law. That is possible because they absorb the experts like Capito and Labeo into their *consilium*, and issue pronouncements that are doubly authoritative, in political power and control of *scientia*.

Time

Knowledge of religious law was, like knowledge of civil law, a specialised branch of knowledge of tradition attributed to the Republican nobility. Priestly control of time may serve as a convenient paradigm for the shifting location of religious authority. In an earlier paper, I suggested that the Roman construction of time was re-ordered around Augustus, whether in the calendar of daily ritual and observance of the *fasti*, or the astral clock of the *horologium*.[42] The process also involves a relocation of authority.

The Republican Roman calendar was under the control of the *pontifices*.[43] The pattern of the year was at once highly complex and to a significant extent arbitrary. The privileged access of the *pontifices* to knowledge of the ways of men and gods had once, before the publication of the calendar by the scribe Flavius, enabled them to dictate by a monthly announcement the rhythm of life: to prescribe, when the Kalends, Nones and Ides would fall, together with *dies fasti* and *nefasti*, the moments at which public speech was and was not possible.[44] By the first century BCE, the main surviving area of arbitrary

---

[40] Schulz (1946), 86; but this is the leitmotif of Part II at 38ff.
[41] For the inadequacies of this viewpoint, see e.g. Veyne (1979), Hölscher (1990).
[42] Wallace-Hadrill (1987).   [43] Radke (1990), 43ff.; Michels (1967), 145ff.
[44] Michels (1967), 19f.

priestly control was the practice of intercalation; and Cicero's anxiety on the
subject in Cilicia sums up the sense of unknowability and unpredictability of
the rhythm of the Republican year.[45] By the end of the Republic, of course, we
witness this as another area for political manipulation and chicanery. Contemporaries could see it as an abuse of authority, an institution, as Cicero puts it,
"wisely set up by Numa which has disintegrated thanks to the negligence of
subsequent *pontifices*".[46] But the vital point here is the way in which authority
over time was traditionally constructed. A narrow social elite, marked off
by exclusive birth and special marriage rituals, claimed as *pontifices* a higher
knowledge of time, as of the proper forms of all relations between Romans
and their gods, and in civil law of citizen and citizen.

The calendar reforms of Caesar (46 BCE) and Augustus (9 BCE) are a classic
example of "rationalisation".[47] Mathematicians, with calculations so accurate
as to be able to survive millennia of cultural change, redefine the rhythm of
the year and put it beyond religious and political control. The incidence of
the equinox is now so accurately correlated with the Roman civil calendar
that it can be relied on to pay tribute to Augustus annually on his birthday –
until indeed an earth tremor displaces the massive gnomon of his sundial.[48]
Simultaneously, the rationalised Roman time can be universalised across
the empire. An eastern Mediterranean which has always operated with local
calendars, variety not only of month names and starting points for the year,
but lack of correlation between the competing rhythms, resolves to make the
"birthday of the god, that is the end of regretting being born and so a new
beginning of life," its New Year's Day.[49] Local traditions and month names
survived even so, and the flattering intentions of the proconsul were not
carried out in full; but now at least it was possible to construct a table cor-
relating the calendar at Rome and at Alabanda.[50]

Knowledge, then, is relocated: from the social authority of a local elite
guarding the cultural specificity of its traditions, to the academic authority of
the experts who can predict the movements of the sun wherever you stand on
the Earth at whatever time in history. It is not, we note, Caesar or Augustus
themselves who lay claim to this superior knowledge, though each takes the title
of *pontifex maximus*, and uses his authority as such to carry through reform.
But rationalisation is an instrument of control. The social and political

---

[45] Cicero, *Ad fam.* 5.9.2; 13.3; 21.4.

[46] Cicero, *De legibus* 2.29; cf. Suetonius, *Jul.* 40, *fastos . . . vitio pontificum per intercalendi
licentiam . . . turbatos*; Macrobius, *Sat.* 1.14.1, alleges bribery by the *publicani*. Cf. Taylor
(1949), 79ff.; Michels (1967), 45f.

[47] Radke (1990), 62ff.; Samuel (1972), 155ff.

[48] So Buchner (1982); but Schutz (1990) brings some of this picture into question, supported by
Barton (1995).

[49] So the decree of the *koinon* of Asia; Laffi (1967).   [50] Samuel (1972), 174ff., esp. 181–2.

authority of Caesar or Augustus is aligned with the academic authority of socially humble experts like the astronomers Sosigenes of Alexandria or Facundus Novius. Augustus ensures that the empire conforms to the knowledge of the mathematician; and reciprocally the mathematician ensures that the stars conform to the power of Augustus, conceived under the sign of Capricorn to re-order the world.

Language

Of all the cultural transformations of this period, for me the most exciting and neglected is that of the Latin language itself, and specifically of Latin grammar.[51] The modern, post-Chomskian, transformational grammarian does not see himself as a legislator, dictating how people may and may not speak, but as an observer of the varieties and changes of usage, dialect and register, stressing the potential of language structures to generate endless improvisation and innovation. The Roman grammarian, by contrast, was an unashamed authoritarian, *custos Latini sermonis*,[52] a "guardian of language" just as much as the soldier was guardian of the frontier; and while the living spoken tongue eluded his control, the effect was to produce a remarkable stability in the official language of literature and administration over many centuries.[53]

This regulated grammar is the product of a first-century BCE revolution. The key document is Varro's *De lingua latina*. At the heart of his discussion of Latin is a major theoretical debate, already started in Latin earlier in the century by his master Aelius Stilo, and deriving from Aristarchus and the grammarians of Alexandria. The issue is precisely the nature of grammar and the function of the grammarian. What is "correct" linguistic usage? Is it merely an observation of *consuetudo*, how people in practice do speak, and so subject to what Greek grammarians called anomaly, or is it regular, rational, logical, patterned, following what they called analogy?[54] Varro does not come down clearly on either side. For him there evidently are logical rules, yet they will not work completely. Above all, he knows that language is subject to constant change, *consuetudo loquendi est in motu*,[55] and one can no more reject linguistic changes of fashion than new shapes of tableware or new styles of clothing.

One reason for Varro's balance, apart from reporting fairly both sides of a Greek academic debate, is that Latin was actually in a state of transition; from what L. R. Palmer called "the morphological uncertainties of archaic Latin, the confusions of gender, the fluctuating forms of declension, conjugation and

---

[51] Cf. Rawson (1985), 117ff.   [52] Seneca, *Ep.mor.* 95.65.

[53] See Kaster (1988) for a perceptive discussion of the social role of grammarians, especially in a later period.

[54] See Rawson (1985), 121ff.   [55] Varro, *LL* 9.17.

word-formation" on the one hand, to the all too well-regulated forms enshrined for us in Kennedy's *Latin Primer*. There is a shift from *consuetudo* to *ratio*. And in that shift is a decisive shift of authority: from the people of Rome, as controlled by their elite, to the grammarian.

The reason for the shift is understood by Cicero discussing the changing role of *Latinitas*, pure Latin, for the orator:

> Hitherto pure Latin was not a matter of reason and science, *rationis et scientiae*, but of good usage, *bonae consuetudinis*. I pass over Laelius and Scipio; in that period men were praised for their pure Latin as for their innocence (though there were those who spoke badly). But virtually everyone in those days who neither lived outside this city, nor was tainted by domestic barbarity, used to speak correctly. But this has been corrupted in Rome as in Greece. Both Athens and this city have received a flood of people from a diversity of origins whose language is polluted (*inquinate loquentes*). This is why our talk needs purging, and some sort of rationality needs to be applied like a touchstone, which cannot be changed, nor are we to go by the perverted rule of usage. (Cicero, *Brutus* 258)

Ratio has won over *consuetudo* because the people of cosmopolitan Rome can no longer be trusted to talk proper Latin. Cicero is talking about Caesar. The old arbiters of pure Latinity were the great statesman, like Flamininus, despite his illiteracy. Now Caesar is applying *ratio* to vitiated *consuetudo*.

Cicero is referring to the lost *De analogia* by Caesar; who wrote, so Fronto tells us, in the intervals of campaign in Gaul, "amidst the volleys about declining nouns, about aspiration between the trumpet blasts".[56] Fronto's wordplay brings out a real parallelism: between conquests that reduced the barbarous Gaul to Roman order, and a treatise designed to rescue Latin from barbarism and reduce language to order.

In the case of law, I observed that it was the traditional custodians of knowledge, the nobles, who themselves transformed the nature of their authority by turning it into an academic discipline. In Caesar too (notably the one Roman-born and the one patrician to contribute significantly to Latin literature), it is a noble who shifts Latin from the control of customary practice to that of rationalised grammar. It was the same Caesar, patrician and pontifex, who took the Roman calendar out of the control of the pontificate, and who planned to reduce Roman law to a written corpus.

Language is one of the most important factors in defining ethnic and cultural identity. When the social and political elite loses control of linguistic usage, it loses control of cultural definition. Suetonius relates an anecdote of the grammarian Pomponius Marcellus, an ex-pugilist, who reprehended Tiberius for the use of a Greek loan-word. The lawyer Ateius Capito springs

---

[56] Fronto, p.221N *scripsisse inter tela volantia de nominibus declinandis, de verborum aspirationibus et rationibus inter classica et tubas.*

to Tiberius' defence, remarking ingratiatingly that even if the word wasn't already Latin, it would be now. "Capito lies", responds the blunt Pomponius; "you have power, Caesar, to grant citizenship to men, not to a word."[57] The patrician Tiberius has to cave in to a low-born grammarian. Emperors put their authority behind that of grammarians, to make an imperial language.

Local and universal knowledge

The argument could readily be extended to other areas: for instance to Roman conceptions of space, illuminatingly discussed by Nicolet, and the shift of organisation of the city of Rome from a tribal (with their implicit structures of social control) to a regional basis.[58] The four areas I have examined, tradition, law, time, and language, all belong to a related area of Roman antiquarian endeavour; scholars from Varro to Suetonius wrote about them. What is at stake is Roman culture in the sense of the set of practices that defined what it meant to be a Roman: *mores*, to revert to Cicero's distinction in the *Tusculan Disputations*, as opposed to *doctrina*, yet reinterpreted and transformed through the agency of *doctrina*.

In his book *Local Knowledge*, Clifford Geertz argues that the sense a culture makes does so at a local level, presenting "to locals locally a local turn of mind."[59] So common sense is a cultural system of shared assumptions at a local level, art inscribes the local perceptions and preoccupations of a society, and law is a form of local knowledge.

If we think about *mos maiorum*, Roman civil law, the Roman calendar, or the Latin language, they do indeed present traces of an essentially local character, stamped with assumptions that ultimately suggest a face-to-face community in Rome itself (not that such a community had existed in a pure form for many centuries). The cultural transformation of the first century BCE offers us the spectacle of a local form of knowledge aspiring, and with some measure of success, to make itself universal. The Latin language cannot become an imperial tongue if one must refer to the Forum Romanum for proper usage; nor can the calendar be followed if it takes months for the news of an intercalation to arrive. Hellenisation and rationalisation are the hallmarks of a universalising culture. Hellenism offered such a powerful model because of its own universalising aspirations, to be the *koine* of the *oikoumene*.

This shift of culture from the local to the universal, driven by the impulse to make Roman conquests Roman, necessitates a revolutionary shift of authority. In a system of local knowledge, a predominantly hereditary elite can act as custodians of knowledge. Their authority in Roman society is indissolubly

---

[57] Suetonius, *De grammaticis* 22; cf. Cassius Dio 57.17.1–3.
[58] Nicolet (1991), 189ff.   [59] Geertz (1983), 12.

linked to their ability to define the Roman: to make authoritative pronouncements on what constitutes Roman tradition, law, time and language. They
must define Roman religion and Roman morals, the Roman family as well
as Roman war and politics. By my argument, the ruling elite has lost control
and authority in all these areas by the fifties of the first century BCE. With the
model of Hellenism, the discourse is transformed, and their authority passes
to specialists who can master increasingly complex and technical fields of
knowledge. The rupture is decisive.

In one sense such an interpretation succumbs too easily to a Roman myth:
of a perfectly ordered Roman society just over the horizon of the Roman past.
The contrasts drawn by Cicero and his contemporaries between the confusion of their own times and the good order of the past are of a mythological,
not a historical order. The society controlled by the noble priest, jurist, orator,
and patron is a simplification that does no justice to the scale of diversity,
contest, and change of earlier periods. We have fallen precisely for an
"invented tradition".

That indeed is a problem that dogs all attempts to understand change in the
late Republic, at the political level too: the lack of contemporary voices from
earlier centuries makes it hard to get beyond the constructions of the past
offered to us by participants in the late Republican crisis themselves. It is the
characteristic flaw in the moralising interpretation of the crisis of the late
Republic offered by authors from Polybius to Sallust: disorder is explained
by the breakdown of a previous order, yet it is incredible that there was ever
a time when the ideal order prevailed, whether one of perfect morals or of
perfect political balance.

But to say these Roman pictures of change are overschematic and simplistic
does not diminish their value as evidence of the perception of fundamental
change. The perfect order of the past should never be read as a statement of
fact; it is rather a mirror image of the disorder of the present. The function of
such constructions, then, is to draw our attention to critical areas of perceived
disorder, in which there is an unacceptable gap between ideology (how things
ought to work, projected onto the past as a fact) and practice.

Such perceptions may make a poor basis for understanding the history of an
earlier period, but they are essential for understanding the period in question.
Perceptions of crisis are themselves part of the crisis, and form the context in
which solutions are formed. Cicero's perceptions of confusion – of ancestral
traditions ignored, the law, the calendar and language out of control – make
possible the "solutions" of Caesar and Augustus.

It is for this reason that it is worth looking beyond the explanations of the
"fall of the Republic" that consider only the political or the socio-economic.
Erich Gruen once saw the collapse of a system as almost a matter of chance;
the Republic was brought down by a combination of circumstances that need

not have occurred.[60] Even now that Gruen has turned to culture and national identity, he still sees the Roman elite of the second century BCE as firmly in control of Roman responses to Hellenism.[61] Yet an elite in cultural control need not have fallen: cultural change is thus no motor of political revolution. From an opposite perspective, Peter Brunt allows little room for the idea of cultural change: nuanced though his treatment of possible factors may be, and sensitive to the metaphysical problems of divining underlying "causes" for major historical transformations, in the end for him the Republic fell because of the political failure of the ruling elite to deal with the social and economic plight of the people.[62] Had they done what Augustus did, they might have survived.

My own picture is not meant to be deterministic (i.e. to argue that the Republic had to fall); but it does give credence to what Cicero and Sallust say, that the republic, in the sense of the whole ideological and cultural system which defined the Roman, had already lost its credibility, even before Caesar's dictatorship. Whether with Sallust you can speak of moral collapse, or with Cicero of social confusion and abandonment of tradition, what is described is the collapse of the cultural structures by which authority had been defined in Roman society. Paradoxically, the agents of destruction of authority were the elite themselves, competing to reinforce their authority. Once the change was made, it was irreversible.

It does not follow that civil war or dictatorship were necessary consequences; but that any political order that attempted to establish itself required as a basis new structures of social authority and cultural definition. Augustus' achievement was not just the establishment of a new political order, but also of a new cultural order. Though it defined itself by reference to the past and to Republican tradition, the new cultural order was differently constructed and reproduced, by *ratio* not *consuetudo*. The Augustan restoration was possible because Augustus understood the change, and used the specialist authority of the experts to reinforce his own political and social authority. He wanted a universalising culture, not local knowledge, to define his empire and a new sense of being Roman.

---

[60] Gruen (1974).   [61] Gruen (1992).

[62] Brunt (1988), 1–92; my summary does little justice to the power and complexity of his picture; yet the "cultural" plays no part in it.

2 The invention of sexuality in the world-city of Rome

Thomas Habinek

In his recent study of the emergence and history of sexuality in the modern world, Don Milligan arrives at the following conclusion: "Sexuality remains what it always was, an entirely responsive ideology produced by the desire to understand and regulate the lonesome and atomised individual spontaneously constituted by all the circumstances of life in modern cities."[1] Milligan implicitly accepts the now familiar characterization of sexuality as a discourse, that is, a means of organizing "sensations, images, desires, instincts, passions" and of producing through their management new knowledge about the individual and society and new channels for the transfer and application of power.[2] Milligan further accepts the view, dating at least to Foucault, that sexuality as a discourse is a modern phenomenon, in other words that what we today regard as sexuality had not yet crystallized as such in the pre-modern era, that erotic sensations, images, and actions were differently interpreted, organized, and regulated in earlier eras, so differently that "the very category 'sexuality,' . . . when imported unwittingly into the ancient world by modern interpreters, seriously distort[s] the meanings of sexual experience indigenous to that world."[3] In the classical world, in particular, on this latter view, sex remained embedded in other social relations and other categories of discourse and was not capable of producing meaning in and of itself. As a result, many of the categories through which sexuality (that is, the distinctively modern discourse of sexuality) produces meaning, especially those of sexual identity and orientation, are quite simply irrelevant to the interpretation of ancient literature and culture.

So much is familiar to anyone who has followed the discussion of sexuality and what for lack of a better term we might call pre-sexuality in the ancient world. (By pre-sexuality I mean the cluster of phenomena which if transported to the modern world would be interpreted according to the categories of sexuality but whose interpretation in their ancient context remains contested.) Where Milligan complicates the discussion is in his assessment of the factors that generate sexuality in the modern world. As is to be expected from the

---

[1] Milligan (1993:111).   [2] Foucault (1978:2:35).   [3] Halperin, Winkler, Zeitlin (1990:5).

brief summary offered above, his work resoundingly rejects the essentialist view which would see a biological foundation for human sexual behavior (and thus deny the validity of the very notion of sexuality as a discourse, not to mention a discourse of modernity). But it also criticizes the social constructivist view, not so much for its epistemology or its historiography (after all, Milligan's summary formulation "an entirely responsive ideology" acknowledges the constructedness of sexuality) as for its failure in its politics to pursue the implications of its own epistemological and historical analysis. What concerns Milligan is the assumption held by many social constructivists that since humans constructed sexuality they can deconstruct it. Such a position, in his view, ignores the larger social forces that have generated sexuality in the modern world, social forces which themselves will not be changed by any attempt, no matter how radical, to reconfigure sexuality today. "The effect of the theory of social construction," he writes "has been to endorse the idea that these gains [i.e. the advances made by the victims of phallocentric sexuality] are the work of radical action, that is, that they are the product of a long tradition of contestation and struggle in which radical strategies seeking self-determination and self-definition have brought about a restructuring of sexuality and a 'deconstruction' of the discourse of sexuality. This is not the case. It is the perpetual flux in all the technical and social circumstances of life, and the perpetual shifting of the locus of the social life of highly industrialized societies towards the individual, and towards the configuration of the consumption and life*style* of the individual, that have found their most startling expression within the reform of sexual manners."[4]

Flux and atomization, specifically, the flux and atomization characteristic of modern cities, are the preconditions of sexuality, at least according to Milligan. The vagueness of the formulation should not be held against it, for while Milligan bases his conclusions on a review of the philosophical, psychological, and political literature of modern sexuality, a comparable notion is adumbrated, although to my knowledge never specifically articulated, in a number of historical and anthropological studies of sexuality. For example, Jeffrey Weeks relates the emergence of sexuality in the nineteenth century to changes in kinship and family structure and to other economic and social changes, including "urbanisation."[5] Ann Rosalind Jones, in a study of early modern Florence and Poitiers, refers to the opportunities and challenges of early modern cities, specifically the need to renegotiate the sex and gender system.[6] Kevin White, in a provocative discussion of the invention of male heterosexuality in late nineteenth- and early twentieth-century America, correlates this development with the great transformation of the US from an agrarian to an urban society, noting that "by 1920, over 50 percent of Americans lived in cities."[7] And Roger Lancaster, whose ethnographic work on

---

[4] Milligan (1993:112).   [5] Weeks (1989:13).   [6] Jones (1991).   [7] White (1993:2).

contemporary Nicaragua traces a distinction between an embedded and a disembedded system of sex and gender very similar to the one I will identify in late Republican and early Imperial Rome, again points to a contrast between rural and urban components of society. His analysis focuses on the contrast between the Nicaraguan *cochón* (a figure closely resembling the ancient *cinaedus*) and the Anglo-American "homosexual," but expresses the contrast in terms of differences between peasant and middle-class urban communities and between a system of evaluation based on honor and shame and one organized around different sorts of ethical and economic considerations.[8]

The work of these historians and anthropologists lends credence to Milligan's insight concerning sexuality and cities, while at the same time posing questions of particular interest to the classicist. Within classical studies, the debate between constructivists and essentialists has in part played itself out as a debate between Hellenists and Romanists, with a group of scholars focusing on Greek material generally suscribing to the view that antiquity transpired "before sexuality," while those focusing on Rome, and specifically literary texts composed in the Latin language, tend to see an ancient configuration of sexual practices and ideologies more closely resembling that of the modern world.[9] While it seems a priori likely that not all of antiquity was characterized by a single configuration of sexual values and practices, scholarly work on other times and places suggests that differences in the organization of sex-life are more likely to correlate with economic differences (e.g. market economy versus gift-exchange) and/or an urban/rural divide than with ethnic or linguistic categories. Thus the work of Milligan and others invites us to re-examine familiar material from the ancient world with an eye to possible differences in the construction of sexuality between the cosmopoleis, such as imperial Rome, Ptolemaic Alexandria, and late imperial Antioch, and other social formations, and with attention to variations in economic organization that may differentiate ancient cities from one another as well as from their hinterlands. Investigations of this sort promise to be of help not only in understanding the ancient world, but perhaps also in refining the discussion of sexuality today: is sexuality to be understood as a product of modernity, of cities, or of factors that happen to be manifest in both? Can we expect the current configuration of sexuality to persist (somewhat paradoxically) as long as flux and atomization are the order of the day? Or are these congested heaps of capital we call cities, with the interpersonal encounters they necessitate, an essential precondition? Closer inspection of the ancient material may help us

---

[8] Lancaster (1992:235ff.).

[9] On the Greek side note in particular Halperin, Winkler, Zeitlin (1990) and Goldhill (1995); on the Roman side Richlin (1992) and (1993). For a more disengaged discussion of essentialism and constructivism as they relate to Roman culture and Latin literature, see Kennedy (1993:24ff.). Already in 1991 Boswell had commented on the difference in approach between Hellenists and Romanists.

begin to untangle the web of causality implied in Milligan's formulation ("entirely responsive ideology produced by the desire to understand and regulate the lonesome and atomised individual spontaneously constituted by all the circumstances of life in modern cities") through comparison with situations that share some characteristics (e.g. mass cities, social flux) but lack others (e.g. industrialization, capitalism).

During the course of the Roman Cultural Revolution, that is the period in which the Roman elites came to terms with their status as rulers of an empire, the city of Rome was itself transformed from an overgrown Italian town to a world capital.[10] Its boundaries remained roughly the same as during the late Republic, yet its infrastructure, administration, demography, and physical appearance were all radically altered. Many of the changes in the city were undertaken not simply for reasons of efficiency, but also out of a sense of rivalry with Alexandria, the leading city of Hellenism,[11] and in an attempt to manifest in the physical environment Rome's political position as center of "the universe."[12] The result was well described by the geographer Strabo who, in reference to the building campaigns of the early Principate, declared: "if one should go to the Old Forum, and see one Forum after another ranged beside it, with their basilicas and temples, and then see the Capitol and the great works of art on it, and the Palatine, and the Porticus of Livia, it would be easy to forget the world outside."[13] Rome had become the world in large part because the world now had to come to Rome: as Ovid put it, with regard to potential erotic conquests, "everything that used to be in the world is now here" (*haec habet . . . quicquid in orbe fuit, Ars* 1.56). During one discrete historical period Rome experienced the swift change and dislocation of the individual that Milligan and others describe as the permanent condition of modern cities.

But it was equally true, or so Augustus would have the Romans believe, that everything that used to be here, i.e. in Rome, was still here: an observation which, while it does not apply to the thousands who lost their lives or status during the civil wars, does do justice to the Latin literary tradition. Indeed, it is the decidedly continuous, even conservative, nature of that tradition that makes it possible to observe changes in the representation and evaluation of human sexual behavior even as they occur. Lacking the police records, psychiatric reports, journals, and interviews that form the basis for

[10] Homo (1951); Jacques and Scheid (1990).   [11] Nicolet (1991); Ceaucescu (1976).

[12] On the relationship between cosmos and empire in Roman thought see Hardie (1986). For the physical representation of this relationship within the Augustan building program see Buchner (1982) which describes recent archaeological discoveries illuminating the cosmic symbolism of the sundial, obelisks, and the Ara Pacis. For further discussion see Bowersock (1990). One guess places the population of Rome in the Augustan era at 800,000 to one million; others place it considerably higher. See Hopkins (1978:96–98).

[13] Strabo, *Geog.* 58 (Loeb translation).

the study of sexual behavior and ideology in later periods, we can nonetheless observe within the ample remains of Latin poetry of the period discursive developments comparable to those associated with the invention of sexuality in other times and places. The isolation of sex as a topic for analysis, the privileging of sexual pleasure as a criterion of personal fulfillment, the construction of distinctive sexual identities based on object-choice, the association of sex with privacy, and the professionalization of advice about sex: all of these can be traced within the literature of the period and linked to other aspects of Roman cosmopolitanism. In particular, the poetry of Ovid, when compared with earlier Latin poetry on sexual or amatory subjects, records both the invention of sexuality as a distinctive discourse and the resistance such a radical development inevitably encountered.[14]

Disembedding sex

If we compare the account of sexual desire and sexual activity to be found in the poetry of Catullus (50s of the first century BCE) with that contained in the elegies and the *Ars Amatoria* of Ovid (composed from roughly 20 BCE through 2 BCE),[15] one salient feature quickly emerges. For Catullus, sex is embedded in a network of political, economic, regional, and affective relationships, while for Ovid it is not. Catullus' expressed desire for a sexual relationship with Lesbia is but one component of his longing for intimacy and personal validation. His negative assessments of Lesbia's behavior employ a traditional vocabulary of honor and shame, loyalty and betrayal, that emanates from a social system in which sex is closely associated with issues of legitimacy, alliances between clans, and male privilege. The other sexual relationships described in Catullus' poetry, despite our tendency to place them in distinctive categories (e.g. homosexuality, pederasty, sadism), in fact are characterized by a similar embeddedness of sexual relations in other sorts of political, social, and economic networks.[16]

---

[14] Cantarella (1988:129ff.) discusses changes in the Roman approach to sexual behavior over time, but is chiefly concerned with the diffusion (or not) of pederasty and the qualities associated with a boy-love. Her study, like many others, becomes enmeshed in a debate between the "reality" and "literariness" of poetic representations. Focusing on sexuality as a discourse and its history as the history of representational strategies makes it possible to avoid such ultimately fruitless discussion. This is not to say that representation and discourse do not affect the way real people live real lives; it is merely to acknowledge the impossibility of reconstructing such real experience except through the study of discourse.

[15] On the dates of composition and/or publication of the works of Ovid see Syme (1978).

[16] Thus in terms of the contemporary definition of sexuality, which implies disembeddedness from other aspects of human interaction, a title such as that of Brian Arkins' (1982) study, *Sexuality in Catullus*, is technically a misnomer. Arkins' book is also noteworthy for its surprising tone of approval with respect to the domineering and phallocentric aspects of sexual activity discussed in Catullus' poetry.

Wiseman's discussion of the provincial nature of Catullus' attitude toward the sexual and other mores of the Roman upper classes is not far off the mark, for the standard of sexual behavior that Catullus brings to bear on his own life and that of his acquaintances is indeed appropriate to an honor-bound, face-to-face society (perhaps as characterized his hometown Verona) as opposed to one composed of independent subjects freed (relatively) of societal and familial constraints.[17] The irony and the anguish of Catullus' position that have endeared him to generations of readers are to be located in his eagerness to be numbered among the *urbani*, or city sophisticates, without simultaneously accepting one of the consequences of *urbanitas*, namely the foregoing of his right to insist on others' adherence to his own ideals of loyalty and honor.

In the poetry of Ovid, the disembedding of sex from other types of human relationships has proceeded to such an extent that the beloved of the *Amores*, unlike the mistresses in the poetry of Catullus, Gallus, Propertius, and Tibullus, has no discernible personality and virtually no name. As *praeceptor amoris* Ovid advises his disciples, male and female, to scour the city for potential bed-mates, since there the erotic riches of the entire world are on display (*"haec habet" ut dicas "quicquid in orbe fuit", Ars* 1.56). Ovid's insistence that his advice is not for matrons or virginal daughters of the aristocracy is a bow to the continuing force of an inherited ideology, but even to acknowledge the possibility of construing sexual behavior as something that might or might not be subject to traditional codes of honorable conduct is to break the appearance of inevitability on which those codes depend for much of their force and to articulate sex as a discrete topic for analysis.

The difference between Catullan and Ovidian representations of sex, honor, and desire has often been imputed to differences in the individual psychology of the two poets or to a perceived tendency toward deconstruction, even parody, within a highly stylized literary tradition. While we cannot entirely rule out such explanations (the latter being more popular today than the former), an important body of external evidence helps us to situate the contrast between the two authors in a broader social context. In 18 BCE and again in 9 CE the political leaders of the Augustan principate imposed a set of laws concerning sexual behavior that are collectively referred to as "Augustan moral legislation."[18] In fact, as David Cohen has argued, this legislation is better described not in moral terms, but as a "massive and deliberate appropriation by the state of a

---

[17] Wiseman (1985).

[18] Recent work by legal historians has described the Augustan legislation less in terms of moral reform (e.g. Galinsky [1981]) and more as the assertion of the prerogatives of persons and of the state at the expense of the family and clan. See Cohen (1991) and Cantarella (1991), who focus on provisions concerning adultery. Wallace-Hadrill (1981) interprets legislation concerning childbearing and inheritance in a similar vein. Richlin (1981) reminds us that legal regulation of sexual activity did not entirely supplant family jurisdiction.

new regulatory sphere: marriage, divorce, and sexuality."[19] "Appropriation" is a crucial term in this description, since it reminds us that in order to assume such regulatory power, the state had to acquire it from some other source, in this instance the family. In effect, the Augustan "moral" legislation disembedded sexual behavior from its traditional familial context, where it had been regulated by forces of honor and shame, and instead described it as a freely chosen activity between legal persons, one subject to scrutiny and regulation in the public sphere.[20]

While the coincidence in approach to sexual activity between the Augustan *leges* and the poetry of Ovid strengthens the argument for the emergence of a distinctive discourse of sexuality, both the legal and the poetic formulations give evidence of the complexities attendant upon such a revolutionary change. The *leges Iuliae* provided explicit exemption from prosecution for adultery to registered prostitutes, a necessary provision if men were to have a sexual outlet outside marriage and not be subject to charges of seduction. It seems unlikely that the legislators were seeking to provide women with such an outlet, yet the loophole in the law permitted precisely that: in a notorious episode in 19 CE the socially prominent Vistilia defended herself against charges of adultery on the grounds that she had registered with the praetor as a prostitute.[21] The legislators' expectation that the traditional disincentive of *infamia*, or dishonor, would be enough to keep a woman from sacrificing her good name ran exactly contrary to the tendency of the legislation to encourage individuals to think in terms of legal, as opposed to honorable, conduct. Vistilia seems to have understood the implications of the disembedding of sex more clearly than did the legislators who had helped to bring it about.

A similar tension between a traditional code of conduct structured around considerations of honor and shame, and the disembedding of sex from precisely such a context, emerges now and again in the poetry of Ovid. Thus, in *Amores* I.10, the *puella* in question is encouraged to have sex with the poet, and offered a legal basis on which to do so: while she should not act like a prostitute by demanding gifts from him, she should feel free to behave in such a manner with regard to a rich lover.[22] Traditional claims of monogamy are set aside and the *puella* is charged with a crime that is no crime (seeking gifts) in a mock-legal brief, while being encouraged to take advantage of a legal loophole to save herself and the poet from the very real charge of

---

[19] Cohen (1991:124).   [20] On legal personhood and the price it can entail see Daube (1978).

[21] The ancient sources pertaining to this episode are Tac., *Ann.* 2.84 and Suet., *Tib.* 35.

[22] The references to prostitution in this poem are explicit: *prostare* (17), *meretrix* (21), *leno* (22), *vendit/emit* (34), *prostituisse* (42). They are also unparalleled in their detail and specificity in earlier Latin love poetry.

adultery.[23] Yet the legalistic tone of the whole proceeding is undercut by the poet's references throughout to honorable and shameful conduct[24] and his implied threat at the end of the poem that the *puella* will be subject to *infamia* if she does not succumb to his wishes.[25] Ovid's employment here of a discourse that is at once sexual and pre-sexual speaks both to the incompleteness of any radical paradigm shift as well as to the nimbleness of the self-interested in taking advantage of the ambiguities inherent in a transitional situation.

In a related poem, *Amores* 3.14, Ovid seeks to reduce to absurdity the new legal specifications for proving illicit sexual behavior. He alludes to requirements for visual evidence (verses 43–6) and to the protocol for identifying oneself as *famosa* (i.e. disreputable because sexually available; verses 3–6). In contrast, the *puella*'s wantonness in displaying her sexual freedom reduces the speaker to the pre-sexual condition of earlier love poets, as a sequence of allusions to Sappho, Catullus, and Propertius makes clear (verses 37–8, 39, and 40 respectively). The privileging of the speaker's own sense of worth and the denigration of the law may seem to mark Ovid as favoring a re-embedding of sex in an honorable context. Yet the elaborate recital of the overwhelming and multiform evidence of the *puella*'s promiscuity reveals that such a pose is at best a humorous acknowledgement of the inevitable. In this, the penultimate poem of his elegiac collection, Ovid exposes the desperation that characterizes attempts to hold back the rising tide of sexuality. Neither the elegiac *puella* nor the disembedding of sex she has come to figure can be contained any longer by concerns of honor – or by the confines of the poet's book.[26]

Sexual identity and sexual pleasure

If we follow Milligan's description of the emergence of sexuality in the modern era, then the disembedding of sex should be accompanied by its valorization as a new and privileged type of connection between atomized individuals. Or to put it differently, the isolation of sex as a discrete activity

---

[23] The legalistic nature of the language in the poem has been remarked by McKeown (1989: *ad loc.*), following Pokrowskij (1907–1910). Neither scholar, however, notes the possible reference to specific provisions of the *leges Iuliae*.

[24] E.g. the triple anaphora in *turpe* at 39–41, the repetition of *gratia* in 42–6, the use of *officium* at 46 and 53, and of *studium fidemque* at 57. All of these terms and phrases are codewords in the aristocratic lexicon of honorable conduct, as outlined in the indispensable work of Hellegouarc'h (1963). See also Earl (1967).

[25] The word *nota* in line 60 would seem to carry the double meaning of "notorious" and "renowned." I grant that the end of the poem concentrates more on the advantages of good *fama* than the disadvantages of bad, but praise here as always derives much of its force from the implication that the speaker also has the power to blame.

[26] The conflation of sexual availability with the commercial availability of the book of poems appears to be a topos in texts of the period: see the excellent discussion of Horace, *Epistle* 1.20 by Oliensis (1995).

and discrete area for discussion and regulation is a symptom of the breakdown of one model of social interconnection, a breakdown that can only be
remedied by the creation of a new model, in which sex itself assumes pride of
place. From the broad societal perspective this paradigm shift becomes manifest in an increased tendency to identify groups of individuals on the basis of
sexual preference or sexual performance; while at the level of the individual
subject a new assessment of sexual pleasure as itself the sign of a meaningful
connection between human beings comes to be promulgated.[27]

In the poetry of Ovid this double response to the atomization of the cosmopolitan city is evident. For one thing, Ovid invents the category of the heterosexual male. In contrast to earlier Roman amatory poetry which represents
the male lover as interested in boys as well as women and, in the case of
Catullus and Propertius, implies or advocates a strong homosocial bond that
may very well contain what we would describe as a sexual element, the
Ovidian *praeceptor amoris* specifically rejects sexual liaisons with boys (*Ars*
2.683–4), while the *ego* of the *Amores* makes no allusion to the sort of
intense homosocial relationship Catullus imagines with Calvus, or Propertius
intimates in his poems to Gallus.[28] Indeed, within the *Ars*, Ovid explicitly
describes a man who seeks to attract another man as "hardly a man at all"
(*si quis male vir quaerit habere virum, Ars* 1.524). The declaration of a character in Plautus' *Curculio*, to the effect that a freeborn adult male can love
"whatever he wants" – just not a bride, a widow, a youth, or a free-born boy
– describes the situation we would expect in a society governed by honor and
shame: issues of status and property, rather than the gender of the one desired,
determined the propriety of a given sexual connection.[29] With Ovid's exclusive interest in the possibilities of coupling between males and females a new
consideration emerges, namely sexual identity.

The creation of a heterosexual identity by Ovid has been overlooked by
scholars in part because of an unspoken heterocentric assumption that it
is homosexuality or bisexuality, rather than heterosexuality, that requires
explanation.[30] In fact, there are traces of an emergent homosexual identity
during the period in question as well, as indicated in the evidence collected by

---

[27] Cf. Kevin White's description of a new sexual morality in turn-of-the century America: "This
new morality stressed instant gratification and fulfillment through consumption and leisure as
a means of assuaging the boredom and aimlessness of twentieth-century life and as a resolution to the seeming irrelevance of the older system and the dullness of corporate life and
concomitant decline of personal autonomy." (White [1993:13]).

[28] Catullus 50; Propertius 1.10, 1.13, 1.20.

[29] Pl., *Curculio* 37–8: *dum te abstineas nupta vidua virgine iuventute ac pueris liberis ama
quidlubet.* Cantarella (1988:155ff.) connects the passage to the praetor's edict forbidding
attempts on *pudicitia*.

[30] The assumption that it is homosexuality rather than heterosexuality that is in need of explanation has been explicitly challenged in recent years: see Katz (1990), (1995) and White (1993).

Amy Richlin.[31] Richlin asserts that "The ordinary Roman definitions of sexual identity remained consistent over at least the 400-year span (roughly from 200 BCE to 200 CE) of the late Republic to the high Empire",[32] but this seems too uniform a reading of the testimonia she herself brings to light. Only beginning in the first century CE in the Roman world do we find individuals identified in terms of the sex of those they desire (as opposed to descriptions, common in all periods, in terms of the type of activity one prefers); and of the passages cited by Richlin, only Juvenal 2 seems to make reference to male homosexuality as a distinctive category. That satire commences with the usual *cinaedus*-bashing (a *cinaedus* is a male dancer who moves in such a way as to arouse his audience; in abusive contexts the term identifies a man who willingly takes the receptive role in male–male intercourse).[33] As the poem proceeds, it makes mention of occupational clustering, same-sex marriage, and distinctive dress on the part of men who have sexual relations with other men. Richlin associates this text with other descriptions of men who prefer the passive role in sexual intercourse, and in fact refers to a "passive homosexual subculture at Rome";[34] but it is difficult to imagine what it is that two exclusively "passive" homosexuals could do to one another that would parallel consummation of heterosexual marriage. In fact, what infuriates the satiric speaker about the "marriage" in question, and about *molles* in general, is their ability to operate on both sides of the various divides that traditional morality seeks to impose. Thus the noble Gracchus, who marries the flute-player (or maybe it is a stiff trumpet that he performs on, the satirist opines) functions as both a *pater-familias*, inasmuch as he provides the immense dowry for the marriage, and as a *nova nupta*, or blushing bride.[35] Similarly the satire's female speaker, Laronia, is outraged that men can argue in court and study the law (unlike women), but also take on the conventionally female tasks of spinning and weaving (51ff.).

The ability of homosexuals to have it both ways extends to sexual activity as well. Indeed, one of the strategies of the satire is to transfer the opprobrium traditionally directed toward *cinaedi* for their willing acceptance of a receptive role in intercourse to all men who prefer sex with men. Laronia complains about the "great concord" (*magna concordia*: 47) the *molles* enjoy among

---

[31] Richlin (1993).   [32] Richlin (1993:531).

[33] On the meaning of *cinaedus* see, in addition to the works cited by Richlin (1993:531n21), the entry under "*cinaedus*" in the *Thesaurus Linguae Latinae*, the article by Colin (1952/53), and Selden (1992:508n137); also the discussion of the *cochón* in Lancaster (1992).

[34] Richlin (1993:548).

[35]   Quadringenta dedit Gracchus sestertia dotem
           cornicini, sive hic recto cantaverat aere;
           signatae tabulae, dictum "feliciter," ingens
           cena sedet, gremio iacuit nova nupta mariti.

                                                    (Juvenal 2.117–20)

themselves and immediately follows her lament with the claim that women do not tongue (*lambit*: 49) other women. The vacillation between active and passive in her own expression (when women do it, it is called "tonguing"; where men are involved, it is "going under" – *subit*) reveals the inadequacy of the old model of penetrator/penetrated or dominant/submissive to the new phenomenon (or newly recognized phenomenon) she is attempting to denounce.[36]

Significantly for the argument of the present paper, the diatribe against homosexuality in Juvenal 2 concludes by linking it explicitly with the life of the capital city.

> What is done now in the victor's city,
> Those we have conquered do not do. And yet one
> Armenian, Zalaces, softer than all the other ephebes,
> Is said to have taken his own pleasure with an ardent tribune.
> Look at the advantages of commerce: he came a hostage,
> But here hostages learn civility. If the boys stay any longer in the city
> No place on earth will lack for lovers.
> Trousers, knives, bridles, and whip will be discarded here:
> Back to Ardaschan they take the habits of Rome's elite.[37]

Richlin, like most commentators on the passage, takes the the phrase *ardenti se indulsisse tribuno* (165) to mean "indulged an ardent tribune."[38] If I am not

---

[36] Thus while I agree with Konstan (1993) in his critique of Courtney (1984), I do not believe that he makes sufficient allowance for the novelty of the satirist's attack in this poem. That *mollis* elsewhere refers specifically to "passives" (Cantarella [1988], Adams [1982]) is no argument against my interpretation of the poem. The vocabulary employed by the satirists has not caught up (or perhaps been made not to catch up) with the social phenomenon it describes. Compare the terms "faggot" and "queer" in English which can refer either to a person who prefers or accepts a specific role in male–male intercourse or to homosexuals more generally; and which can be applied as insults or as terms of self-identification by those so insulted.

[37]   Sed quae nunc populi fiunt victoris in urbe
      non faciunt illi quos vicimus. Et tamen unus
      Armenius Zalaces cunctis narratur ephebis
      mollior ardenti sese indulsisse tribuno.
      Aspice quid faciant commercia: venerat obses,
      hic fiunt homines. Nam si mora longior urbem
      †indulsit† pueris, non umquam derit amator.
      Mittentur bracae, cultelli, frena, flagellum:
      sic praetextatos referunt Artaxata mores.

                                   (Juvenal 2.163–70)

Leo and others propose a gap of two half lines between *pueris* and *non umquam*. My translation of "*hic fiunt homines*" with reference to civility, as opposed to manliness, takes note of the distinction in Latin between *homo* ("person, human being" as opposed to beast) and *vir* (high-status male as opposed to lower status boy/woman/girl).

[38] Richlin (1993:553).

mistaken, the Latin is better regarded as ambiguous: it can mean either that Zalaces bestowed himself on the tribune (i.e. made himself available for the tribune's pleasure and thereby assumed a "passive" role) or that Zalaces "took his pleasure of the tribune" (as I have translated it) and thereby assumed an "active" role.[39] The first reading is the expected one in view of the traditionally subordinate relationship of captive youth to Roman official; but it is the second that is picked up on by the rest of the passage. There would be nothing surprising about a captive being taken advantage of by a tribune: what is shocking is that the tribune now lets the youth take advantage of him. Having come to Rome a hostage, the Armenian there "becomes civilized" (*fiunt homines*, as the satirist sarcastically puts it). The longer he and others like him remain in Rome to learn new customs, the less likely that any place will lack for *amatores* – a term that specifically describes agents of affection rather than objects of lust. Through the anecdote of Zalaces and the tribune the satirist repeats his claim that one rotten apple can spoil the whole barrel (or, as he puts it, one sick pig fells the herd);[40] it must be emphasized, however, that the contagion he imagines as spreading throughout the world is not passivity, but homosexuality – the preference of men for other men as both agents and objects of desire.

Along with a new sense of personal identity, whether self- or other-bestowed, on the basis of the sex of the erotic object, there also develops in the literature under consideration a focus on sexual pleasure, especially shared sexual pleasure, as an end in itself. This new focus on pleasure as the *telos*, or aim, of sex is apparent in the structure of Ovid's *Ars Amatoria*, as Duncan Kennedy has recently pointed out: both book 2, which is addressed to men, and book 3, which is addressed to women, culminate with description and praise of the possibilities of mutual orgasm.[41] Pleasure for both parties is presented as the only relevant aim of both the poetry and the pursuits it describes. A similar emphasis on sexual climax is apparent in the opening book of the *Amores*, where four elegies pass before Ovid names and describes the object of his lust: Corinna. Within poem 5 she does not speak and barely acts: instead the poet describes his undressing of her, their foreplay, and – who does not know the rest? (*cetera quis nescit?: Amores* 1.5.25). The act of intercourse is the reason for Corinna's existence and the climax of the poem: all that remains

---

[39] For the two meanings of *indulgere se* see *Oxford Latin Dictionary* s.v. *indulgeo*.

[40]   Dedit hanc contagio labem
    et dabit in plures, sicut grex totus in agris
    unius scabie cadit et porrigine porci
    uvaque conspecta livorem ducit ab uva.

(Juvenal 2.78–81)

[41] Kennedy (1993:60).

is post-coital repose and the wish for a repetition of the events that have just been described. The contrast between the first appearance of Ovid's *puella*, and the introduction of the mistress in Catullus, Propertius, and Tibullus, has been well noted by many readers. The emphasis in Ovid on sexual pleasure, especially pleasure constructed on the model of male orgasm, is but a more specific version of the disembedding of sex from other relationships that was described above.

Ovid's valorization of orgasm is apparent on the basis of comparison not only with other Latin love poetry but also with biological and other ancient texts that make reference to sexual pleasure.[42] In Aristotle, references to pleasures of sex, whether equal or unequal for men and women, occur as observations of human experience that must be accounted for, explained away, or ignored, by biological theorizing.[43] His interest, like that of other ancient biologists, is in the mechanics of reproduction and in the status relationship between men and women sustained or implied thereby. Pleasure is an issue only insofar as it relates to one or both of those topics. In at least some of the Hippocratic texts, pleasure is less the product of biology than an independent force that must be reckoned with. But that reckoning consists not in its maximization, as in Ovid, but in its regulation and subordination to broader anatomical and social goals. Thus according to one such text, women should have intercourse as often as possible whether they enjoy it or not. The goal is not to maximize pleasure, but to stabilize the womb which will wander away unless it is fixed in place by a penis and its emissions.[44] Ovid's poetic predecessor Lucretius, in his description of the science and ethics of sexual desire, represents pleasure as a dangerous force, one that disrupts the psychic equanimity of the would-be philosopher in addition to posing a threat to social harmony.[45] Even Cleitophon, the eponymous hero of Achilles Tatius' Greek novel, whose discourse on the relative advantages of women over boys as sexual partners shares certain similarities with Ovid's discussion, is exclusively concerned with the effect a woman's behavior during orgasm has on her male partner rather than with the maximization of the shared pleasure of the sexual encounter.[46]

---

[42] For the ancient biologists' accounts of the origin and function of sexual pleasure, see Laqueur (1990) and Dean-Jones (1992). My discussion in this section is greatly indebted to their research.

[43] See, for example, his discussion at *Gen. An.* 1.20.1 (727b).

[44] *Mul.* 2.123–26, *Nat. Mul.* 2.3 and 2.8 (texts cited by Dean-Jones [1992:n. 35]).

[45] *DRN* 4.1058ff.

[46] Achilles Tatius, *Cleitophon and Leucippe* 2.37. For a discussion of this and related passages in Greek novels, epigrams, and moral literature see Goldhill (1995:82ff.). Goldhill eschews a sociological interpretation of sexuality in the novels on the grounds that their provenance is indeterminate. A similar difficulty does not afflict the study of Ovid.

Ovid, who seems well aware of the ancient scientists' debates over the causes of pleasure and the relative pleasure enjoyed by men and women, makes use of their language and arguments but precisely so as to deny the instrumentality of pleasure which they take for granted and to establish the maximization of shared pleasure as an end in itself: what a student of a later period of sexuality refers to as "fulfillment through consumption."[47] Thus at the climax of book 2 of the *Ars,* Ovid sings the praises of older women as partners in heterosexual intercourse on the grounds that "with them, orgasm is felt without stimulation: let the woman and the man experience pleasure to an equal degree." (*illis sentitur non inritata voluptas/ quod iuvat ex aequo femina virque ferant, Ars* 2.681–682). The phrase "without stimulation" expressly contradicts the Hippocratic claim that a woman does not experience sexual pleasure unless and until she is penetrated by a man.[48] The inference in Ovid is not just that women are independent participants in sexual exchange, but that the lessened need of the man to perform in the case of an auto-orgastic older woman will allow his pleasure to equal hers. At the conclusion to the third book of the *Ars,* the biological subtext to Ovid's teachings becomes even more apparent. There, after recommending equal orgasm and chatter during or after sexual intercourse, the preceptor advises women who have no sensation of orgasm (*sensum Veneris,* 3.797) to feign pleasure with deceitful moan. As if to account for the existence of so *rara* an *avis* as an unorgastic female, he proceeds to declare: "unfortunate the girl for whom that spot is sluggish and unresponsive, a spot through which equally a man and a woman ought to take pleasure" (*infelix cui torpet hebes locus ille puella/quo pariter debent femina virque frui, Ars* 3.799–800).

The expression *infelix cui torpet hebes locus ille puella* situates Ovid firmly in the camp of the one-sex theorists of ancient biology who regard female anatomy and female pleasure as homologous to male.[49] In fact, the Latin line disguises the gender of its subject until the final word: read up to *puella,* it could equally well describe an impotent man. Moreover, the adjective *hebes,* meaning "unresponsive," but also "incapable of penetration,"[50] as of a blunt sword or dagger, or conceivably a phallus, assimilates "that spot" on a female to "that thing" on a male. Earlier in the same passage, Ovid advises women to "experience sexual pleasure from the inmost marrow" (*ex imis medullis, Ars* 3.793): again an invocation of a biological explanation for sexual pleasure,

---

[47] White (1993:13) (see note 27 above).

[48] [Hipp.] *Gen.* 4.1 (= Lonie [1981:2]) states that the woman's pleasure commences when the womb is disturbed during intercourse. According to the same text, her pleasure continues "until the man ejaculates."

[49] On one-sex versus two-sex models of anatomy and ontology see Laqueur (1990).

[50] *Oxford Latin Dictionary* s.v. *hebes.*

this one as old as Plato, who refers to marrow as the source of the fluids emitted during sexual intercourse.[51]

Ovid's focus on pleasure, and in particular on the mutuality of pleasure as enjoyed by men and women in heterosexual intercourse, is an attempt to privilege the pleasure of sex at the expense of other factors that might persuade or dissuade an individual from participating in a given act of intercourse. In particular, Ovid makes use of the argument from equal pleasure to dissuade women from seeking gifts in exchange for sex. This point is made explicit in *Amores* 1.10, where the seducer inquires "when sex pleases both to an equal extent, why should one buy and the other pay?" (*Am.* 1.10.33–34) and is implied at the end of *Ars* 3 where a recommendation for equal pleasure (796) is followed a few lines later (805) by a reminder to women that they should not ask for a present after performing in bed. In both cases Ovid associates sexual performance with aristocratic *noblesse oblige*: each party must feel free to bestow benefits on the other. To insist upon engaging in sex on a contractual basis (*certo aere*: 21) is dishonorable (*turpe*: 39, 41). The advantage gained by the male in adopting this position should be obvious: since pleasure constructed on the basis of male experience and honor is a quality that functions in large part to protect his own privileged position, denying the woman the option of negotiating a contract prevents her assertion of her own subjective desires or needs. As Terry Eagleton puts it with respect to a similar conflict over law and generosity in *The Merchant of Venice*, "[Portia's] gratuitousness is a deeply ambivalent quality . . . those who wield power can afford to dispense with exact justice from time to time, since they, after all, control the rules of the game . . . The victimized need a fixed contract, however hard-hearted that may seem, precisely because they would be foolish to rely on the generosity of their oppressors."[52]

Ovid's deployment of the argument concerning mutual pleasure in heterosexual intercourse to the advantage of the para-aristocratic male poet, is thus another example of his ability to manipulate the discourse of sexuality even as it first emerges in his poetry. Rather than accepting the logical consequences of the disembedding of sex from traditional relationships of honor and shame, he seeks to make sexuality one more area for exercise of aristocratic prerogative. Because women remain in so many ways inferior to men in the Roman world despite their changing legal status, insistence on the mutuality of pleasure between men and women in heterosexual intercourse poses no particular threat to the power relationships that prevail in other aspects of society. Such is not the case where sexual relationships between men are concerned, and indeed we can trace the growing recognition of the destabilizing potential of

---

[51] Plato *Timaeus* 86c, 91b; Hipp. *Gen.* 1.1 (= Lonie [1981:1]).   [52] Eagleton (1986:41).

homosexual relations between the poetry of Catullus and that of Juvenal. In Catullus, the mutuality of the homosocial bond is stressed in poem 50, where Catullus and Calvus are said to engage in an equal exchange of poetry and desire (note the expressions *modo hoc modo illoc* and *reddens mutua* at 50.5–6).[53] Because, according to the argument of this paper, a distinctive discourse of sexuality has not yet emerged, or at least not been entered into by Catullus, the possibility of a sexual relationship between Catullus and Calvus remains just one aspect or expression of the allegiances expected between men of similar station. When specific sexual acts are described by Catullus, they are always manifestations of relationships of power, usually unequal power. Ovid transfers the notion of mutuality from homosocial to heterosexual relations and concretizes it in an exhortation to equal enjoyment, but the net effect is to disembed sex from its traditional context without disrupting other aspects of that context that he has an interest in preserving. The Ovidian *amator*'s pretense that his mistress can love him as freely as Calvus can love Catullus flies in the face of everything we know about the asymmetrical distribution of power between men and women in the historical Rome. By Juvenal 2, the possibility of the mutual pleasuring of men, independent of the traditional relationships of power and domination, strikes terror into the heart of the satirist. The marriage treated with such scorn is not just between two men: it unites the rich and noble Gracchus with a mere horn-player. And the relationship between the tribune and the Armenian ephebe subverts hierarchies of both rank and ethnicity. The "great concord" to be found among homosexuals, especially if transported from the cosmopolitan capital to the frontier provinces, threatens to undo the patterns of oppression and domination on which the entire empire is and has been built. The resulting disruption spreads Rome's dishonor even among the dead (149ff.).

Privacy and professionalism

One manifestation of the disembedding of sex from other kinds of relationships is a new emphasis on creation of a private space for performance of sexual acts.[54] When a given subject's sexual privilege or sexual availability is but a consequence and expression of relative status more broadly conceived, then there is no particular need for sexual desire or sexual behavior to be kept hidden from the public view. In a pre-sexual context, to the extent that sexual liaisons are expected to be conducted in private, it is because certain sorts of

---

[53] On the homosocial and homoerotic aspects of Catullus' poetry and of the later literature it has inspired see Fitzgerald (1995).

[54] Weeks (1989:13) mentions privacy as an aspect of sexuality overlooked by Foucault, "Sex, that is to say, is the essence of our individual being which asserts itself against the demands of culture."

liaisons, specifically those within marriage, are exclusionary in order to secure the legitimacy of potential offspring. In ancient Athens, sex within marriage is kept private, but sex at a symposium, whether with women or boys, is not. A noteworthy Cynic epistle in which the philosopher describes the negative consequences of his public masturbation at the sight of a beautiful youth refers to a deliberate violation of the decorum of the gymnasium and a provocative display of desire toward a free-born male rather than reflecting any preference for keeping sex private, on the part of either the Cynic or his critics.[55] The distinctive privilege of public nudity and aggressive display of the phallus accorded to free-born males in democratic Athens suggests that some degree of public display and public acknowledgment may even be essential to the propagation and enforcement of a traditional sexual status system.[56] In Rome, the toga, rather than nudity, is the costume that marks the sexually privileged adult male,[57] while the wearing of an apotropaic *bulla* distinguishes sexually unavailable free-born boys from their less privileged counterparts.[58] The use of the toga to advertise sexual privilege explains its assignment to prostitutes and actresses alone among Roman women: they, like elite males, albeit for opposite reasons, can engage in sex *ad libitum* with impunity.

The potentially public nature of sexual activity is evident in the poetry of Catullus. Catullus' enemies are subject to public ridicule and publicly threatened with sexual abuse, and in several poems, public sex is graphically described. The habitués of the *salax taberna* in poem 35 are criticized more for their corruption of the poet's girl than for the public nature of their carryings-on, while Lesbia's masturbation (if that it is) of Remus' descendants on street-corners and in back-alleys (poem 58) is objectionable not as public sex but as public humiliation of Catullus, who regarded her as his own (*Lesbia nostra, plus quam se atque suos amavit*: 58.1, 3). Catullus' own intrusion into the sex-play of a couple he finds *in flagranti* is a source of laughter rather than embarrassment (poem 56), while his invitation to Lesbia (poem 5) to love him without regard for the opinions of judgmental elders (*rumores senum seueriorum*, 5.2) and to share kisses beyond number so as to confound the envious (*ne quis malus invidere possit*, 5.12) presupposes a public context for their extravagant osculation. Indeed, the poem in question (number 5) invokes the familiar image of a circle of *aestimatores*, or judges, of aristocratic display (*aestimemus*, 5.3),[59] if only to turn it around by proposing that the lovers assess their assessors. The one poem in which Catullus seems to privilege a

---

[55] The letter in question is Diogenes 35, available in Greek and English in Malherbe (1977: 144–47).

[56] On phallic display at Athens, see Keuls (1993/1985); elsewhere Fehling (1974/1988).

[57] I owe the concept of nudity as a costume to David Leitao.

[58] On the nature and function of the *bulla* see Daremberg and Saglio (1877–1919).

[59] On *aestimatio* see Habinek (1990a) and (1992).

private context for sexual relations, number 68, concerning the house of Allius, is an exception that proves the rule, for it specifically assimilates Catullus' affair to marriage through invocation of the mythological paradigm of Protesilaus and Laodamia (*coniugis . . . flagrans . . . amore*, 68.73) In Catullan poetry, as in a pre-sexual context more generally, the relative appropriateness of the public versus private performance of sexual acts can only be evaluated in terms of the relative status of the participants involved.

In contrast to Catullus' more complicated protocol concerning public displays of affection, Ovid is adamant about the need for sexual liaisons to be conducted in private. In *Amores* 2.19 the poet criticizes a husband who too obviously leaves his wife available for an adulterous affair. The lack of challenge, but also the elimination of the element of deception, are regarded by the poet as violations of the rules of the game. In 3.14 he exactly reverses the traditional logic which requires that only sex in a context of marriage be kept private. Here Ovid admits that he has no claim to exclusivity with respect to the object of his affections, yet nonetheless insists that his *puella* keep her promiscuity to herself: "no girl sins who is capable of denying that she has sinned: only public confession destroys her reputation" (*non peccat, quaecumque potest peccasse negare/ solaque famosam culpa professa facit*, Am. 3.14.5–6). In poem 1.5 Corinna's first appearance is to the poet in a darkened private room. While he gladly – and necessarily, since otherwise there would be no poem – shares virtually everything about her with his reading/listening public, he leaves undescribed the sexual act itself. This same emphasis on discretion recurs in the *Ars Amatoria*, where the preceptor exhorts his audience not to brag about sexual conquests any more than they would have sex outside the bedroom: better for girls to be off-limits altogether than to be the topic of boastful accusations (*Ars* 2.601–40). Even the advice on comportment during the act of intercourse is hedged about with admonitions concerning privacy: at *Ars* 2.704 the Muse is instructed to wait outside the closed doors of the bedchamber; while the description of intercourse near the end of *Ars* 3 is preceded by reference to the poet's sense of modesty (769–70) and finished with an admonition not to let too much light in through the bedroom windows (807–08).[60]

The privatization of sex that characterizes Ovid's poetry goes hand in hand with the publicization of sexuality. As sex becomes removed from public observation and disembedded from a broader network of social relations, it becomes the topic of public conversation and public advice on the part of a newly emergent class of experts. While we have little evidence concerning the sexual acculturation of youths in pre-cosmopolitan Rome, the literature and art

---

[60] The privatization of sex would seem to be a characteristic of the visual arts of the period as well: see sources cited at Habinek (1982); also Clarke (1991); Myerowitz (1992).

of the archaic and classical Greek symposium point to a semi-public context for initiation into the sexual aspect of elite male behavior.[61] It seems likely that certain rituals served a similar purpose for young women in both Greece and Rome.[62] Ovid imagines a completely different mode of acculturation in the form of lessons from a professional sexologist. Parents, mentors, and local elders are noteworthy by their absence from the education of both the male and the female audience for the *Ars Amatoria*. We can draw no conclusions concerning the real importance of book-learning in shaping the first sexual experiences of young Romans on the basis of Ovid's witty and sophisticated manual for lovers. Indeed the work presupposes familiarity with the task at hand: the most the reader will get is expert advice on particulars and a systematic account of what she or he may already know by experience. Yet the mere possibility, whether intended seriously or not, of reducing pursuit, seduction, foreplay, and intercourse to a set of learnable rules is a reflection of the proliferation of specialized discourses that characterizes the late Republic and early Principate at Rome – i.e., the period during which the city became a cosmopolis. The case of Ovid makes it appropriate to expand Andrew Wallace-Hadrill's account of the development of expert discourses of time, tradition, law, and language to include an expert discourse of sex as well.[63]

Recent articles by Holt Parker (on *anaiskhuntographoi*) and by Molly Myerowitz (on erotic wall-paintings, or *tabellae*) remind us of some of the means (other than Ovid's *Ars*) through which a cosmopolitan Roman might have learned to bring technique to bear on his or her love-life.[64] In addition, the application of the language of disease to homosexuality, as discussed by Amy Richlin,[65] may constitute further evidence for the development of a professional, in this case, medical, discourse concerning sexual behavior. (With regard to the later re-emergence of sexuality in industrialized Europe, Arnold Davidson will argue that modern sexuality cannot exist in the absence of psychiatric reasoning.)[66] In this respect, Ovid's *Ars* bears somewhat the same relationship to the discourse of the specialists as Virgil's *Georgics* does to agricultural handbooks. At the same moment that it testifies to the development of sex (or agriculture, in the case of Virgil) as a discrete and problematical topic for analysis and to the concomitant rationalization of the subject, Ovid's *Ars* also represents the co-optation by the elite (in this case a member of the literary elite) of the skills and competencies of the professional class. It is precisely such a co-optation, or subordination, of technical discourses to larger cultural projects that Wallace-Hadrill describes as characteristic of the reign of Augustus.[67] In the case of the *Georgics*, the poet's incorporation of both

---

[61] Bremmer (1990).   [62] Dowden (1989).   [63] Wallace-Hadrill (this volume)
[64] Parker (1992); Myerowitz (1992).   [65] Richlin (1993).   [66] Davidson (1987).
[67] Wallace-Hadrill (this volume).

traditional and expert lore suggests an uneasiness over the totalizing claims of rationalization, and may constitute a subtle intervention in political and philosophical debates of the time.[68] In the *Ars*, Ovid cheerfully, yet with tragic consequences, miscalculates the extent to which rationalization has replaced considerations of honor and shame, at least in the official line emanating from the imperial household: if we are to believe him, a *carmen*, most likely the *Ars*, was one basis for his relegation by the emperor to the shores of the Black Sea.[69]

We must not confuse the immediate biographical impact of the *Ars* with its broader social implications. This work, together with the *Amores*, articulates sexuality as a discourse in the world-city of Augustan Rome. The differences between Ovidian amatory poetry and earlier works in the same vein cannot adequately be described in terms of variation within a literary tradition. In the poetry of Ovid, sex emerges as a discrete topic of discussion, investigation, and rationalization, independent of its significance as marker of other sorts of social relationships. This disembedding of sex manifests itself in an emphasis on shared pleasure as an end in itself, in the creation of distinctive sexual identities (heterosexual and homosexual), and in the insistence on the private performance and private significance of sexual intercourse. Paradoxically, the invention of sexuality as a distinctive discourse and a privileged basis for the construction of human relationships is best understood as the product of a new set of social and economic conditions, much as Milligan has argued with respect to the modern period. The breakdown of traditional ties of loyalty and community, the atomization of the individual, and the rationalization and commodification of human relationships are all features of the world-city, in antiquity as in the modern era.[70] In the case of revolutionary Rome, the limitations imposed on traditional expressions of male competitiveness and dominance heightened the importance of performance in the sexual sphere and fostered a need to differentiate the true *vir* from the *male vir*. What the ancient city lacked that the modern city depends upon is a capitalist system of economic organization, a difference that may in part account for the resistances to the development of sexuality also traced in this paper: peasant concepts of honor and shame retained relevance in an urbanized Roman

---

[68] Schiesaro (this volume).   [69] Rudd (1976).

[70] In this respect my argument parallels that of Konstan (1994), who seeks to connect the distinctive emphasis on sexual symmetry between male and female lovers in Greek novels to the changing social conditions under which they were composed. Konstan's discussion is helpful to my case for its clear delineation between the culture of city as polis and the culture of city as node in an imperial system. More problematic are his reading of the novels as "response" to changed social conditions and his failure to identify differences between Roman and Greek experience that might account for the differences he perceives between Roman and Greek novels.

society still largely organized around patterns of patronage and clientage. In the modern world, it is capitalism, together with technology, that generates and requires the rapid pace of change to which an attempted stabilization of sexual identity responds in the modern city. In Augustan Rome change was also swift, albeit for other reasons.

The social, political, spatial, and economic changes that characterize modern cities as well as Augustan Rome, produce, and are in turn intensified in their impact by, changes in discourse of both a literary and a non-literary sort. It is as a result of historical accident that in the case of cosmopolitan Rome we must read these changes chiefly in the imaginative creations of the poets, as opposed to the journals, police records, and medical reports available to researchers in later periods of history. But difference need not imply incommensurability: in the case of the ancient city, as this paper has argued, it is possible to trace discursive developments comparable to those more readily manifest in the historical record from other places and times. Moreover, the very literariness of the Augustan discourse of sexuality gives it a distinctive transhistorical force. As Labate, Kennedy, and others have argued, Ovid's poetry contributes to the valorization of culture in the Roman world and in later periods of Western history that look to Rome for inspiration and authorization.[71] The glamor of the poets' representation of human sexual relations makes of their texts one of the pressures that determine the particular configurations of sexuality as it re-emerges under comparable conditions at different moments in the history of the West. In the poetry of Catullus we have eloquent testimony to the alienation produced by relocation to the *urbs*; in the writings of Ovid we trace the inscription of perhaps the most powerful response to that alienation yet invented: sexuality.

[71] Labate (1984), Kennedy (1993).

3   *Recitatio* and the reorganization of the space of public discourse

Florence Dupont
(translated by Thomas Habinek and André Lardinois)

During the Roman Republic, *oratio*, or public discourse, constitutes the means by which the ideal citizen enacts and confirms his status or *dignitas* within the socio-political hierarchy of the state. For the Roman nobleman, the opportunity to use language in such a manner and thereby gain access to high honors is the essence of *libertas*. Because the places in which *oratio* is performed – the forum, the Campus Martius, and the Senate – are public places, or places of the *populus*, the public discourse conducted in them reactivates the collective memory, whether mythical or historical, that is inscribed upon the topography of the city. Political discourse at Rome is thus associated both with *libertas* and with a political/religious arrangement of the city's space. The exercise of the public discourse of *libertas* involves the whole collective memory of Rome. It lies at the very heart of Republican culture in that it ensures the continuation of the political class, their rootedness in both space and time, and their communication with the rest of the *populus senatusque Romanus*, whose presence as addressee or spectator is prerequisite to the performance of a speech.

As a practice, oratory is thus situated firmly within a culture of orality. The impact of *oratio* on the orator, that is its social efficacy from the standpoint of the subject, cannot be accomplished except through performance. A written discourse has no effect. The subject of the text cannot replace the subject of the performance; nor can the reader or *lector* play the part of the orator. An *oratio* is always an *actio* (or performance), orally delivered and improvised. To prepare a speech is not so much to compose it in advance as to rehearse for its performance.

The practice of oratory is a fundamental institution of Republican *libertas*. It determines the worth of the members of the *nobilitas*. What becomes of it under the Empire?

With Augustus' seizure of power, the spaces for the performance of *oratio* disappear, together with the political context. Power is now exercised neither in public places, such as the forum and Campus Martius, nor in public buildings, such as the curia or temples, but in the interior of the palace of the princeps on the Palatine. The emperor monopolizes the power of political speech, while at the same time redefining it, for he no longer uses speech as a means of persuasion. He has no reason to persuade, since his word, or his decrees, which are extensions of himself, have the force of law. Oratory of the traditional sort is reduced to ancillary status, consisting of either speeches on command, such as panegyric of the emperor, or pleadings of a technical nature before minor tribunals. In neither case does oratorical discourse survive as the institution of liberty through which the nobility demonstrates its worth and secures its prestige.

But another institution emerges during this period, namely, *recitatio* or public reading. At the same time, literature, and with it, the publication of books of poems, history, and even speeches, continues to expand. Other prestigious modes of discourse would thus seem to take the place of the old Republican *oratio*; but these modes imply the use of writing. Does the transition from the Republic to the Principate perhaps also entail the transition from an public discourse that is oral to a public discourse that is written? Let us attempt to answer this question through an investigation of *recitatio*.[1]

Public discourse? Private discourse? Ludic discourse? The ambiguities of *recitatio*

Asinius Pollio, who was a contemporary of Augustus, is reputed to have been the first to organize *recitationes* as they come to be known during the Empire. "Public reading" is a bad translation of the Latin term *recitatio*, since there is nothing public about *recitationes* in the civic or political sense of that word. To the contrary, *recitationes* constitute a private form of oratorical (or poetical) discourse, a discourse that bestows social prestige and thus substitutes, at least in part, for the traditional *oratio*.[2]

In a *recitatio*, the writer of a treatise reads the text aloud to a small circle of friends. We are dealing here with a real "writer," that is someone who has entrusted his text to the page, whether he actually traced the letters himself or had a slave do it. This text can be a lyric or epic poem, a scene from the theater (i.e. a dramatic poem), a historical narrative, or even a speech.[3] Excluded are public readings of works commonly referred to as *sermones*,

---

[1] I can never express adequately my debt throughout this study of *recitatio* and publication under the Empire to the works of Emmanuelle Valette-Cagnac, in particular her 1993 thesis (EPHE, fifth section), entitled *Anthropologie de la lecture dans la Rome antique*.

[2] On Asinius Pollio and the history of *recitationes* see Quinn (1982) and Pennacini (1989). Under the Republic, recitation, as practiced for example by Cicero, was merely a training exercise for public speaking and not yet a social institution. On the Republican orators' awareness and manipulation of the symbolic significance of the venues of their speeches see Vasaly (1993).

[3] Pliny, *Ep.* 7.17.1–4.

such as philosophical dialogues, since *sermones* constitute the degree zero of writing for the Romans, that is a purely instrumental use of language sustained by an ideal of transparency and resistant to a reading that focuses on style as opposed to content. (Indeed, philosophy prided itself on doing without style.)[4] In addition, the text that constitutes the object of a *recitatio* is always unpublished, so that each reading is unique and the *recitatio* itself becomes something of an event.

A private performance

This event, as was noted above, takes place within a private space: the house of the author or a friend, [5] or an auditorium hired especially for the occasion. The space is always within the city of Rome, at least at the beginning of the Principate. And even later, when provincial capitals develop their own public readings, Rome remains the only place where one can obtain literary fame. This is why Seneca the Elder leaves Spain, together with his children and household goods, and heads for Rome.

The organization of the space of *recitatio* and the behavior of its participants makes it an ambiguous realm, one that resembles at once the theater, the curia, and even the courtroom.[6] Despite the presence of an *orchestra* and a *pulpitum*, all is arranged so as to avoid having the reading of a text turn into its theatrical staging. In particular, the speaker remains seated, which of course prevents him not only from staging his text, but even from making use of such gestures as an orator might legitimately employ. It is a motionless body

---

[4] On *sermo* as instrumental, see Cicero, *Orator* 61 and 113.

[5] A reading that takes place in a public location and before the entire *populus* is unusual at Rome and in my view to be distinguished from *recitatio* on the basis of both its social effect and its performative nature. Virgil's verses, it is often pointed out, were applauded in the theater, but can this performance be regarded as a *recitatio*? Tacitus (*Dial.* 13) is quite precise: *auditis in theatro Vergilii versibus*. In addition, he observes that Virgil found himself at the performance by chance and as a spectator: *forte praesentem spectantemque Vergilium*. As will become clear below, this is hardly the customary position of an author during a *recitatio*, where, in fact, his attendance is required and he makes himself available to the public's gaze, whether he actually reads his verse or not. At a *recitatio*, the author is not among the spectators. Thus the event described by Tacitus must be a performance of Virgil's verses, most likely the *Bucolics*, complete with singing and dancing. We have testimony to such an occurrence in Suetonius' *Life of Virgil*, 102–03 (*Bucolica eo successu edidit ut in scaena quoque per cantores crebro pronuntiarentur*) and in Servius' note on *Buc.* 6.11 (*Dicitur autem ingenti favore a Vergilio esse recitata adeo ut cum eam postea Cytheris cantasset in theatro*). These theatrical representations follow recitation or publication (which itself presupposes a preliminary *recitatio*).

[6] Juvenal 8.38–53.

that delivers the text, never a performer such as a lawyer or a comic actor. The audience is seated in hierarchical fashion, the most important people in the front on chairs, the others, both free and freedmen, in the back on benches. There may even be a paid clapper among them. This hierarchical seating of the audience makes the *recitatio* look like a political gathering, such as the Senate, and distinguishes it from the traditional theater, where undifferentiation had until the time of Augustus been the rule (see Suet., *Aug.* 44). It makes it clear that the audience is not the licentious spectatorship of the *ludicrum*; rather, an appeal will be made to their judgment, or *iudicium*, as happens in a political assembly or a *consilium*.[7] And the audience of the *recitatio* is in every respect private, since it consists of invited friends,[8] and a stranger would not normally enter the gathering.[9] This audience is in any event indispensable to the *recitatio* since it urges the *lector* on by its cries and even determines the length of the session. Without an audience there can be no *recitatio*.[10] In this respect, the *recitatio* resembles traditional oratory, whether political or judicial, for which an audience is also indispensable, even when it is not the addressee. Cicero makes note of his own need for the *corona*, or public attendant upon the proceedings in the forum, including friends of the advocate. Without the *corona*, the orator loses an essential component of his success, as happened to Cicero when he tried to defend Milo. But note the difference: in a *recitatio*, the *corona* itself is the target of the presentation, whereas in an *oratio*, the real audience consists of the judges.

A social event

From the standpoints of time, space, and audience, the *recitatio* is a private performance. It has no place either in the calendar or in the political organization of the city's space. Nevertheless, a *recitatio* is very different from the rhetorical exercises that occupied men of affairs and constituted a prelude to the main event in either the Senate or the Forum. The *recitatio* is a social event in itself, and is not followed by any other oral performance in a public

---

[7] In response to the Julian laws the theatrical *cavea* was also organized and disciplined in accordance with social criteria (Suet., *Aug.* 44), but it never assumed the role of a *consilium*. The theater remained the locus of "licentious" pleasures.

[8] Invitation is a defining custom with regard to space in the Roman world. No one is permitted to enter a house unless *invitatus*. To do otherwise is to commit an act of violence or *vis*. The importance of this custom is attested by the number of letters of invitation to dinner, fictional or otherwise, that recur throughout Latin poetry.

[9] It is surprising that Claudius takes the initiative to enter the auditorium since he heard the public outcry from the exterior. See n. 11 below.

[10] Pliny often asks his correspondents to find an audience for him when he is getting ready for a *recitatio*: e.g. *Ep.* 5.12.2.

space. The City takes an interest in *recitatio* in and of itself, as is shown by the fact that public approval at times literally could not be contained within the house in which the reading took place. Pliny reports that Claudius, having heard the noise from a *recitatio* of Nonianus, proceeded at once, unannounced, to the event.[11] The anecdote shows that it was easy to find out who was giving a *recitatio*, the more so since recitations were always held in the city: texts written in the countryside are subsequently presented in the city through a *recitatio*.[12] Although the populace at large is never invited to a *recitatio*, nevertheless performance at a *recitatio* is an honorable and even prestigious activity, one of which the City is quickly informed – in contrast to a funeral oration delivered at the private ceremony known as the *funus indictivum*.[13]

In the same manner, the imperial palace keeps close track of the *recitationes* given by members of the senatorial or equestrian orders. This activity loses its political neutrality precisely to the extent that rumor overtakes it. In Tacitus' *Dialogus* the friends of Maternus are disturbed both by the negative effect of his *Cato* on Vespasian and by the widespread discussion of the work the day after Maternus' *recitatio*:

> It was the day following that on which Curiatius Maternus had given a reading of his *Cato*, when court circles were said to have taken umbrage at the way in which he had thrown himself in the play heart and soul into the role of Cato, with never a thought of himself. The thing was the talk of the town . . .[14]

An event of little consequence

While the *recitatio* is a self-contained feature of the life of the City, in many cases it is nothing more than a prelude to the publication, in the form of a book, of the text being delivered. Pliny the Younger tells us that *recitatio* provides the author with the opportunity to correct his text, which is always provisional. In contrast, the publication of a text gives it a new status in society: from private discourse it becomes public discourse. The book that

---

[11] *Cum (Claudius) in Palatio spatiaretur audissetque clamorem, causam requisisse cumque dictum esset recitare Nonianum subitum recitanti inopinatumque venisse*: Plin., *Ep.* 1.13.3.

[12] Plin., *Ep.* 1.13.6.

[13] The *funus indictivum* differs from the *funus publicum* which is a public event, a "state funeral" so to speak. At the latter the *elogium* of the deceased and his ancestors is pronounced in the forum. Pliny (*Ep.* 3.10) gives a public reading of his *elogium* of Vestricius Cottus without even inviting the family who constitute, at a real *laudatio funebris*, the official audience of the speech, together with the deceased's predecessors who are present in the form of *imagines*, or death masks.

[14] *Nam postero die quam Curiatius Maternus Catonem recitaverit, cum offendisse potentium animos diceretur, tamquam in eo tragoediae argumento sui oblitus tantum Catonem cogitasset, eaque de re per urbem frequens sermo haberetur . . .* Tac., *Dial.* 2, tr. W. Peterson (Cambridge, Mass. 1946).

emerges from the *recitatio* has as its potential audience the Roman people in their entirety: hence the use of the verb *emittere*, to send forth, to describe publication. The shift in potential audience is worth calling attention to, even if we have become accustomed to the implicit democracy of publication. As Pliny says, "I remember having read to a few what I wrote for many" (*memini quidem me non multis recitasse quod omnibus scripsi, Ep.* 3.18.9). The book offers the author a larger audience, giving it a republican dimension, which is why an emperor could tolerate the public reading of the *Cato*, but could not permit its publication.[15] Secundus, who the day after the recitation finds Maternus with the manucript of the *Cato* in his hands, remarks: "Has the talk of your detractors no terrors for you, Maternus? Does it not make you feel less enamored of that exasperating *Cato* of yours? Or is it with the idea of going carefully over it that you have taken your drama in hand, intending to cut out any passages that may have given a handle for misrepresentation, and then to publish your *Cato*, if not better than it was at least not so dangerous?"[16] The political powers ascribe to the discourse of the *recitatio* less weight than to the text of a book. The *recitatio* is a source of irritation rather than anxiety, and so it remains under the empire a tolerated venue for senatorial opposition.

The relative inconsequentiality of the *recitatio* has to do with the fact that it is always defined by lacks and absences, which make of it a deficient fiction. When pressed by his friends to give a reading of an oration which he has already delivered before a real tribunal, Pliny hesitates, for, as he writes, "Speeches, when recited, lose all their force and intensity, even their identity as speeches" (*actiones quae recitantur impetum omnem caloremque ac prope nomen suum perdere, Ep.* 2.19.2)." And if the reading of a speech renders it cold and lifeless, to the extent that it is no longer recognized as a speech, it is because a speech requires the performative context for which it was composed. As Pliny continues in the passage cited above: ". . . their fire is fed from the atmosphere of court: the bench of magistrats and throng of advocates, the suspense of the awaited verdict, reputation of the different speakers, and the divided enthusiasm of the public."[17] All of this transforms the *oratio* into an occasion experienced as such by its participants, who constitute the only

---

[15] Plin., *Ep.* 7.19.5 speaks of a certain Senecion, condemned by a *senatus consultum* for having written a biography of the senator Helvidius, who was celebrated for his republican virtues.

[16] *Nihilne, inquit, Materne, fabulae malignorum terrent quo minus offensas Catonis tui ames? An ideo librum istum adprehendisti ut diligentius retractares et sublatis si qua pravae interpretationi materiam dederunt, emitteres Catonem non quidem meliorem sed tamen securiorem?* Tac., *Dial.* 3, tr. W. Peterson.

[17] *ut quas soleant commendare simul et accendere iudicium consessus, celebritas advocatorum, exspectatio eventus, fama non unius actoris diductumque in partes audentium studium, Ep.* 2.19.2 tr. B. Radice (Cambridge, Mass. 1969).

adequate audience. And it is the occasion itself that bestows its reality on oratorical discourse, which has no existence independent of the unique performative context. Furthermore, it is the subject of the performance, namely the orator,
who establishes by the play of his body and his physical presence (*actio*) the
link between the speech and its referent. It is he who connects with the social
reality and makes of his speech an event. And so what is lacking in the *recitatio*
is the entire performative mechanism of *oratio*, as a result of which the text as
such becomes inaudible. The listener at a *recitatio* does not "hear" at the
reading of an oration what those who attend an authentic trial, whether as judges
or as spectators in the *corona*, hear. Which is why the *recitatio* must rely on
another form of reception, in order for the listener to hear anything at all.

A ludic performance

The reception in question is ludic. Like theatrical discourse, the discourse of
the *recitatio* is received with attention paid to its strictly formal aspect. The
morality of the matter (*res*) is not of concern, which is precisely the Roman
definition of ludism.[18] Thus Pliny mentions in one of his letters (5.17.1) that
he was present at the first *recitatio* of Calpurnius Piso at which the young
nobleman read a poem concerning astronomy. The audience was enchanted
not by the scientific knowledge of the boy but by the excellence of his verses
and the beautiful variety of his style. The stars were but a pretext for a literary
exercise. The young man demonstrated his perfect command of the language,
that is of the technical competencies of an orator, just as he might have in an
exercise at school (*ludus*). His concern was to convince the audience not of
the truth of what he was saying, but of his own rhetorical virtuosity. In other
times his performance might have marked the beginning of a beautiful career
in the forum. In the case of Pliny's own *oratio*, what he fears, with justice, is
that his speech, which is more argumentative than oratorical, might bore his
listeners (*Ep.* 2.19.5). He is concerned that listeners at *recitationes* are incapable of situating themselves within a fictive performance, of constituting in
their imaginations the context of a case or, as is of course impossible, of playing
the part of the judge so as to be the fictive recipient of an absent *oratio*.

Presented out of context, the texts read at recitations are without social
reality. There is always a gap between, on the one hand, the text and performance implied by it, and on the other, the recitation. There is no text that
corresponds to the type of performance that constitutes *recitatio*. Each type of
text performed at a *recitatio* clearly belongs to another performative context,
as Pliny tells us explicitly at 7.17.3: "I should like to ask them why they allow
(if they do allow) readings of history, whose authors aim at truth and accuracy

---

[18] On the concept of ludism, see F. Dupont, *L'acteur-roi* (Paris 1985), pp. 48ff. (English translation in preparation University of California Press).

rather than at displaying their talents, and tragedy, which needs a stage and actors rather than a lecture-room, and lyric poetry, which calls for a chorus and a lyre instead of a reader."[19] It is this discrepancy between the performance implied in the genres of tragedy, lyric, or oratory, and the performance of the *recitatio* that robs the text that is read of its social reality and therefore of its power. As a consequence members of the audience cannot judge the effects of the text, its impact as a performance, but can only appreciate its *compositio*, i.e. the way it is put together. Their function is professorial, in that they can criticize the text as if it were an exercise with regard to which they express merely a technical judgment.

As a result, the *recitatio* is always on the verge of becoming theater, that other pole of ludism. The text, which is always exploited for its formal qualities, becomes the basis of a vocal exhibition in which the appreciation of a rhetorical piece of writing disappears in favor of a spectacular interpretation on the part of the speaker which in turn calls for a musical and sensuous reception of the text. A passage from Persius illustrates the point:

> It is understood that you will read
> this product publicly: combed, fresh laundered, white,
> wearing a carnelian – decked out, in fact,
> as though it were your birthday – on a lofty
> rostrum, in a flowing recitativo,
> from nimble, liquid gullet, and rolling
> over the audience an orgastic eye.
> Soon, you can see enormous Toms and Dicks
> off good behaviour: their voices fog over,
> they begin to flutter as the chant enters
> via their backsides and their insides are tweaked
> by twitching verses.[20]

This text, of singular obscenity yet with the clarity characteristic of satirical exaggeration, shows how a *recitatio* may lose its primary function of presenting the naked utterance, in the absence of any *mise-en-scène* (recall the seated position of the *lector*), and instead be led astray by the musicality and vocal

---

[19] Plin., Ep. 7.17.3 (tr. Radice).

[20]
> Scilicet haec populo pexusque togaque recenti
> Et natalicia tandem cum sardonyche albus
> sede legens celsa, liquido cum plasmate guttur
> Mobile conlueris, patranti fractus ocello
> Tunc neque more probo videas nec voce serena
> Ingentis trepidare Titos cum carmina lumbum
> Intrant et tremulo scalpantur ubi intima versu.

Persius, *Satires* 1.15–21, tr. R. E. Braun in *Roman Poets of the Early Empire*, ed. A. J. Boyle and J. P. Sullivan (Harmondsworth 1991).

play of this same *lector*. The pleasure of the audience is thus typically that of the audience in the theater: the passive, musical pleasure of a body both abandoned and possessed. This type of reading in fact belongs in the theater and ought not to be confounded with *recitationes*. There, at least, in order to make the text more pleasurable to the audience, actors, singers, and dancers are employed, as was the case with the performance of Virgil's *Bucolics*.[21] To a certain degree the *recitator* "cheats," for he tries to acquire to his advantage but by illicit means the prestige associated with a successful *recitatio*. At the same time, there is no great distance between theatrical ludism and professorial ludism since in both cases the mode of perception is purely formal, directed toward the language of the text rather than its content.

Recitatio *and the senatorial opposition*

Recitatio in the imperial period differs from both theatrical and civic (whether judicial or political) discourse, while at the same time situating itself in a social space that transcends the limits of purely private pleasures. Located between the public and the private realms, the discourse performed at a *recitatio* partakes of the intimacy of a conversation among friends at a country estate as well as of the extended publicity of a published book. For these reasons it can serve as an expression of political opposition, one to be tolerated by emperors claiming to be republican, such as Augustus. The *recitatio* also holds the middle ground between the pure orality of Republican *oratio*, which is always improvisatory, and epistolary writing, which implies the absence of the writer during the reading of the letter. For while *recitatio* takes for granted the existence of a written text, which is to be read, it also presupposes a degree of orality and demands the presence of the writer, who will also be the reader, in order to make the text perceptible to its recipient.

Recitatio **as autonomous social practice**

Having recognized in the *recitatio* a concrete social practice that marks the transition from Republic to Empire, we have now reached the point in our analysis at which we must cease to define *recitatio* either in negative terms or in terms of its intermediary status and proceed instead to study it as a self-contained and distinctive social institution.

A gathering of friends

Recitatio, as we have seen, requires the presence of *amici*, or "friends," and is therefore one of the social expressions of clientelism. To go to the public

---

[21] Cf. n. 5 above.

reading of a friend, particularly of a patron, or conversely, to lend one's audit-orium, is a duty of friendship,[22] an obligation at once moral and social.[23] Nor is it simply a question of attending a reading: one must give judgments on the quality of the text.[24] As a consequence the *recitatio* puts to the test the qualities of friendship of each and every attendee: intellectual rigor, honesty, and directness are sought from the listeners; lucidity and modesty from the reciter, who is to accept criticism and correct his text as a result of it. There is an ethics of *recitatio* that determines whether a man is truly possessed of the qualities of *libertas*, whether he has an *animus liberalis*. Such a man never refuses to attend the public reading of a friend even if it takes up all of his time, just as he would never refuse to assist him at a trial or in other *negotia*. He must even encourage a friend to give recitations, to overcome his (more or less feigned) modesty, which is, after all, but a lack of ambition.[25] Similarly, together with the rest of the audience, he will encourage the *recitator* to continue with the reading and demand that he proceed until the very end, even if that takes several days. Finally, when he himself has written something worthy of being heard he will not solicit his friends, as if requesting payment for a debt, but will wait for them to force him to hold a recitation through their urgent remonstrations.

On the other hand, the reader will not cease to proclaim his debt toward his friends, affirming that in the final analysis the text he is to publish is a collect-ive creation, not his personal achievement.[26] He will repeat again and again that alone he is capable of nothing, that solitary genius is always inferior to collective mediocrity.[27] This animadversion is nothing less than an expression of republican faith and a rejection, at least in theory, of tyranny. It evokes the origin of this rejection in Republican Rome, where complete confidence was placed in the collegiality of power and decision-making, a tendency apparent in the collegiality of magistracies and in the fact that, in a less institutionalized but nonetheless important way, every Roman would involve his friends in his decisions. The friends who constituted a *consilium amicorum* offered advice, by way of obligation, or *officium*, to any magistrate, general, or provincial governor who was their friend.

The *recitationes* therefore comprise a practice that truly realizes the old values of the republican elite, creating a community founded on gift and counter-gift,[28] and implying thereby a type of reciprocity. Each listener is also

---

[22] For example, Plin., *Ep.* 1.18.2.

[23] Hor., *Ars* 419–52; Sen., *Ep. Mor.* 122.11; Plin., *Ep.* 8.12.1.

[24] Plin., *Ep.* 3.15.3. This is why the listener must be careful not to be seduced by the musicality of the text.

[25] Plin., *Ep.* 2.10.1.ff. and 2.19.1ff.   [26] Martial, *Epigrams praef.* 12 and Plin. *Ep. passim.*

[27] Plin., *Ep.* 7.4.10.

[28] On the socializing function of gift and counter-gift, see Mauss (1950) and more recently Godbout (1992).

a potential *lector*, and vice versa. The practice of public writing/reading helps to preserve the unity of the Roman political elite, particularly of the senatorial class. As a collectivity this elite supplies to its members mutual recognition at each *recitatio*, while celebrating common values, of which the most important is the rhetorical mastery of language.

The requirements of honor

Those listeners who do not respect the social demands of the *recitationes* commit a mistake that goes far beyond simple rudeness. Should their behavior become customary, the *recitatores* who "cheat" by buying a clapper to stimulate the applause of the rest of the audience or who try to seduce the listener, like the dirty old man in Persius' satire,[29] would pose a threat to one of the new foundations of the *nobilitas*: hence the legitimate indignation of Pliny, who regularly reminds us that there is an incompatibility between the *officium* of the *recitatio* and pure pleasure.[30] To assist in a *recitatio* is a labor, demanding effort and constancy.

But the worst thing for a *recitator* to encounter is indifference. He is exposed, trembling, to the judgment of an audience of friends, the pertinence of whose judgments and criticisms he takes for granted.[31] He interprets the amorphous silence of the audience as a denial of his very existence, a denial that cannot be tolerated,[32] that must be understood in the social context as an insult (*offendas*), a rupture of friendship. As Pliny observes, "whom you greeted as a friend, you depart from as an enemy" (*ut inimicum relinquas ad quem tamquam amicissimum veneris*, Plin., *Ep.* 6.17.3). This type of offense, which criticism, of whatever sort, would not produce, is, according to Pliny, attributable to the jealousy, or *invidia*, of the listeners, who are themselves always potential *recitatores*. But this jealousy, Pliny tells us, is absurd, for it has the effect of destroying the system by which everyone's value is determined:

And so, whether you stand above or below or equal, praise your inferior or your superior or your peer: your superior, because unless he is praiseworthy you cannot be praised, praise your inferior and your equal because it adds to your glory if those you precede or match seem as great as possible.[33]

---

[29] Cf. above and Juvenal 7.38–53.

[30] Plin., *Ep.* 8.21.5–6. Pliny defines his listener-friends as a *sodalitas* who assemble not for pleasure but to support him. Cf. Hor. *Ars* 438ff. On rudeness at a *recitatio*, see Plin., *Ep.* 6.17.1ff.

[31] Plin., *Ep.* 7.17.3 recounts how at the mere thought of performing a recitation his hairs stand on his head in terror, just as Cicero says happens at the thought of speaking before judges.

[32] Plin., *Ep.* 6.17.2–3.

[33] *Denique sive plus sive minus sive idem praestas, lauda vel inferiorem vel superiorem vel parem, superiorem quia nisi laudandus ille non potes ipse laudari, inferiorem aut parem quia pertinet ad tuam gloriam quam maximum videri quem praecedis vel exaequas* (*Ep.* 6.17.4).

Pliny's arithmetic of praise implies a solidarity of all those aspiring to glory, for praise is always relative.

A *rite of passage*

The *recitatio* is constitutive of noble identity under the Empire inasmuch as the first public reading by the young descendant of a grand aristocratic family serves as a rite of passage for entrance into the rank of adulthood, just as once, under the Republic, the first legal case in which a young noble attacked the enemies of his family served the same function.[34] Pliny recalls, as we have seen above, the *recitatio* of the astronomical poem at which a certain Calpurnius Piso (of the famous Pisones, of whom one, the censor in 120 BCE, published seven books of *Annales*, not to mention the friends of Horace) was put on display.

Pliny's account of the event is incisive and sensitive to its social significa-tion. He tells us of the anguish and the elation of the family as they decipher the reaction of the audience and come to realize that their young man has acquitted himself favorably – that he will travel the glorious path of the ancestors. Pliny himself rejoices in this assurance of the continuity of a great house and the renewal of its nobility both here and in his account of other recitations, where the efflorescence of a new generation of *recitatores* is a sign, so he says, of the liberalism of the Princeps.[35] The senatorial class is in good condition.

An *institution of* libertas

If the recitation of a speech can be regarded as a feeble and devalorized version of *oratio*, with the recitation serving as a deceptive substitute for Republican oratory and as the literary phantom of liberty, the inverse is also possible, as Pliny proposes with respect to his panegyric of Trajan (*Ep.* 3.18). At the commencement of his term as consul, Pliny pronounced the customary eulogy of the emperor before the Senate, in fulfillment of his duty or *officium*.[36] The target of praise is the emperor, but the senators are also in attendance. Pliny respects the performative context, speaking in accordance with the place and time (*ad rationem et loci et temporis*, 3.18.1); afterwards, however, he prepares a separate text, which, having been corrected, will be published in the form that survives for us under the title *Panegyric of Trajan*. The only

---

[34] Thomas (1984b).   [35] Plin., *Ep.* 1.13.1.

[36] At a time when a consulate typically lasted two to three months, Pliny was consul together with Cornutus Tertullus throughout the year 100 CE.

true and beautiful version, says Pliny, is the latter, that is to say, the false one. The meeting in the Senate was irksome, as always under such circumstances. Pliny spoke and his listeners listened in a constrained environment. But the false panegyric, refashioned for recitation and lasting three days, was free and therefore beautiful. "This is yet another tribute to our Emperor: a type of speech which used to be hated for its insincerity has become genuine and consequently popular today."[37] The procedure in question is a subtle one. The discourse of *recitatio*, being external to the political institutions of the empire but anchored in the social practice of *libertas*, is a free discourse which proves the liberalism of the princeps who permits it to flourish. It alone can offer to those it praises a true and sincere *elogium*. What is more, the false panegyric breaks free of rhetorical constraints, and the amount of time it occupies (three days!) corresponds not only to the magnitude of the subject but also to the desire of the auditors, since Pliny's friends insist on hearing it through to the end.[38] In his letter describing the occasion, Pliny continually emphasizes the perfection of an event at which each participant gives evidence of his extraordinary *libertas*. The auditors were scarcely even invited, but came, as it were, spontaneously – and despite the bad weather at that. Nor did they yield to easy pleasure but preferred instead the most sober sections of the panegyric. The attention of the audience like the modesty of the reciter made of this false panegryic a success such as the true one did not and could not achieve. And so the false panegyric of the *recitatio*, false since it presupposes a performative context that will not be the context of its performance, is truer than the true panegyric which, because the praise of the prince is required, cannot be the expression of a sincere admiration such as a captive discourse is incapable of providing.

It is clear then that *recitatio* is indeed a form of social practice that permits the existence of a truly free discourse on the margins of the new institutions wherein discourse is definitively constrained. This liberation results from a fictive performance which makes it possible to produce a speech that is only realized in a performance to which it does not correspond, namely, the *recitatio*.

The mortal glory of the book

The published book, anticipated by a public reading, interrupts the process of communication that makes possible the *recitatio*. In fixing the text, publication kills the reciter in order to honor him as a writer.

---

[37] *Accedet ergo hoc quoque laudibus principis nostri quod res antea tam invisa quam falsa nunc ut vera ita amabilis facta est*, Plin., *Ep.* 3.18.7, tr. Radice.

[38] Plin., *Ep.* 3.18.4.

The life and death of the recitator

The *recitatio* requires the physical presence of the author, for the latter is defined not as the subject of the performed text but as the subject of the performance – even when he does not read his own book. Pliny tells us that he reads verse badly and thus has one of his freedmen take his place at a recitation (*Ep.* 9.34.1–2). But what shall Pliny do, under the circumstances? How shall he conduct himself? "Should I sit focused, mute, and inactive?" he asks, "or should I, as others have done, accompany the reading with murmuring, expressive looks, and gestures? Yet I think I am no better at pantomime (*saltare*) than at reading (*legere*)."[39] This amusing passage demonstrates that the *recitator* is first and foremost the physical presence of a living body. It makes a difference that he undergoes this social examination, that he confronts the judgment of his peers, accepts the image they return to him, receives their advice, and makes corrections in consequence thereof, if he intends to enjoy the fruits of his labors, i.e. the social prestige linked to the exercise of public discourse. Only in this way will the circle of his friends expand – a circle composed of other writer–reciters. Indeed, Pliny boasts of having as his friends all of the authors who count at Rome: "for there are very few people who care for literature without caring for me, too."[40]

Normally every recitation leads to a publication, with the result that the book supplies a new amplitude to the words of the *recitator* who becomes thereby both author and proprietor of his text.[41] But this expansion of the audience, which might conceivably earn for the author the glory acquired by the Republican orator in addressing a truly political people, is in fact accompanied by a new performative loss. The *recitatio* deprives the text of an adequate performative context, but establishes a true performative subject – the reciter – and true recipients – the audience (who, it should be noted, continue to be designated by the term *populus*) – and generates a type of social communication between them. It is this communication between *lector* and *auditor* that the book destroys, since the two become confounded, and the author, isolated from performance, becomes at best a name on an object.

Thus publication is the death and burial of the author for the sake of his own extended glory.

---

[39] *Cogito recitaturus familiaribus amicis experiri libertum meum. Ipse nescio quid illo legente interim faciam: sedeam defixus et mutus et similis otioso? an ut quidam quae pronuntiabit murmure, oculis, manu, prosequar? Sed puto me non minus saltare quam legere*, Plin., *Ep.* 9.34.1–2.

[40] *neque enim est fere quisquam qui studia ut non simul et nos amet, Ep.* 1.13.5, tr. Radice.

[41] Plin., *Ep.* 2.10.3.

The book as tomb

In order to convince a friend to publish his work, Pliny relies on a *locus communis*: we are all mortals, and only glory, that is the memory of human-kind, helps us escape that harsh condition (*habe ante oculos mortalitatem a qua deserere te hoc monimento potes, Ep.* 2.10.4). What is noteworthy here is that the monument that will assure the memory of the poet is the published book.

The book is in effect a monument, an object offering to the hands and eyes of all who read it the name which it commemorates. *Exegi monumentum aere perennius*, writes Horace at the end of a book which he has deliberately put together from his odes (*Carmina* 3.30.1). And as Pliny also says, the glory that attends a book corresponds to the dimensions of the empire, since the book is offered to all who know Latin, a condition that suffices to make of one a recipient, as long as Rome and its culture endure.[42] But who is the *ego* commemorated by the book, if not the subject of the poem and the name inscribed on the cover of the book?

Very strange business. A Roman tomb does not commemorate the sculptor but the one interred within. The text that one reads inscribed on the stone speaks the name and rank of the deceased, listing his accomplishments. Here, in the case of a book, the tomb is, in a certain sense, the monument of the sculptor whose sole glory is to have fashioned his own tomb. But in this way the poet/sculptor situates himself in the place of death. For he is the eternal absent, while the book is what speaks in his place, as often Greek funerary inscriptions do.[43] What is more, the eternal absent, the author of a book, has existence only through his absence. He is condemned to muteness, and is himself turned into a talking statue. And this is how his readers perceive him, since, after arriving from the outskirts of the empire, enthusiastic admirers come to visit him in Rome, and gaze on him as they would on a statue (*si quis requirit ut semel vidit, transit et contentus est ut si picturam aliquam vel statuam vidisset*, Tac., *Dial.* 10.2). All social interchange, at least such as is accomplished through his work, has for the author become impossible.

Discourse in stone

Finally, what does the reader of a book read and why does he read it? In one of his best-known letters to Tacitus, Pliny insists that a written discourse is the archetype of oral discourse, which he calls *actio* (*est enim oratio actionis exemplar et quasi arkhetypon, Ep.* 1.20.9). That is how one can find in speeches

---

[42] Plin., *Ep.* 2.10.2 and Hor. *C.* 3.30.5ff.   [43] Svenbro (1988:33–52).

that have never been delivered (e.g. the later *Verrines*) expressions characteristic of improvised speech.

The reader will therefore be once again placed within a fiction, for he is
collectively and anonymously the sole recipient of the book and of what is
written, the treatises themselves implying a fictional performance, where the
audience will be the judge. While he cannot appreciate the effects directly he
can reconstitute them in an imaginary fashion. What is the point of such a
book except to furnish exemplary speeches, like those composed in the schools,
whose imaginary impact owes nothing to chance or to the clumsiness of the
adversary, speeches written according to the rules?

Besides the monumentalized author and the obliterated reader, there is also
the petrified text. The book at Rome is not an instrument of social communication. What is the purpose of reading the undelivered speeches of courtroom speakers? Why, to write others, petrified in their turn, and to assure the
continuation of a discourse that is politically dead yet survives in the social
practice of *recitatio*. Reading makes it possible to write and then to read out
loud more imaginary speeches. The book becomes an instrument of memory,
but of a memory that is itself dead. In order to assure the repetition of the
pattern read–write–read the techniques of the production of texts are maintained, in the absence of any adequate performance.

Last, the problem with reading a book, the reason it is invalid as an honorable
practice, is that it does not permit a reciprocity of exchange, such as is found
among peers and present in the *recitatio*. Even when Pliny writes to Tacitus
about the latter's works, he puts himself in the position of a corrector, that is
to say, an *auditor* at a *recitatio*: "I have read your book and marked as carefully
as I could the passages which I think should be altered or removed."[44] He asks
Tacitus, to whom he has sent his own book, to render him the same service
in return.

This exchange is the basis of an extraordinary friendship, one that manifests
itself in reciprocity and in the practice of the traditional values of aristocratic
friendship: "O delightful, O magnificent exchange! How it thrills me to think
that if posterity has any concern for us, everywhere will be told the story of the
candor and the loyalty by which we lived."[45] Two writers, during their lifetime,
succeed in overcoming the constraints of the book, thanks to epistolary writing,
which allows dialogue and thus a symmetry between reader and writer. They
accomplish the rare feat of reconstituting, under the Empire and by means of
writing, a space for *libertas*.

---

[44] *Librum tuum legi et quam diligentissime potui adnotavi quae commutanda, quae eximenda
arbitrarer*, Plin., *Ep.* 7.20.1, tr. Radice.

[45] *O incundas, o pulchras vices! quam me delectat quod si qua posteris cura nostri usquequaque
narrabitur qua concordia, simplicitate, fide vixerimus!* Plin., *Ep.* 7.20.2.

II

Texts and Contexts

4   The boundaries of knowledge in Virgil's *Georgics*[1]

Alessandro Schiesaro

The drama of knowledge: Aristaeus and Proteus

1. Didactic poetry fashions its primary goal as that of imparting knowledge, metaphorical or practical, to an internal addressee and by extension to the larger world of interested readers. The nature and boundaries of knowledge naturally represent a significant theoretical concern of the didactic poet and, by extension, the reader and the critic: thus the ideological connotations of knowledge – as well as its limits, dangers, and hopes – inevitably impact the themes that such poetry deals with, and should form an integral part of our overall interpretation of didactic texts. The problem of knowledge – where, how and especially why it can be obtained – certainly plays a prominent role in the *Georgics* and in two other didactic works to which I will often refer, the *De rerum natura* and the *Works and Days*.

In this essay I will investigate the most important epistemological procedures that govern Virgil's understanding of the phenomena he purports to explain. This should contribute, I hope, to a better understanding of the *Georgics* as a didactic work, and more specifically of the ways in which Virgil's idea of didacticism might or might not have been different from that of his most immediate and most influential predecessor, the author of *De rerum natura*. Inevitably, such an analysis will end up confronting some of the questions most frequently asked of the *Georgics*, and will be unable to steer clear of the exegetical controversies that have animated the debate on this poem, especially in the past few years. If I offer a partial apology for this aspect of my work it is not because I would like to advocate a separate status for this kind of research, as if it could be located in an impossibly higher or pre-ideological stage of reading, but because I would not want it to appear as necessarily dependent on a specific reading of the poem. In fact, I think that looking at the nuances and modulations of intrinsically ideological yet less obvious items such as the paradigms of knowledge can help find a way out

[1] Thanks are due to Francesca Antonini, Alessandro Barchiesi, Denis Feeney, Deirdre von Dornum and Anonymous Reader for their much appreciated help with this paper, and to my co-editor and co-organizer, Tom Habinek: it was fun working together.

of the polarized critical alternatives that now risk stifling interpretation of the *Georgics*.

Throughout this paper the term 'knowledge' will refer to a series of practices by which the text finds, elaborates, and communicates an understanding of events, broadly intended. This rather vague definition aspires to be as inclusive as possible, although I will have to limit my remarks to some specific topics. Under its heading I would include any explicit methodological remarks which the poet offers on the issue, as well as our decoding of the epistemological protocols which he employs: I operate on the assumption that any statement can be analyzed from an epistemological point of view, since we might inquire about the sources it draws upon, the claim on authority it may or may not make, and the communicative practices it resorts to in dealing with its audience. In the case of a didactic poem this research is at the same time easier and more fruitful not just because we are likely to encounter more explicit remarks, but also because these particular issues constitute an essential component of the signifying strategies of the text.

I will start from the end of the poem, by reading in the epyllion that concludes book 4 a dramatization of the process of knowledge and the problems by which it is characterized. I will then devote the bulk of my paper to the two most important aspects of the epistemological procedures of the *Georgics*, the use and function of signs and the poem's complex attitude towards the determination of causes.[2] Due to lack of space I will have to defer to another occasion the treatment of the interplay of truth and falsehoods in some of the most famous sections of the poem, a topic which has received a great deal of attention recently.[3] Finally, I will offer some remarks on the connection between the conceptualization of knowledge and the structuring of power relations in the text.

I gladly admit right away to a propensity for reading the poem as an extended and sustained reaction to the other great attempt at didactic poetry of the first century BCE, Lucretius' *De rerum natura*. This reaction extends over a number of different levels. Virgil reacts to the theology, or indeed the quasi-non-theology of Lucretius, by reasserting as vocally as possible the active

---

[2] I will not analyze in this paper the poet's appeals to direct observation, nor his method of formulating theoretical hypotheses.

[3] I am well aware that this topic is very closely connected with my own, and regret the need to separate the two treatments. Virgil's position in respect to traditions such as the *bougonia*, for instance, and his judgment of their truth-value, forms an integral part of his overall attitude towards knowledge. While it is exceedingly risky to summarize in a couple of lines an argument that is necessarily much more complex, I will anticipate here that I find less than convincing the theory that Virgil deliberately misleads his readers as far as grafting and *bougonia* are concerned, since the ancient evidence on both accounts seems to me much less uncontroversial than it would have to be in order to make such deception work in the text.

presence of the gods in all aspects of life. He reacts as well to the overall ideology of *De rerum natura* by focusing much more than Lucretius had done on the shared values of the community rather than on the individual's attempt to reach *ataraxia*, or at least by trying to demonstrate that these personal goals can be attained only in a social context. Finally, Virgil proposes a model of life that privileges active labor rather than contemplative reflection. And both Lucretius and Virgil, of course, share the belief that poetry is the appropriate medium for their message.

2. The second half of the last book of the *Georgics* describes Aristaeus' painful and complex search for knowledge, specifically for information on why his bees have been destroyed, and in so doing it dramatizes effectively the procedures and problems involved in the search for truth. The specific status of the episode, however, poses some problems. This epyllion is not only a clearly marked section unto itself, but it also differs from the surrounding context because of its nature as a narrative inset. Here for the first time in the poem the Muses are invoked as the source of information by the georgic poet. If this late appeal to the Muses echoes at least in part a similar move on Lucretius' part – in the *De rerum natura*, too, Muses are not invoked before book 6 – it is also a clear signal of change in the texture of this part of the poem. This shift of status turns the episode into an appealing mythological enactment of the problems of knowledge but inevitably raises questions as to whether and how directly any insights we might glean from it can be applied to the rest of the poem, non-mythical and non-narrative as it is. This is a quandary for which no easy solution is at hand, but I will nonetheless point out the intriguing analogy between the role and behavior of Cyrene in her dealings with Aristaeus and those of the georgic poet who instructs the farmer in the rest of the poem.

The Aristaeus episode as a whole is articulated into three sections, each representing a separate attempt at knowing and understanding undertaken by different characters. At the outset, the narrator invokes the Muses in order to learn more about the origin of the *bougonia*: *quis deus hanc, Musae, quis nobis extudit artem?|unde nova ingressus hominum experientia cepit?* (315–16: "Which god, o Muses, which one has revealed this technique to us? Where did this new experiment have its beginning?"). The answer to this initial question is embedded in the long narrative that unfolds immediately afterwards: the narrator of the *Georgics* can in fact offer a very detailed explanation of who first resorted to *bougonia* and for what reason.

In the second section, the beginning of the narrative proper, the poem follows Aristaeus in the initial moves of his search for an explanation for the disaster that has just befallen him and eventually for a remedy. His anguished invocations to Cyrene transfer the scene from a human to a divine setting, as his mother finally grants him permission to be admitted into the underwater abodes of the Nymphs: "bring him, bring him to us; lawful it is for him to tread the divine threshold" (358–9: *duc ad nos; fas illi limina divum|tangere*).[4] The detailed description of how the waves withdraw to let Aristaeus – *mirans* (363) and *stupefactus* (365) – proceed in his *katabasis* stands as an appropriate reminder of how extraordinary and exceptional this permission actually is (359–63):

> simul alta iubet discedere late
> flumina, qua iuvenis gressus inferret. at illum
> curvata in montis faciem circumstetit unda
> accepitque sinu vasto misitque sub amnem.

and withal, she bade the deep streams part asunder far, that the youth might enter in. And lo, the wave, arched mountain-like, stood round about, and, welcoming him within the vast recess, ushered him beneath the stream.

The consultation between Cyrene and her son takes the form of a religious ritual which opens with an invocation to Oceanus (380–1: "Take the goblets of Maeonian wine; let us pour a libation to Ocean"; *"cape Maeonii carchesia Bacchi;|Oceano libemus" ait*), and the taking of a favorable *omen* (386). Cyrene herself, however, is not the repository of any relevant information, but refers Aristaeus to the *vates* Proteus, who alone will be able to provide a satisfactory explanation, cautioning him all the while about the cunning expedients he will have to employ in order to gain the information he is seeking. Proteus will try to disguise himself in a thousand different shapes before yielding to Aristaeus, who will even have to use force and tie up the *vates*.

The third section of the narrative relates the meeting between Aristaeus and Proteus, who after countless escape attempts finally reveals the reason for the divine wrath which has provoked the extermination of the bees. It will only be thanks to a more specific explanation on the part of Cyrene, who addresses Aristaeus after the seer has concluded his story, that Aristaeus will learn the procedures he must follow in order to regain his swarm.

Several elements of this story are worth focusing on, and I will start by calling attention to a general characteristic that can best be gleaned by intertextual comparison. The encounter between Aristaeus and Cyrene is close in many details to the Iliadic scene which describes Thetis' dialogue with her son Achilles in book 18. There it is the mother who spontaneously comes to her son's rescue after hearing his cries (lines 65–9), consoles him (70–7) and volunteers to procure the weapons which will help him fight Hector (136–7). In the *Georgics* it falls to Aristaeus to look for his mother and beg for help.

---

[4] Translations from the *Eclogues* and the *Georgics* are by H. R. Fairclough in the Loeb collection, with modifications.

In fact he must follow a very difficult and tortuous path which reaches its peak when Cyrene finally shares with him the details that reveal how she could probably have answered his question from the beginning anyway.[5] In this episode all knowledge comes from divine actors: Aristaeus is granted permission to seek his mother's help thanks to the gods, and it is on their order, *deum praecepta secuti* ("following the instructions of the gods," 448) that he addresses Proteus. Proteus, the divine *vates* who knows everything, delivers a *responsum* laden with the uncertainties and ambiguities that traditionally characterize divine utterances.

Although it is tempting to identify Proteus with the poetic narrator of the *Georgics*, this solution entails considerable difficulties. Unlike Proteus, the narrator shows his ability to deliver a complete and understandable answer to the question he asks of the Muses at the beginning of the epyllion. It is Cyrene who, like the narrator, imparts *praecepta* both when she orders Aristaeus to seek Proteus' advice and when she explains what to do in order to restore the bees (548). Here again knowledge is sought thanks to and explained through the active intervention of divine powers. Similar in this respect to Cyrene, the narrator of the *Georgics* is not only the indispensable link to a world of knowledge which lies outside the reach of the common mortal, the knowledge of the Muses or of Proteus, but he is also able to distill it into practical and valuable *praecepta*. Like Cyrene, who yields to Aristaeus' loud cries, the poet takes pity on the unaware mortal, and, "pitying the farmers" (1.41: *miseratus agrestis*), proceeds to divulge the knowledge they need.

This episode highlights a series of tensions that are central to the representation of knowledge in the *Georgics*. Knowledge is a divine possession, and the gods decide if and how much of it can be bestowed on mortals. It is arguably the georgic poet who, mediating between the human and the divine, manages to overcome the otherwise insuperable chasm that separates the two realms. There is no illusion that he might be the autonomous discoverer of such knowledge: on the contrary, he is but one link, albeit an indispensable one, in the chain that connects all the actors of this drama of knowledge. Aristaeus' tears are "idle" (4.375: *inanis*) until Cyrene decides to hear his pleas. The adjective conveys the helplessness and ultimate futility of the farmer's cry, which can find a useful response only in the providential intervention of the gods.

Knowledge is a tortuous and indirect process in which every stage is inevitably charged with complex power relations. Aristaeus has to be granted permission in order to pursue his search, his desire has to be considered *fas* by

---

[5] This scene could be usefully compared with a similar one in *Ecl.* 6.18–9: there, too, Silenus yields to Chromis and Mnasyllus after they have tied him up (and he has asked them to be set free).

Cyrene; it is only on the strength of that authoritative sanction, coupled with the use of wit and force, that he can overcome Proteus' resistance. In this scene the georgic poet appears to be endowed with a demiurgic power, one that can translate Proteus' narrative into practical *praecepta*.

Signs for knowing

3. The episode of Aristaeus, Cyrene and Proteus highlights some of the problems connected with the search for truth in the *Georgics* and offers precious insights about the characteristics and limitations of this process. An exploration of specific procedures which the georgic narrator employs in the bulk of the poem will yield a more satisfactory and complete image of the epistemological protocols of the *Georgics*, and should also better situate them in the lively cultural debate on knowledge, truth, and the nature of divine power which takes place in the first century BCE.

Such an analysis should begin by looking at the role and importance of signs, which not only play a very significant and varied role in the first book of the poem, but also provide a benchmark to compare Virgil's epistemology with that of other authors. Signs are an integral component of the knowledge which the *Georgics* try to impart. In the first book we are immediately confronted with the two main headings under which they can be grouped: first, signs which, on the basis of experience and observation, anticipate future events which are causally connected with them, such as weather signs or, later in the poem, symptoms of disease; and, second, extraordinary occurrences which presage extraordinary events with which they are not causally linked, such as the *portenta* following Caesar's death.[6]

4. The Aratean and ultimately Hesiodic section on weather-signs begins with a firm statement about the reliability of god-given *signa* (1.351–5).[7] The structure of the passage, articulated by a series of indirect questions (*quid, quo, quid*) recalls the typically didactic beginning of the poem as a whole (1.1–4: *quid, quo, quae, qui, quanta*).[8] What we see is indeed a new beginning, under the double aegis of Iuppiter and Hesiod as "fathers" (353: *pater*) in their respective domains:

> atque ut haec certis possemus discere signis
> aestusque pluviasque et agentis frigora ventos,

---

[6] Weather signs: 1.229; 351; 439; 463; symptoms: 3.440; 503; 4.253; *portenta*: 1.471.

[7] A fine analysis of this passage is offered by Farrell (1991), 79–83.

[8] For the use of indirect questions and other structural devices as markers of the didactic style see Brown (1990), esp. 316–18.

> ipse pater statuit quid menstrua luna moneret,
> quo signo caderent Austri, quid saepe videntes
> agricolae propius stabulis armenta tenerent.

and that through unfailing signs we might learn these dangers – the heat, and the rain, and the cold-bringing winds – the Father himself decreed what warning the monthly moon should give, what should signal the fall of the wind, and what sign, oft seen, should prompt the farmer to keep his cattle nearer to their stalls.

The certainty of the signs guaranteed by Iuppiter stands in direct contrast with the unreliability of the weather in the fall season which the narrator had mentioned in the preceding section (311–50): in that season special attention should be exercised in order to forecast sudden storms (313). The narrator himself (316 *ego*) has often noticed devastating storms caused by the rage of Iuppiter (328–34), and it is out of fear of such disasters that the farmer should carefully observe the signs of the sky and honor the gods. That the last two concepts are strictly connected is made clear by their rapid succession at line 335ff.:

> hoc metuens caeli mensis et sidera serva
> frigida Saturni sese quo stella receptet,
> quos ignis caelo Cyllenius erret in orbis.
> in primis venerare deos, atque annua magnae
> sacra refer Cereri . . .

in fear of this, mark the months and signs of heaven; whither Saturn's cold star withdraws itself and into what circles of the sky strays the Cyllenian fire. Above all, worship the gods, and pay great Ceres her yearly rites . . .

Hoc metuens at line 335 refers both to the storm which destroyed the crops, and to the divine rage that provoked it; the exhortation to observe the signs at 335 and to venerate the gods at 338 is the joint answer to both aspects of the problem. After a description of the rites in honor of Ceres at 338–50 the narrator proceeds to state that Iuppiter has established signs which enable the farmer to forecast the weather. The beginning of line 353, *ipse pater statuit quid menstrua luna moneret* ("the Father himself decreed what warning the monthly moon should give"), recalls line 328 (*ipse pater media nimborum . . .*), where *ipse pater* at the beginning of the line introduces the description of the storm. The implicit assumption established by this connection is that scrupulous observation of weather-signs and religious rites are closely linked, and that both should be carried out by the fearful farmer. Virgil does not explicitly say, nor of course could he say, that careful weather forecasting can avert the storm, and it is meaningful that at 355 he directly points out that the cautious farmer can at most learn when to keep his animals close to the shed. This is a danger he can avoid; the crops, if their destruction by a storm can be avoided at all, will perhaps have to be trusted to divine benevolence such as the protection of Ceres.[9]

This close connection between religious ritual and observation of the signs is a very important aspect of the use of *signa* in the poem. An equally remarkable feature of georgic signs in general, and weather-signs in particular, is the frequency – five times out of seven – with which they are qualified as "certain" or "undoubtable." At 1.229, the first appearance of signs in the poem, the narrator guarantees that Bootes will offer clear signs, *haud obscura . . . signa*, of the best time for sowing beans. Similar assurances about the reliability of signs occur in different contexts, ranging from the *certissima signa* (1.439) furnished by the sun, to the *non dubia . . . signa* (4.253) announcing the onset of a disease among the bees. This reiterated trust in the certainty of signs should be evaluated *vis-à-vis* the use of *signa* in the empirical epistemology of Lucretius, where the interpretation of signs is a complex process, and plausibility is often regarded as a satisfactory result. The higher degree of certainty that the narrator of the *Georgics* presumes to extract from signs could be taken to imply an advancement over the function and effectiveness of signs in the *De rerum natura* were it not for the fact that it directly derives from the providential architecture of the world. *Signa*, like everything else, are integral components of a *kosmos* providentially arranged by God, and, as 1.351–5 make abundantly clear, epistemological practices are enabled by and subordinated to a religious view of the universe. There is no clash between the "scientific" approach of Virgil and his religious convictions, because he refuses to deal with any topic or method which can potentially disrupt those convictions. Unlike scientific explanation, passive observation of the sky is part of the traditional, pious life of the farmer, whom Virgil promises in the very first line to tell "beneath what star it is well to turn the soil" (1.1–2: *quo sidere terram\vertere*), and to whom he recommends the observation of "the months and stars of heaven" (1.335: *caeli mensis et sidera*).

It is worth reflecting further on the differences between Lucretian and georgic signs. In Virgil's poem the divine guarantee backing the complete reliability of signs radically subverts the hierarchical implications of this epistemological procedure. In Lucretius, the reliability of signs is rooted in the knowledge of natural laws which have emphatically nothing to do with divine power, and in fact justify reduced belief in such power. Signs act as free and open-ended probes which reach a level of reality not immediately evident, and equate humans to gods as far as the knowledge of nature is concerned. By

---

[9] That the section on the respect for religious rites is to be seen as at least a partial response to the disasters listed in 316–27 is also pointed out by the connection established by the detail mentioned at line 318 (*et fragili iam stringeret hordea culmo*) and picked up at 347–8 (*neque ante\falcem maturis quisquam supponat aristis*): a successful cropping should not begin before the rites have been performed.

stressing the fact that gods send and guarantee signs, Virgil deprives them of any disruptive potential: signs will let human beings know and understand just as much or as little as the gods decide. The ability to interpret signs correctly is in itself a gift of the gods, and the poem will not put forth properly scientific rules valid under all circumstances, irrespective of the attitude of the observer. This shift in the power connotations of the epistemological process alters in a significant way the role of the poet as well. Lucretius casts himself as the demiurge who makes accessible to a large (Roman) public the astonishing discoveries of Epicurus' "divine" mind; once revealed, though, the knowledge of the laws of nature puts any mortal on the same level with the *prōtos heuretēs* and his interpreter. As Lucretius remarks, each person should continue in his or her pattern of search and inquiry armed with the unlimited epistemological potential furnished by Epicurus. Virgil, too, selects for himself the role of an intermediary, but one of a markedly different nature. All he can do is hand down a set of carefully detailed pieces of information, and assure human beings that they all originate from a superior and ultimate power. While he declares his necessary subordination to the gods who enable him to communicate their knowledge, the poet of the *Georgics* inevitably recreates an equally rigid and incontrovertible power structure in his relationship with the readers.[10]

5. The close connection between signs and divine power raises questions about divine benevolence and providence: why do the gods send signs to men if not in order to help them? Do they actually succeed in their intent? Is it reasonable to expect them to do so? The main danger incumbent on these and similar questions is the temptation to connect them immediately with the debate on the overall ideological inclination of the *Georgics*, and to phrase one's answers in terms of "optimism" or "pessimism." While this is certainly an option, I believe that it is hardly the only one available, and that it is methodologically more promising to try to define Virgil's own ideological propensities only after a larger background picture has emerged. It will be only against that background that Virgil's *Weltanschauung* will acquire full meaning. In the cultural debate of the mid first century one can observe different conceptions of the gods and their attitude towards human beings. I refer not only to the clash between Epicureans and Stoics, a shouting match that can sometimes obscure equally interesting, if more nuanced contrasts. Other lines of tensions surface, not only among the Stoics themselves, but also between the Stoics and the Neoacademics, for instance, or, at another level, between a more rationalistic and perhaps even "enlightened" approach to traditional Roman religion[11] and a more conservative one.

---

[10] A fuller treatment of this topic in Schiesaro (1993).
[11] Timpanaro (1988), xxvii-xciv, esp. lxxxiii.

That Virgil is aware of the complexities of the discussion over the nature and meaning of signs and of its far-reaching implications *vis-à-vis* the nature of the gods can be clearly understood by looking at the extended commentary that follows the description of a specific weather-sign. Beginning at 1.393, Virgil explains how to forecast, thanks to *certa signa* (394), dry sunny days after a rain: at the conclusion of a detailed list of signs, Virgil recommends the observation of the behavior of ravens (410–14):

> tum liquidas corvi presso ter gutture voces
> aut quater ingeminant, et saepe cubilibus altis
> nescio qua praeter solitum dulcedine laeti
> inter se foliis strepitant; iuvat imbribus actis
> progeniem parvam dulcisque revisere nidos.

Then the ravens, with narrowed throat, three or four times repeat their soft cries, and often in their nests, joyous with some strange, unwonted delight, chatter to each other amid the leaves. Glad are they, the rains over, to see once more their little brood and their sweet nests.

This description is followed by several lines of explicit reflection on why birds such as ravens can in fact announce changes in the weather (415–23):

> haud equidem credo, quia sit divinitus illis
> ingenium aut rerum fato prudentia maior;
> verum, ubi tempestas et caeli mobilis umor
> mutavere vias et Iuppiter uvidus Austris
> denset erant qüae rara modo, et quae densa relaxat,
> vertuntur species animorum, et pectora motus
> nunc alios, alios dum nubila ventus agebat,
> concipiunt:

not, I believe, that they have wisdom from on high, or from Fate a larger foreknowledge of things to be; but that when the weather and fitful vapours of the sky have turned their course, and Iuppiter, wet with the south winds, thickens what just now was rare, and makes rare what was now thick, the phases of their minds change, and their breasts now conceive impulses, other than they felt, when the wind was chasing the clouds.

Although the observation of weather-signs is an empirical *ars*[12] which is not necessarily connected with divination (supporters of the latter, however, often compare the two), the disclaimer at 415–23 can be fully understood only in the context of the debate on the possibility and reliability of divination which reached great intensity in the middle of the first century BCE. It is worth noticing that Virgil inserts these lines immediately before beginning, at line 424, a section devoted to the signs which can be gleaned from the sun. This section, which opens with an eclipse of the sun, leads in turn to the

---

[12] Such as navigation and medicine, as Quintus says in *Div.* 1.24; cf. 1.111 and 1.112. The most explicit analogy occurs at 1.128. Cf. also 2.14.

description of the *portenta* surrounding the death of Caesar (463–97), that is to a set of phenomena which are clearly part of divination proper.

Cicero's *On Divination* is our fullest guide to the intricacies of the debate about divination and its cultural and political implications. The opposing views of Quintus and Cicero in, respectively, the first and second books center on the existence of divination and its connection with divine power. Quintus argues from a Stoic point of view, not the more restricted one of Chrysippus, which postulated a direct divine causation for each and every sign, but the refinements probably suggested by Posidonius as a way to rebut Carneades' scorn on the older theories.[13] According to this strain of Stoic thought, divinatory signs are valid and reliable as part of a "global causality"[14] determined by the gods since the beginning of the world. In this manner the Stoics, and Quintus with them, strive to find a way out of the problematic alternative which Cicero points out in the introductory chapters of the work: a hasty discussion on divination, as opposed to a reasoned and detailed analysis, he warns, can indeed present the danger of wholesale denying of divination and religion and thus siding with the *impia fraus* of Epicurus, or accepting it in its less enlightened form, and becoming prey to "old women's superstition" (1.7: *anilis superstitio*).[15] Neither solution is acceptable to Cicero. The Epicurean denial of divination is part of the overall denial of any divine intervention in things human, while Stoic thought on divination could hardly resist the rationalistic – if not altogether sceptical – feelings that had by this time conquered a significant sector of the Roman elites.

Virgil, too, reacts to the notion that ravens possess, thanks to the gods (*divinitus*), "a deeper understanding of reality" (416: *rerum prudentia maior*), and offers a scientific and rationalistic explanation of why they signify the imminent improvement of the weather. By denying this direct divine causation of the signs coming from the ravens, Virgil is also taking a position on the use of birds, and specifically of ravens, in the context of artificial divination. *Auspicium* and *augurium* form the most important part of traditional Roman divination, and the one most closely connected with Roman political procedures: a fateful *auspicium* is prominently recorded, after all, at the very foundation of the city.

It is important to grasp fully at the outset that Virgil's position, here as elsewhere, discourages rash simplifications. Even if referred more directly to divination proper, these explicit rationalistic remarks would not prove its impossibility. Certainly the notion that the gods were directly responsible for

---

[13] Panaetius had pushed his critique of Chrysippus towards a complete denial of divination; cf. *Div.* 1.6, 1.12, 2.88.

[14] Timpanaro (1988), 319.

[15] Cicero's solution to this dilemma, as Timpanaro, *passim*, points out, is first to distinguish between religion and divination, and then between a social use of divination and its (impossible) theoretical justification.

each and every *signum* attracted a considerable amount of incredulity and even scorn among anti-Stoic polemicists, but a Stoic such as Quintus was able to keep his critics at bay by framing the issue of divine causation in more flexible terms, as we glean from his irritated remarks at the beginning of his apology for divination. At *Div.* 1.12, for instance, Quintus takes issue with the polemical attitude that the Peripatetic Carneades, and to a certain extent the Stoic Panaetius as well, had formulated against divination, and rebuts the argument that divination is in fact an essential form of communication between men and gods. It is wrong, Quintus argues, to think that the gods are directly and explicitly responsible for each and every event, including the birds' singing, that can be construed as a sign, although in general it is safe to assume that they guarantee the overall reliability of predictions based on such signs (1.117–18). Quintus, who connects divination very closely with other forms of quasi-scientific techniques such as medicine, meteorology and agronomy (1.12–16), does not offer any specific explanation of why signs act as they do, but limits himself to observing their repeated reliability. Birds, for instance, anticipate changes in the weather, and yet no explanation of this phenomenon is readily available; frogs, too, have a similar gift (1.15). His remarks on birds and frogs deal directly with the issue which Virgil addresses in his *excursus* on the raven. On the other hand Cicero, speaking out of his Neo-Academic convictions, carefully distinguishes between the rational ability to forecast the weather, and the tendency to interpret signs such as liver patterns or the raven's song, which are causally unrelated to the events they are supposed to predict (2.16).

Virgil's position in the context of the intense debate we have briefly exposed is nuanced, indeed almost tormented. There is little evidence in the *Georgics* for any sympathy with the "impious" Epicurean view that the gods are utterly oblivious to human vicissitudes, and none can be gleaned from the passage about ravens. While repeated efforts are made, as we will see, to uphold the notion that proper religious behavior is an essential component of an ordered society,[16] Virgil demonstrates an explicit willingness to separate himself from a reductive assessment of the relationship between gods and signs.

The evaluation of intertextual connections can add one more item to the dossier. Line 415 offers the only instance of the use of *divinitus* in Virgil, an adverb which plays a key role in Lucretius' poem.[17] Placed emphatically in the first line of Virgil's methodological preamble, *divinitus* functions as a "motto" which alerts the reader to the Lucretian implications of the passage, which is itself reminiscent of the discussion of the birds' voice in *De rerum natura* 5.1083–6:

---

[16] This is particularly true of sacrifice: cf. Habinek (1990b).
[17] Cf. 1.116, 150, 736; 2.180; 4.1278; 5.52, 198, 1215.

> et partim mutant cum tempestatibus una
> raucisonos cantus, cornicum ut saecla vetusta
> corvorumque greges ubi aquam dicuntur et imbris
> poscere et interdum ventos aurasque vocare.

and some of them change their harsh notes with the weather, as the long-lived tribes of crows and flocks of ravens, when they are said to cry for water and rains, and anon to summon the winds and breezes.[18]

Muto and *tempestas* of line 1083 reappear in Virgil at 1.417–8: *verum ubi tempestas et caeli mobilis umor|mutavere vias et Iuppiter uvidus Austris.* . . . Lucretius refers to the ravens' forecasting ability in the context of a discussion on the origin of language, and does not take any explicit position on the issue, but the intertextual connection need not surprise. The Epicureans had introduced into the cultural debate on religion and divination rationalistic elements that could not be ignored even by authors who would never explicitly collude with that sect. Cicero, whose rejection of Epicureanism is blunt,[19] clearly takes much of that criticism into account in *De divinatione*, a text which, as Timpanaro has recently argued, stands as a powerful attempt to reconcile traditional religion and enlightened rationalism.

6. The connection between divine power and *signa* acquires a new aspect in the case of signs which are part of divination proper, such as the *portenta* that surround Caesar's death at 1.463–97. The narrative attempts to establish a seamless transition between the two topics by exposing the double value of the signs offered by the sun both for forecasting the weather and also for anticipating terrible events (461–6):

> denique quid Vesper serus vehat, unde serenas
> ventus agat nubes, quid cogitet umidus Auster,
> sol tibi signa dabit. solem quis dicere falsum
> audeat? ille etiam caecos instare tumultus
> saepe monet, fraudemque et operta tumescere bella;
> ille etiam extincto miseratus Caesare Romam . . .

In short, the tale told by even-fall, the quarter whence the wind drives clear the clouds, the purpose of the rainy South – of all the Sun will give you signs. Who dare say the Sun is false? He often warns us that dark uprisings threaten, that treachery and hidden wars are upswelling. He also had pity for Rome after Caesar died . . .

There follows an impressive list of extraordinary occurrences which lead up to the disaster of Philippi (489–90). This is the only passage of the poem that explicitly explores the value of signs as part of divination,[20] and just as in the

---

[18] C. Bailey's modified translation.

[19] Cf., in the introductory chapters (1.5), the attack against Epicurus' "blabbing about the nature of the gods" (*balbutientem de natura deorum*).

[20] A failed attempt at divination is mentioned at 3.489–91 in the context of the Noric plague.

case of weather forecasting the narrator does not voice any explicit doubt about the reliability of these signs, nor about the expectation that they could be properly understood. The syntax of the passage makes it clear that the signs follow Caesar's death and presage civil war, even if historiographical records inform also that Caesar was repeatedly warned by ominous signs.[21]

Virgil's signs find a precise counterpart in several sections of *De divinatione*,[22] and offer numerous connections with the long fragment of his own *De consulatu* which Cicero quotes in the first book of the essay. At 1.17–22 Quintus, in his attempt to prove to his brother that divination does exist, and that Cicero himself in fact had believed in it, offers as proof the section of *De consulatu*[23] in which the Muse Urania describes the extraordinary signs announcing Catiline's rebellion, and other *portenta* and prophecies similarly connected with the events of 63 and Cicero's successful intervention. It is significant that in both *De consulatu* and *Georgics* these *signa* lead to civil unrest:[24] thus the coincidences between signs mentioned in the two passages acquire a pointed relevance even if some of them are predictably rather traditional. Virgil and Cicero both refer to the appearance of nocturnal ghosts, comets, lightning in a clear sky, and earthquakes, and both mention the eclipse of the sun at the beginning.[25]

The reference to *De divinatione* enlarges the scope and significance of the use of these signs in the *Georgics* beyond the somewhat restricted boundaries within which recent critics have tried to constrain them. For instance, Christine Perkell, in an interesting study about "the poet's truth," argues that the uniqueness and strangeness of the signs related in the passage ultimately convey the worthlessness of signs as means of knowledge:[26] unique and unnatural signs would be devoid of any practical utility because they could not be recognized and interpreted. This assumption, however, is at odds with the fact that it is precisely extraordinary *portenta* that can anticipate extraordinary events, and they are understandable not in spite of, but because of their uniqueness.

---

[21] Timpanaro (1988), 320; cf. *Div*, 1.119.   [22] Setaioli (1975), 14 n.2.

[23] Probably written around 60 BCE: Timpanaro (1988), 245.

[24] Cicero, *De consulatu*, lines 49–53. Cf. Virgil's reference to *caecos tumultus* (464), *fraudem* (465) and *operta bella* (465), with Setaioli (1975), 17 and n.1.

[25] The exact meaning of *Phoebi fax* has however been disputed: cf. Setaioli (1975), 17.

[26] Perkell (1989:157): "The conception of the reliability of signs and of the predictability of routine, seasonal, or annual events forms the very basis of the assumption of a knowable world and of georgic endeavors ... It therefore seems of great significance that two of the most dramatic events in the *Georgics*, the portents after Caesar's death (1.463–97) and the Noric plague (3.478ff.), both marked by signs, are represented by unique and unnatural occurrences, for which there is no rational, material, natural or atomic explanation." A similar conclusion is reached from another point of view by Thomas (1988:144), who insists on the fact that these *signa* occur only "after" Caesar's death, and are therefore worthless. However, they are valid as signs of the civil turmoil that follows Caesar's death.

In any event, Virgil's *portenta* are hardly unique and unprecedented. Almost all of them had been mentioned in *De consulatu*, and each one of them has a distinguished background specifically connected with social and political unrest.[27] The specific value of these *signa* existed not only in the collective memory preserved by tradition, a tradition which was at least theoretically held to be true, but also as an integral part of a specifically literary tradition.[28]

Just as in the weather-signs section, the logical texture of this passage suggests a manner of argumentation that is at once proleptic and *ex negativo*. Terrible storms can destroy the crops, *but* certain precautions, both practical and religious, can be taken to partially avoid such disasters. In the case of the civil war it is worth noting the contrast between the past life of "impious people" (468: *impia . . . saecula*) who were forewarned by unusual signs, but failed to interpret them properly and thus avoid the dire consequences they anticipated, and the new mode of life that will perhaps be made possible by Caesar's intervention (498–504). By evoking these signs and their literary antecedents, and by contrasting the "impious generation's" inability to interpret and exploit them with his own correct interpretation (even if *ex eventu*), Virgil reinforces the notion that the ability to take advantage of signs is rooted in the observer's respect for the religious hierarchy that governs the world. It is significant that the conclusion of the section, and thus of the book, hinges once again on an invocation to traditional Roman deities, who are asked to enable Caesar to carry out his mission of salvation (498–501).

The signs mentioned by Urania in *De consulatu* were all correctly interpreted by Cicero, who was thus able to prevent a full-blown disaster. In Virgil's passage the signs are considered equally reliable and effective, and if they fail to prevent the civil war it is mainly because the *impia saecula* are exactly that, *impia*: the ability or inability of the observer to interpret the signs and act accordingly is factored into the chain of events that must necessarily unfold as destined. I believe it is unwarranted to extrapolate from the passage relating the *portenta* after Caesar's death an overall sceptical attitude towards divination – and even more towards signs in general – on Virgil's part. It is worth observing, however, that by carefully inserting in the narrative line a complex intertextual connection Virgil considerably complicates and nuances our evaluation of his attitude.

The second book of *De divinatione* is a vibrant refutation of the defense of divination that Quintus had eloquently offered in the first half of the essay.[29]

---

[27] Ample information is supplied by Pease (1920–23), *ad loc.*

[28] Mynors (1990:92) thinks they might have been already present in Ennius' poem.

[29] The relationship between the two parts of the essay, and its overall interpretation, has recently received much attention: cf. Denyer (1985), Beard (1986), Schofield (1986), with Timpanaro (1988), xcvi.

Cicero takes up his brother's arguments one by one, and rebuts them from the viewpoint of Neo-Academic scepticism towards divination, which is seen as an untenable and irrational banalization of the gods' power. Cicero's refutation of the position expressed in *De consulatu* and in the third Catilinarian oration is clear in points of detail, as he proves that all the supposed *portenta* are natural and casual, and that they do not have any necessary connection with the conspiracy. Much less forthcoming is Cicero's explanation of his different attitude towards divination in the different contexts of the poem and the dialogue. One could perhaps invoke the passing of time, but if the explanation were this simple we would expect Cicero to bring it up himself. What he offers instead is a rather elliptical and hazy rejoinder (2.46):

"Tu igitur animum induces – sic enim mecum agebas – causam istam et contra facta tua et contra scripta defendere?" "Frater es; eo vereor. Verum quid tibi hic tandem nocet? Resne quae talis est an ego qui verum explicari volo?"

"Will you then – for thus you pleaded with me – will you then persuade yourself to take sides against me in this discussion, in the face of your own writings and of your own practice?" "You are my brother, and on that account I must respect you. But what, pray, is causing you distress in this matter? Is it the nature of things, which is what I said, or my insistence on finding out the truth?"

The passage is so obscure that textual corruption has often been suspected: emendations, however, could hardly transform it into an explicit and comprehensive response. It is better to take reticence for what it is, and follow Timpanaro's persuasive suggestion that Cicero is here stopping short of admitting clearly that his use of *portenta* in the *De consulatu* and the Catilinarian oration was based on *Realpolitik* rather than on philosophical conviction.[30] Divination, as *De legibus* amply attests, is an integral and untouchable component of the traditional Roman religion which Cicero, an augur himself, will do nothing to undermine and question as far as the real power relations within the state are concerned. On the other hand, from a detached, philosophical point of view, he cannot suppress his impulse to subject it to a stringent rationalistic critique.

The connection between the *Georgics* and *De divinatione* represents a singularly interesting case of intertextuality, since the explicit reference to the *portenta* described by Urania in the first book of the essay cannot be separated from the deconstruction of that description volunteered by Cicero in book 2: Virgil's allusive gesture telescopes both the apology and the critique of divination. As usual, differences between the original context and the alluding text signal meaningful elements. The *Georgics* repeat the *portenta* listed in *De divinatione* and refer them to a different, subsequent historical situation.

---

[30] I follow here Timpanaro (1988)'s translation (145) and interpretation (lxxvi–lxxxiii; 353–4) of the passage.

The events that anticipated the Catilinarian conspiracy of 63 BCE also warned of impending civil unrest in 44 BCE, but the second time they went unheeded. The context seems to offer at least a partial explanation of why they were not effective, namely that they fell on unreceptive and impious interpreters. Thus the book ends with a complex and ultimately open view of divination: the *portenta* Virgil lists encode, thanks to the bifurcated intertextual model, both a confident assessment of the human ability to interpret such signs and to act accordingly, and also the cautionary notion that such interpretation is not always guaranteed or even possible at all. The complexities of the passage definitely set Virgil apart from a Stoic view such as the one Quintus outlines, without, on the other hand, making him share Cicero's rationalism. Once again the possibility of reading signs correctly and profiting from such an activity seems to be connected more with the piety of the interpreter than with any general rule valid for all time. In this particular respect Virgil is closer than one might suspect at first sight to Cicero's own position in book 2. Cicero reiterates that divination cannot eliminate personal responsibility, and that certain moral choices ought to be made irrespective of the favorable or ominous signs that precede them: King Deiotarus was justified in rushing to help Pompey regardless of what the birds were telling him. By putting a strong emphasis on the immorality of the *impia saecula* Virgil points out that divinatory signs cannot be the automatic solution to all human problems, and that a thorough moral renovation is in order if Romans hope to take advantage of the *portenta* they are given to observe.

7. The numerous connections between the *Georgics* and *De divinatione* not only underline the great importance that Cicero's reflection must have had in Virgil's eyes, but also exhibit at least a partial affinity in the two writers' overall attitude. Virgil found in Cicero's essay a rich, if in turn problematic, articulation of several crucial issues: the nature and limits of divination, the power of the gods, and how to respond to the Epicureans' attacks on traditional religion without siding with wholly unscientific and indefensible positions. However, Cicero's practical, unapologetic distinction between a set of religious beliefs which the masses had to respect, and the enlightened scepticism of the ruling classes appears to lose ground, in the *Georgics*, in favor of a less divisive intermediate solution.

Since the audience Virgil envisaged for his poem was typologically similar to Cicero's, the *Georgics*' careful mixture of traditional rites and beliefs with discernible, yet controlled, elements of rationalistic critique must be seen as a different answer to the same set of problems. In this way, Cicero's own rationalistic excesses are implicitly criticized and scaled back, although, as I will show in the next part of this essay, the ultimate champion of rationalistic *hybris* will be unsurprisingly identified with Lucretius.

In the *Georgics'* new world order signs can be certain because they come from god, but the very insistence on their certainty ultimately transforms them into *praecepta*, that is into a predetermined set of fixed indicators which the narrator reveals thanks to his superior knowledge and which the farmer ought to master with deference. In the process, *signa* completely lose the liberating and theoretically unlimited potential they display in Epicurus' and Lucretius' epistemology. The farmer is told exactly how much he can know, and no attempt is made to empower his epistemological ability in a way which could eventually dispense with need of further instruction. The georgic *signa* are, in this respect, a true and accurate embodiment of the power structure that underlies the rural world envisaged by the poem: as the gods will grant power to Caesar, so they will, if duly asked and honored, grant knowledge to the farmer.

In this perspective one can more readily make sense of the connection that the repetition of *miseratus* in two sections of the poems strongly suggests. The verb is used to describe the sun's eclipse after the death of Caesar at line 1.466, but had already concluded Virgil's invocation for Octavian's help at 1.41: "and, pitying with me the farmers who know not their way, enter" (*ignarosque viae mecum miseratus agrestis|ingredere*). In what sense are both the sun and Caesar supposed to "take pity?" The connection lies, I believe, not in the attempt to equate the sun and the ruler, but rather in the fact that both serve the same function towards knowledge in their respective contexts. The sun "takes pity" on Rome not just by hiding the shameful sight she offers, but by sending a clear, if unheeded, sign of the impending catastrophe of civil war. Virgil and Octavian will "take pity" on their Roman readers by a similar act of instruction. Both the parallel use of the verb, and its intrinsic connotations, effectively reinforce the notion that knowledge is granted by the gods and thus inevitably hierarchical.

The final scene of the book crystallizes this connection in the image of the chariot out of control and dragged off its path by unrestrained horses. The chariot embodies the comprehensive war that is raging in the world, the *res publica* in desperate need of direction, and the poem itself, which is ostensibly determined to redress the lack of a *dignus honos* (507) for the plough. We will have to unroll the next scroll to discover in the terse, prosaic style of the beginning of book 2 an implicit solution to this dramatic situation.

Causal knowledge

8. The analysis of signs has highlighted the well-marked boundaries within which they are allowed to operate in the *Georgics*, and especially the ideological lines of tension which can be detected in Virgil's procedures. Signs are

– or at least should be – closely connected with the identification of causes which provoke certain events. In the empirical tradition represented in first-century Rome by Lucretius, signs enable the observer to penetrate a level of reality at which ultimate causes can be identified; through signs, among other factors, we can detect the workings of natural laws on the basis of which causes can be safely determined.

Any discussion of causes in the *Georgics* is bound sooner or later to face the exegetical problems created by the debated *makarismos* at the end of book 2. The traditional interpretation of this passage[31] sees in the exclamation of lines 490–92, *felix qui potuit rerum cognoscere causas* . . . ("happy he who was able to understand the causes of things"), a reference to the Epicurean philosophy of Lucretius, and in the following lines, beginning at 493 with *fortunatus et ille deos qui novit agrestis* ("blessed too the man who knows the gods of the countryside"), a reference to Virgil's own *Georgics*. However, Richard Thomas[32] has recently claimed that it is wrong to consider Lucretius as the primary object of lines 490–2, which according to him refer to the *Georgics*, while 493–4 express "contentment with a pastoral world, the world represented by the *Eclogues*": Virgil first expresses his "wish for the success of the poem" he is writing, then "a compromise within (his) aspirations." Thomas argues that lines 490 to 92 "fit perfectly the aims of the *Georgics*," since it is " 'understanding' of nature – *cognoscere causas* – that is the goal throughout the poem".[33]

I believe, on the contrary, that the presence of Lucretius in these few lines is explicit, substantial, and specific, and raises significant issues. The first (and foremost) question to face is whether it is really possible to describe the epistemological procedures of the *Georgics* as an attempt to "understand causes." Secondly, can Virgil claim for his own work, even only as a hope, the overcoming of "all the fears," "inexorable fate" and "the thunder of greedy Acheron" (491–2: "has cast beneath his feet all fear and unyielding Fate, and the howls of the hungry Acheron"; *atque metus omnis et inexorabile fatum*|*subiecit pedibus strepitumque Acherontis avari*)?

The word *causa* is used five times in the *Georgics*.[34] Setting aside one instance which is not immediately relevant,[35] and, at least for the moment,

---

[31] For a a persuasive, recent treatment see Hardie (1986:33ff.), who also directs to the relevant bibliographical items.

[32] Thomas (1988), 252.   [33] Thomas (1988), 253.

[34] I cannot deal here with the equally important case of *ratio*. The epistemology of the *De rerum natura* revolves around the notion of *ratio*, a word used hundreds of times in the poem. *Ratio*, in its multiple meanings, indicates both the inner workings of nature and the doctrine which reveals them, and *ratio* is the gift that the poet transfers to his readers. This word appears not a single time in the *Georgics*.

[35] 2.455: *Bacchus et ad culpam causas dedit.*

2.490, it is worth looking again at the episode of Aristaeus, where *causa* figures twice, towards the beginning and the end of the passage. At 387–414 Cyrene instructs Aristaeus to meet Proteus, since "the *vates* knows everything" (392: *novit omnia vates*), and he will be able to "explain the whole cause of the disease" (396–7: *omnem | expediat morbi causam*). The word *causa* is again on Cyrene's lips in her second speech, when, after Aristaeus' successful – if unclear – meeting with Proteus she explains in more explicit terms what the *vates* meant: "this is the whole cause of the plague" (532: *haec omnis morbi causam*).

In all these instances *causa* does not introduce a scientific, rational explanation of events based on the inductive discernment of invisible causes, but a form of revealed knowledge that only divine benevolence can hand over to mortals. The very opposite is true of 2.490, where the knowledge of causes is directly linked to the ability of freeing oneself from fear, destiny, and the power of Acheron: far from being a way of liberating humans from the power of gods and *religio*, the understanding of *causae*, in the Aristaeus episode, is clearly seen as a divine prerogative that reinforces the subordination of mortals to gods.

Only once in the whole poem is *causa* used by the narrator himself, who pledges, at 3.440, to point out "the causes and signs of the diseases" (*morborum quoque te causas et signa docebo*), that is, of the diseases which befall cattle. This association of *causae*, *signa* and *morbi* rings truly Lucretian, but the reader who expects anything similar to Lucretius' elaborate explanation of the causes of the plague in *De rerum natura* 6.1090–132 is soon disappointed, since Virgil relates a series of symptoms and connections between visible events (like cold weather and rain) and the insurgence of disease in the stock (3.440–4):

> morborum quoque te causas et signa docebo.
> turpis ovis temptat scabies, ubi frigidus imber
> altius ad vivum persedit et horrida cano
> bruma gelu, vel cum tonsis inlotus adhaesit
> sudor, et hirsuti secuerunt corpora vepres.

Diseases, too, their cause and tokens, I will teach you. Foul scab attacks sheep, while chilly rain and winter, bristling with hoar frost, have sunk deep into the quick, or when the sweat, unwashed, clings to the shorn flock, and prickly briars tear the flesh.

The narrator does not push his analysis beyond the level of evident facts such as that cold is dangerous and does not make use of signs or scientific hypothesis in order to account for the atomic modifications that cause the disease according to Lucretius. Unsurprisingly, such a form of superficial awareness based on experience and simple observation is matched by a correspondingly empirical set of precautions and remedies which can supposedly help counter the plague (445–51):

dulcibus idcirco fluviis pecus omne magistri
perfundunt, udisque aries in gurgite villis
mersatur, missusque secundo defluit amni;
aut tonsum tristi contingunt corpus amurca
et spumas miscent argenti vivaque sulphura
Idaeasque pices et pinguis unguine ceras
scillamque elleborosque gravis nigrumque bitumen.

Therefore the keepers bathe the whole flock in fresh streams; the ram is plunged in the pool with his dripping fleece, and let loose to float down the current. Or, after shearing, they smear the body with bitter oil-lees, blending silver-scum and native sulphur with pitch from Ida and richly oiled wax, squill, strong hellebore, and black bitumen.

Virgil raises in the reader the expectation of an epistemological approach similar to the one employed by Lucretius, who used *signa* as *opsis tōn adēlōn*, "image of hidden things," as a means to understand non-evident causes, but immediately frustrates it by proposing instead a form of knowledge that relies heavily on fixed, limited *praecepta*: truly causal knowledge is not the kind of knowledge that is attempted or encouraged in the *Georgics*, while it is exactly the main objective of Lucretius' poem.

It is true, however, that at least the first themes listed at 2.477–8 can also be Virgilian, indeed georgic. *Caeli viae et sidera*, "the roads of the sky and the stars," is a pertinent reference to the Aratean part of book 1, and Virgil does indeed recommend, at 1.335, that the farmer observe "the months of the sky and the stars" (*caeli mensis et sidera serva*). *Defectus solis variae lunaeque labores*, "the sun's lapses, the moon's many labors" is more problematic, since the line is closely modelled on Lucr.5.751 "eclipses of the sun and the moon's occultations" (*solis item quoque defectus lunaeque latebras*), and *defectus* – a rare word – is used only once in both authors; still, eclipses are dealt with in the *Georgics* at 1.351–464 and 1.466–8, where they are all interpreted as signs which can be used to forecast the weather. On the contrary, the four themes that are formulated in a truly causal way by the words *unde*, *qua vi*, *quid* and *quae mora* (479–82),[36] are prominent and well recognizable Lucretian themes which never find their way into the *Georgics*, where there is no discussion of earthquakes (479 *unde tremor terris*),[37] sea-tides[38] (479–80 *qua vi maria lata tumescant/obicibus ruptis rursusque in se ipsa residant*), and "variations in the lengths of day and night."[39]

It is in the context provided by these facts that the allusion embedded in line 490 assumes a particular relevance. The clausula *cognoscere causas* is not paralleled elsewhere in the *Georgics*, but is taken, with a change in case,

---

[36] Cf. n.8 above.   [37] Cf. Lucr. 6.287 *inde tremor terras graviter pertemptat*.
[38] I think it is preferable to think of sea-tides here rather than storms: cf. Mynors (1990), 167.
[39] Mynors (1990), 167.

from one of the most significant sections of *De rerum natura* book 5, where Lucretius explains why primitive humans developed a belief in the existence and omnipotence of gods (5.1183–7):

> praeterea caeli rationes ordine certo
> et varia annorum cernebant tempora verti
> nec poterant quibus id fieret cognoscere causis.
> Ergo perfugium sibi habebant omnia divis
> tradere et illorum nutu facere omnia flecti.

Moreover, they beheld the workings of the sky in due order, and the diverse seasons of the year come round, nor could they learn by what causes that was brought about. And so they made it their refuge to lay all to the charge of the gods, and to suppose that all was guided by their will.

The absence of rational, causal explanations of natural phenomena is what forced early human beings to – as Lucretius puts it – "hand everything over to the gods," to believe that nothing could be explained if not in terms of divine power. Virgil is not simply picking up a *clausula* from Lucretius, but alluding to the specific conceptual framework he establishes, namely the direct connection between the human's ability to offer causal explanations and their rejection of traditional *religio*. The terms of the relationship are the same, but Virgil's answer is diametrically opposed to Lucretius': human beings cannot possibly achieve a truly scientific, causal explanation of phenomena; gods not only do exist, but are also responsible for the ordered connection of events about which they reveal as much or as little as they deem fit. All mortals can undertake is a limited exploration of macroscopic phenomena in order to recognize evident patterns of regularity that can be of help in their daily activities. This is a form of epistemological restraint, whose ultimate effect is to reinforce, or at the very least not to challenge, a belief in the pervasive power of gods and their comprehensive intervention in every aspect of human life.

9. Lucretius and the Epicureans are not the only ones who display scepticism towards a vision of a world in which absolutely every aspect of nature could be taken only as a reflection of the divinity, and every action would be subjected to the inexorable fate that Virgil seems to be defending by default in the passage. A similar form of restraint characterizes, as we have seen, the position taken *vis-à-vis* divination by Quintus, who early on in his speech claims that: "of all these things [prophecies, prodigies and the like] ... the results more than the causes should be examined" (1.12: *quarum quidem rerum eventa magis arbitror quam causas quaeri oportet*), and insists on the opportunity that mortals accept some evident facts, such as the curative power of certain medicines, for instance, without inquiring further why such powers

exist. The theoretical underpinning of Quintus' position is clearly rooted in Stoic determinism: things are the way they are because of the gods' decision, and all causes ultimately return to the *primum mobile* of all causation. Inquiring about specific causes is, in a sense, an idle exercise.

Virgil's position, once again, is discernibly more nuanced. The juxtaposition of *felix qui potuit* and *fortunatus et ille* seems to lend almost equal value to the two options obtainable in the field of scientific didactic poetry, and to justify the preference for the non-causal one with fear rather than theoretical impossibility. Unveiling all the causes is a victory that does indeed "equate us to the sky," as Lucretius put it (1.79 *nos exaequat victoria caelo*), but also provokes *horror* together with *divina voluptas* (3.28–9). Restraint is in order, Virgil rejoins, if we are to escape both the emotional stress of *horror* and the intrinsic impiety of that kind of *voluptas*. Thus the world of the *Georgics*, and the ideal of life and knowledge it envisages, consistently shrink away from the "greatness" of Lucretius in all its literary and philosophical implications. Still, while it is impossible to agree with the iconoclastic scientific program of the Epicureans, it would hardly be better to embrace wholeheartedly the Stoic position advocated by Quintus.

The complexity of Virgil's epistemological assumptions lies in the need to preserve intact to the greatest possible extent the foundations of traditional religion without appearing hopelessly out of touch with the revolutionary insights of the rationalistic critics. Lucretius' vocabulary of causation and signification can after all be adopted, but cleansed of its formidable disruptive power.

10. I return by way of conclusion of this section to the *Georgics'* intimation to "observe the *caeli mensis et sidera*" (1.335). Similar concerns play an important role in Hesiod's *Works and Days*, a poem sealed with a solemn and comforting blessing (826–8), one whose dissembled items provide an instructive allusive overtone to the contrast between *felix* and *fortunatus* drawn by Virgil:[40]

he is truly blessed (*eudaimōn*) and rich (*olbios*) who, knowing (*eidōs*) all these things, does his work, guiltless before the gods, observing omens and avoiding wrong.

Hesiod displays complete confidence that the knowledge of values and norms guaranteed by tradition, and the pious respect of gods enable men to lead a fulfilled, happy, and righteous life. Man will thus be *eudaimōn* and *olbios* at the same time, will know what matters, and act accordingly. By analogy the poet will face no painful alternative between two different modes of singing didactic poetry. At the end of the second book of the *Georgics* it is

---

[40] This connection is mentioned by La Penna (1962), 244.

precisely this solidarity between *eudaimōn* and *olbios*, of *felix* and *fortunatus*, that is shown to be in an irreversible state of crisis, as the two terms come to describe irreconcilable alternatives both for the life of the farmer and the work of the poet. This is why the georgic way of life described at length in 2.493–540 constitutes a joint answer to the same problem.

More than anything else, the Epicurean lesson taught in *De rerum natura* shattered the mutually reinforcing bond in which Hesiod had firmly believed: *felix* and *fortunatus* now describe two opposite alternatives to the problem of knowing and believing, and Virgil is fully aware of the fact that after Lucretius' attack the primeval innocence of the Hesiodic position cannot be simply restated. The connection between knowledge and happiness which Hesiod had framed in traditional and religious-oriented terms has in fact become just the opposite, a powerful weapon in the hands of a determined rationalistic attack against *religio*. Virgil could restore – to a degree – the ideal solidarity of values praised by Hesiod, and hope to overcome these rationalistic strictures not by ignoring, but by fighting the methodological lesson of *De rerum natura*, and showing that at least a certain kind of scientific poetry and traditional beliefs could coexist. It is not knowledge *per se*, but the aspiration to understand causes, the "reasoning Pride," in Pope's words, that should be abandoned.

Tempted as he may be to follow the Lucretian way of writing didactic poetry, and wish that the Muses might teach him how to do so, Virgil has to step back and follow an alternative path in order to preserve the very power of inexorable fate that Lucretius tried so hard to break (Lucr.2.254: *fati foedera rumpat*) with a form of scientific poetry which Virgil explicitly wishes he could follow but which he soon realizes is an impossible dream (*G.*2.477: *accipiant*).

Knowledge, power and the order of poetry

11. I will conclude – as I began – with the analysis of a narrative passage that encodes important elements for understanding the process of knowledge. I will look back to the beginning of *Eclogue* 1, where Meliboeus and Tityrus discuss their respective errors of knowledge. Meliboeus laments that the oaks "often touched from the sky" (17) had in fact predicted an impending disaster, but he did not pay due attention to these signs, because his own mind was "ill-fated" (16: *si mens non laeva fuisset*). As we have noticed in connection with the *portenta* announcing the civil war, the signs sent by the gods do not relieve humans from their responsibility to interpret them correctly and act accordingly. Tityrus, on the other hand, was ensnared in an analogical fallacy: he thought he knew that small things could provide a reliable image of larger things (23: *sic parvis componere magna solebam*), that he could imagine Rome

on the basis of the nearby small town. This is very much a Lucretian error, the very foundation of the analogical method of *De rerum natura*. Unlike Meliboeus however, who finds no remedy for his misjudgment, Tityrus does discover a way to overcome his mistake. His "conversion" arrives when he is finally able to "recognize the favorable gods" (41: *praesentis . . . cognoscere divos*), ask the famous *iuvenis* for a *responsum* (44), and engage in the pastoral activities recommended by the *iuvenis* (45: "feed, youths, your oxen as of old; rear your bulls"; *"pascite ut ante boves, pueri; summittite tauros"*) In this way Tityrus was able to gain the *fortuna* to which Meliboeus immediately refers in his answer: *fortunate senex . . .* (46).

It is not the analogical science praised by Lucretius that can help Tityrus, but a form of knowledge that depends on mutually reinforcing bonds between social and religious powers, a form of knowledge that ultimately recognizes its subordinate status and learns how to "know the gods," as Virgil will repeat at *G*.2.493. *Fortuna* can derive only from "knowing the helpful gods," *praesentis cognoscere divos*, that is the *praesentia numina* of *G*.1.10 (Virgil refers *praesentis* to divinities only in these two passages before the *Aeneid*). That is why Virgil exclaims at *G*.2.458 "o happy farmers, o too happy should they realize their blessings!" (*o fortunatos nimium, sua si bona norint,*|*agricolas*): their happiness is there for them to grab, provided they understand the hierarchical structures that shape both the relationship among humans, and the relationship between them and the gods. The proud illusion of *cognoscere causas* should be replaced by the willingness to *cognoscere curas* (1.117),[41] to listen to the poet and his practical, consciously limited precepts based on elementary forms of connection between visible phenomena.

The epistemological procedures of the *Georgics* take issue directly with the confident exploration of invisible phenomena undertaken by Lucretius, and put forth an alternative mode of knowledge emphatically aware of its limitations. The narrator of the *Georgics* sides with the empirical, limited, religious-oriented knowledge of the *agrestes*, and further develops their "naturally" righteous beliefs. This is an operation that Virgil carries out with a remarkable degree of subtlety, one that does not lend itself to sweeping characterizations. But it is essential to insist on the fact that Virgil's program proceeds more by way of incremental assimilation than outright confrontation, and that it actually leaves room for at least a modicum of epistemological diversity: after all, those who strive to "understand the causes" are praised from a distance rather than criticized harshly.

The *Georgics* is a subtle attempt to redefine the tools and scope of the farmer's knowledge on the part of the poet, to present a notion of *praecepta* that does not reject wholesale rational modes of knowledge and yet does not

---

[41] The two clausulae crystallize a pervasive ideological difference: Schiesaro (1993), 142–3.

unduly challenge established religious truths.[42] At the end of the poem the reader, and the farmer, should be persuaded that knowledge, too, is a divine gift just as the plough donated by Neoptolemus, and that the poet has usefully and generously absolved his duty as a precious demiurge. In the process, the reader should also have learnt, even if that name has not been named once, and no direct attack has been waged, that Lucretius' attempt to provide a lay concept of knowledge is off track, and its theoretical respectability does not translate into any practical usefulness. As the Hesiodic allusion in the *makarismos* at the end of book 2 strongly suggests, Virgil does try to provide a unified model, where knowledge, belief and practical life can coexist in a mutually dependent relationship, and where the activities of the farmer, just as his ways of knowing, can find a superior ethical justification. Whether or not this "theodicy of knowledge" is "optimistic" or not is less important a consideration than the fact that Virgil has intensely striven to overcome the cultural and ideological rifts that for decades had been so evident among the Roman cultural elites.

12. While it might nowadays sound slightly obvious to repeat that knowledge is power, I believe it is hardly unwarranted to claim the peculiar pertinence of that axiom for texts such as *De rerum natura* or the *Georgics*. Lucretius' fight against the oppressive power of religion is waged through a systematic revision of the forms of knowledge to which men can resort, and by a powerful defense of empirical evidence *vis-à-vis* the unsubstantiated tales of mythology. In the *Georgics*, since Virgil establishes early on a precise parallelism between the task of the narrator and Caesar's role in the taming and ruling of the world, it is legitimate to infer that the protection of the epistemological superiority of the narrator is intertwined with and dependent on the preservation of the *status quo* in the political domain. In the *De rerum natura*, Epicurus' mental flight into the skies enables him to penetrate the secret workings of nature, and to return among men with a clear notion of what can be produced and what cannot, that is with the basic elements of Epicurean physics thanks to which every man will be able to understand reality (1.62–80). In the *Georgics*, Caesar is asked to "take pity" on farmers, and to help the poet in his benign task of handing down useful *praecepta* (1.40–2).

Andrew Wallace-Hadrill has rightly pointed out the central role that the new cultural order of the Augustan age assigns to specialized and rational knowledge, safely entrusted in the hands of magisterial figures whose expertise is separate

---

[42] I must disagree with Perkell (1989) 190 who argues that the "poet's truth" in the *Georgics* is at odds with what she defines as the "iron age" values of *praecepta* and rational analysis. The pointed contrast between the poet's "mystery" and the farmer's *praecepta* which Perkell suggests obliterates the important process by which the poet does in fact offer his own set of *praecepta* and imposes his own magisterial role.

from, but available to, the political powers that be.[43] It is interesting to compare this general tendency with Virgil's fashioning of the narrator of the *Georgics* as an expert *geōrgos*, a repository of technical knowledge who is at pains not to reject rationalistic tendencies. Although he guarantees that he can relate many *praecepta veterum*, the georgic narrator's very act of teaching signals the necessity to reconceptualize a supposedly traditional knowledge and disseminate it through markedly different channels of communication. Virgil's knowledge is available to all interested in listening, but now is imparted *ex cathedra*, is authorized and backed by a close and compelling political structure, and carefully mixes rationalism with arguments from authority: it is a complex form of knowledge which eloquently testifies to the revolutionary ferments which have by now seeped deeply into the culture of the Romans.

[43] *Supra*, pp. 11ff.

5 *Ut arte emendaturus fortunam*: Horace, Nasidienus, and the art of satire

Ellen Oliensis

Though separated by only a few years – book 1 is generally dated to 35, book 2 to 30 BCE – Horace's two books of satires are, in many respects, worlds apart. One obvious difference has to do with their subject matter. While book 1 is peppered with references to dinner parties and dining habits,[1] it can boast nothing comparable to the discourses on dining, both theoretical and practical, that preoccupy fully half of the eight satires of the second book.[2] The most striking difference between the two books, however, is one of narrative technique. Whereas Horace himself dominated the satiric stage of book 1, in book 2 he prefers to play a supporting role, speaking relatively few words *in propria persona* and ascribing the bulk of his satire to someone else. Rather than delivering philosophical diatribes, for example, as in book 1, he is now their somewhat exasperated recipient. In a sense, in poems such as these, Horace ceases to be the satirist of his own satire. The effect has been analyzed with some precision by Mario Labate (1981:26), who compares the second book to a shattered mirror which yields only fragmentary and partial truths. But the significance of this shift remains underanalyzed. What moves Horace to shatter the mirror? How are we to understand his abdication of the role of satiric speaker?

The argument of this essay is that Horace's change of satiric subject matter and technique at once manages and exposes the anxieties attending his social ascent. The times rendered that ascent especially problematic. In the chaotic closing decades of the Republic, the shifting fortunes of civil war blurred once-secure distinctions. Proscriptions, expropriations, the favor or anger of a few enormously powerful men, destroyed many men and made as many others. It was difficult, in such circumstances, to sustain the traditional image of meritorious ascent. Writing a few years before Horace, the historian Sallust lamented that "new men" seeking the honor of the consulate, men who in the

---

[1] The most interesting passages are 1.1.117–19; 1.3.4–8, 90–4; 1.4.86–9; 1.5.71–6; and 1.6.114–18. All references are to the Oxford text of Wickham and Garrod (with one exception, noted below).

[2] 2.2, 2.4, the second half of 2.6, and 2.8. On the significance of food in *Satires* 2 see Gowers (1993), 126–79; Hudson (1989).

90

past relied on *virtus*, now advanced "by secret dealings and brigandage rather than noble arts" (*furtim et per latrocinia potius quam bonis artibus, Jug.* 4.7); the same accusation could be leveled against men who achieved wealth and distinction while remaining private citizens. The stock figures of the greedy miser and the extravagant spendthrift against whom Horace measures his own moderate *modus vivendi* in *Satires* 2.6 – "if I have not increased my property by base means (*ratione mala*), if I am not about to diminish it by waste or neglect (*vitio culpave*)" (2.6.6–7) – had a special charge in a period which saw ambitious men accumulate and spend fortunes, whether to raise armies or their own individual social profiles, with frightening speed. Throughout his early poetry, Horace labors to defend himself against the accusation that his fine art of satire is, in the Sallustian sense, a "bad art" of time-serving ambition.[3] Let me underscore at the outset that the aim of this essay is not to establish "the truth" about Horace's ascent – a truth that may have eluded Horace himself – but to explore how his satires register his intense awareness of the hard things that could and would be said about him.

I begin with a simple question: Who are the satiric speakers of the second book, and what, if anything, do they have in common? In some cases, the speaker is little more than a proper name, a peg on which to hang a satiric discourse. All we know about Catius, the man who recites the culinary precepts that fill up *Satires* 2.4, is that Horace claims him as a friend (*per amicitiam*, 2.4.88); all we know about Cervius, the garrulous gentleman who recounts the fable of the country mouse and the city mouse which concludes *Satires* 2.6, is that he is Horace's neighbor (*vicinus*, 2.6.77). About the book's three chief philosophizers, Ofellus, Damasippus, and Davus, we are more fully informed. As it happens, these three satirists do have something in common: they are all the victims of misfortune. Ofellus, the rustic philosopher of *Satires* 2.2, has lost his farm, a fact that Horace reveals, as if incidentally, near the end of the poem (2.2.112–15): "I knew this Ofellus when I was a little boy, and he didn't spend any more when his fortune was intact than he does now that it is clipped. You can still see him, with his livestock and his children, working undaunted as a tenant on the little farm that was taken over by the surveyors" (*metato in agello|cum pecore et gnatis fortem mercede colonum*).[4] Like the farm of Meliboeus in Virgil's first eclogue, Ofellus's farm is one of the indirect casualties of the civil war. The misfortunes of Damasippus, the man who delivers the lengthy diatribe of *Satires* 2.3, are set not in the country but in the city. As he himself reports (2.3.20–5), and as

---

[3] On the defensive disposition of Horatian satire, see now Lyne (1995), 12–20. Horace's self-defense also helps construct the moral authority of the "Augustan age"; see DuQuesnay (1984) and Kennedy (1992).

[4] The phrase "working undaunted as a tenant" is borrowed from the translation of Rudd (1979), 93. Unless otherwise indicated, all translations are my own.

we know from Cicero's letters,[5] Damasippus was a dealer in antiques and expensive real estate, renowned for his sharp eye for what would sell. For reasons unspecified, his business has gone bust (*postquam omnis res mea Ianum\ad medium fracta est*, 18–19; cf. *male re gesta*, 37). Davus, the featured speaker of *Satires* 2.7, identifies himself at the outset as one of Horace's slaves (*servus*, 2.7.1) – as a man, that is, deprived not of his property but of his *libertas*. The story of his or his ancestors' enslavement is not told; it is as if he were a slave by nature, not fortune. Indeed his very status as a slave occludes the history of his enslavement. But Horace, whom the invidious liked to describe, so he tells us, as "the son of a freedman,"[6] perhaps knows otherwise. The dispossessed farmer, the bankrupt businessman, the slave: all have suffered (or inherited) a reversal of fortune, a diminution of status.

And this is precisely why they turn to satire, why they need satire. It is no accident that two of these satires take place during the Saturnalia, a festival which temporarily annuls status differences, granting the slave a "December license" (*libertate Decembri*, 2.7.4) that frees his tongue if not his person.[7] Like the Saturnalia, satire levels society by bringing the master down. Horace may condescend to don the mask of the free-speaking freedman satirist so as to unmask the pretensions of others; for those of lower status, satiric discourse has a different meaning. For Ofellus, it is a tonic that both fortifies and consoles. As he reminds his sons – sons who will not inherit their family farm – a man who lives modestly and moderately has little to lose (2.2.126–8): "Let Fortune rage and stir up new storms; how much can she take from our simple pleasures? How much leaner is our life, my sons, since the new occupant arrived?" They are not the first or the last to suffer dispossession, he adds: the new owner will be driven out in his turn, if not by another man then in the end by death, the ultimate leveler (129–32). Philosophy is also a comfort to Damasippus, who claims to have been rescued from the very brink of suicide by the Stoic philosopher Stertinius, who consoled him (*solatus*, 2.3.35) by proving that all men, with the exception of the Stoic sage, are equally insane. This lecture, which Damasippus proceeds to recite for Horace's benefit, not only restored the bankrupt businessman's self-respect, it also equipped him, as he reports, with a means of self-defense (296–8): "These are the weapons (*arma*) given to me by my friend Stertinius, the eighth Sage,

---

[5] *Fam.* 7.23.2; *Att.* 12.29.2, 12.33.1.

[6] On Horace's status, see Armstrong (1986) and now Williams (1995); Williams mounts a strong case against taking the reiterated tag "born of a freedman father" literally, suggesting that Horace's father was among the rebel Italians captured or enslaved during the Social War and enrolled after the war as full Roman citizens.

[7] It is significant that the slave Davus awaits Horace's express granting of this license before launching into his tirade. On the practical limits of Saturnalian license, see D'Arms (1991), 176; on Horace's Saturnalian satire, Freudenburg (1993), 211–23.

so that from now on if I'm abused I can take my revenge – whoever says I'm crazy will hear the same from me!" The equalizing thrust of satire is most clear in the case of Davus, who uses his moment of Saturnalian license to announce that his master is no less a slave than he is (2.7.75–7): *tune mihi dominus?* "*You* play master to *me*? – you, who are so utterly subject to the bidding of men and of circumstance? You, who will never be freed, no matter how often the wand of freedom waves over you, from wretched fear?" Horace is in effect, Davus claims, the "fellow-slave" of his slave (*conservus*, 80) – which makes Davus the fellow-master of his master. The fact that it is their own misfortune that opens the eyes of these philosophers to the leveling truths they propound does not deprive their discourse of authority, but it does open it to the accusation of impurity. Misery – the uncharitable might say – loves company. By situating his satirists as he does, Horace exposes satire for what it "really" is: not a disinterested revelation of timeless philosophical truths, but a consolation prize awarded to life's losers. Satiric leveling is how the satirist gets even.

But stoic endurance, fortified by stoical reflections, is not the only way of responding to fortune's blows. The man laid low by fortune can also use his wits to better his lot. When Damasippus delivers his harangue, he may be angling not only for respect but also for sympathy and, perhaps, an invitation to dinner. The cheerful polypragmatist, who arrives uninvited at Horace's country retreat, is one of a long line of meal-cadging philosophers whose great original is Socrates, known to his enemies not as the father of philosophy but as "the *scurra* of Attica," as Cicero reports.[8] Perhaps Damasippus even hopes to win himself a position in Horace's household as a philosopher-in-residence. The former dealer in antiques is now marketing another kind of cultural capital.

How closely do these down-and-out philosophers resemble the man who records their words of wisdom? Very little, it would appear. The autobiography furnished by Horace's *Satires* presents no "reversal of fortune" to be satirically faced down or corrected. Book 1 depicts Horace's life story as a relatively smooth ascent from humble beginnings,[9] to the honor of the military tribunate (Horace does not specify the circumstances), to a well-deserved place within the exalted circle of Maecenas; book 2 continues the curve, remarking Horace's intimacy with the young Caesar and establishing him on his new Sabine farm. I do not mean to suggest that we should take Horace's satiric autobiography at face value but to draw attention to what is missing from his earliest self-portrait. Horace insulates his autobiography and his

---

[8] *Nat. D.* 1.93, cited by Corbett (1986), 3.

[9] But not too humble: as argued by Williams (1995: 310–11), the same satire that brands Horace a "freedman's son" comes close to stating that his father was in fact freeborn (e.g., with *ingenuo si non essem patre natus*, "if I were not born [sc. but I am] of a freeborn father," 1.6.21).

satiric practice from the influence of fortune by erasing his own famous
reversal of fortune. This reversal is most memorably recorded in the capsule
autobiography of his late epistle to Florus (*Epistles* 2.2). On his return from
Philippi, where he fought on the Republican side, Horace found himself
deprived of his family property (Venusia was one of the Italian towns designated for the resettlement of veterans).[10] How was the struggling young man
to repair his fortune? The wry answer offered in the epistle to Florus is – by
writing poetry (*Epistles* 2.2.49–52): "After Philippi discharged me, leaving
me earth-bound, my wings clipped, stripped of ancestral house and lands, bold
poverty spurred me to compose verse" (*paupertas impulit audax | ut versus
facerem*). Horace's exposé of the satirist in book 2, which displaces these
autobiographical "facts" onto a series of surrogates, also retroactively exposes
the satirist of book 1. Like Ofellus, Horace forfeited his family property to
the resettlement program of the triumvirs; like Damasippus, he has betaken
himself to the profession of satirist; like Davus, and this is the hardest truth
of all, he has forfeited his freedom in the service of another man.

This last charge is explicit, leveled by the slave against his master in
Satires 2.7. When Horace hasn't been invited anywhere for dinner, according to Davus, he praises "carefree cabbage" (*securum holus*, 2.7.30), posing
as a devoted adherent of the simple life, a real Ofellus, so to speak. But
the moment he receives an invitation from his patron Maecenas, however
belated, he is off like a shot, leaving his parasites (*scurrae*, 36) to exit with
empty stomachs, heaping curses on their host, who is himself a parasite at a
richer man's table.[11] The slave's tirade culminates, forty lines later, in the
bitter figure of the marionette (80–2): "The truth is that you, who give orders
to me, are yourself someone else's miserable slave, and you dance like a
wooden puppet on strings that another controls" (*tu mihi qui imperitas alii
servis miser atque | duceris ut nervis alienis mobile lignum*). As Michael André
Bernstein (1992:45–7) has pointed out, the image of the marionette seems
designed to illustrate Horace's "enslavement" not to sexual desire – Davus's
ostensible subject here – but to Maecenas. And as Davus renews his attack,
the slippage between sexual and social enslavement becomes all too apparent
(89–94): "A woman demands five talents from you; she scolds you, she turns
you away from her door and douses you with cold water, and calls you back
again: withdraw your neck from the vile yoke, 'I'm free, I'm free!,' come,
say the words! You can't do it. A harsh master (*dominus*) rides your mind,
applies sharp spurs when you're worn out, and reins you around, though you

---

[10] Syme (1939), 196.

[11] In the eyes of well-bred and well-disposed readers, Horace's haste will bespeak his devotion
not to his patron's table but to his company; but there are also those invidious outsiders,
including Horace himself in certain moods, who share the slave's base perspective. For a
stimulating deconstructive treatment of the parasite, see Serrres (1982).

say no." It is indeed not the mistress but the master, the *dominus*, who is at issue here.[12]

Horace's relation to Maecenas is also subjected to the stern scrutiny of Damasippus in *Satires* 2.3. The charge leveled by the once-successful businessman against Horace is, appropriately, not servile self-abasement but self-inflating social ambition. "What's my particular form of madness?" Horace foolishly asks, after Damasippus has concluded his lecture. Damasippus has his answer ready (2.3.307–9): "First, you're busy building, which is to say imitating tall men, though you're hardly two feet from head to toe." Damasippus has in mind one "tall man" in particular (312–13): "Is it right for you to do whatever Maecenas does, you, who are so unlike him and so far out of his league?" (*tanto dissimilem et tanto certare minorem?*). He follows this with the fable of the frog and the calf, the moral of which is that no matter how hard Horace works at puffing himself up, he'll never be as big a man as Maecenas (*non si te ruperis ... |par eris*, 319–20).

In a sense, however, it is Damasippus, not Horace, who is the over-inflated frog of this puffed-up poem. One of Horace's best jokes is that this overstuffed satire, which covers more than twice as much paper as its closest rival (1.4, with 143 lines), opens with Damasippus charging that Horace writes too little (*sic raro scribis*, 1). Not only the form but the content of the satire is enlarged and exaggerated. The miser who insists on drinking vinegar has a cellar stocked, Damasippus reports (115–17), "with vintage Chian and Falernian, a thousand jugs full – that's nothing; make it three hundred thousand!" The enthusiastic revision may be taken as a figure for the relation between this garish diatribe and the diatribes of book 1, a relation encapsulated in the joke with which Horace finally silences Damasippus in the last line of the poem (326): "Let the greater lunatic spare the lesser!" (*o maior, tandem parcas, insane, minori!*). The joke does concede, however, that the difference between the two is a difference only of degree.[13] Like the slave, the aspiring client at once paints and himself embodies a satiric caricature of Horace, the *amicus* of Maecenas. Such hyperboles overshoot the mark but describe its general location.

The analogy these satires put into play – Damasippus and Davus are to Horace as Horace is to Maecenas – holds not only for the content of these relationships but for their discursive form. Within the narrative situation,

---

[12] The "wooden puppet" of this satire is cousin to the figwood statue of Priapus in *Satires* 1.8, once "a useless piece of wood" (*inutile lignum*, 1), since put to use protecting the new gardens on the Esquiline against intruders. Here as in 2.7, the issue of the speaker's subordination to Maecenas, the owner of these gardens (and of the Priapus that watches over them), is displaced by a struggle for mastery against female opponents, a struggle that Priapus eventually wins.

[13] Note the clustering of comparatives (*maiorem, minus, minorem, maior dimidio, magis atque magis, par*) and terms denoting size (*longos, moduli bipedalis, ingens, magna*) in 308–20.

Damasippus and Davus stand in the same relation to Horace as Horace stood to Maecenas in the diatribes of the first book. This is another way of describing the shift in narrative technique which provided the starting-point for this essay, a shift I can now describe more precisely. In the diatribes of both books, a speaker of inferior status addresses someone of superior status. In the second book, this narrational dyad is transposed downward on the social scale: Horace takes the seat formerly occupied by his patron Maecenas, passing the satiric megaphone to his social inferiors.[14] This transposition not only elevates the Horace of book 2, it also and simultaneously demotes the Horace of book 1, situating him among the horde of men displaced, declassed, or dispossessed by the vicissitudes of the civil wars, men on the make, men scrambling to repair their fortunes. If Horace is less inclined to play the satirist in book 2, one reason is that he has already repaired his fortunes; a landed gentleman once again, he is the proud owner of a Sabine estate which, as we learn in the epistles (1.14.1–3), is extensive enough to support five families of tenant farmers – farmers such as Ofellus, perhaps, who lacked Horace's luck or skill in social advancement. The fiction of the second book is that Horace, being a made man, no longer needs or deigns to wear the satiric mask. Book 2 is a rereading and rewriting that at once disavows and exposes the impure ambitions of the upwardly mobile satirist of book 1.

It may be suggested that such a reading is already included within the first book; that Horace, from the very beginning, turned a satiric eye on his own progress. This argument, made with great flair in James Zetzel's classic article on *Satires* 1, has since been developed in rich detail by Kirk Freudenburg, who claims, following Zetzel, that the satirist of book 1 is "himself the chief object of satire."[15] It would be foolish to argue that the first book is entirely unconscious of its ambitions, nor is such an argument necessary for my purpose, which is limited to reading book 1 from the perspective of book 2. Still, the bumbling ethos of the satirist, so well described by Freudenburg, is something more than an artful creation, a mask to be donned and doffed at will. From a sociolinguistic perspective, this ethos has a precise social function. "In societies all over the world," as Penelope Brown and Stephen Levinson point out in their study of the sociolinguistics of politeness, "members of dominated groups or lower strata express deference to dominant members by bumbling, by the kinesics, prosodics, and language of slow-wittedness or buffoonery" (1987:186). When Horace strikes this pose in a satire that is directly addressed to Maecenas, he is – however exaggeratedly, however ironically,

---

[14] Pressed to its logical conclusion, this satiric argument discloses Horace's patron as but one more puppet and parasite. This is a disclosure that Horace avoids but that Caesar, the ultimate puppet-master, can treat as a joke, as in the letter to Maecenas preserved in Suetonius's life of Horace (*veniet ergo ab ista parasitica mensa ad hanc regiam*).

[15] Freudenburg (1993:21), following Zetzel (1980).

however artfully – "expressing deference" to a social superior. Social interaction is itself a complex form of role-playing, and the "real" Horace is no
more or less on display in Maecenas's dining-room than within the pages of
his poetry.[16]

The new-critical claim that the author Horace and the character Horace
share nothing more than a name is as ill-founded as the naive historicist claim
that they are one and the same. Readers such as Zetzel and Freudenburg give
Horace too much credit when they ascribe every false step to Horace's persona, postulating a godlike author smiling somewhere high above as he pulls
the puppet's strings. It is sometimes the author, not his persona, who stumbles.
In *Satires* 1.9, Horace describes his encounter with an impossible social
climber who is desperate to penetrate the circle of Maecenas. In the course
of this encounter, the man offers Horace his support in exchange for an
introduction (1.9.45–8): "You'd have quite an ally to back you up, if you'd
just open the door for me; I'll be damned if you wouldn't push all the others
aside." In reply, Horace delivers an impassioned defense of the moral integrity
of Maecenas's circle (48–52):[17]

> non isto vivimus illic
> quo tu rere modo; domus hac nec purior ulla est
> nec magis his aliena malis; nil mi officit, inquam,
> ditior hic aut est quia doctior; est locus uni
> cuique suus.

We don't live there at all the way you think; no house is more free of those faults;
it doesn't bother me, I tell you, if another man is richer or better educated than I am;
each of us has his own place.

According to Zetzel, this defense is liberally seasoned with irony: "The ninth
poem does not just cast a bright light on Maecenas and his companions, . . .
it questions their self-satisfaction as well."[18] I do not believe that this poem is
critical of Maecenas and company or even of Horace's persona, who is distinguished in this poem not by rudeness, as Zetzel claims, but by his almost
total inability to be anything but polite. Horace is trapped because he cannot
bring himself to break off the conversation without a decent pretext, which he
appears to be sadly incapable of inventing.[19] His defense of Maecenas's circle
is represented as a spontaneous outburst, provoked by the social climber's offens-
ive insinuations, and authenticated by the dislocated word order characteristic
of excitement. This staged rupture of discursive and social norms is rounded

---

[16] Similarly Schrijvers (1992), 254. For a lucid deconstruction of the opposition between "persona" and "self" in Horace's poetry, see Martindale (1993), 16–17.

[17] Following Klingner's Teubner edition, I treat *inquam* as part of Horace's outburst.

[18] Zetzel (1980), 71. Cf. Freudenburg (1993:208): "the speaker's self-satisfaction is tainted," etc.

[19] Henderson (1993:85–6) points out that Aristius Fuscus has no such trouble shaking off
Horace at the end of the satire.

out by Horace's ungraciously curt reply to his interlocutor's incredulity (52–3): "'What an amazing story, I can hardly believe it.' 'But that's how it is.'" A moment later, Horace regains his self-control, reverting to the distancing, ironic courtesy that his anger momentarily ruptured. The outburst, which is designed for Maecenas as well as the emulous outsider, is meant to sound genuine.[20] My point is that the smugness and elitism detected by Zetzel cannot simply be ascribed to Horace's persona.

At moments such as these, Horace shows too much of the work that went into solving the problem posed by his individual reversal of fortune. The denial is too obvious, the attempt to differentiate himself from his vulgar double too crude.[21] In his second book, Horace is much more consistently evasive, much more defensively self-conscious, anticipating and as it were inoculating himself, not without pain, against every charge of artful ambition and self-serving opportunism. The encounter with the social climber is recast, accordingly, in the mock-epic dialogue of *Satires* 2.5, a dialogue from which Horace is entirely absent. In this satiric addendum to the Homeric *nekuia*, Ulysses consults Tiresias not as a seer but as a financial prognosticator (2.5.1–3): "Add to your tale, tell me this too, Tiresias: what arts can I use to repair the fortune I've lost?" (*quibus amissas reparare queam res | artibus atque modis*). Though set in the epic past, the poem is thoroughly topical. The generic "impoverished aristocrat" represented in the guise of Ulysses may well be, like Ofellus, a victim of the civil war – not an expropriated farmer, of course, but an impoverished senator. Unlike Ofellus, however, Ulysses does not view his poverty with the complacency of a philosopher; "without assets," he complains, "breeding and character aren't worth a damn" (*et genus et virtus nisi cum re vilior alga est*, 2.5.8).[22] In response to the request of his money-hungry friend, Tiresias offers instruction in the fine and thoroughly Roman art of legacy-hunting, a specialized and degraded form of the art of friendship. The irony is blatant, but the alternative perspective of true friendship goes unexpressed. Is Horace an honest Ofellus, content with his lot, whose farm has been miraculously restored, or a Ulysses who has worked hard and deviously to accomplish such a restoration? In terms of the satire that follows, is Horace a country mouse or a city mouse?[23] While Horace might like to fancy himself

---

[20] On the oblique compliment, see Rudd (1982), 81–2.

[21] On the multiple links binding Horace to his unnamed other in 1.9, see Henderson (1993).

[22] Translation following Rudd (1979), 110.

[23] This famous fable, which concludes the poem that celebrates Horace's restored fortune (the acquisition of the Sabine farm), preaches the virtue of resting contented with one's lot: the country mouse who goes to the city "rejoices in his changed lot (*mutata sorte*) and, while times are good, plays the happy dinner guest" (2.6.110–11) until misfortune strikes, in the guise of the returning master and his dogs. Insofar as Horace identifies with the country mouse, he succeeds in representing his own *mutata sors* as not a deviation but a return to the *status quo*.

an Ofellus, he knows that others might like to accuse him of being a Ulysses. By making the implicit comparison first himself, Horace precludes their attack and shows himself to be nobody's fool.

In *Satires* 2.8, Horace's final variation on the theme of loss and recovery, the comic poet Fundanius regales Horace with a description of a dinner party at the house of one Nasidienus Rufus. This is in fact the most detailed description of a *cena* in Horace's satires; Fundanius tells Horace not only what the guests said and what they ate but also just where they all reclined – information that conveys something about the guests' relative status (the different locations on the three couches of the Roman *triclinium* had precise social meanings). By contrast, when Horace describes a rustic dinner party at his own Sabine villa in *Satires* 2.6, or a dinner he enjoyed in company with Maecenas, Virgil, and others en route to Brundisium in *Satires* 1.5, he refrains from recording the seating arrangements. Guests at these dinners, we are to understand, are too busy enjoying the true pleasures of conviviality to worry about who reclines where. Horace's defensive representation of Maecenas's *amici* as men who know and are happy with their assigned places (*est locus uni|cuique suus*, 1.9.51–2) similarly naturalizes the social hierarchy into invisibility. Against this blandly idealizing backdrop, Fundanius's specifications in *Satires* 2.8 serve as an index of Nasidienus's obsession with relative status.[24]

The diners of *Satires* 1.5 are diverted by the antics of two buffoons; the rustic company of *Satires* 2.6 enjoys a simple meal and ethically enriched conversation. In *Satires* 2.8, however, the dinner – the food and its elaborately theatrical presentation – is itself the entertainment, ready-made material for Fundanius's subsequent comic narration.[25] Nasidienus believes that the measure of a dinner party's success resides in the quality of the food and the artfulness of its preparation, and the conversation is accordingly dominated by the intrusive culinary glosses supplied by Nasidienus and his hanger-on Nomentanus, for example (2.8.43–4): "This eel was caught when it was pregnant; the flesh is not as good after they give birth." These exquisitely irrelevant refinements might be comedy enough, but Horace cannot resist adding a bit of slapstick. The evening declines to follow Nasidienus's script. He has just finished describing his special recipe for fish sauce when a dust-laden tapestry suspended above the table falls down into the platter on whose virtues he was discoursing (*ruinas|in patinam fecere*, 54–5). At this tragic turn of events, the host covers his head and weeps as if at the death of a son. This is in effect

---

[24] Nasidienus's arrangements are unusual – he yields the host's place to one of his hangers-on, as if unsure of his own ability to entertain his guest of honor, Maecenas. On the ethos of equality vs. the reality of social discrimination at the *convivium*, see D'Arms (1990).

[25] On actual performances of comedies at Roman dinner parties, see C. P. Jones (1991), 192–3.

Nasidienus' "reversal of fortune" – a domestic and hilariously trivial variation on the reversals suffered by Ofellus, Damasippus, and Ulysses.

Like its counterparts, *Satires* 2.8 is in part a meditation on the proper response to calamities (*casus*, 2.8.71; compare *casus dubios*, 2.2.108). Nasidienus
is consoled by the "sage Nomentanus," who universalizes his plight (2.8.61–
3): "Alas, Fortune, what deity is more cruel to us than you? How you delight in
making sport with the affairs of men!" Nomentanus is seconded, with heavy
irony, by Balatro, one of the attendant *umbrae* brought along by Maecenas
(65–72): That was just the way of things; here Nasidienus had labored so hard
to be sure that everything would be just so; and then accidents like this
happened. But even this dust-cloud, he reminds his disconsolate host, has a
silver lining (73–4): "Adversity (*res adversae*) enables a host, like a general,
to display innate qualities that remain hidden when things are going well."
These edifying reflections are designed to recall the attitude of the second
satire's stalwart farmer, who recognizes that Fortune is a tempestuous goddess
and counsels his sons to meet adversity with fortitude (*novos moveat Fortuna
tumultus*, 2.2.126; *fortiaque adversis opponite pectora rebus*, 136).[26] But unlike
Ofellus, Nasidienus does not resign himself to his misfortune. Revived by his
philosophical counselors, rather as Damasippus is revived by the sage Stertinius,
Nasidienus rushes out of the room, only to return triumphant, a few lines later,
leading a procession of slaves bearing platters laden with food no less extraordinary than that destroyed by the calamitous tapestry. Fundanius announces
this return with a mock-epic apostrophe (2.8.84–5): "You re-enter, Nasidienus,
with a changed brow, like a man bent on mending misfortune by means of
art" (*Nasidiene, redis mutatae frontis, ut arte\emendaturus fortunam*). Like
Ulysses, Nasidienus seeks to restore his fortune with art, the art in this case not
of false friendship but of gastronomy.

But the attempt is not successful, as Fundanius gleefully reports in the
poem's closing lines (2.8.93–5): "We paid our host back by taking off without even tasting his dishes, as if they'd been tainted by the breath of Canidia,
more poisonous than the snakes of Africa." Canidia, whose name decorates
the final line of this satire, is one of the witches encountered by the figwood
statue of Priapus in *Satires* 1.8. *Satires* 1.8 and 2.8 both end with hasty
departures, but the perspective is reversed: whereas Priapus takes his revenge
(*non testis inultus*, 1.8.44) by driving the witches out of Maecenas's gardens,
Fundanius and his friends take theirs by abandoning Nasidienus's table. The
allusion to Canidia thus turns the dinner party of Nasidienus inside out. It

---

[26] Cf. further the ironic warning against complacency at 2.2.106: "naturally you will be uniquely
blessed with constant good fortune" (*uni nimirum recte tibi semper erunt res*). In 2.7, Davus
defines the man who is truly *liber* (2.7.83) as one who cripples all attacks of fortune (*in quem
manca ruit semper fortuna*, 88).

exposes the would-be insider as a double of the ultimate outsider, the witch who uses the art of magic, a kind of perverted cookery, in a vain attempt to win friends and influence people.[27] Unbeknownst to Nasidienus, the real party, the in-crowd, can only be somewhere else.

The punishment meted out to Nasidienus is not only the desertion of his table; the *coup de grâce* is struck by Horace, whose satire publishes and fixes the host's exclusion from the company he so longs to keep. In this regard, the most obvious double for Nasidienus in the first book is the social climber who fastens onto Horace in *Satires* 1.9. Just as Nasidienus advertises the excellence of the food he serves, so this would-be insider promotes his wares, such as they are, with a blithe and almost endearing lack of finesse (1.9.7): "You should get to know me," he tells Horace; "I'm an intellectual."[28] "If I know myself," he adds, with unintended humor, "you'll find I'm worth as much to you as your friends Viscus and Varius. Who can produce as much verse as I can, and in as little time?" (22–4). In the very act of seeking to purchase Maecenas's friendship with talents such as these, these men unwittingly expose their social impossibility; their eager display of their qualifications in itself disqualifies them. In both poems, moreover, Horace's exposé of these inept pretenders is motivated. It constitutes his delayed vengeance – on the social climber, for persecuting him with unwelcome attentions, and on Nasidienus, contrariwise, for failing to invite him to dinner, a dinner whose guest list, as Horace gradually discovers, included not only Fundanius but also Maecenas, Varius, and Viscus. Why wasn't Horace invited, when so many friends of his were?[29] It seems that the talented freedman's son is still not a big enough fish to merit a place at the table of the *nouveau riche*. The satire is, then, both Horace's revenge and his vindication. For if the house of Nasidienus was graced by this eminent company on this one memorable and disastrous occasion, Horace enjoys a day-to-day intimacy with these men, an intimacy to which the easy interchange of *Satires* 2.8, with its assumption of shared values, itself testifies.

But Horace is not only a frustrated guest, he is also, significantly, a frustrated host. The poem opens with Horace's question (2.8.1–3): "How did you

---

[27] On Nasidienus's witchy feast, see now Freudenburg (1995); for a comparison of the culinary art of Nasidienus and Canidia, see Gowers (1993), 176–7.

[28] Translation by Rudd (1979), 75.

[29] Horace's mortification is sketched in just under the surface: it is after Fundanius incidentally reveals that Maecenas was one of the guests (16) that Horace interrupts to ask who else was there (18–19). On Horace as "the uninvited *scurra*," see Freudenburg (1993), 232–3. Baker (1988) attempts to rescue Horace from the charge of unfeeling rudeness by arguing that his absence from the meal indicates his desire to distance himself from the behavior of the guests; but Horace, here as elsewhere, succeeds in having it both ways – at once claiming and disowning the satire he ascribes to Fundanius.

enjoy dinner *chez* the blessed Nasidienus? Yesterday, you know, when I was hoping for your company, I was informed that you'd been drinking there since midday." It was when he was trying to get Fundanius to come to dinner at *his* house (*mihi quaerenti convivam*, 2) that he learned of his prior engagement. The hospitality extended by Nasidienus displaced whatever entertainment Horace had in mind. If the witch of *Satires* 1.8 and the social climber of *Satires* 1.9 are close relations of Nasidienus, the third and last double for Nasidienus is, of course, Horace himself,[30] and in particular the Horace of *Satires* 1.10. With *Satires* 2.8, Horace thus rolls the three last satires of his first book into one – an exercise in compression that itself retrospectively reveals the latent affinities between the discrete protagonists of the earlier satires.

In *Satires* 1.10, Horace identifies the select readership to whose delectation he offers up his satires. The list includes all the eminent names on Nasidienus's guest list, and then some – a gesture aptly characterized by Niall Rudd (1986:139) as a "piece of blatant name-dropping." Just as Nasidienus is thrilled by his dinner guests, Horace is thrilled by his readers; both men are proud to have won the attention of these luminaries, and almost pathetically eager to please. But the protagonists of the two poems have more in common than this unfortunate propensity to self-promotion by association. As Fundanius remarks near the end of *Satires* 2.8, the dishes carried in by a procession of slaves might have been "delicious, if only their master hadn't lectured us on their origin and nature" (*suavis res, si non causas narraret earum et\naturas dominus*, 92–3). *Satires* 1.10 is also a didactic discourse, a collection of precepts on the proper way to write satire. The poem opens a door to the satiric kitchen, showing us how Horace prepares his poetic effects, and exposing his poetic *sprezzatura* for the calculated, cultivated illusion that it is.[31] One might imagine Horace's elite audience yawning in dismay: "Dear Horace, your poetry would be delightful, if only you didn't insist on telling us just exactly how it was done!" Like Nasidienus, the Horace of book 1 re-enters society with a new face, *mutatae frontis*, equipped with the art of satire, an art that mends both faces and fortunes.

It is the distressed recognition of this likeness that fuels the second book of satires. Horace's second book is the product of second thoughts, an attempt to write over and thus blot out his earlier production. And yet in the process Horace inevitably retraces, and with a heavier hand, the original design. If Horace no longer addresses his patron directly, it is nonetheless clear that

---

[30] For different versions of this comparison, see Gowers (1993), 167–70; O'Connor (1990); Freudenburg (1995), 217–18.

[31] On the social significance of such "backstage" spaces as the kitchen, see Goffman (1959), 106–40.

the satires of the second book are designed for Maecenas's overhearing. The proliferating screens of the second book shield Horace but do not render him invisible. Horace is still writing satire – still aiming to please the discriminating palates of his powerful friends. Nasidienus's dinner is served, after all, on Horace's page.

I close with one final question: what is the relation between the art of satire and the art of dining? At the end of his very first satire, Horace compares the wise man, the man who understands how life should be lived, to a *conviva satur* (1.1.119), a dinner guest who knows enough to leave the table when he has eaten his fill. As many readers have remarked, the second book of satires comically misreads this image by taking it literally: whereas book 1 purports to teach us how to live, book 2 devotes much of its energy to teaching us how to eat.[32] One model for this shift is provided by an exchange between the stern father Demea and the slave Syrus in Terence's *Adelphoe*. In this scene, Demea's description of his son's moral education is punctuated by the slave's ironic congratulations (414–17):

> DE. I leave out nothing, I get him used to it, I advise him to gaze, as if into a mirror, at the lives of men, and to profit from the example of others: "Do this!"
> SY. That's the way!
> DE. "Don't do that!"
> SY. Brilliant!

After a little more of this, the slave finally interrupts (419–29):

> I swear I don't have time right now to listen. I've got hold of just the fish I was after: I must take care it doesn't get spoiled. For it's as much of a disgrace for me to neglect my duty as it is for you to neglect yours; so far as I'm able, I lecture my fellow slaves in just your style: "This is well-sauced, this is burnt, this isn't clean enough; that's right, now; next time, remember." I take great pains to instruct them, as I can, with what wit I have: and then I advise them to gaze, as if into a mirror, upon the platter, Demea, and to think what needs to be done.

The passage is often cited in connection with Horace's account of his own father's educational technique in *Satires* 1.4.[33] Like Demea, Horace's father directed his son's attention to living examples of virtue and vice, for example (1.4.109–11): "You see how badly off Albius' son is, and how Baius is bankrupt? There's a great lesson there to deter a man from wasting his inheritance." It is from this technique, moreover, that Horatian satire purports to be derived: as a grown man, Horace claims, he introjects the figure of his father and carries on the good work, scrutinizing his fellow man with a satiric eye in the admirable hope of improving his own character.

---

[32] See above all Gowers (1993:126–79), who considerably complicates this generalization.
[33] See Leach (1971), Anderson (1982), 51–5.

We must take – we are expressly invited to take – this self-characterization, which plays a strategic role within the polemics of *Satires* 1.4, with a large pinch of salt. And yet it is only in book 2 that Horace makes space for the kind of thorough-going parody that is delivered within Terence's play by the slave Syrus; it is in book 2 that Horace realizes the implicit self-deflating critique of book 1. Syrus's response to Demea may be taken as an emblem of the relation between Horace's two books of satires. Book 2 takes down or de-grades both the content and the speaker of book 1, substituting gastronomy for philosophy, the slave for the master. This is not a gratuitous exercise but a defensive strategy. Having exposed his foundational satiric narrative of misfortune and its artful amendment – a narrative he will have the distance to apply to himself only a decade later – Horace cannot but abandon the satiric role.[34]

[34] I would like to thank T. N. Habinek and Alessandro Schiesaro for inviting me to be part of this revolution, and the conference participants for their comments on the paper I presented there. I am particularly indebted to Niall Rudd, John Shoptaw, and Gordon Williams for their incisive criticisms of various versions of this essay.

6   Horace and the material culture of Augustan Rome: a revisionary reading

Eleanor Winsor Leach

Scholars seeking traces of Augustan Rome in the landscape of *Odes* 1–3 have often approached their investigations with preconceived ideas about finding some vatic equivalent of the program of monuments mapped by Zanker and Kellum, or at least some kind of propagandistic notice given to brick changing into marble.[1] The absence of any such commemorations sparks disappointment and leads in this instance to the question: what sense of an Augustan cultural revolution exerts its physical presence in the *Odes*? As a preliminary, one must remember that the greater number of the monuments associated with Augustan policy, the Horologium, Ara Pacis, great porticoes and Forum Augusti, had not been undertaken by 23 BCE, the year to which the completion of the three books is commonly assigned. Yet even existing places receive short shrift. Perhaps the allusion in 3.1 to elections in the Campus should call up the Saepta Julia, Agrippa's contribution dedicated in 26 BCE, but the emphasis is on competing candidates, not architecture. Augustus' major public building of the period, the Palatine Temple of Apollo, is present in *Ode* 1.31 except that we do not see it clearly because Horace makes a gesture that is quite singular and not at all diffident. As self-ordained *vates* approaching the newly dedicated temple, he stands before the altar blocking the view. Without mention of the splendid architecture, or even the occasion, he pours a libation and makes a request seemingly modest were it not for the immodesty of its being for himself: a prayer for the continuing vitality of his talents.[2] Not only the absence of description, but also the personal intrusion are especially surprising if we compare Propertius' description of the temple through an admiring spectator's eyes (Fantham, this volume, pp. 126–8). Perhaps the self-reflexive

---

[1] Leopold (1936); Bedon (1988), looks at circuits and neighborhoods, but does not distinguish the modes of representation or focus in the lyric poems from those in the hexameter to which he most frequently refers. Most recently Dyson and Prior (1995:255–63), in an historically positivist examination, review the allusions to monuments without consideration of literary contextualization.

[2] Even more, the posture assumed by the poet as sacrificer echoes that of the sculptured representation of Apollo himself who, according to reconstructions based on the "Sorrento base", carries a lyre and holds out a patera. Kellum (1986:175–6) describes the image.

approach might suggest that both poet and *princeps* were still finding their public image and voices at this moment.[3] For the poet the challenge of *carmen Latinum* posed in the succeeding ode (1.32) demands all his lyric inventiveness along with the full co-operation of his lyre. More intrusively and with less diffidence in the epilogue Ode (3.30) the poet from Apulia obstructs the view of an Augustan landmark as he establishes his *monumentum aere perennius* to endure alongside the Capitoline. In the background we may glimpse a rival *monumentum*, the Mausoleum which was the first of the *princeps'* public structures, combining his aspirations by way of a public image with his melancholy fears for the end of it all.[4] With this Horace now competes in duration.

To return then to the question: is there no identifiable presence of an Augustan Rome in the poems? In contrast to the prevailingly negative answer I will consider several aspects of Horace's construction of a contemporary Roman environment. First its centrality to Empire; secondly its persistently Republican character, and thirdly the views that Horace does vividly present, specifically in book 2, of the personal environs of many addressees.

In focusing this discussion on *Odes* 1–3, I follow the principle that Horace's physical worlds are constructed in accordance with an idea of the decorum of genre.[5] Approaching lyric as a challenge of adaptation, Horace emphasizes the intrinsically elitist coloring of the genre originating within the homogenous intimacy of the Greek symposium while foregrounding its sense of obligation to the public sphere.[6] Whatever the nuances of the voice, it is essentially a performative voice engaging in discourse to be heard, not private meditations overheard.[7] The rhetorical self-staging involved should not be regarded as

---

[3] Yavetz (1984:1–6) points to a change in Augustus' strategies of self-representation indicated just after the Cantabrian Wars (25/24) when he abandoned his unfinished, self-justificatory *Autobiography*, and took up the *Res Gestae* instead.

[4] Yavetz (1984:6), suggests that the monument symbolized the emperor's pledge that "as opposed to Antonius, Octavian and his family were to be buried in Rome." Syme (1986:38) speculates that a written text, anticipating the *Res Gestae* had already been prepared to distinguish the "huge and regal monument constructed on the Campus Martius waiting to receive his ashes". The possibility lends meaning to Horace's *aere perennius*. Zanker (1988a:72–7) fully explores the implications of the monument as an expression of power, albeit one whose lack of a coherent architectural vocabulary left it also without a coherent message.

[5] Contrary to the more common approach, as exemplified by Leopold (1936), Bedon (1988), that treats both lyric and hexameter poems as semantically equivalent representations of reality, the latter, of course, containing the more numerous and more specific descriptive notices. For a distinction between the scope and nature of the worlds represented in lyric and hexameter with reference to the Sabine Farm, Leach (1988).

[6] Gentili (1988:55–6) stresses the sense of limitation to the members of a given social group or milieu that especially characterizes lyric.

[7] Thus, in spite of his belief in the essentially private nature of Horace's artistry, Johnson (1982:126–7) notes Horace's success in achieving "an overwhelmingly persuasive illusion of music for these spoken poems, and, through music, an illusion of performance." Gentili

candid confession.[8] What we need to consider is neither the nature and quality of Horace's experience of the city, nor his contributions to an understanding of urban dynamics, but rather the selectivity of his representation and the messages this communicates. Here again we may look for a significant contrast with Propertius. Professor Fantham has illuminated what might be regarded as a subversively counter-revolutionary emphasis that colors Propertius' reconstruction of the primitive landscape amidst the spectrum of monuments (Fantham, this volume, pp. 124ff.). Unlike the elegist, Horace neither foregrounds early history nor creates a "new city". Nowhere does he supply any such panoramic overview as the erstwhile erotic poet develops in 4.1 when setting himself up to be poet of Rome. All the same, Horace's Rome does exhibit a topography comprised of allusions and associations whose totality makes a picture one may consider strategic even if it is not systematically laid out.

Rome is the representational field that gives meaning to the public character of the *Odes*. Images of the River Tiber in the second and the penultimate poems delimit the collection and bring its civic and communal concerns to the fore. In the overview that heralds closure, we contemplate vicariously through the eyes of Maecenas the noise, smoke and resources of *beata Roma* (3.29). Throughout the course of the poems military events that function as time markers, but also as occasions for movement out of and into the city, place Rome at the center of a broad geographical world.[9] Horace's Mediterranean and Near Eastern geography displays a territorial consciousness, shared with many of his contemporaries, that the social historian Claude Nicolet defines as a new political self-consciousness of Empire,[10] a consciousness that found its eventual embodiment in Agrippa's itineraries and *orbis pictus* in the Campus Martius.[11]

(1988:55–7) stresses the mimetic relationship between performance and text. Nagy (1994:415–17) places Horace within a tradition of lyric performance that he defines as a mimesis or re-enactment of the entire series of dramatic occasions that are his poetic predecessors with one qualification: ". . . following the pattern of Alexandrian poetics, the occasion may not be 'real' – to the extent that there need not be a real performance, Still, the occasion is presented by the poet as absolute, and it is indeed 'real' on the strength of that presentation."

[8] Bakhtin (1981:131) characterizes ancient rhetorical autobiography in a very relevant manner: "The important thing is . . . preeminently, that exterior real-life chronotope in which the representation of one's own or someone else's life is realized either as verbal praise of a civic-political act or as an account of the self."

[9] Nicolet (1991:29), citing Fraenkel 426ff.

[10] Luisi (1987:95–6); Nicolet (1991:29), citing Fraenkel, 426ff., mentions Horace's commitment to Augustus' mission. White (1993:159–69) treats the theme of Empire with emphasis on the way in which Augustus is "drawn into" a previously existing structure after the battle of Actium, but concomitantly noting the lack of detail with which Horace treats the campaigns.

[11] Pliny 3.17; Richardson (1992:319). With its completion and dedication only in 7 BCE, the map was too late for Horace as it was also for Agrippa, but Luisi (1987:91–2) assumes his familiarity with the work-in-progress. Nicolet (1991:29–47) also describes the geographical research carried out by predecessors of Agrippa.

In considering the influence of this awareness on the city, Horace implies divided sentiments. Personally he is not shy about placing his talents at the center of Roman cultural development. The imaginative aerial journey on which he is about to embark in transformed swanlike guise in 2.20 is one of double effect. Appropriating the far-flung vision of Icarus striving for the zenith, the speaker surveys the Mediterranean from Africa to Asia, from Spain to the Hyperboreans; yet his voyage also carries his fame as an object of wonder to barbarian peoples: Colchians, Dacians and Geloni. While the declaration is as much exaggerated for its humorous effect as the journey itself is fantastic, it bespeaks confidence of achievement within a stable cultural milieu. This is a vicariously derived power that it is the Roman poet's particular pleasure to enjoy.

All the same it is an advantage of the poet's privileged existence that he can contemplate empire with equanimity, free from the anxieties that trouble his associates of the political world from whose point of view empire extends not so much in terms of territories, although geographical names are important, but rather as peoples whose identities are polarized by their relationship to Rome. As a center of contemporary civilization, the city is frequently defined in relation to a disorderly or threatening other: Cleopatra in her moment of ascendancy, but continually those nationalities beyond the borders: Medes, Parthians, Dacians, Cantaberi, Britons, even Chinese. Preoccupation with the threats they pose is a price of leadership. Expeditions against such troublemakers in the name of the nation are a laudable enterprise; it is better to fight Medes than Romans. However, for individuals such as Iccius, who contemplates a journey to Arabia with apparent thoughts of its legendary riches (1.29), such campaigns may admit questionable motivation. Conduct verging upon the self-serving of the merchant poses a potential compromise with the professions of Stoic allegiance that Iccius' extensive, elegant library represents.

International politics may entail compromises. The return of Phraates, deposed King of Parthia, to his ancestral throne exemplifies expedient patronage, yet the man himself falls short of real merit (2.2). Whatever the *plebs* may think, *Virtus* rejects him from her catalogue of the blessed (*eximit numero beatorum*). Sustaining Roman conduct in alien surroundings is important. Regulus perceived this necessity in defeat (3.5.5–40); it is of equal consequence in success. The harshest view of Roman society declares that Scythians and Getes lead more upright lives (3.24.9–20). Returns to Rome are celebrated by feasts of social integration at which the art of the symposium is cultivated (1.36; 3.14). The equation develops between Augustan victory abroad and pleasure at home.

Specific references to events in progress locate the awareness of power in the Augustan moment, yet empire itself is a legacy from the Republican past. Likewise the environment where the center of world power resides. Looking more specifically at the spatial and architectural locations of Horace's Roman city, we find a pronounced emphasis on traditional landmarks defining the framework of the poet's rhetorical "public square." Threats to venerated places can be taken metonymically as threats to national survival as when flood waters menace the sacred precincts of the Forum in 1.2, or the Cleopatra of 1.37 plots *ruinas Capitolio*.[12] Unthreatened these monuments are signs of stability. Juno concedes the triumphant pre-eminence of the Capitoline (3.3.42–42 *stet Capitolium fulgens*). Although it may witness mercurial surges of public enthusiasm (3.24.45–46: ... *in Capitolium|quo clamor vocat et turba faventium*),[13] its stability re-emerges in the final poem along with the Vestal and Pontifex. Additionally a Roman audience might well think of the Area Capitolina as the space in which Horace arrays his catalogue of gods, heroes and Romans in the Pindaric celebratory *Ode* 1.12.[14]

Several visual rubrics in the Roman odes sketch traditional places. Candidates for public office compete in elections in the Campus (3.1.10–14); Regulus, leaving the Senate House, walks resolutely through the protesting crowd outside its doors (3.5.50–56). Temples needing restoration move our attention over the entire city (3.6.1–4). Emphasis on historical continuity is appropriate to the civic focus of these six odes spoken in an indeterminate moment of present time shown in its relationship to national traditions of legend and history. In certain other poems, public monuments are associatively drawn into the narratives of personal lives. The grandiose theater that was Pompey's self-commemoration becomes the location of still another individual memory when it resounds with popular acclamation of Maecenas (1.20.3–8; 2.17.26–27). Its outline merges into Rome's natural topography as the applause rebounds from the river banks and the Vatican Mount (1.20). In this context the Tiber, as *flumen paternum*, evokes Maecenas' Etruscan ancestry.[15] Later we see the tawny stream as the setting of Quintus Dellius' pleasant villa (2.3.18–19). Especially it is mentioned, along with the Campus, Strabo's Augustan Park, in poems addressed to young lovers as a place for displaying prowess in athletic routines traditionally regarded as the initiatory threshold of the military/civic

[12] Cleopatra's threat was not invasion, but competition. By relocating the seat of empire in Egypt she would have robbed the Capitoline of its power. Bedon (1988:28), makes the point that the Capitoline is a metonymy for Rome as a whole.

[13] The allusion is puzzling, and generally taken to refer to the *aerarium* in the Temple of Saturn beneath the Capitoline to which the treasures (triumphal booty?) of vss. 47–9 are to be dispatched. Quinn (1980), 285, *ad loc.*

[14] Richardson (1992:31–2), s.v. Area Capitolina: The gods are Jupiter, Liber, Hercules and the Kings of Rome. The heroes do not coincide, but our list is by no means complete and many were moved by Augustus. The poem concludes with Jupiter in his chariot. Nisbet and Hubbard (1970:145), discuss parallels with Virgil's procession of heroes in *Aeneid* 6.

[15] Cairns (1992:96–8), noting the Etruscan connection of the Vatican side, is to the point here. "The fact that Maecenas has been acclaimed in Rome, and that the Vatican had echoed this acclaim, almost implies a return to the Etruscans of their lost territory."

career (1.8; 3.7.27–28; 3.12.7.).[16] Finally its subsidence from late-winter violence to seasonable placidity is assimilated to individual consciousness (3.29).

The Roman landscape of the *Odes* is that of an essentially Republican Rome, not, like that of Propertius, a reconstruction of Republican origins, but rather a contemporary city essentially the same as that which the young Apulian had entered some twenty-five years before. The sub-textual message of this topography is one of stability. With all its revered landmarks, Horace's city is a place where extraordinary historical events are assimilated into the ordinary rituals of life. In this sense its image may serve to provide reassurance amidst the anxieties of the difficult year plagued by flood, famine and Augustus' precarious health in which the collection of *Odes* as we know it was assembled,[17] but it also reinforces the message of the restored Republic in terms of that "relocation of authority" that Andrew Wallace-Hadrill has called characteristic of the merging of politics and life that constitutes an "Augustan Cultural Revolution".[18] The Rome that frames Horace's occasional tributes to Augustus is a city that values its traditional past amid a new and responsible consciousness of geographical and ideological domination.

That this still Republican Rome is not a nostalgic refusal of the present, but rather its strategically crafted endorsement may become clear when we consider the topics and images of book 2, the book that addresses itself most searchingly to the complexities of living in the Augustan present. This is primarily because the book foregrounds persons rather than events. In this respect readers have noticed a kind of consistency, if not precisely unity, in the tone and texture of its twenty odes.[19] Composed primarily of poems of direct address, the book encompasses a range of persons that varies from the obscure, the unidentifiable and possibly fictional to figures of historical prominence. Nisbet and Hubbard's description of the majority as "significant personalities of the second rank" catches a sense of immediate presence within the grouping, but still underplays the cross-sectioning that makes it a kind of contemporary social geography.[20] As these commentators note, the poems blend exhortation with encomium, but in a proportion that subordinates compliments to advice intended to influence actions and attitudes (Nisbet and Hubbard [1978:3]). Noting the metrical consistency of Sapphic and Alcaic poems making up the greater portion of the book, as well as the relatively similar length of the poems,

---

[16] Nisbet and Hubbard (1970:113) provide documentation concerning the nationalistic symbolism of young men's athletics.

[17] Syme (1986:385), notes how much confidence in the present order was needed in this year.

[18] Wallace-Hadrill, "*Mutatio morum*", above, pp. 11ff.

[19] Nisbet and Hubbard (1978:1–5) comment on its coherence in terms of subject matter, tone of voice and arrangement.

[20] Syme (1986:386) notes two other senators in book 2, Valgius Rufus, a member of Messalla's circle, and Quinctius Hirpinus.

they attribute a *mediocritas* in the essential sense of the word, but less easy to define when it is not quantifiable. *Aurea mediocritas* as it comprises the substance of Horace's temporizing advice to Licinius has claimed its share of attention, but with greater emphasis on the moderation of *mediocritas* than on its oxymoronic golden tone. The quality that the commentators describe in negative terms as an "avoidance of grand themes and manner" (Nisbet and Hubbard [1978:1]) may in fact be inverted to appear as a positive endorsement of the themes it embraces.

References to the public areas of the city are absent from the odes of book 2, but they are replaced by a thick texture of references to personal circumstances and surroundings. From the constructive potential of Sallustius Crispus' wealth to the slave girl (who might just be a captive princess), fancied by "Xanthias of Phocis" the majority of the addressees have something to value, to use or to enjoy. Added to possessions, the symposium fostering sociability with its luxuriance of wine, flowers and fragrances is also a positive employment of material resources. Recommendations to enjoy life are of course the substance of the *carpe diem* theme for which several of the poems are noted. The import of this theme is as practical and material as it is philosophical, and one cannot consider it in isolation from the circumstances of those persons to whom it is addressed. It is of no small consequence that the men to whom the first three poems of the book are dedicated, Asinius Pollio, Sallustius Crispus and Quintus Dellius, came through the civil wars with a history of shifting allegiances, and are now enjoying their immediate comforts and a measure of freedom as beneficiaries of Augustan *clementia*.[21] Seneca grouped these survivors as members of an inner court circle recruited *ex adversariorum castris* (*De clementia* I.10.I). To these three can be added a lesser personage, but closer associate, Pompeius, Horace's *commilito* under Brutus, whose return from exile the poet welcomes with reminiscences and a call to forgetfulness of the past (2.7). The conjunction of such personal histories suggests some modification of the statement that Nisbet and Hubbard have made concerning the apolitical character of *Odes* 2.[22] As Seneca said to Nero about Augustan *clementia*, "your grandfather pardoned his enemies, for had he not done so, whom would he have been able to rule?" Although it may be true that themes in the grand manner are avoided and wars are fought at a distance from Rome, this should not obscure the fact that the implications of the book are political in the subtlest manner possible: that it exercises its hortatory and cautionary advice in illuminating the advantages of life in the contemporary

---

[21] The point is frequently observed. Syme (1986), 384–5; Santirocco (1987), 84–5.

[22] Noting that the personal backgrounds of these figures make the three poems a kind of "testimonial to the clemency of the new regime," Santirocco (1987:84) is one of very few scholars who see a political stance that "goes beyond the usual safe advocacy of campaigns abroad and reforms at home."

Augustan world. Amidst its gallery of personalities and life-styles, the poetic speaker establishes his own firm presence highlighting characteristics that stress his affinity to other figures: civil war participation in the past and the owner-ship of property in the present.[23] This bonding of common experience makes his advice cogent, constructing his role across lines of economic difference as a kind of reversed patronage (2.18:10–11: *pauperemque dives | me petit*).

Material property and possessions fill out the social topography as a land-scape of contemporary private Rome in a manner that challenges traditional scholarly notions of the poet's desire to propagate ideals of simplicity, no mat-ter whether these are construed as personal or programmatically "Augustan".[24] To begin with two of the more notable hortatory poems in which domestic backgrounds figure prominently, we may identify a certain conduct pattern involving the presence of a circumstantial or psychological obstacle to enjoy-ment that remains only imprecisely defined. The addressees, Dellius of *Ode* 2 and Postumus of 14, may resemble a figure whom Lucretius caricatures in *DRN* 3. 1063–7, the restless villa owner whose anxieties or ambitions preclude his enjoyment of his property. This is a "man escaping from himself". The difference with Dellius, at least, is that the cause of his malaise appears to be external. The opening lines counsel equanimity amid difficult circumstances as fully as amid favorable ones (*rebus in arduis . . . non secus ut bonis*). The possibility of a gloomy withdrawal is raised. Certainly present circumstances must have constituted a kind of withdrawal for Dellius, Cicero's *desultor bellorum civilium* who had, in the words of Nisbet and Hubbard, "gained Augustus' favor but scarcely further employment" (1978:51–3). But in the garden that Dellius owns the very trees exemplify sociability (2.3.9–10 *qua pinus ingens albaque populus | umbram hospitalem consociare amant | ramis*). From the tendency to create an underworld before his time Dellius stands admonished by the reminder of the real goods he will relinquish in death: his purchased fields, the villa that the golden Tiber washes, and his heaped-up wealth.

A similar reminder of present commodities is given in *Ode* 2.14 to a different kind of man, the dutiful Postumus. As Commager indicated, the revealing glimpse of this personality occurs in the poem's concluding image of exquisite wines locked away with a hundred keys to await the "splendid

---

[23] Leach (1992:271–302) considers the symbolic implications of the Sabine property as mode of self-representation in the *Odes* and in the hexameter poems. Although the focus of descrip-tions and vignettes differs greatly from one to the other form of poetry, certainly in both cases we may understand that the poet has selected details of a kind that give self-presentation precedence over literalism with a variety of symbolic values. The farm which we see in the *Odes* is at one moment a sacred precinct offering magical divine protection to the artist and at another an atrium from which the poet addresses all Rome as his clientship.

[24] Santirocco (1987:83) coordinates simplicity with an attack on luxury.

profligacy" of a free-living heir (Commager 1962:286). Save for the hoarded wines, the material comforts that Postumus is able to enjoy are less ostensibly luxurious, more orthodoxly Roman: *tellus*, *domus*, a pleasing wife and a garden that is assiduously cultivated with a variety of trees. Because the historical identity of Postumus, unlike that of Dellius, is uncertain and the possibility of his being fictive could always be entertained,[25] it is difficult to conjecture the rationale of his restrictive conduct. Readers have seen the poem as melancholy for its insistent imagery of death, yet the dread of the future appears inherent to the subject himself. Horace introduces Postumus in an attitude of *pietas*, feeding his fears of death by the sacrifice of 300 bulls to Pluto. Does this observance of ritual perhaps carry Augustan emphasis on religious scruple too far?

Still another personage whose identity Horace defines within the context of property is Pompeius Grosphus, a wealthy Sicilian equestrian holding large estates in Agrigentum, whose family standing may stem from the period of the Punic Wars.[26] His portrait as an established land-owner concludes the poem in the penultimate quatrain. We see Grosphus positioned at the center of his own small empire. His hundred herds of Sicilian cows surround him mooing; chariot horses lift their whinnies in his honor and the wool "twice dipped in purple dye" that clothes him shows how the produce of his estate supports his equestrian status.[27] Grosphus presents a more relaxed appearance than Dellius and Postumus, but this ease is in keeping with the rhetoric of the poem in praise of *otium*, a good which many desire and few can truly enjoy.

It is perhaps worth asking why Horace selected Grosphus as the recipient of an ode on this topic. The answer should lie in the combination of personal security and detachment from Roman politics that Grosphus' situation represents.[28] This ode differs from the two above in picturing its addressee as an example of the good life enjoyed, rather than one who must be nudged towards appreciating it. Fraenkel's suggestion that the thrice repeated *otium*

---

[25] Commager (1962:285–6) raises the suggestion that the name may define the character type. The common view identifies him with the young man, Propertius Postumus of Propertius 3.12, but P. White (1995:151–60), argues on the ground of this Postumus' apparently advanced age that a more likely bearer of the name will have been Curtius Postumus, an ambitious adherent of Caesar, whose self-promotion roused Cicero's deepest antipathy. Following this suggestion we may see still one more figure whose history as a survivor of wars gives the poem a political significance, but whose career may well have reached its effectual limits.

[26] Nisbet and Hubbard (1978:252–3) cite an established agricultural Grosphus in Verrines 3.56, and a military Grosphus of the second Punic War in Silius Italicus 14.208.

[27] Referring to Grosphus' "admiring cows" Nisbet and Hubbard (1978:2), do not miss the humor of this godfather image. Although many interpreters (e.g. Commager [1962:37; 333]; Davis [1990:205–11]) regard the comparisons as negative, this opinion reflects their more general premise that Horace writes to oppose luxury.

[28] *Epistle* 1.12 attests to the dependable honesty of Grosphus' character: "nil Grosphus nisi verum orabit et aequum."

introduces an intertextual reworking of Catullus' negative characterization of a debilitating *otium* in poem 51 is fruitful; the allusion foregrounds a climate in which the significance of the word has altered from a young lover's defensively apolitical life-style to an advantage conferred by a politics that fosters the personal life (Fraenkel 1957:211–13). Along with the stereotypical strangers to *otium*, merchant and soldier, the poem includes figures more relevant to recent history: the exile who, in fleeing his country, cannot escape himself. The extrapolation "nothing can be wholly felicitous" (26–8) is a sentence that appears to extend beyond the immediate subject. As a Sicilian whose private holdings constitute his own independent kingdom, Grosphus does not need the forms of recognition that the majority of Roman aristocrats crave. Horace addresses him as one who shares in the ability to appreciate a freedom from mental agitation and from cares that neither wealth nor consular authority can banish. Thus in the final lines of the ode Grosphus' territorial self-sufficiency and Horace' own artistic self-sufficiency within the limits of his rural property appear in unconflicted alignment.

These images that unite owner with property draw their cogency from the traditional Roman status equation, classically articulated by Cicero, of the public figure with his house.[29] Perhaps Horace's most standard application of this principle occurs metaphorically in the Licinius Ode where the parameters of *aurea mediocritas* are delimited in imagery of housing. A man living *tutus* and *cautius* neither suffers the degradation of an *obsoletus tectus* nor flaunts the grandeur of an *aula* provoking envy. Within architectural vocabulary *aula* is a word of even regal connotations not regularly applied to the ordinary aristocratic house.[30] With its implications of receiving clientage on the grand scale it implies a world apart from the more private villa environment that Horace has been picturing as the epitome of a well-adjusted contemporary life removed from the center. Horace associates this villa world with the symposium (Murray 1985:43–4). Notably the sympotic vignettes of *Odes* 2 tend to present the settings of such occasions as apparently private gatherings in contrast to books 1 and 3 where many public occasions demand such festivity. Thus even to Hirpinus Quinctius, an ostensible sympathizer with Augustan military enterprise, Horace commends the sympotic life as the antidote to public concerns, to *aeterna consilia* (2.11).

---

[29] The standard formulation is in *De officiis* 1.139–40, where Cicero comments on the decorum of housing hinting that a properly appointed house can even contribute to a candidate's political success. While a house should enhance the dignity of its owner, he must be careful that it does not exceed his dignity, for, in the last analysis, the owner ought to distinguish the house and not the reverse.

[30] In Vitruvius, *De architectura* 5.6.8, *aulae regiae* are the palaces represented in the decoration of a tragic stage.

That the value of possessed property should stand out in these odes is not difficult to understand in view of the threat of confiscation that had hung over governmental changes since Sulla's time. In this practice Augustus had done his share, but confiscation is no longer his policy, a point to which the comforts of a former opponent like Dellius bear witness. The Pindaric emphasis upon wealth in action that opens the Sallustius poem is followed by the example of Proculeius who divided his share of his patrimony among brothers deprived by the civil war.[31] The transfer of property to chosen recipients or heirs is in itself a sign of political stability. In the Grosphus poem the idea of living well "with little" is epitomized by the image of an inherited object (*paternum|splendet in mensa tenui salinum*). The gleam of the salt cellar evidences its material value, yet the fact of its being inherited suggests the inherently Roman principle that continuity of possession is essential to well-being. On the other hand, inheritance for Dellius and for Postumus, perhaps by reason of their having no children, is seen in coldly negative terms as an alien appropriation of what the owners themselves have failed to use to the fullest, but for this the *princeps* can scarcely be held responsible.[32]

Emphasis upon material comfort in these poems as a benefit of the Augustan climate of life should prompt rhetorical reconsideration of the ode most specifically concerned with villa property, 2.15. Focusing with sustained description upon a place rather than a person, this poem foregrounds images of a pleasurable environment often cited as a condemnation of *luxuria* in the name of Augustan simplicity, yet a careful reading will reveal a more complex point of view.

The highly pictorial text of this ode urges readers to answer descriptive wordings by a visual response. The opening two stanzas describe the transformation of a landscape (15.1–8):

> Iam pauca aratro iugera regiae
> moles relinquent, undique latius
>   extenta visentur Lucrino
>   stagna lacu platanusque caelebs.
>
> evincet ulmos; tum violaria et
> myrtus et omnis copia narium
>   spargent olivetis odorem
>   fertilibus domino priori

---

[31] The information is supplied by Porphyry. What may be surprising is that he performed this gesture during his lifetime, and not merely by will.

[32] The expression seems particularly clear in view of Champlin's (1991) presentation of the emotional basis underlying Roman testation.

An old villa farm is becoming a new villa park. All the elements of the description – *moles, stagna, platani* and *myrtus* – belong to the vocabulary of domestic landscaping. The phrase *domino priori* makes clear that remodelling follows from a change of ownership. Such campaigns of alteration were common enough from the late Republic to early Empire with the transfers of property that took place in the aftermath of civil wars and proscription (Rawson 1976:87). This change is assimilated to a contrast of present and past with a luxurious character inferred for the present by the mention of the Lucrine Lake with its particular connotations of gastronomic pleasure,[33] and by the sensuous quality of the garden planted to yield its *copia narium*. At the same time words emphasizing a decline in productivity: the narrowing of plowlands, the infertile character of the plane tree *caelebs*, in implied contrast both with the marriageable elm and with the previous fertility of the olive groves, appear to make luxury encroach upon profit. The contrast sharpens in the succeeding stanza where a further image of landscaped comfort, thick laurel shielding from the hot sun, prefaces an abrupt turn of attention to the past (2.15.10–12).

> non ita Romuli
> praescriptum et intonsi Catonis
> auspiciis veterumque norma.

With the appearance of unshaven Cato – symbol of unamenable virtues – a spare and more abstract financial vocabulary displaces our images of the pleasing villa. Presumably we readers will adopt an attitude of righteous moral superiority. All the same the poet allows us to linger for a moment within the shade of a porticus catching up the Northern breezes before being reminded how our ancestors did not scorn to build their houses of cheap and readily available turf. While Horace may have granted the moral upper hand to civic asceticism, still he has furnished the case with singularly unengaging weapons of argument. However strongly recommended Cato's austere style, one can scarcely imagine that the reader will be inspired with a desire to emulate it.

Urging us to adopt a civic-minded view of the poem, Nisbet and Hubbard observe that this description outlines "one particular aspect of the problem of luxury building: its effect on agriculture." Even so they are not deeply convinced of the urgency of the case, whose hyperbolic expression they find disproportionate to actual circumstances.[34] Thus, as they observe, "The virtual

---

[33] Although the lake was famed for its oysters it was also a productive source of fish, and one must remember that most large *piscinae* were developed for raising fish. Mielsch (1987), 23–36.

[34] For historical confirmation, however, of the existence of such a problem, they are able to cite nothing more conclusive than a parallel passage in Seneca's *Controversiae*, as likely as not to be derived from the very poem. Nor are they themselves deeply impressed by the urgency

disappearance of agricultural land under the palaces of the rich, the extravagant hyperbole is appropriately stated not in the present tense, but in the form of a dire prophecy." Hyperbole, as they see it, effectively undermines the poet's genuine message: "It is easy to point out that Horace's fears are illusory, but this is to miss the feeling of the poem."

Is the situation really so confused? Suppose, to the contrary, that the initial image is neither generalizing nor hyperbolic, but specific in its reference to a particular property being remodelled. If the reader constructs a mental picture of the farm that luxury has truncated, that same picture frame must include the innovations that alter its aspect. Now I think that a reader will have to approach this poem with a rock-ribbed resistance to pleasure in order to escape the seductive charm of the images. After the initial wording which privileges the old landscape over the new one, the present-day images crowd so insistently into the foreground that the reader cannot help but savor the charm of pools, plane trees and myrtle even while acknowledging the price demanded by such change. The result of this competition or confrontation of images is by no means an unequivocal condemnation of luxury, but rather a sublimated debate wherein the aesthetics of a commodious present day confront a stern and primitive negativism of austerity. The choice of a winner in this competition, I propose, depends upon the reader's judgment. Whatever the underlying pressure of morality, the case has been put in such a way that allegiance to what Nisbet and Hubbard call "the frugal virtue and public spirit of former days" must emerge as a species of self-deprivation.

Horace's subtle and ambiguous rhetoric weighs a commodious present against a revered, yet far less ingratiating past in such a manner that we are invited to question which of the two images the Augustan regime truly fosters. Can any form of past culture be recovered? The image of Cato's disciplined life and also of public benefaction may evoke thoughts of a vanished competitive system carrying a level of civic responsibility that no longer pertains to the Roman aristocrat. In the face of present-day realities, nostalgia and the use of nostalgia as a political ideology seem futile. At the same time, the plane trees, the myrtle and the heady-scented flowers are the same features that Horace has commended in his portraits of Dellius and Hirpinus as the amenities sweetening contemporary life.

Naturally the pressure to enjoy such amenities is situated in temporal consciousness. As a form of intangible wealth that must, like Sallustius Crispus'

---

of the case which they find no less contrived than that in Seneca. The message that the commentators have felt compelled to transmit here is a prime example of the way in which a history of reading can be influenced by extrinsic concerns. Evidence for an Augustan agricultural crisis and a corresponding laudation of the old ways of agriculture has been desired and Horace can be construed to supply it.

silver, take its *color* through use, time itself emerges as a resource for living. Thus Horace's evocations of place are pervaded by an awareness of time by every definition: dramatic, biographical, and historical. The speaker himself, nearing forty, professes that age has distanced him from erotic involvements (2.4). As often in erotic discourse, lovers polarize past and future; some, like Xanthias (2.4) and the anonymous lover of Chloe (2.5), enjoy positive prospects, but an irrationally self-pitying Valgius must be urged to forget the disappearance/desertion of his beloved. Such personal poems position the present moment against others, often encouraging flexibility in an acceptance of change. Both nature and mythology offer constructive models to Valgius, while politics opens a compensatory field for his talents in celebrating the trophies of Augustan victory. Isn't this consolation in the extreme?

Forgetfulness on a larger scale is the blessing of the Massic wine (*oblivioso Massico*) that Horace broaches in honor of his comrade Pompeius returning at last from the exile imposed by his civil-war partisanship. In view of their shared experience, the poet airs his own military adventures: the awkward loss of a shield, a miraculous translation from the field of battle. That these events are shaped from a merging of lyric and epic tradition gives them a certain humorous speciousness that does not so much diminish as it highlights the hortatory theme of burying dangerous experience.[35] Again the sympotic image subsumes the present moment. The urgency to recognize positive changes amid the fluidity of events is most intense in the warning to Licinius to steer his course prudently between the stormy deeps and the treacherous shore (2.10). In this poem the motif of time is linked with positive alterations. Apollo does not always stretch his bow, but sometimes rouses a taciturn Muse with his lyre. That the description seems to fit Scopas' image of the god in the Palatine temple robed in dignity and sounding his cithera as a vicarious image of the dedicator's pacific policy might appear to fix the figure of a benevolent Augustus as a centerpiece for the book.[36] It is also in keeping with the politics of the book that Horace should incorporate this warning to Licinius, in company with the more positive exhortations to other addressees, at a point when it might still, if heeded, have averted personal disaster.

The conjunction of personal time with national events currently transpiring acquires its significant resonance from a larger temporal consciousness that places collective Roman experience in an historical perspective. This appears both immediately and insistently in the opening address to Asinius Pollio

---

[35] Santirocco (1987:92–3) notes denial of the past in two poems with political content.

[36] Propertius 2.31.15–16 is the direct witness to this attitude. On analogy with the Sorrento base and a later coin of Antistius bearing the legend "Apollo Actius," Zanker (1988a:85–6 *et passim*), and Kellum (1986:174–6) have reconstructed the statue as holding a patera in one hand, but this is in contradiction to Propertius' description. See now Gurval (1995), 123–6.

praising the vividness of his Civil War history with an *enargeia* that plunges the reader into the sounds and sights of battle. As a review of dramatic high-lights in which the voices of speaker and historian become indistinguishably blended together, the poem evokes a performative occasion such as a *recitatio* to air the new work.[37] Horace's dramatization tempts the hearer's inclinations towards heroizing the past as combatants soiled with *non indecoro polvere* come before us and the fierce spirit of Cato stands upright with the whole world around him subdued. Yet the spirited tone of the recreation vividly illumines the perils of awakening memory. The historian "marches over fires buried beneath treacherous ash" and heroic determination becomes more culpable with the progress of the poem when Roman enemies rejoice in the slaughter and Roman blood paints shores and seas. From such images in attributed discourse, the poet turns suddenly away, summoning the *Musa procax* into the more congenial atmosphere of a "Dionean grotto". In accordance with the rhetorical confusion of voices, this "importunate Muse", whose voice threatens to slip into dirges (*neniae*), might be Pollio's as well as his own, while the Dionean *antrum* has also a double implication, uniting the erotic preserve of lyric with the regime of Dione's descendant Augustus. This summons serves as the reader's invitation to the book whose contents are dedicated to the very task of deflecting the emotions of regret and nostalgia for the past that Pollio's history dangerously excites.

Consideration of this lyric summons returns us to questions of performance and audience. In conclusion I want to extend the concept of unity to propose that this central book of the *Odes* appropriates the dramatic shape of a sym-posium. As an occasion of rhetorical self-staging for the performer's voice, it provides a complementary staging for his audience. Enacting the role of a host with the traditional Roman gesture of entertaining his guests, the speaker constructs a hypothetical dramatic presence shaped around the portraits of individuals addressed. In the order of address or arrangement we may notice something closer to the Greek symposiast freedom of ignoring social gradations than to the Roman sense of hierarchy.[38] Pollio occupies first place, although Maecenas, as a closer friend, has finally the greater share of attention, being mentioned in three poems, two of which place him in a direct comparative relationship with the speaker himself. Some have attributed the selection of persons to the diplomacies of patronage. Nisbet and Hubbard propose an

---

[37] Quinn (1980) 197, *ad* 17–24, characterizes the ode as Horace's imaginary response to such an occasion. Conventional opinion, e.g. Fraenkel (1970:234–9) assumes only Horace's her-alding of a "forthcoming" literary production.

[38] Murray (1985:40), although, as he notes, the Romans did not always adapt the form grace-fully. Rather than the traditional nine participants, hierarchically placed, the group includes twelve counting Horace, and assuming that Xanthias, twitted for his love interest in Phyllis, might be a male attendant while Barine is the hetaira of the evening.

overarching theme of *amicitia* with emphasis on the manner in which Roman social structure supplies the guidelines of interassociation among persons of unequal status.[39] But even if this principle pertains, it need not be construed as the exclusive rationale governing Horace's choice of persons. As we survey the differences of these figures, they may well seem to be strategically chosen to represent not only a variety of life-styles but also a variety of attitudes.[40]

An immediate dramatic moment for the symposium is supplied by the speaker's confession of age. He measures his nearly forty years in civic terms (2.4.23–4 *cuius octavum trepidat aetas | claudere lustrum*). The year is 25 BCE and two references to Rome's still inconclusive Spanish campaigns against the Cantabri reinforce the date.[41] Horace's contemporaries will have recognized that this year is not the present one – 23 BCE Instead, the symposium with its elements of unity stands as a framed centerpiece to the collection: a past moment recreated amidst passing time, a year whose prosperity contrasts with the present year that the *Odes* in general are designed to address with their demonstrated proofs of stability.

In addition to its allusions to current affairs and topics, the discourse is spiced with the amatory interest requisite to the symposium: a patronizing tease for Xanthus; a lascivious reflection upon Chloe and a warning against Barine, the unscrupulous hetaira whose perfidy imperils not only all the men present but also the virtuous womenfolk left at home (2.8). The parts of the discourse are knit together with the speaker's characterizations of himself, all of them including references to his role as performer. With Maecenas he debates a choice of subject (2.12). Relating a personal anecdote of his narrow escape from the death-dealing tree on his own property, he incorporates a glimpse of his lyric predecessors still binding their spells among the underworld shades. From the penultimate ode with its vision of the inspirational Dionysus whose heady influence fills verses with streams of wine, milk and honey, the book progresses to a triumphantly bibulous climax in the self-staging of its

---

[39] Nisbet and Hubbard (1978:2). To this may be added Habinek's remarks (1990a) on social inequality as the context that enabled candid advice.

[40] White (1995) has recently amplified the idea that Horace's selection of ex-contestants in the civil wars represent a variety of allegiances with an eye to some manner of verbal reconciliation.

[41] Nisbet and Hubbard (1978:93–4). The corresponding historical keynote is the address to Septimus on his way to aid Rome in mastering the troublesome Cantabri in Spain (2.6: indoctum iuga ferre nostrum). Augustus' Cantabrian campaigns extend from 26–24 BCE. In Ode 2.11 Quinctius is exhorted to put the plans of the Cantabri and Scythians out of mind and concentrate on the pleasures of youth and the symposium. These two poems in which the Cantabri are unconquered but an object of attention would seem to belong to the years of the campaign from which the *princeps'* victorious return is celebrated in Ode 3.8. Chronologically also they may be located after the reference in 1.26, the invocation to Fortuna of Antium on behalf of campaigns that never occurred. Additionally 25 BCE has been suggested as a probable year for the amnesty that brought about Pompeius' return.

final cygnian/Icarian metamorphosis. If Bacchus returned from the underworld with Cerberus licking his calves (2.19.29–32), likewise the Bacchic symposiast discovers his means to rise above the "Stygian wave." A second command to silence *neniae* brings the collection/symposium/performance back to its start but now the voice that had ambiguously blended with Pollio's speaks out confidently for itself.[42] This half-facetious claim of immortality anticipates the sober, genre-specific declaration of the *monumentum aere perennius* (3.30.1–2). One should not overlook how the Epilogue poem reconfigures its opening paradox as it hypothesizes a duration for the collection co-terminous with that of the city, yet conceptualizes the life of the city itself in terms of state monuments and rituals (3.30.8–9: *dum Capitolium ꘑ scandet cum tacita virgine pontifex*). This second paradox might best be understood by the fact that the collection at once creates and contains the city and is the medium in which the city itself will be preserved. Thus the immediate programmatic persuasive mission of the *Odes* of urging acquiescence in the Augustan political revolution is a message on behalf of the continuity of Roman culture, a message addressed as fully to Augustus as to his subjects.

---

[42] I thank Tom Habinek as editor for urging me to make something of the *neniae* in this sympotic context.

7 Images of the city: Propertius' new-old Rome

Elaine Fantham

If ever Rome was full of unfinished buildings, it must have been in the years after, or even before, Actium, when the new monuments were rising on the Palatine, and the Campus Martius was taken over by temples and theaters and porticoes and the towering Augustan Mausoleum. It is not as though major elements of the city had been destroyed, as they were in the Sullan assault of 83, and would be again in Nero's great fire and five years later in the battle between the supporters of Vitellius and those of Vespasian. The stimulus for this fever of construction came instead from an ambitious vision of the city, a desire shared by Caesar and his heir, to emulate Alexandria and other Hellenistic imperial capitals. Augustan poets hailed the gilded roofs and luxurious statuary, but as Rome's residents watched the heart of their city transformed, they must have passed years living in an extended construction site, with the old disfigured and the new still incomplete or raw.

I have chosen Propertius as my witness to this process, although he is not, like Virgil, the originator of the classic contrast of Then and Now, because the genre of elegy permits him both a realistic evocation of city scenes and activities, and the chronology of his four books is well enough defined to allow a sense of his evolving vision. Let me see how much it is possible to deduce his attitude to the changes taking place around him from his representation of the old city as well as his allusions to the new.

Inevitably any interpretation of the poet's response must be to some extent conditional. In the first place we have to take into account the influence upon Propertius of his poetic predecessors: indeed it would be totally misleading to reconstruct his representation of Rome without mapping on to it the landmarks offered by the poetic models available to him. Luckily elements of imitation in the relationship of Propertius' account of the early city to the *Ur-Rom* of Virgil and Tibullus have been traced, and expertly traced, by La Penna, Solmsen, and others,[1] while Buchheit has examined in detail the dependence of Propertius' fullest contrast of *Einst und Jetzt* in *Elegy* 4.1a on Tibullus' virtuoso *Elegy* 2.5, and on book 8 of the *Aeneid*.[2]

---

[1] See La Penna (1977), esp. part II ch.4 "Scoperta poetica della città e d'intorni, 176–82, 187–91 and on formal echoes, La Penna (1950) and (1951). Solmsen (1961); K. Weeber (1978).
[2] V. Buchheit (1965).

Virgil's way had been to evoke Rome in her first miraculous beginnings with the few scattered cottages of Evander's idyllic settlement in the eighth book of the *Aeneid*. With Evander's retrospective narrative these passages from book 8 provided inspiration for the pastoral vignettes of *Ur-Rom* in Tibullus' elegy for young Messalinus. Indeed it seems to me highly likely that besides *Aeneid* 2, 4 and 6 – known to have been recited to Augustus in 23 BCE – Virgil would have chosen to compose and recite these passages with their immense appeal to local patriotism as early as possible in his epic undertaking.[3] Certainly much of the *Aeneid* and probably of Tibullus' second book was known to court circles of Rome before 19, when both poets died, and it is easy to show that one important elegy of Propertius' third book (if not also his salute to Virgil in 2.34[4]) is familiar with the parts of the *Aeneid* that introduce early Rome.

---

[3] We need not go all the way with Grimal (1952) to accept his conviction that Virgil himself composed the Roman scenes of book 8 as an early homage to Augustus.

[4] Pillinger (1969:195) argues that 2.34 shows Propertius' "familiarity with the Actium motif in the *Aeneid* then in progress," noting also that beside 4.6 "several passages elsewhere in book 4 point to his special interest in the eighth book of Virgil's epic."

I would go beyond his argument to suggest that 2.34 is Propertius' response to the books opening the second half of the *Aeneid*. It defines the *Aeneid* in four lines before hailing it with an accolade that could also be read as a lictor's proclamation to clear the way for a triumphal procession. *Nescioquid maius nascitur Iliade* ("Something even greater than the *Iliad* is coming to birth" suggests, not Virgil's first proem, but his second, from the seventh book, just as the references to the Actian shore of guardian Phoebus and gallant ships of Caesar (2.34.61) mark his acknowledgement of the great image on the shield of Aeneas in book 8. Here the poet is saluting the *Aeneid* in terms of the *Iliad*, that is, the warfare of its second half: he even borrows the comparative from Virgil's proem to book 7 *maior rerum mihi nascitur ordo|maius opus moveo*," a greater series of events is coming to birth: I attempt a greater task." But while Virgil is only asserting the greater grandeur of his war narrative over his Odyssean wanderings, Propertius has changed the context of the comparative to make Virgil a more extravagant compliment.

Propertius will develop the nexus between the arms given to Aeneas by Venus and the ships that bring Caesar victory without any fundamental change of direction in 4.1. 39–40 and 45–8. His description of Virgil's present task in 2.34.63, echoing the metrical form but not the syntax of *Aen.* 2.618, has adapted the phrase *arma suscitare* "raising up arms" to suggest the warfare of *Aeneid* 7–12 rather than the voyages of 1–5. By its wording it also points to Aeneas' literal *arma*, the shield on which is depicted the panoramic battle scene of Actium. As a result he has put the cart (or triumphal chariot) of Augustus' Actian victory before the horse of Aeneas' warfare and role as founder. Rome's walls are the natural symbol of the foundation and undoubtedly "the arms of Trojan Aeneas and city-walls raised on Lavinian shores" (2.34.63–4) echoes "arms and the man who first . . . came to Italy and the shores of Lavinia" (*Aen.* 1.1–3). But Propertius has telescoped into a single phrase places and times that Virgil set apart: the shores of Lavinium and the walls, not of Lavinium but of Rome herself (*atque altae moenia Romae, Aen.* 1.1–7). It is these walls that will symbolize the city throughout its appearances in Propertius' text.

Balancing the great *Recusatio* to Maecenas in book 3, the Cleopatra elegy
3.11 foreshadows much in book 4, and I shall make it my point of departure
for understanding how Propertius came to write his poems for Rome ("give
me your favor, Rome, this work arises on your honor" *Roma fave: tibi surgit
opus* 4.1.67), and evoke his "ancient names of places" *cognomina prisca
locorum* (4.1.69).

When I come to consider book 4 itself, I want to argue that not only the
opening guided tour, 4.1a and the etiological elegies (4.1; 4.2; 4.4; 4.9 and
4.10) but the whole book was designed to reflect the shape and life of the
city. In particular I believe that Propertius' image of Rome was shaped by
Varro's conception of Romulus' archetypal city, which would also be known
to him through its transformation in the opening chapters (1–12) of Livy's
first book, composed between 29 and 25 BCE.

With one conspicuous exception Propertius makes few references to the
new city of gold and marble: instead he invites us to deduce his response to
the *new* city from his imaginative devotion to the *old*. Indeed, in the proud
evocation that opens book 4, contrasting Rome's greatness with the earliest
settlement shared precariously between man and nature, his symbol for the
mature city is itself old: "Wolf of Mars, best of nurses for our community,
what walls grew up from your milk!" (4.1.55–6).

Rome's greatness is symbolized by the walls she had in Propertius' time
long outgrown, so that the city he is celebrating is not the new metropolis;
instead he presents himself as the poet planner founding or marking out the
old city: "for I would attempt to lay out the walls in loyal verse" *moenia
namque pio coner disponere versu* (4.1.57). Propertius sees himself as another
Amphion, the poet architect first mentioned in the second Ponticus elegy
(1.9.10) then cited with Orpheus as a model for Propertius' creative power in
3.2.5–6: "men say Cithaeron's rocks were driven to Thebes by his art, and
of their own accord were fused into its walls."

Thus the poetic city Propertius creates is a nostalgic counterpart of Augustus'
physical creation of the new monuments.

But the first occasion on which Propertius presents the city of Rome as a
symbol of patriotism[5] is *Elegy* 3.11, which is also his first certain allusion to
the eighth book of the *Aeneid*. The opening theme of the poem is his own
submission to the tyranny of his lover: this leads to the denunciation of
female tyranny whose worst and last example, Cleopatra, is evoked in lines
41–6:

She who dared to pit the barking Anubis against our Jupiter, and force the Tiber to
endure the threats of the Nile, to drive back the Roman bugle with the rattling sistrum

---

[5] Propertius has portrayed the social amenities offered by Rome to the lover in 2.32, and evoked
the primeval Rome of Romulus in 3.9.

and chase the Liburnian prows with Egyptian puntpoles, and cast vile mosquito nets towards the Tarpeian rock and lay down the law between the statues and trophies of Marius.

Besides the obvious echoes of Horace's famous Actium epode (*Ep.* 9) and the Cleopatra ode (*C.* 1.37),[6] these lines draw specifically on *Aen.* 8.696 and 698 for Anubis and the *sistrum*. Propertius draws again on the shield ecphrasis for the image of the protective Nile offering refuge in 3.11.51:" yet you fled to the wandering streams of the fearful Nile" *fugisti tamen in timidi vaga flumina Nili* (cf. *Aen.* 8.711–3). There can be no doubt that this elegy reflects Virgil's representation of Actium and his association of Augustus' victory with the triumph of Italy and Rome herself. But in contrast with Virgil's Actium vignette, Propertius' poem foregrounds the physical city of Rome. Here too his inspiration may be Virgilian. Virgil's craftsman god depicted the early city in the shield ecphrasis at 635 and 647 (*urbem*) and made the Capitoline the visual focus of the climactic scene of Gallic assault at 652–4, alongside Romulus' Palatine hut at 655. Again, in the culminating triumph vignette Vulcan shows Augustus Caesar first entering the city walls in triple triumph, *triplici invectus Romana triumpho | moenia* (714–15) against a backdrop of three hundred shrines, then finally at his destination on the snow-white threshold of gleaming Phoebus (720).

In 3.11, the city itself becomes ever more important for Propertius as the elegy advances. Thus initially Propertius damns women by representing them as threatening to control the male world of the community. He prepares the way for Cleopatra with Semiramis' foundation of Babylon (21, 25) and her commands to Bactria to submit to her *imperium* (26). Cleopatra herself is designated but needs no naming. The symbol of her arrogance is her demand for Rome's walls and the subjection of her Senate:

> Romana poposcit
> moenia, et addictos in sua iura patres.

The sedes of *Romana . . . moenia* echoes that of *Aen.* 8.714–15: the enslaved senate recalls Caesar in *Aen.* 8.679 advancing "with Senate and people" *cum patribus populoque*. For Propertius the walls of Rome, celebrated by Virgil in *Georgics* and *Aeneid* alike,[7] signify the prize of contention and frame his meditation on the naval victory. After the walls the Tiber (42) and the Capitoline (*Tarpeio . . . saxo* 45) are evoked to symbolize the city and its defences,

---

[6] Compare *foeda . . . conopia* (45) with *turpe conopium, Epode* 9.15–16, and the threats to Jupiter Capitolinus, *Iovi nostro* (41) *Tarpeio . . . saxo* (45), and demand for the city, *coniugis obsceni Romana poposcit | moenia* (31–2), with *dum Capitolio | regina dementes ruinas . . . parabat Odes* 1.37.6–8.

[7] Cf. *G.*2.535 "and set around her seven hills with a wall" *septemque una sibi muro circumdedit arces = A.* 6.783; and the walls that symbolize Rome's power in *A.*1.7 and 276.

followed by its natural defences "high on her seven hills" (57).[8] Propertius also names other sites of defensive resistance, the cistern in the Forum recalling Curtius' death, and the path commemorating Horatius' demolition of the bridge, before he brings his poem back emphatically to the walls, founded by the gods and still to be preserved by them:

> haec di condiderant, haec di quoque moenia servant:
> vix timeat salvo Caesare Roma Iovem. (65–6)

These walls the gods established; these they also keep safe. Rome would scarce fear Jove himself while Caesar thrives.

The next and last site to be mentioned is the temple of Leucadian Apollo (69).[9] The Augustan temple on the Palatine wins pride of place as climax and conclusion to Propertius' evocation of the city. After the walls, the river, the citadel and seven hills that together defended Rome, comes finally the votive temple of victory commemorating the end of its need for defences: *tantum operis belli sustulit una dies* "one day abolished such a struggle of warfare" (3.11.70).

There is a further signal that already in this book Propertius was preparing to make the city his theme. The elegant *recusatio* of 3.9, includes among Propertius' promises, always contingent on Maecenas setting him an example, the promise that he would write a national foundation epic of his city:

> eductosque pares silvestri ex ubere reges (51)
>   ordiar et caeso moenia firma Remo (50)
>   celsaque Romanis decerpta Palatia tauris (49)[10]

I shall tell of equal kings reared by a woodland udder and walls made safe by Remus' slaughter, the lofty Palatine grazed by Roman cattle . . .

The proposed, but postponed, celebration of Rome will begin with Romulus and Remus and honor the walls and the safe heights of the Palatine. In 3.9 the Palatine is singled out as the original walled community of Romulus (matching that of Livy 1.7) and associated by etymology with the original pastoral economy of Rome: but when the temple of Leucadian Apollo culminates the evocation of Rome in 3.11, there is no need to name its Palatine site, for the temple and its porticoes must have been the best known and most celebrated of Octavian's new monuments even before he entered Propertius' poetry as *tuus . . . Caesar* in the dedicatory poem of book 2 (2.1.25).

---

[8] On Rome's natural defences, note Cicero's account in *Rep.* 1.5 stressing the advantages of the Tiber and the *nativa praesidia* of steep hills enhanced by the Romulean walls. Tiber, hills, and walls will constitute the city for Propertius.

[9] Propertius is cited from Fedeli's text, in which only 67–8 are transposed to precede 59.

[10] Here I go against Fedeli, retaining Peiper's transposition of 51 and 49.

Let us give a moment to Propertius' ecphrastic encomium of this temple and its porticoes, the pointedly short and symmetrical 2.31.

You ask why I am late for you? The golden portico of Apollo has just been opened by Caesar. It was so great a sight, articulated by Punic columns, the female brood of old Danaus set between them.

Here indeed I thought the marble likeness of Apollo more handsome than the god himself, mouthing its song to the silent lyre: and round the altar stood Myron's herd, four crafty oxen, lifelike images.

Then at its center rose the temple in brilliant marble, dearer to Apollo than his natal Delos: as its features there was the sun-chariot above the roof-ridge, and the doors, the famous work of Libyan tusk;

one panel showed the Gauls cast down from the peak of Parnassus, the other mourned the death of Tantalus' daughter. Then finally the god himself, between his mother and his sister, clad in the long robe sounds out as Pythian his songs.

Scholars have been grateful to this elegy for its documentation of the appropriated Greek cult statues and iconographic scheme of the ensemble. We in turn know from our historians the occasion in October 28 BCE recorded by Propertius.[11] But this poem is filled with representations of gods and divine acts, not with the monument itself or its setting. Since the temple itself had already been consecrated at Caesar's triumph in 29, one would expect Propertius to focus on the newly finished porticoes, and he certainly devotes ingenuity to evoking the range of Numidian *giallo antico* columns with Danaus' daughters (their daggers half-concealed beneath their robes) filling the intercolumnar spaces.[12] In lines 5–6 the poet concentrates on the statue of Apollo, set apparently before the altar in front of the temple around which were set the famous lifelike heifers of Myron.[13] The hyperbolic compliment "almost more beautiful than the god himself" has naturally led scholars to assimilate this statue, not otherwise identified, to the image set by Octavian in the library complex, reported by a scholiast on Horace *Epistles* 1.3.17 to have had Octavian's face and deportment.

So far each artistic element has had its couplet. In the second half of the poem the temple briefly looms in the foreground, dazzling in its marble, and exalted as the god's new favorite place of worship. With the distich describing the cult statue of Apollo Citharoedus by Scopas (15–16), this distich frames

---

[11] Dio 53.1.3 "Moreover he completed and dedicated the temple of Apollo on the Palatine, the precinct surrounding it, and the Libraries."

[12] Cf. Ovid, *Ars* 1.71–6; *Tr.*3.1.60–2 "I am led to the shining white temple of the unshorn god, where stand the foreign statues between the columns, the daughters of Belus and the father with drawn sword." Also see Kellum (1986).

[13] Cf. Pliny, *NH* 34.57. Both the Apollo and the cattle are praised in terms of their naturalism, which was a famous aspect of Myron's art recorded in many epigrams.

four lines devoted to the frontal ornamentation, one to the sun-chariot on the roof-ridge (or possibly to a pedimental relief),[14] the other three to the ivory-panelled doors celebrating two acts of vengeance by the leader's patron god.

Does such an enumeration of respected works of the best Greek classical period make a good poem? Does it even offer a natural sequence of visual experiences as they would affect the onlooker? To me this seems a frigid and unelegiac elegy, without flow or climax, and troubled by extraordinary ellipses, such as the yoking of the mourning for the children of Niobe with the presumably unmourned Gauls, or the odd zeugma *in quo* of 11, combining the statuary group aloft with the doors as part of the temple itself. Finally, as commentators have noted, the superlative praise of the first statue outshines the simple description of the cult statue that should have formed the climax of the poem. It would be easy to transpose lines 5–6, harder to justify the transposition, or to explain the ensuing leap from the Danaids to the insufficiently located altar. The poem gives the modern reader little pleasure: what aesthetic appeal, beyond that of a Baedeker, would it have for Propertius' Hellenized readers? Did Propertius regret it? Is that why he does not attempt any similar architectural ecphrasis again?

Was he trying to conform to the new ideology? Inevitably allusions to the Palatine suggest to the modern reader the ideological conflict between the Augustan Palatine and Republican Capitoline hills – a contest that would be played out in other Augustan public acts, such as the ritual of the Secular Games in 17. The Secular hymn with its stress of the new Palatine triad would be sung in more than one place, but certainly in front of this same temple, within the residential precinct of Augustus himself. Most readers of Propertius seek to interpret in these political terms the poet's choice of sites for celebration, scrutinizing his poetry for a hint of polarisation or even favoritism between the two focal hills.

Keeping in mind these oppositions of old and new, architecture and nature, Imperial and Republican symbols, we come at last to the image of the city offered by the Romano-centric fourth book. Although the opening line of 4.1: *Hoc quodcunque vides ... qua maxima Roma est*, "all that you see here, where mighty Rome extends" introduces the most expansive representation of the city, past and present, I suggest that we begin by following Propertius' urban topography through the sequence of poems 4.2 to 4.10 that form the body of the book.[15]

---

[14] La Penna and others have referred this to the (otherwise unknown) subject of the pediment, but archaeologists (Coarelli [1980:257], Zanker [1988a:85]) refer Propertius' language to the rooftop chariot sculpted by Lysias, in which both Apollo and Diana ride. Propertius himself is the primary source for many details, but the classical sculptors of most of the statuary are identified in Pliny's chapters on the history of sculpture, *NH* 36. 24 (on the shrine) and sections 13, 32 and 34–5. See now Richardson (1992), 14 and figure 64.

[15] Scivoletto (1981) offers little assistance.

First a word about those walls, so prominent in 2.34 and 3.9 and 11. Remnants of the Servian walls still survive and were surely more fully preserved in the Augustan era, but by Propertius' life-time the old Romulean walls must already have been purely conceptual, defined only by the surviving gates of the Palatine itself, since even the ritual Pomerium had been expanded by Sulla and Caesar. Yet in 4.1, as in 2.34 and 3.11, the walls of Rome serve repeatedly to symbolize the city.

> optima nutricum nostris lupa Martia rebus
>   qualia creverunt moenia lacte tuo
> moenia namque pio coner disponere versu

Wolf of Mars, best of nurses for our history, what walls grew up sustained by your milk! For I would try to lay out the city walls in loyal verse. (4.1. 55–57)

Reformulating his promise to celebrate the city, Propertius makes its walls a symbol of his own ordering and constructive powers (*disponere versu*) and expresses his rise to metropolitan fame by contrasting Rome's fortifications with the walled hilltops of his native Assisi (65–6, cf. 125–6).[16] In contrast, the story of Tarpeia in 4.4., Propertius' counterpart of Virgil's vignette of the Gallic capture on Aeneas' shield, marks the importance of Rome's walls by stressing their absence and the Romulean city's reliance on its natural defences: *murus erant montes*, "the hills served as its wall" (4.13); compare their pointed omission and substitution in Tarpeia's mock farewell in 4.35–6: *Romani montes et montibus addita Roma | et valeat . . . Vesta*, "farewell you Roman hills and Rome attached to its hills, and Vesta . . .".[17] Only the slope of the "Tarpeian rock" (remember 3.11.45) defends Rome, and Propertius' elegy purports to honor Tarpeia's tomb and tell how she gave the cliff her name.[18]

Varro's *De Lingua latina* is neither a *descriptio urbis* nor a periegesis but a word list, in which the ordering of the place-names and their origins is still likely to reflect his perception of their spatial and historic sequence, and more systematic accounts given in other works now lost. After introducing the *septimontium* (not our seven hills but the multiple crests of Palatine and

---

[16] Propertius' *creverunt moenia* seems to have no parallel in Latin, but for the emotive connotation of walls cf. *Aen.* 1.365–6 and 4370 *fortunati quorum iam moenia surgunt*: " Happy are those whose walls are now | already arising!" Outside Virgil *crescere* and *surgere* are found with *moenia* only in Ovid's imitations at *Heroides* 7.11 and *Met.* 15.452.

[17] Goold has recently been inspired by the precedent of *Murus erat montes* to revive the conjecture *et Tiberis nostris advena murus erat* in 4.1.8.

[18] Wiseman (1978) has shown that the *rupes Tarpeia* refers specifically to the south-east face of the summit by the arx overlooking the Forum. Since there was not yet any temple of Jupiter on the other crest, Prop. 4.4.2 *antiqui limina capta Iovis* must be an anachronism. The naming of the summit after Tarpeia may be pointed by the text of 4.4.29 if we adopt Palmer's transposition "et Tarpeia sua . . . ab arce" stressing the etymology of the place name, rather than the paradosis *sua Tarpeia* which construes *Tarpeia* (abl.) with *arce*.

Capitoline with the Velia) Varro starts his list with the Capitoline and explains its name from the mythical omen of the head discovered by the Tarquins laying the foundations of the temple of Jupiter. He adds that it was previously called Mons Tarpeia from the crime and death of the Vestal Tarpeia, and even now the cliff is called *Tarpeium saxum* (5.41): before that again it was *Mons Saturnius*, just as Latium had been called *Saturnia*. Virgil elaborated this last etymology in *Aen.* 8.347–58; Propertius turned to its successor.

From the Capitoline Varro proceeds *not* to the Palatine but to the Aventine and Velabrum (5.43–44). The ritual of the Argei leads him to the first listing of the four names of the urban, district-based, tribes *Suburana, Esquilina, Collina* and *Palatina*, then to his account of the Mons Caelius and Vicus Tuscus "in which stands the Statue of Vertumnus" (5.46), and of the Carinae (47, cf. *Aen.* 8.361). It is then he treats the Palatine with its various etymologies, and its two crests, Cermalus and Velia. For Varro, writing in 47 BCE, the Palatine was simply the wealthy residential area occupied by such as Cicero and Hortensius: only its role as a district naming one of the tribes (the list is reprised at 56 with *Palatina* in second place) seems to earn it any special attention.

In contrast, Livy's chronological narrative starts with the Palatine as Evander's original settlement, first walled by Romulus, who extended the "city," but set up his asylum or reception center for fugitives between the two crests of the unenclosed Capitoline (1.7). In fact Livy's next few chapters are focused on the Capitoline: 1.10 reports Romulus' dedication of his *spolia opima* to the sacred oak of Jupiter Feretrius and demarcation of a site for the future temple, 1.11.6–9 describes how Tarpeia as daughter of the garrison commander on the Arx betrayed the cliff access to the Sabines, and 1.12 sets the Sabines on the citadel, from which they descend to fight the Romans in the open valley of the future Forum between the two hills, *in media convalle duarum montium* (1.12.10).

Propertius follows Livy's configuration of early Rome for the betrayal, defeat and victory of the Sabine war in the valley between the two hills evoked in his Tarpeia elegy: but Propertius' fantasy, like Dionysius of Halicarnassus' archaizing history,[19] reforests the terrain: it starts from a Grove of Tarpeia (*Tarpeium nemus*[20]) and generates a clearing by the Tiber inlet where Tatius

---

[19] Compare DH 2.15 "He consecrated the place between the Capitol and the citadel . . . 'the place between the two groves', a term that was really descriptive at that time of the actual conditions, as the place was shaded by thick woods on both sides where it joined the hills" and 2.49 "after cutting down the wood that grew on the plain at the foot of the Capitoline and filling up the greatest part of the lake . . . they converted this plain into a forum." (Tr. Cary, LCL)

[20] There is no reason to adopt Kraffert's conjecture *Tarpeium scelus* as do Camps and Goold; even without the transposition Propertius is clearly referring to three places, two of which relate to the Varronian aetiological tale: Tarpeia's grove, her tomb and the ancient shrine of Jupiter (? Feretrius). See below for Propertius' stress on the wooded aspects of unpopulated early Rome.

can camp and exercise in view of the citadel, and Tarpeia goes to fetch water for the service of Vesta. Livy has other topographical features – the old gate of the Palatine, the marsh that bogs down Mettus Curtius – but essentially it is his Romulean city that Propertius portrays in 4.4, as also in 4.1.

Yet it is a mistake for modern readers of Propertius to look for Propertius' Rome only in the overtly etymological elegies. Consider the locations named in successive elegies from 4.2 to 4.10. Pride of place in 4.2. is given to the Forum – *Romanum satis est posse videre forum* (4.2.6) – and the old river inlet of the Tiber, associating his name with the river bend (*Vert-amnis*) and Velabrum (7–10). But the poem lingers in the crowded Vicus Tuscus, linking the site with the legendary force of Caelius Vibenna as in Varro. The third elegy, like Arethusa, is confined to her home until she makes her votive journey to the Porta Capena between Caelian and Aventine to meet her returning husband. After the Capitoline emphasis of 4.4, the fifth elegy takes us through the red-light district and outside the city to the burial grounds of the poor; no place is named except for a swift allusion to the waste ground beyond the Colline gate as source of *Collinae herbae* (4.5.10–11). The adjective should not be passed over, since it names one of the four districts of the urban tribes. Subura and Esquiline, the eponyms of two more tribes, are named in the great Cynthia elegies 4.7 and 8.[21] Between them comes the commemoration of Actium, Propertius' most elaborate variation on the great Virgilian theme with its focus on the temple of Palatine Apollo (11). This is indeed the only time that Propertius will call Apollo *Palatinus*,[22] and he may have chosen to do so precisely to evoke the fourth of the urban tribal districts, offering the sequence Collinus, Palatinus, Subura(nus), Esquili(nus) in 4.5 through 8. The poem itself, like Virgil's shield, transports the reader to Actium and thence to the Nile before returning to the god's *monumenta* in Rome.

Now to 4.9 and 4.10.[23] The former perversely displaces the traditional Aventine associations of Cacus with a conspicuous early allusion to the Palatine (4.9.3 "the sheep-rich Palatine, unconquered hills") before the expected reference to the Velabrum and river shallows (9.5–6), the Forum Boarium (9.19–20), and Ara Maxima (67). Hercules' promise in 19–20 is ambiguous, for as he invites the oxen to sanctify the *arva Bovaria* with a mighty moo (*longo . . . mugitu*), he promises that their pasture will become the *nobile . . . Romae . . . Forum*: not, then, the region of the Forum Boarium but the future republican forum. These displacements seem designed to edge the scene of Hercules'

[21] Cf *vigilacis furta Suburae*, 4.7.15, and *Esquilias . . . aquosas*. 4.8.1.

[22] Compare 4.1.3 *Navali stant sacra Palatia Phoebo* "where stand the Palatine buildings sacred to Phoebus of the ships," and contrast 2.31 (*Phoebus* 3 times, *Pythius* once) 3.11.69 (*Leucadius*) 4.6.67 (*Actius*).

[23] On 4.9 see Anderson (1964), Pillinger (1969:182–9), and Cairns (1992a), with response by Anderson (1992).

thirst towards the far end of the Palatine: the whole episode, including his final curse excluding women from the Ara Maxima, is again moved away, set not at the celebrated altar, but in this imaginary secluded spot where the birds sing in the abundant shade as the long-branched poplar marks the ruined shrine. This pastoral setting, worthy of a Third style wallpainting, replaces the topography of Roman legend, excluding from the text both traditional heroic events, the battle with Cacus and the founding of the altar, and both their traditional sites.

Propertius' final aetion is almost equally coy about the site of Romulus' dedication to Jupiter Feretrius. His readers knew, as Livy did, that the altar and temple stood on the Capitoline, but the poet speaks only of the city's gates (7), her territories (10), her towers (13), and Romulus' humble home (*parvo . . . Lare* 18). From this first Palatine settlement he radiates outwards to Veii and the villages of Cora and Nomentum, before moving away from the Tiber to the Rhine (39) and Marcellus' victory over Brennus' descendant, Virdomarus.[24] Unsatisfactory as the brusque narrative may seem to the modern reader, the elegy depends for its effect as much on spatial as on temporal advance, from the first defence of the original city to the victory that ensured the safety of Italy itself from the barbarian.

There remains the resumptive opening poem with all its problems. Guey (1952) imaginatively converted the first part of the elegy (up to line 50) into a walk around the summit of the Palatine, but of the four alleged viewpoints only the first and second, at the foot of the Cermalus and on its crest near Augustus' Palatine precinct, seem to be needed. If we read the first fifty lines without transpositions or reinterpretation, they offer a view of Rome that pans in from an opening focus on the grassy hills of the entire city ("all that you see," 4.1.1) to the Palatine temple and, facing it, the once bare Tarpeian rock, now bearing the gilded gables of the temple of Jupiter Optimus Maximus. Below it lies the Tiber, opposite again *domus ista Remi* (4.1.10: despite the reference to "rising on steps" not the temple of Romulus on the Quirinal, but the *casa Romuli* rebuilt on the Cermalus in the 30s). Beneath in the Forum area is the new Senate house where the old senators once met in the open, and the Comitium of the Quirites; beyond, the new theaters of Marcellus and Pompey with their awnings lead towards the Campus Martius, now being adorned by Augustus with monuments to himself and his family.

With this poem Propertius is doing more than reconstruct his image of the old city: he is renewing the foundation of Rome. His final invocation "be favorable to me, Rome; this work arises for you" and appeal to his fellow citizens for fair omens and good auspices (*candida . . . omina . . . dextera*

---

[24] That Propertius has Virgil's vignette of the Gallic capture in mind is clear from his adaptation of the Gaul's striped breeches *virgatis . . . bracis* of 4.9.43, from the striped cloaks *virgatis . . . sagulis* of *Aen.* 8.660.

cantet avis 68) surely recalls Romulus' celebrated auspices and rounds off his earlier claim "I would attempt to lay out your walls in verse".[25] Here then is a new and living portrait of the Rome of old.

La Penna has argued that Propertius must have felt even more acutely than most of his generation the contradictions between the old models based on the standards of an agrarian society, and the convenience, pleasures and attractions of the Hellenized urban community he now lived in.[26] Most recently Martindale, speaking of Virgil's *Ur-Rom* in *Aeneid* 8, sees Virgil's "blurring of epic with pastoral" in Evander's Rome as a necessary "contradiction within the spiritual idea of Rome, which is simultaneously the *caput rerum*, the metropolis which Augustus found brick and left marble, and an idyll of primitivism and rural simplicity." But he transforms this fair description of conflicting sentiment into an imputation of disingenuity, of "an (attempted) erasure of conflict, in the interests of Roman identity and Augustan ideology".[27]

If this opposition of images and values of Rome then and now does not require us to read disingenuity into Virgil, why should we give a different reading to Propertius, treating him as either hypocrite or dissident? Do his images of the old city discredit the new monuments that express Augustan pride in renewal? Given his double inheritance of pastoral nostalgia from both Virgil and Tibullus, even the cattle, hides and straw littered around 4.1[28] may be as traditional as the earthenware gods of 4.1.5. Ovid would develop these rustic textures further in the *Fasti*, suppressing the elegant contempt that he had expressed for such primitive rusticity in *Ars Amatoria*.[29]

The nostalgia that rejects modern landscaping as part of luxury and corruption is very real in Juvenal's third satire, where Umbricius seems to incriminate the marble of Egeria's cistern for the degrading of her grove:

we went down to the valley of Egeria and her grottoes so unlike the real caves. Her divinity would have been so much more vividly present, if grass fringed the waters with a green border and no marble violated the native tufa stone![30] (*Sat.* 3.17–20)

[25] Cf. Ovid, *Fasti*. 4.827–36, in which Romulus' prayer is followed by good omens, the citizens lay the foundations and in a brief space of time the new wall came into being *et novus exiguo tempore murus erat*.

[26] La Penna (1977), 182.

[27] Martindale (1993b) 51. The contrast between early pastoralism and Virgil's *Romano ... foro et lautis ... Carinis* (The Roman forum and the elegant Carinae, *Aen.* 8.361) or Propertius' *aurea templa* (golden temples, 4.1.5) is proper to the different stages in Rome's organic growth and is cause for neither conflict nor embarrassment.

[28] Cattle, 4.1.4 and 22; straw 4.1.19; hides, 4.1.12 and 25.

[29] *Ars* 3.113–22. Ovid's deprecation of ancient primitive conditions (*simplicitas rudis*) inherited in part from Propertius' recognition of the past as irrecoverable, cf. 2.32 "he who looks for the Tatii and Sabines of old, has only recently set foot in our city." (cited by La Penna [1977] 182).

[30] The preceding allusion (3.16) to the Camenae being evicted from their grove and the wood reduced to beggary also maintains the note of regret for the numinous world of woodland.

However, as Eleanor Leach shows in her paper "Horace and the Material Culture of Augustan Rome," we cannot assume a simple monolithic attitude to urban change on the part of our poets, or of Augustus himself.[31] Horace reflects in *Odes* 2.15 the appeal of the very pleasure gardens he is deprecating, and his enjoyment of material luxury colors many other poems. Augustus too cultivated his reputation for simple living[32] and certainly condemned the ostentation of private luxury in building: the demolition of Vedius Pollio's palace was as much a reaction against the man's luxury as against his notorious cruelty.[33] But however modest Augustus' private living space, his precinct, once enhanced by the Apolline temple and its libraries, and later the shrine of Vesta, took on the glory of a public monument, and the *princeps*, with a personal wealth from inheritance and spoils equal to or greater than that of the state treasury, would add further monuments from his own pocket.[34]

I think we forget that what Augustus was replacing may have once been woodland and hills, but surely was no longer green by the time he purchased the ground needed for the new Rome. Most probably the contemporary Republican city was nothing for a sentimentalist to regret. Hence Propertius may well have had no cause to feel or conceal resentment of the fine new public buildings, but at the same time his poetic imagination turns away from the city around him in nostalgic distaste. His imaginative preference for the distant past emerges from details, such as the epithets in 4.1a: alluding to primitive materials and textures (earthenware, artless, skin-clad (twice!), rustic, bristly, lean, cheap and rough) and to modest scale and simplicity (*nuda, parva*)[35] all associated with emotive words like *prisci, patrio, annua.*

The elegist is clearly not unhappy with the unofficial city of Vertumnus, the Subura and his well-watered Esquiline; and he is careful to give praise

---

[31] Pp. 105–21 of this volume, esp. 116–18.

[32] Cf. Suet., *Aug.* 73: "he later lived on the Palatine but in the modest house of Hortensius, conspicuous neither for its expanse nor its adornment, having only short porticos with Alban columns and inner rooms without any marble or notable mosaic pavement." The "house of Augustus" certainly has a simpler decor than the later Julio-Claudian and Flavian palaces, but Hortensius was in his day a by-word for luxury.

[33] On Vedius' palace, and his *luxuria*, cf. Ovid, *Fasti*. 6.640–4, *quia luxuria visa nocere sua* "because it seemed corrupting by its luxury" and Tac., *Ann.* 1.10.5.

[34] Much of his wealth came from his father. As Lucan would comment on Julius in 49 BCE, "now *for the first time Rome was poorer than (a) Caesar*" (*BC* 3.163) For money paid out from Augustus' private purse, cf. *Res Gestae* 16–18, and add 19–21 for public monuments restored or built "from the proceeds of booty."

[35] La Penna (1977:90), is more justified in speaking of Propertius' love of rustic purity and poverty than in attributing to this fourth book the association of contemporary splendor with excess and corruption. Poems in Propertius' earlier books denounce the present *mores* chiefly in connection with sexual licence and infidelity. The only criticism of current behaviour that I find in book 4 is the implied condemnation of foreign cults in 4.1.17.

to Augustus' new Palatine precinct in 2.31 and 4.1. But Propertius' recurring evocations of natural untilled land, in particular the *loci amoeni* of 4.4. and 4.9 24–30, are reinforced by his encomiastic use of *Natura* (cf. 2.18.25, 3.22.18) and the adjective *nativus* for the natural beauty of seashells (1.2.13), the lush natural couch of grass (*nativus torus* 3.13.36), and the natural springs (*nativae . . . aquae* 4.4.4) of Tarpeia's grove. Propertius' old Rome is full of trees, undergrowth and brooklets, exploiting to the full the traditional picture of wooded hills that we find in Dionysius of Halicarnassus (2.15.4 on the grove of the asylum) and *Aeneid* 8 (of the copses and brambles of the Capitoline): Virgil's brambles and thickets (*dumi, Aen.* 8 348, repeated 657; *vepres*, 8.645) are recalled by Propertius' hairy brambles *hirsuti . . . rubi* (4.4.27): his Capitoline is moist with dew and rivulets (4.4.48, 50), his Palatine and Capitoline alike blossom with epithets of natural abundance, rich in ivy, foliage, cattle, and shade (*hederoso, ramosa, pecorosa, umbroso*: 4.4.3; 4.4.5; 4.9.3; 4.9.24) a pastoral world also recalled in more overtly idyllic settings like the passage on the happiness of former young country people in 3.13.25 (*felix agrestum quondam pacta iuventus*) mentioned above. The best evidence for Propertian regret of the present built-up city and its marble monuments is this sensual delight in the unsettled wilderness surrounding Rome's first citizens.

Propertius is not, after all, aiming to write bucolic poetry:[36] neither his Tarpeia nor his Hercules is represented as enjoying the spring and shade of the pre-civic landscape. Yet without any generic pressure to enhance the wilderness the poet has let his image of Rome be dominated by groves and grottoes and waters that outbid the glitter and luxury of the new Augustan city: against the ostensible glorification of the gilded and marble temples and their precincts, the lost – and irretrievable – natural innocence of the unpopulated pre-urban community emerges as the world privileged by both the former dissident and the ostensibly reconciled composer of patriotic elegy.

---

[36] But La Penna (1977:86), rightly stresses the bucolic setting of Tarpeia's passionate love.

8   Livy's revolution: civic identity and the creation of the *res publica*[1]

Andrew Feldherr

In the opening paper of this collection, Andrew Wallace-Hadrill maps the intellectual frontiers of Augustus' *imperium*: the *princeps'* appropriation of political power coincides with and depends upon the rationalization and codification of knowledge about Rome and her institutions that made such information uniform, capable of dissemination throughout the empire, and independent of the social authority of the *nobiles*. The result of this decoupling of systems of knowledge from local authority was nothing less than a "new sense of being Roman." At almost the same time that Augustus consolidated his political control over the Roman world, another similarly ambitious attempt at creating a unified and comprehensive picture of the totality of the Roman state was under way: the historian Livy, whose own city had just received full Roman citizenship in 49 BCE, and who from the beginning of his text advertises the fact that he is not a member of the *nobilitas*, nevertheless promises to "write out in full the history of the Roman people from the origin of the city" (*praef.* 1). The expression not only suggests the comprehensiveness of his account but also lends it the character of a final, official version; the same verb, *perscribere*, is also used of the written record that gave legitimacy to senatorial decrees.[2] So too Livy ends his preface with a prayer to the gods that recalls the practices both of the poets who glorified Rome's origins and of a consul setting out on campaign.[3]

---

[1] This paper was developed from parts of my 1991 dissertation at the University of California, Berkeley. In that form it profited from the criticism of my advisers, E. S. Gruen, T. N. Habinek, T. G. Rosenmeyer. I am also grateful to my wife Deborah Steiner and to the participants of the "Roman Cultural Revolution" conference at Princeton, in particular to Richard Saller, for their many helpful suggestions. The flaws that remain are my own.

[2] Cf., e.g., Caes., *B.C.* 1.6, Cic., *Cat.* 3.13, and for the procedure Mommsen (1888:3.1003ff.). The verb also helps define Livy's place in the historiographic tradition: Sempronius Asellio in his preface (fr. 1 *HRR*) contrasts authors of *historiae*, who attempt to narrate events thoroughly (*perscribere*) with the producers of *annales*, which merely recount "what was done and in what year it happened."

[3] Ogilvie (1965:29). Cf. especially 45.39.10, *maiores vestri omnium magnarum rerum et principia exorsi a dis sunt, et finem statuerunt.*

The place of Livy's text in an Augustan "cultural revolution" has been among the most debated issues in Roman historiography and has yielded an astonishing variety of conclusions. Livy has appeared as Augustus' "improving publicist," in Syme's notorious phrase, and conversely as a staunch republican.[4] What all such approaches share, however, is a presumption of the priority of political action over literary creation. Whether Livy approves or disapproves of the Augustan regime, he can only react. Yet not only does Livy's preface fail to mention any political figure; as we have seen, it also appropriates the language of political activity to describe the historian's task. Thus a more productive starting-point takes seriously Livy's claim that his *History* can act autonomously as an instrument of social and political change.[5] The aim of this paper is to illustrate how Livy's text can perform such a function through an analysis of his narrative of perhaps the single most significant transformation to affect the Roman state in his text, the end of the monarchy and beginning of the republic. The "revolution"[6] accomplished by L. Junius Brutus in 509 BCE was the event that brought into being a distinctively Roman ordering of political authority. However, as we shall see, the constitutional aspects of this change depend upon a more profound shift in each Roman citizen's sense of civic identity, the nature of which mirrors first-century anxieties about the individual's place in the Roman state. Within Livy's text, this revolution in consciousness can in turn be correlated with a change in the systems of communication and representation by which the individual is brought into contact with the collective authority of the state. The public spectacles staged and orchestrated by Brutus serve as the means through which the new state is built and finally provide a model for how Livy's narrative, by representing the same events, can itself generate "a new sense of being Roman" among its own audience.

---

[4] For recent surveys of the range of positions that have been taken see Badian (1993), Deininger (1985), and Kraus (1994:6–8). The phrase "improving publicist" will be found in Syme (1959:76).

[5] Cf. the comments of Kraus (1994:8–9): ". . . the historian's project parallels/rivals Augustus' own building of a new Rome via (re)construction of its past. . . . But a shared project does not necessarily mean a lack of independence." Starting from a different perspective, Miles (1995:8–74) has recently argued that Livy's demonstration of the ultimate unreliability of the records upon which any narrative of the past depends serves both to undermine any attempt to create an authoritative account of how things actually happened and correspondingly to emphasize the moral function of history, its capacity to shape and perpetuate an image of national identity. This strategy also redresses the inequality in social status which placed Livy the Paduan at a disadvantage in comparison with aristocratic historians.

Luce (1990) offers a particularly striking demonstration that Livy's *History* did not constitute an official Augustan version of the past by pointing out the variations between the *tituli* inscribed on the statues of Roman heroes in the Forum Augustum and Livy's accounts of their deeds.

[6] Given the cautions of Wallace-Hadrill, the phrase is used advisedly. Livy's term for the transformation is "*libertatis origo*" (2.1.7).

The fundamental principle of the new order that followed upon the expulsion of the Tarquins can be found in the first sentence, indeed in the first word, of Livy's second book, which begins just after the end of the *regnum: liberi iam hinc* (2.1.1). *Libertas*, the power of law exceeding the power of men, defines the Republic against the monarchy. Yet the semantic range of the word *liberi* extends beyond the simple absence of a tyrant to describe the civic status of each individual Roman as a free citizen as opposed to a slave.[7] Later in this introduction Livy highlights the interdependence between the transformation of the state as a whole and the personal development of each Roman as citizen, both of which are implicit in the word *liberi*. *Libertas*, according to Livy, was only possible when Rome had already been in existence long enough for the original population of shepherds and exiles to feel a sense of communal loyalty sufficient to survive the storms of faction (2.1.5). Thus the state cannot achieve its final form until its individual members develop a sense of belonging to the community, and correspondingly Livy's narrative integrates the creation of the Republic with the development on the part of the individual of a new sense of civic identity. Livy's *regnum* and republic epitomize radically different views of the hierarchy of social bonds that construct identity. This difference in turn affects every level of social organization and is particularly revealed in the tension between family and state as *loci* of loyalty and affection. For yet a third meaning of *liberi* is children, and it is through Brutus' execution of his own *liberi* for conspiring to recall the Tarquins, that the establishment of *libertas* is completed.[8]

Reasons why issues of belonging and civic identity should permeate accounts of Rome's origins written in the late first century are not far to seek. The citizen population had grown from 395,000 in 115 BCE to about 1.5 million in 28 BCE, according to a conservative estimate.[9] Not only did this vast population of new Romans, who were already *cives* of their own cities, have to think of themselves as members of the Roman *patria*, but in the face of such expansion the very term *civis*, which originally described a participant in a tangible community of peers, required redefinition for all citizens.[10]

---

[7] On the connections between *libertas* and *civitas* see especially Wirszubski (1950:3ff.).

[8] For another analysis of the implications of this passage for Livy's conceptions of "the process of social unification," and particularly of how the importance of connections to family and locality for the consolidation of the state figures in Livy's narrative of the monarchy, see Phillips (1979).

[9] See Brunt (1971:13–14) for the statistical evidence. The census figure for 28 BCE is given at *Res Gestae* 8.2 as over four million, which Brunt assumes is only conceivable if it includes women and children.

[10] On the vast problems of citizenship see the standard treatment by Sherwin-White (1973) and particularly Nicolet (1988:21–3). The meaning and derivation of *civis* are discussed by Benveniste (1969:1.335–7).

Nor is it inappropriate to adopt the perspective of the individual citizen here. The Romans themselves recognized that the subjective dimension, the individual's identification of himself as a Roman citizen, was fully as important as issues of law and public procedure in questions of citizenship. Thus Cicero in the *Pro Balbo* claims that "our *ius civitatis mutandae* ... depends not only on public laws but also on the will of the private citizen." (*Pro Balb.* 27).

The choice to accept Rome as his *patria* is one that Livy as a new citizen himself would have faced. A member of a well-connected Paduan family, the historian was fully conversant with the local traditions and history of his birthplace, and, unlike any of the other non-Roman Augustan writers, he died in the city where he was born.[11] Livy's Paduan origins not only provided ammunition for his contemporary rival, Asinius Pollio, who criticized Livy's style for its *Patavinitas*,[12] they also manifest themselves in his text and give a particular significance to the starting-point he chooses for his narrative. Livy begins his history of Rome with an account of two Trojan exiles: in addition to Aeneas' settlement in Latium, another Trojan, Antenor, successfully fled to Italy and became the ancestor of the Veneti. Therefore just as the Roman state has its origins in the loss of a previous fatherland, Troy, so too the creation of Livy's text depends on the historian's own decision to tell the story of his Roman *patria* rather than the alternative narrative of his native people the Veneti. The displacement of an earlier *patria* similarly affects other outsiders incorporated into the Roman state during the first book, most notably the Albans whose Romanization coincides with the actual destruction of their native city (1.29).

Cicero's philosophical writings show how the changing definition of citizenship could affect the individual and help to define the Romans' conceptualization of the relationship between patriotism and loyalty to the family and other social groups. Although Cicero was a Roman citizen by birth and even the *pater patriae*, he is still at pains to define what that *patria* is. As book two of the *De legibus* begins, Cicero and Atticus are wandering by the river

---

[11] The importance of Livy's ties to his native city are stressed by Leeman (1961) and especially Bonjour (1975b:185, 249–50). Within the history, Paduan local traditions emerge not only at 1.1, but also in the description of the failed Laconian expedition into Paduan territory at 10.2.4–15, commemorated both by the spoils displayed at Padua in the temple of Juno, and by an annual re-enactment of the naval battle. More strikingly, in his account of the battle of Pharsalus, Livy includes a description of the prodigies that announced the battle at Padua, and were interpreted by a local augur, C. Cornelius, who was a relative of the historian (Plut. *Caes.* 47).

[12] Quint. *I.O.* 1.5.56, 8.1.3. The scholarship on the precise implications of this charge is vast. A recent survey will be found in Flobert (1981), who argues that the primary thrust of the term lies in its contrast not to *latinitas* but to *urbanitas*.

Fibrenus on Cicero's native estate at Arpinum. Atticus is surprised to hear Cicero refer to Arpinum as his *patria*, and Cicero responds by asserting that "everyone from the towns has two *patriae*, one of nature, and one of citizenship" (*De leg.* 2.5). The hoary distinction between law and nature has a special significance for the *De legibus*, but it also parallels the link between public laws and private will that we saw in the passage from the *Pro Balbo*. It would be one thing if Cicero's two *patriae* could be neatly divided into the spheres of legality and affection, if Roman citizenship simply constituted an extra level of obligation that was distinct from and not in competition with pre-existing loyalties to the natural *patria*.[13] But patriotism involves affections as well as obligations. "It is necessary," Cicero continues, "that the *patria*, where the name of *res publica* is a marker of our common citizenship, stand first in our affections; for which we ought to die and to which we ought to devote ourselves entirely and upon which, as upon an altar, we ought to set and as it were sacrifice all our goods. However, the *patria* which bore us is dear in almost the same way as that which receives us" (*De leg.* 2.5). Thus the same criterion of affection, *caritas*, is used to measure the bonds to both the smaller and the larger *patria*.[14]

It was not only the native town that could offer a challenge to civic identity. A passage of Cicero's *De officiis* locates the Roman male at the midpoint of a concentric pattern of social entities, extending from the family to the entire species, all of which placed demands on his affections and loyalties. In this passage too there is a tension between a motion inwards, by which the nearest bond of family ought to prevail, and a motion outwards, by which every outer layer of society, because it encloses the nearer bonds, requires greater obligations. "No association is graver, none is dearer than that which binds each one of us to the Republic. Our parents are dear (*cari*), our children are dear, but one *patria* embraces all the affections of all men; on behalf of which what good man would hesitate to seek death, if he might benefit her?"[15] On the one hand civic loyalty is a natural extension of all

---

[13] This is the view of Nicolet (1988:45–7), who claims that the Romans avoided such a conflict of obligations by creating "two levels of citizenship."

[14] For a further analysis of this passage and Cicero's treatment of the conflict of loyalties it reveals, see Bonjour (1975b:78–86).

[15] Cic. *De off.* 1.57. Bonjour (1975b:59–65) similarly describes the inherent ambiguity of terms like *pietas*, *caritas*, and *amor*, which were used to describe sentiments toward both the fatherland and the family. On the word *caritas* see Hellegouarc'h (1963:148–9). Based largely on Cicero, *Part.* 88, scholars have proposed various distinctions between the terms *amor* and *caritas*. Both may be applied to family, but while *amor* is the natural result of *usus* and *familiaritas*, *caritas* implies some choice and is therefore especially suitable to affections towards more distant or abstract persons and organizations. But for our purposes it is enough that *caritas* too describes an affective bond which is here applied both to the family and to the *patria*.

other affections. If you love your wife and children you will necessarily love the Republic which encompasses and protects them. Except you have to love the Republic more. It is not enough to serve the Republic simply as a means of preserving your family; at a certain point you must measure the Republic on the same scale of *caritas* as the family, and the Republic must prevail.[16]

The schema put forward in Cicero's writings, by which *caritas* is built outward from the inner core of the family to include the state, directly informs Livy's discussion of loyalty to the *res publica* in the preface to book two. The factors that have sufficiently bound the wandering peoples to one another are "love of wives and children and the *caritas* of the place itself" (*pignera coniugum ac liberorum caritasque ipsius soli*, 2.1.5). Livy's first book includes a clear illustration of how love of children and wives can bind citizens to one another. After the rape of the Sabine women, Romans and Sabines are united as a people because of their mutual affection for the Sabine women who are wives to the Romans and children to the Sabines.[17] And in the later books of Livy's narrative many mutinies will be quelled by the sight of wives and children, most famously Coriolanus' in the middle of the second book itself. *Caritas ipsius soli* will form the theme of Camillus' great speech at the end of the first pentad.[18]

But beyond simply reproducing the Ciceronian model of patriotism, Livy has devoted his second book to the tensions inherent in the conflicting claims of more immediate groups and the new conception of the *res publica*. Indeed in his narrative of the transition from monarchy to Republic, Livy also chronicles that crucial moment in the education of every citizen at which the Republic becomes dearer than family. The structure of the book highlights the individual's struggle between family loyalty and state loyalty. Thus Brutus'

---

[16] Cf. Bonjour (1975b:64) on the relationship of the two *patriae*: "Il est évident que le *de legibus* (2.5) ne fait qu'une différence quantitative, et non qualitative dans la *caritas* selon qu'elle se rapporte à la grande ou à la petite patrie."

My purpose is not to suggest that the family is an exclusively private entity. The work of Thomas (1984) in particular has demonstrated the extent to which family relations were always public in the sense that they were recognized, controlled by, and integrated into the public life of the state. The point is rather that according to the subjective terms used by Cicero and Livy, the integration of family and civic roles becomes a locus of tension and conflict; it cannot be taken to be self-evident and unproblematic.

[17] 1.13, a passage whose connection with the preface to book 2 is confirmed by similarities in language. For example, with *animos . . . consociassent* (2.1.5), compare *regnum consociant* (1.13.4). So also Phillips (1979:89).

[18] For appeals to wives and children cf., e.g., 7.40.12. On the Coriolanus episode, 2.39–40, see especially Bonjour (1975a). Bonjour (1975b:66–8) gives other examples of how ties to family are accentuated in patriotic exhortations throughout Livy's text. *Caritas ipsius soli* is especially emphasized at 5.54.1–4.

execution of his sons forms the beginning and Coriolanus' abortive mutiny occurs at the center. This event is followed ten chapters later by the scene in which the Fabian *gens* undertakes the Republic's war with Veii, almost at the cost of its own destruction (2.48–50). Livy also includes parables which are used within the text explicitly to educate citizens to think of the state not only as the protector of the family but in the same terms as family and even body. Thus in a kind of prelude to the education of Coriolanus, the plebeian Titus Latinius receives a prophetic dream warning him of a danger to the state if there is not a ritual repetition of improperly performed *ludi*.[19] Latinius is afraid that he will be laughed at if he tells anyone and so disregards the dream. A few days later his son dies. When he hesitates even longer, his own body is stricken with disease. The event implies more than the interconnectedness of family and state, it suggests an analogy between them. The *res publica* is a family or body in macrocosm. This is also the point of the famous parable of the belly and the limbs, which the patrician Menenius Agrippa tells to a group of plebeians who are trying to sever the bonds to the state which Livy stresses in his preface to the second book (2.32.8–12). When the limbs, or plebeians, begrudge food to the belly, which represents the patricians, they themselves begin to fail. Here again the image of the body is used as part of a rhetoric of inclusion.

Thus what is at stake in the transition between monarchy and Republic is not simply a system of government nor even liberty as opposed to tyranny but a fundamentally different interaction between the individual and the social entities that enclose him, and therefore a novel conception of individual identity. So too Livy's portrait of the Tarquins emphasizes a sense of obligations that is directly the reverse of the Republican citizen's. The last Tarquins continually overprivilege the family against the state. When the Tarquins first appear in book one, they are wanderers who have come from Corinth to Tarquinia to Rome (1.34.1–2). Thus they are just like all the other original Romans, also exiles. Yet the Tarquins ultimately fail to make the connection to place that other Romans have, and they leave the narrative just as they entered it, wandering among the cities of Etruria seeking aid for their clan. Tarquinius Superbus gains the throne by the deposition and murder of Servius Tullius. He justifies this act on the grounds that he is the son of Tarquinius Priscus. Tarquin claims that "he has occupied the throne of his father, and much better the king's son be the heir to the kingdom than the king's slave" (*se patris sui tenere sedem; multo quam servum potiorem filium regis regni heredem*, 1.48.2). Not only does he define public status on the basis of domestic status, but in so doing he reverses one of the great models

---

[19] 2.36; cf., Cic., *De div.* 1.55.

of inclusion formulated under the monarchy, the adoption of Servius Tullius. Tarquinius Superbus is as devoted to his sons as he is to his father.[20] As a ruse to overcome the town of Gabii, Sextus Tarquinius pretends that his father the king has finally turned against his own family and forced him into exile (1.53.6). The young Tarquin's lie to the Gabines only highlights the essential closeness between father and son. The contrast between Tarquinius Superbus and Brutus in this regard receives its final illustration when, after Brutus has watched his own sons executed for plotting against the state, Tarquin is immediately described begging his Etruscan allies "not to allow him to perish before their eyes with his adolescent sons."[21]

The transition from monarchy to Republic could have been construed as a simple dynastic transition; both of the first consuls, Collatinus and Brutus, were related to the Tarquins.[22] What is more, Brutus' motive for hating Tarquinius could have been portrayed as revenge for the murder of his own father and brother.[23] Yet unlike the accession of Superbus, the creation of the Republic is not the result of either revenge or family ambition. In fact the first appearance of Brutus in the narrative occurs in a context where his values are explicitly contrasted with the Tarquins'. A terrifying portent occurs; a snake emerges from a wooden column and causes panic in the royal

---

[20] The importance of this theme in Livy's account of the reign of Tarquinius Superbus is also highlighted by Dumézil (1949), who argues that the indulgence shown by Tarquin toward his sons contrasts specifically with Roman ideals of fatherhood and thus helps delineate the Etruscan character of their reign.

[21] *cum liberis adulescentibus*, 2.6.2. The same phrase was used to describe Brutus' sons two chapters before at 2.4.1.

[22] For Brutus and Collatinus as dynastic successors of Tarquinius Superbus, see Gantz (1975: 546–8).

Bettini (1991:48–52) uses the legends about Brutus and Collatinus as an illustration of the opposition between the affectionate *avunculus*, represented by Collatinus who desires to spare his sister's sons the Vitellii, and the disciplinarian *pater*. What is remarkable is that Livy's version seems to de-emphasize the role of family bonds. The two avuncular relationships sketched in Livy are those between the Vitellii and the sons of Brutus (2.4.1), where I will suggest that it contributes to the characterization of the conspiracy's anti-republican nature, and that between Tarquin himself and Brutus' brother, whom he puts to death (1.56.7). The latter case is treated by Bettini as the exception that proves the rule: Tarquin is so monstrous that he even kills his sister's sons. The reference to family relationships in this passage also perhaps contrasts with Brutus' perspective, if the point of the Delphic embassy is the redefinition of the term *mater*. On this see below.

[23] Indeed the whole episode was the subject of a tragedy by Accius which seems to have begun with Tarquin recounting a dream in which he sacrificed one of two brother rams and was then butted and knocked down by the survivor (Acc., *Prae.* 17–38 Ribbeck = Cic., *De div.* 1.44). But even here the emphasis seems less on revenge as such than on the deceptive appearance of the sheep, which corresponds to Brutus' deceptively harmless exterior.

palace.[24] Tarquin, typically confusing the boundary between public and private, refuses to summon the haruspices, as he ought to do for a public prodigy, and instead sends his sons to consult the Delphic oracle.[25] Brutus, who has always pretended to be a fool in order to protect himself, is sent along with them, as Livy says, more as a source of fun, a *ludibrium*, than as a companion. The oracle's response to the king's inquiry is not recorded. But when the sons themselves ask who will be the next to rule at Rome, they are told that it will be the next to kiss his mother. Brutus, correctly solving the riddle of the oracle, realizes that the earth is the common mother of all mortals, feigns stumbling and kisses the ground. The riddle is of course an ancient one, with parallels in Herodotus and elsewhere,[26] but in this context it takes on a particular significance; it drives home the point that whereas the Tarquins think only in terms of the family, Brutus has made the conceptual leap to apply the vocabulary of family to larger communities. Correspondingly the imagery of the family is transformed from something exclusive, which differentiates Tarquins from others, to a means of inclusion:[27] the earth is a common mother. In fact the language used to describe the earth, *communis mater omnium mortalium* recalls Cicero's argument for the supremacy of the larger *patria*.[28] Thus the passage may be related to the Ciceronian transition by which the largest community supersedes the smaller in the individual's affections.

The first two events of the Republic, the expulsion of Collatinus and the execution of Brutus' sons, confirm and extend the process of redefinition of state and family. In the versions of these events given by Plutarch and Dionysius the sequence is reversed: the banishment of Collatinus follows after and results from the trial of Brutus' sons for treason.[29] After Brutus has executed his own sons, Collatinus wishes to spare his nephews, who were also involved in the conspiracy. This is the reason that his own loyalty to the

---

[24] Ogilvie (1965:216) suggests that the manuscript reading *in regiam* be retained in place of Bauer's *in regia* and that therefore the portent did not occur in the *regia* itself. He supports this on the grounds that there were no wooden columns in the original *regia*.

[25] 1.56.4ff. Ogilvie (1965:217) points out that even if the prodigy did occur in the *regia*, it ought still to have been considered public. However he attributes the error not to the king but to the annalistic tradition. Thus the "tendentious" language of 1.56.5 indicates that an earlier annalist felt the need to justify grafting the episode of the Delphic embassy onto the occasion of the snake portent. I would argue that Livy's emphasis serves to highlight the confusion of public and private within the narrative.

[26] Herodotus 6.107. Cf. also the dream of Julius Caesar, Suet., *Caes*. 7.

[27] Brutus' natural mother was in fact a Tarquinia and thus the source of his familial connection with the king (1.56.7).

[28] Thus the *patria iuris* must stand first in our affections because it is a universal bond (*universae civitatis, De leg*. 2.5). So too at *De off*. 1.57 the large *patria* "embraces all the ties of all men," (*omnes omnium caritates*).

[29] Dion., *Ant*. 5.7.4ff; Plut., *Publicola* 4.3–5.2.

state came under suspicion. In Livy's version, however, Collatinus has done nothing to deserve banishment. His only offence is his *nomen*, Tarquinius. Thus the effect of Livy's order is to highlight the issue of family membership in the expulsion of Collatinus. Furthermore, the conspiracy of the sons of Brutus to recall the Tarquins is not simply a monarchist plot but results from the entire civic and social outlook that we have defined as typical of the last kings. Whereas Livy virtually defines the Republic as a time when the rule of law was more powerful than the rule of men, *imperia legum potentiora quam hominum* (2.1.1 and 2.3.3–4), the conspiracy of the sons of Brutus prefers a man, *homo*, to laws. "A man can be entreated, when there is need of justice or injustice, favor and obligation have some scope, a man can get angry and forgive, a man knows the difference between a friend and an enemy."[30] In other words a man is subject to all sorts of influences which depend upon his personal, as opposed to his public status. He is prone to precisely the same impulses that bind a man to family rather than to state. Similarly, the young conspirators are bound to the conspiracy because of their birth and family connections. Thus the sons of Brutus are admitted into the conspiracy by their maternal uncles, the Vitellii (2.4.1).

In contrast to their conspiracy, the execution of the sons of Brutus represents the final rejection of the social conceptions of the *regnum*, and, through Livy's explicit description of the event as an *exemplum*, establishes a timeless model of the values underlying Roman citizenship. In presiding as a magistrate over the execution of his sons, Brutus adopts the role defined by his position in the state rather than in the family. (It is as magistrate that Brutus acts, there is no question of *patria potestas* here.)[31] Furthermore the execution cannot be understood in isolation, but is complemented by the grant of *libertas* and *civitas* to Vindicius, the slave who revealed the conspiracy (*ut in utramque partem arcendis sceleribus exemplum nobile esset*, 2.5.9). The Republican concept of civic identity, unlike a hierarchy which privileges only birth, allows for the incorporation of new citizens. Hence Vindicius, who was a slave within the *familia*, becomes a citizen in the same ceremony in which Brutus' children are executed (2.5.9–10). The connection of the two actions also provides a final demonstration of the inseparability of individual *libertas*, that of the new *civis* Vindicius, and the collective *libertas* of the state, which the defeat of the conspiracy secures.

---

[30] *regem hominem esse a quo impetres ubi ius, ubi iniuria opus sit; esse gratiae locum, esse beneficio; et irasci et ignoscere posse; inter amicum et inimicum discrimen nosse*, 2.3.3. The references to *beneficia*, *gratiae*, and *amicitia* recall particularly the language of political competition among the Republican aristocracy and thus give a special relevance to Livy's diagnosis of the threats to *libertas*. Ogilvie (1965:243) detects a Late Republican patina in the language of the entire episode.

[31] First observed by Mommsen (1889:22). See below, pp. 152ff.

The shifts in public forms and individual values encoded in the expulsion of the Tarquins are accompanied by yet another transition, which is signaled most clearly in Livy's narrative of the rape of Lucretia and its aftermath. This transition involves the manner in which public and private, individual and state, are brought into contact through media of public display. Not only do the figures within the text manipulate appearances in characteristic ways to control public opinion, but Livy himself associates the monarchy with a distinctive genre of public spectacle, drama. Brutus' expulsion of the Tarquins, on the other hand, depends upon the effective use of spectacles to engender within his audience precisely the sense of civic identity upon which the Republic is predicated.

Under Tarquin the emphasis on the private as opposed to the public and common creates a disjunction between what the king intends and what he allows to be publicly perceived. The king's intentions recede from public view. In war Tarquin relies on deception and guile, as Livy says, the least Roman arts (1.53.4). Hence the strategy for the conquest of Gabii (1.53.4–1.54.10). After Tarquin's son, like Zopyrus at Babylon, has cunningly won the confidence of the Gabines, he sends a messenger to his father. Tarquin, strolling through his garden, makes no response to the messenger but begins to knock off the heads of poppies with his staff. The messenger gets bored and leaves, assuming there is no message, but the son of course understands and has the most important Gabines killed. In this story, father and son alone share a secret language (*tacitis ambagibus*) which is inaccessible to any outside observer.

No event better illustrates the connection between the inversion in social perspective and the inversion of public spectacle under the reign of Tarquin than the overthrow of Servius Tullius. As we have seen, Tarquin's claim to the throne is based upon inheritance. In considering Servius a slave rather than a king, Tarquin defines him by his position within the family rather than his position within the state. The supremacy of the private, family space also appears in the setting of the story. Tarquin must be persuaded to kill the king by his wife, Tullia (1.47.1–6). These exhortations, though they will influence the course of public events, are known only to Tarquin and Tullia. Thus what Tarquin says and does in the Forum when he usurps the royal throne results from motivations that are hidden in two senses. The constitutional justifications that he quotes serve only to conceal his personal ambitions, and these ambitions are kindled in private conversations removed from the gaze of the state (1.47.8–12).

The eruption of family ambitions into public life also manifests itself in a violation of the decorum of public spectacle which occurs just at the moment when Tarquin takes power. At this instant Tullia herself not only appears in her chariot in the middle of the Forum, but actually calls Tarquin forth from the Senate and becomes the first to proclaim him king (1.48.5–6). The impropriety of her appearance in public is emphasized by Livy's comment that she feels no shame at appearing before an assembly of men, and Tarquin himself orders her to leave.

The incongruous prominence of Tullia in the narrative may be connected with another aspect of the historian's presentation of the *regnum*. Livy describes the death of Servius as a tragic crime, produced by the royal palace itself, which also functions almost as a stage set through which Tullia enters and exits (*tulit enim et Romana regia sceleris tragici exemplum*, 1.46.3). Far from simply exemplifying what we might call tragic history, the seamless absorption of tragic techniques to intensify historical narrative, Livy's reference to tragedy actually serves to set his account of this reign apart from the events that surround it. Thus this disruption in the fabric of the narrative corresponds to the improper appearance of Tullia as a sign of the rift that divides this regime from the rest of Roman history.[32]

If the spectacles of the last king concealed private motives from the eyes of the people, then the foundation of the Republic, by which the true center of civic power is restored to the public sphere, is accomplished through an opening outward, a process of revealing what has been concealed. Thus the end of the monarchy depends upon driving Tullia, the symbol of the hidden dynastic machinations of the Tarquinii, out of the palace. The fall of the dynasty is predicted by a serpent gliding out of a wooden column. The motif of revelation appears particularly in Livy's presentation of Brutus himself. Brutus had pretended to be slow-witted and took his name, which means stupid or sluggish, "in order that under the concealment of that *cognomen*, the spirit that would be the liberator of the Roman people might lie hidden, biding its time" (1.56.8). Brutus represents his character by means of a sign he carries with him, a cornel-wood staff that has been hollowed out to contain a gold wand (1.56.9). This sign operates through riddles, *per ambages*, and it is in the solution of another riddle, that of the Delphic oracle, that Brutus' succession is itself confirmed. This emphasis on riddles is significant because concealed or hidden meaning was one of the characteristics of the Tarquins' communication. Tarquin speaks to his son in *ambages*; Brutus, himself a riddle to be solved, succeeds through his skill at understanding hidden meanings. In fact since the prodigy of the serpent appearing from the wooden column is never actually interpreted, I would suggest that it signifies Brutus himself, whose sign is the gold wand in the wooden staff.

This cluster of images is concentrated two chapters before the central revelation that leads to the overthrow of the monarchy, the revelation of the body

---

[32] Woodman (1992) has shown that Tacitus similarly excises the tyrannical reign of Nero from his narrative by treating it in an anomalously Herodotean style.

of Lucretia. When Tullia pollutes her Penates with the blood of Servius Tullius, their anger is said to insure that this *regnum* will have an end like its beginnings (1.48.7). And indeed the episode which brings about the end of the Tarquins' power is also marked by a transgression of the boundaries of public and private, family and state, which symmetrically answers the disruptions by which the Tarquins gained the throne. Then Tullia, riding out of the *regia*, had not felt shame at appearing before the assembly of men (*nec reverita coetum virorum*, 1.48.5). The Lucretia episode begins when a group of men, leaving the battlefield, enter a *domus* which is inhabited by a truly modest wife. Within the tale, the initial intrusion of Tarquinius is balanced by the exposure of Lucretia's body to an ever expanding circle of spectators. Sextus had threatened that if Lucretia did not consent to his attack, he would put a naked slave next to her corpse to make it seem as though she had been unfaithful (1.58.4). This may be read as the dynasty's final attempt to use appearances to conceal rather than reveal. Lucretia on the other hand kills herself openly, in the presence of her family; her death is combined with a revelation of the secret deeds of the prince. Her body is then carried out of the house and put on display in the forum at Collatia, the ancestral village of the Collatini; next Brutus goes on to narrate her violation in public at Rome itself. Not only does this process generally predict the expansion of individual loyalties described in the preface to the second book, the particular locations where the public revelation takes place even correspond to the levels of communal bond described in Cicero's *De officiis.* The *familia* is succeeded by Collatia, the *patria loci*, or native *patria*, which is followed finally by Rome the center of the *patria civitatis.*

The process of publication in the case of Lucretia also involves a shift in the type of spectacle by which the crime is represented. As a recapitulation of the entire *regnum*, it is appropriate that the rape of Lucretia begin as a drama. Ogilvie and other commentators have invoked both comedy and tragedy to describe the episode. In particular, the idea of a contest of wives has been referred to New Comedy.[33] Here it suffices to observe that Livy both describes the event as a *ludus* and inserts expressions appropriate for stage dialogue, such as *satin salve?* and *age sane.*[34] Yet as the narrative progresses, the dramatic beginning, which corresponds to the motion from battlefield to *domus*, is replaced by the spectacle of the corpse itself on display in the forum. But there is another dimension to this shift, which takes an event of essentially private significance, and invests it with historical consequences for the entire state; here the paradigm of sacrifice is introduced as a new means of portraying Lucretia's death. The reconception of her suicide as a sacrifice

---

[33] Ogilvie (1965:219 and 222), who cites parallels.

[34] *ludus*, 1.57.11; *age sane*, 1.57.8; *satin salve*, 1.58.7. The last two are only the most striking examples of dramatic turns of phrase catalogued by Ogilvie.

is accomplished through the gesture of the oath which Brutus, who chooses this moment to reveal himself, forces the other spectators of the suicide to swear. "As the others were absorbed in mourning, Brutus snatching the knife from the wound and holding it, still dripping with blood, before him says 'By this blood, *castissimum* before the royal injustice, I swear, and I make you gods my witnesses, to drive out with fire, sword and whatever force I might, Tarquinius Superbus together with his criminal wife and children'" (1.59.1). Both gesture and language contribute to the sacralization of the scene. An oath sworn by blood is rare in Roman religion,[35] but where blood is used in ritual, it often derives from sacrificial victims or appears in a sacrificial context.[36] And *coniurationes* were usually confirmed through sacrifice.[37] The word *castissimum* is also relevant here; though Lucretia as an *univira* was sexually chaste, the adjective *castus* is also used for ritual purity. In fact this is its customary meaning in Livy.[38]

But Lucretia's blood is no longer *castus*; her sacrifice is an impure one. The sacrificial interpretation of her death thus becomes another means of representing the impropriety of her violation, but now in a medium that affects not

---

[35] Ogilvie (1965:226).

[36] For the ritual use of sacrificial blood see Fowler (1911:33–4). In Dionysius' narrative after the expulsion of the Tarquins, when the first consuls swear what is virtually the same oath as that proposed by Brutus in Livy, they do so "standing over the remains of sacrificial victims," Dion. Hal. *Ant.*, 5.1.3.

[37] Bleicken (1963) has argued that two series of coins, one Roman from the time of the Second Punic War and one minted by the Italian rebels, both of which depict soldiers with swords surrounding a sacrificial victim, are depictions of *coniurationes*. A literary description of such a rite among Italic peoples occurs in Livy's description of the Samnite oath at 10.38; the connection with the coin scenes was made by Instinsky (1964). Alföldi (1971) agrees that the Italian coins show a *coniuratio* but claims that the Roman coins in fact represent a treaty between Aeneas and Latinus.

The most famous *coniuratio* to be confirmed by blood and/or sacrifice was Catiline's. According to Dio's account a boy is actually brought in, sacrificed, and subsequently eaten by the conspirators, 37.30.3. Sallust's more restrained version has Catiline mix human blood with the wine that was circulated among the conspirators in *paterae*, Sal., *Cat.* 22.1–2. Consciousness of this hideous crime was meant to insure the fidelity of the participants. Sallust connects the ritual element with the gesture of circulating wine, *sicuti in sollemnibus sacris fieri consuevit*. But it is unclear what particular rites are meant; McGushin (1977:152–3) adduces the wine-oaths of Caucasian tribes, but the words *sollemnibus sacris* ought to refer to official Roman rituals. Latte (1960:391) points out that under certain circumstances, such as the festival of the Bona Dea, it was customary for the priests to taste the blood of the sacrificial victim although there is no mention of wine. For the drinking of sacrificial blood in real and imaginary Greek oath rituals, see Herter (1966).

[38] The only other occasion where a word related to *castus* is used of sexual purity is earlier in the Lucretia episode (1.57.10). Otherwise cf. 7.20.4; 10.7.5; 10.23.9; 27.37.10, 39.9.4. See also Moore (1989:121–2).

only the *domus* but the entire state. And indeed it is an impure sacrifice that motivates the expulsion of the kings as it was ritually re-enacted every year at the festival of the *regifugium*. In this ritual, which took place on 24 February, the very date Ovid assigns for the rape of Lucretia, a surrogate for the king, the *rex sacrorum*, performs a sacrifice in the Forum and immediately flees the area.[39] Scullard, using the analogy of the Greek *buphonia*, where the sacrificer is also forced to flee, assumes that the *rex* takes on himself the guilt of an impure sacrifice.[40]

Within the narrative it is precisely at the moment of the oath by blood that the importance of the death of Lucretia is redefined as something greater than a family misfortune. Brutus, one of the two outsiders present, takes the lead, and the other spectators turn from mourning, the act of a father and husband, to anger. Similarly, whenever the body is displayed, the first reaction of the spectators is to weep, out of sympathy for the father, but then Brutus, as a *castigator lacrimarum*, forces them to perceive themselves not so much as members of a family but as members of the state. He urges them to do what befits men and Romans.[41]

Thus the introduction of sacrifice facilitates the moment when the individual spectator establishes his civic identity in the manner highlighted in the preface to book two. But how can we understand the meaning of sacrifice in this process? According to René Girard, sacrifice is predominately a social act, in which the concerted violence against one individual, mediated in certain crucial ways, becomes a means of establishing social coherence.[42] Cicero in his descriptions of collective identity also refers to the role of sacred rites, *sacra*. These for him constitute one of the natural bonds that unite both family and by extension the *patria naturae*.[43] And when we look back at Cicero's description of the relationship between the individual and the larger *patria*, there too we find an image of sacrifice. It is the *patria civitatis* "for which we ought to die and to which we ought to dedicate ourselves entirely, and upon

---

[39] Ovid, *Fasti* 2.685–856.

[40] Scullard (1981:81); on the *buphonia* see Burkert (1983:136–43). For a discussion of other Roman rituals that may have been connected specifically with the expulsion of the Tarquins, see Mastrocinque (1988:47–8).

[41] *tum Brutus castigator lacrimarum atque inertium querellarum auctorque quod viros, quod Romanos deceret arma capiendi contra hostilia ausos*, 1.59.4.

Cf. the similar conclusion of Phillips (1979:90): "violation of family ties, by outraging a sense of community based in part on such ties, leads directly to the destruction of established political forms."

[42] Girard (1977). For a fuller description of the socializing function of sacrifice in Roman culture, and its particular importance in Augustan iconography and literature, see the discussions of Gordon (1990), Habinek (1990b), Elsner (1991), Hardie (1993), and Feldherr (1998).

[43] Use of the same rites unites the family at *De off.* 1.55, and at *De leg.* 2.3 Cicero identifies Arpinum as the location of his sacred rites, *hic sacra*.

which we ought to set out and as it were consecrate all that we have."[44] This striking series of images suggests that the citizen is both the one who makes the offering and is himself the victim who must die for the Republic. So not only is the role of *sacra* emphasized as a source of collective feeling but the act of joining the *patria* is conceived of in sacrificial terms.

Lucretia's death constitutes a negative image of sacrifice. Rather than participate collectively in the killing, the spectators are bound by sympathy with the victim and revulsion for the society responsible for her death The beginning of the Republic by contrast offers other examples of collective action where the citizens band together to punish or expel transgressors. The expulsion of Collatinus, while not explicitly described as sacrificial, can be profitably understood according to the logic of sacrifice established in the Lucretia episode. In fact, Livy links Collatinus' banishment directly to Lucretia's death by depicting it as an extension of the oath he swore by Lucretia's blood (2.2.5). The other Tarquins were expelled by violence, but Collatinus is persuaded to go by Brutus. The first words of Brutus' exhortation are *hunc tu tua voluntate* (2.2.7). Collatinus, rather than be subjected to violence must leave of his own will, in a manner that will absolve the state of any blame, just as the sacrificial victim too must be a willing victim.[45]

Brutus' adoption of sacrifice as a paradigm for representing the death of Lucretia also has implications for Livy's own aims in representing the crimes of the monarchy. First the opposition between sacrifice and drama as forms of spectacle needs an additional qualification because the two phenomena are not exactly comparable. It is only Livy's comment as narrator which depicts the murder of Servius Tullius as tragic. Tarquin and the other characters within the narrative are at pains to conceal the "dramatic" nature of the event. Thus when Tullia, the inspiring Fury who has actually caused his crime, appears in public, Tarquin must drive her back into hiding. To Livy's audience, Tarquin is a character in a drama but from the perspective of the audience within the text, this dramatic interlude has taken the place of real government. On the other hand the transition to sacrifice is accomplished through the intervention of Brutus, a figure in the narrative. When viewed in this way, the actions of Brutus the revolutionary and Livy the historian both operate

---

[44] *pro qua mori et cui nos totos dedere et in qua nostra omnia ponere et quasi consecrare debemus*, Cic., *De leg.* 2.5.

[45] Other legends too connect the figure of Brutus to transformations in Roman sacrifice, and one in particular presents him as effecting a shift away from the alienating sacrifices instituted by Tarquinius Superbus. Macrobius, *Sat.* 1.7.34–35, tells that Tarquin originally instituted the practice of sacrificing young boys during the festival of the Compitalia in response to the injunction of the Delphic oracle that "*pro capitibus capitibus supplicaretur.*" Brutus cunningly re-interpreted the oracle by substituting the "heads" of poppies for those of boys. For an analysis of this and other religious reforms connected with Brutus, see Mastrocinque (1988: 37–65).

towards the same end of exposing what the Tarquins would conceal. The value of the sacrificial paradigm used by Brutus is to reveal the deeds of the Tarquins in a context which makes them emphatically public as opposed to private crimes. Livy, by staging the whole reign as a drama, makes of it a negative example whose ultimate function is to define by contrast the proper conception of the *res publica*.

The essential equation of Livy and Brutus as producers of spectacle receives confirmation when we find Brutus himself acting as an historian. After having displayed the body of Lucretia in the forum at Collatia, Brutus moves on to the Roman Forum where he delivers an oration which not only describes the rape of Lucretia, but also refers to the murder of Servius Tullius, even the digging of the *cloaca maxima* (1.59.7–11). In other words, he recapitulates much of Livy's own narrative. In fact Livy says that Brutus recalled even more horrible deeds which are difficult for the historian to relate (*his atrocioribusque, credo, aliis quae praesens rerum indignitas haudquaquam relatu scriptoribus facilia subiecit, memoratis . . .*, 1.59.11). However, this difference in content, even the necessary distancing created by such an authorial aside, is less significant than Livy's implication that at this moment Brutus' action and his own are comparable. Brutus' speech cannot be separated from the historical events it describes; his narrative acts upon its audience as a catalyst in effecting the change in governments and in social structures. As we have seen, this change is not a unique event of purely historical significance, nor does it merely reflect concerns which had a particularly vivid impact on the experiences of Livy's own time, when vast numbers of new citizens, including the historian himself, were coming to think of themselves as Romans. Every citizen, even Cicero, experiences the shift in values that Livy makes responsible for the creation of the Republic. And Livy's narrative, as another representation of that transformation, can have an impact no less vivid nor forceful than the words pronounced by Brutus.

One of the implications of this similarity in function between the historian and the consul is that under the Republic a different relationship obtains between the historian's text and the events it narrates. No longer do the illegitimate spectacles of a Tarquin require exposure; the historian can align his representation of the past with the public displays of the new magistrates in a manner that perpetuates their effect and expands their audience. The first fully described events of the new republic, particularly the execution of the sons of Brutus, reproduce and resolve the tensions between family and civic identity, but now in the form of a public spectacle which Livy's text, rather than exposing or discrediting, strives to recreate for its own audience. In the case of the execution of the sons of Brutus, we shall see that the dynamics of the spectacle described by the historian, where the killing of guilty victims takes place at the command of a presiding magistrate whose presence draws the attention of the crowd away from the execution itself, recall the visual aspect of sacrifice, the very ritual whose successful manipulation by Brutus was crucial for the creation of the republic.

The climactic moment of the execution, when Brutus watches his sons' death with "a father's spirit shining forth in the execution of public duty," can be read as an epiphany of Ciceronian patriotism. As Yan Thomas interprets the scene, it is not a question of Brutus suppressing the duty of a father in order to do his duty as consul. Rather the two social roles are integrated. Both consular *imperium* and *patria potestas* come together in authorizing the execution.[46] The consequent unity of two levels of social authority both illustrates the civic aspect of the Roman father's power of life and death, and simultaneously establishes a new relationship between the consul and the *populus* whereby the magistrate becomes the "father" of the people. This interpretation is explicitly attested by Florus for whom Brutus' execution of his sons indicates that he has "adopted the people in the place of his sons."[47] To accept a paternal relationship with the people also implied the rejection of another model of absolute power also present in the *domus*, that of master to slave. The link between the *dominus* and the tyrant, already developed in Greek political theory, perhaps gained a special importance for the Romans who, as Thomas points out, made their unique construction of the father–son relationship a distinguishing characteristic of their own society.[48] Thus in Livy's text Brutus' absorption of the role of *pater* is coupled with a rejection of that of *dominus* implicit in the liberation of his slave Vindicius.

The motif of the consul as a public father shapes the brief remainder of Brutus' life. He dies in battle fighting in single combat with Arruns, one of the sons of Tarquin.[49] After his funeral the married women of Rome mourn for him for an entire year, just as they would a parent, "because he was such

---

[46] "Un lien s'établit entre la *vitae necisque potestas* et *l'imperium*. Un même visage incarne deux pouvoirs dont l'exercice, aux yeux du peuple romain, offre le même et terrifiant spectacle," Thomas (1984a:518). Cf. also the argument of Mastrocinque (1988:121ff.) that the *regnum* of Tarquinius Superbus was associated with a breakdown of paternal authority over the *iuventus* and that thus Brutus' restoration of civic order goes hand in hand with his restoration of the proper hierarchical relationship between the generations.

[47] *ut plane publicus parens in locum liberorum adoptasse sibi populum videretur*, Florus, 1.3.5, in Thomas (1984:531–2). Cf. also the crowd's description in Livy of the consulate as "born from the Junian house," as though in substitution for Brutus' natural offspring (*consulatum ortum ex domo Iunia*, 2.5.7).

[48] For the uniquely Roman aspect of the father's power of life and death, see Thomas (1984a:503ff). The link between the tyrant and the master, and correspondingly between the good king and the father, is developed by Aristotle, *Pol.* 3.8.2, 3.14.15, etc. The comparison also appears in Cicero's treatment of the just king in *De rep.* 1.64. Cf. also *De rep.* 3.37.

[49] In Dionysius' more prolix account of the duel, Arruns calls Brutus a wild beast for putting his sons to death, Dion. Hal., *Ant.* 5.15.1.

a fierce avenger of outraged chastity" (*quod tam acer ultor violatae pudicitiae fuisset*, 2.7.4). This claim reveals another link between Brutus' expulsion of the Tarquins and the execution of his sons. To guard the chastity of the women of the household was pre-eminently the responsibility of its male members.[50] In this sense Brutus' transformation of the rape into a national matter, like punishing his sons as a consul, unites family and political authority in a manner directly opposite to that of the Tarquins, who made the public personal.[51] The transition from father to consul is reiterated when Sp. Lucretius Tricipitinus, Lucretia's real father, replaces Brutus as consul (2.8.4).

But Livy's narrative makes it impossible to separate the "adoption" of the state from the loss of the family. As a sign of this reciprocity, the final battle between Brutus and the "son" is nothing if not ambiguous. Arruns and Brutus "careless of protecting their own body provided they wound the enemy," each die by the other's spear. Both the action itself and the sentence in which Livy describes it are as synchronized as a formal dance (*contrario ictu per parmam uterque transfixus duabus haerentes hastis moribundi ex equis lapsi sunt*, 2.6.9). In his analysis of the execution, Thomas assumes that only the public construction of the father's power over his children, the *vitae necisque potestas*, is involved in Brutus' execution of his children and consequently that the *animus patrius* he revealed has nothing to do with affection but only with discipline.[52] But Livy makes it clear that the fact of Brutus' paternity is a hindrance to the performance of his duty by stating that if he were not consul but only a spectator he would be removed (*qui spectator erat amovendus, eum ipsum fortuna exactorem supplicii dedit*, 2.5.5). The consul Manlius Torquatus, who must also execute his own son and compares his situation to Brutus', makes his love for his son explicit: "Natural affection (*ingenita caritas*) for children moves me" (8.7.18). And this language reminds us that without "natural affection" the formation of the state would never have been accomplished. Thomas rejects the notion that the subjective response of Brutus as individual should be given too much prominence,[53] but by isolating Brutus within the narrative, by focusing the eyes of the crowd on him alone, it is as an individual that Livy forces his audience to see him.

---

[50] Cohen (1991:117).

[51] Although this part of Livy's work probably appeared a good seven years before 18 BCE, the connection to the issues involved in Augustus' adultery laws seems inescapable.

[52] Thomas (1984a:518).

[53] "Il est pourtant clair que la force de cette scène n'est pas limitée au débat sentimental qui agite subjectivement un *pater*. Des institutions sont en jeu, un droit se fonde et se manifeste, et des fonctions – paternelle et consulaire – sont mobilisées: l'image d'un individu souffrant ou surmontant sa souffrance n'est assurément pas le meilleur point de départ pour tirer la leçon de cet exemplum," Thomas (1984a:516, n.36).

But the point of this qualification is not to restore sentimentalism *per se*,[54] much less to imply that Livy intentionally undercuts the patriotic force of the scene; it involves the fundamental techniques of Livy's narrative. The emphasis on perspective, on the perceptions of the onlookers, is not a device for reinforcing a patriotic "moral" with the greatest possible vividness but a means of allowing his own audience to experience subjectively the shift in values upon which the creation of the Republic is predicated. As in so many of the publicly performed rituals of the Roman state, particularly sacrifice, resolution and harmony can only be achieved through the recreation of tensions and disorder. Thus Livy uses the climax of the revolution to rearticulate the oppositions in social organization and the construction of individual identity that inform the whole narrative, but now in a form that approximates the very ceremonies in which civic leaders presided over similar "refoundations" of the Roman state.

As a spectacle the episode is focused on Brutus, whose presence makes the execution *conspectius* and whose face at the very moment of death usurps the attention of the crowd, and consequently of Livy's audience. It is in his countenance that the tensions of the scene are represented: *eminente animo patrio inter ministerium publicae poenae*. This moment where civic and familial roles are held in balance and equally accessible to the gaze of the viewer can be read as the true climax of the process of revelation effected by Brutus since his first appearance in the narrative.[55] It must thus be interpreted as a reversal of, for example, Tarquin's deposition of Servius Tullius where the disjunction between the personal and the public is emphasized.

However, Brutus is initially described not as a spectacle but as a hypothetical spectator. In fact Brutus occupies in every sense an intermediate point relative to the execution. Unlike the narratives of Dionysius and Plutarch where Brutus must actually persuade an unwilling crowd to go through with the execution,[56] here his participation is limited to a presiding role: he takes his place as consul and gives the command for the execution although even this moment of active participation is elided by Livy's shift to the passive voice (the lictors *were sent* to exact the punishment).[57] This treatment subtly emphasizes the structural resemblance between the execution and public

---

[54] Compare, for example, the conclusions of Tränkle (1965:327–29) that Livy's particular aim in this scene is to render the character of Brutus more sympathetic and human.

[55] It is precisely this sense of revelation that distinguishes Livy's version from that of Valerius Maximus. Here the father's spirit "shines forth," but Valerius reverses the image and has Brutus "slough off the father to play the consul," *exuit patrem ut consulem ageret*, Val. Max. 5.8.1.

[56] Dion. Hal. *Ant.*, 5.8.3; Plut. *Publicola*, 6.1.

[57] *consules in sedem processere suam, missique lictores ad sumendum supplicium. nudatos virgis caedunt securique feriunt, cum inter omne tempus pater voltusque et os eius spectaculo esset eminente animo patrio inter publicae poenae ministerium*, 2.5.8.

sacrifice, where the killing itself is carried out by subordinates commanded by the presiding priest. It also lends an impersonality and lack of specificity to the proceedings which contrast with the extreme personal involvement of Brutus as *pater*. The description of the execution juxtaposes a simple five-word statement in the historical present emphasizing the ritual instruments of consular power with an adversative *cum* clause describing how the crowd turned their attention to Brutus' reaction. Again at the instant he becomes the object of the crowd's attention, Brutus is also an onlooker.

What is the point of this narrative complexity? As a spectator Brutus occupies the same position relative to the event as the rest of the crowd and perhaps of Livy's own audience as well. Yet at the same time he is distinguished by taking as it were the place of the victim. The effect both highlights the "subjective" experience of Brutus and, by confusing the distinction between Brutus and the rest of the audience, puts every spectator in his place. The recreation of spectacle through the text thus offers a means for every citizen to experience as a participant the ritualized moment that more than any other provides an aetion of Roman citizenship. Cicero had expressed this transformation as a sacrifice where the individual subject occupies the dual role of presider at a sacrifice and of victim. Thus in Livy's treatment the execution of Brutus' sons balances the impure sacrifice of the death of Lucretia that ended the monarchy. And like Brutus exposing Lucretia's corpse in the Forum, Livy offers a spectacle which modulates sympathy with the father into civic participation.

Livy's use of sacrificial spectacle in these episodes as an instrument for allowing his own audience to experience the transition to full participation in the *res publica* provides a final correspondence between the methods of the historian and those of the *princeps*. A crucial aspect of Augustus' self-representation, and one which possessed a decisive impact for the iconography of all subsequent emperors, was the number of statues, coins, and public monuments which placed the emperor at the center of religious ceremonies, particularly as sacrificant.[58] As Elsner has recently demonstrated in his interpretation of the *Ara Pacis*, such representations, far from simply denoting the abstract *pietas* of the emperor, served to recreate and reproduce the sacrificial experience, placing the viewer in the place of participant and making the emperor the focal point of the event.[59] Nor was this experience limited to

---

[58] Cf. the comments of Zanker (1988a:127): "Certainly from the time of the Secular Games in 17 BCE, and probably much earlier, in the 20s, the princeps must have made it known that henceforth he preferred that statues put up in his honor show him togate at sacrifice or prayer."

[59] Elsner (1991:52): "In looking at the altar Roman viewers did not simply see images of a sacrifice that once happened. They saw a cultural process in which they themselves became involved."

Roman viewers; the diffusion of these images in Italy and the provinces provided a prototype for religious activity throughout the empire and helped create a network of cult practices grounded in the authority of Rome and of the *princeps* himself.[60] In his own adoption of sacrifice as a means of "Romanization" and the use he makes of visual images to recreate ritual, Livy again anticipates the techniques of empire; but in place of the emperor stands, in this case, the figure of Brutus,[61] and the medium through which the image is propagated is no coin, stamped with the mark of imperial or senatorial power, but the historian's text.

---

[60] The thesis of Gordon (1990).

[61] Gordon's description of the sacrificial panel on the arch of Trajan at Beneventum provides a striking parallel for the visual priorities in Livy's configuration of Brutus' execution of his sons (1990:202–3). In this panel, the sacrifice is presented at one side of the image, while the emperor *capite velato* dominates the other. Yet none of the spectators in the background observe the sacrifice: all have their heads turned to face the emperor, who alone directs his gaze toward the *victimarius* opposite him. In the same way, it is Brutus who attracts the attention of both the crowd and the reader in Livy's narrative and provides sole access to the execution itself.

9   Concealing/revealing: gender and the play of meaning in the monuments of Augustan Rome

Barbara Kellum

The interrelatedness of gender and power is key to an understanding of the monuments of Augustan Rome. As someone who has long pursued an understanding of the ways in which visual meanings were constructed in Augustan context,[1] I have found that gender can be a useful category of analysis precisely because it tends to destabilize our understanding of the past.[2]

As I hope to demonstrate in examining the first of three structures that I will discuss, gender encodings, even at the most basic level of reading, are not transparent. The scene depicted on figure 1, one of a series of terracotta Campana plaques from the Temple of Apollo on the Palatine, has sometimes been identified as Apollo and Diana crowning a sacred pillar. The source of the identification is not difficult to trace: Apollo is a god who sometimes wears the peplos and both he and his sister Diana were honored at the temple; besides, the best and most widely available published illustration of the plaque, from which most slides in collections worldwide were made, is so labeled.[3] Nonetheless, a consideration of hairstyle and costume and a recognition of the central device establishes that this is a *pas de deux* for two maidens, decorating an aniconic representation of Apollo Agyieus, a type of critical importance to Augustus and to the Palatine complex.[4] In context, the repeated plaques were self-consciously juxtaposed with their masculine counterparts, Apollo and Hercules, locked in contest over the Delphic tripod (figure 2).

Both sets, at the time the temple was dedicated in 28 BCE, must have looked to contemporary viewers simultaneously old and new. Terracotta revetments and sculpture typified the oldest temples in the city, and, from the second century BCE on, such ornament was supposedly disparaged by many Romans once they had laid eyes on the glistening marble temples of the Greek East.[5] The former antitheses were here combined, since the Temple of Apollo on the Palatine, although it alluded to Etruscan temples in its form, was one of the first built of solid marble, from the newly discovered Luna quarries.

---

[1] Kellum (1985); (1990); (1994a); (1994b); (1996).   [2] Scott (1986).
[3] Andreae (1977):122 (plate 40).   [4] Carettoni (1973):78–80, & n.24; Strazzulla (1990):22–9.
[5] Livy 34.4.4; cf. Plin. *NH* 36.6–7.

158

Fig. 1. Archaizing maidens crowning an aniconic representation of Apollo Agyieus, terra cotta Campana plaque from the Temple of Apollo on the Palatine, Rome.

In motif, as in material, the two sets of plaques harkened back to "archaic" models. The "archaistic" maidens-composition was newly generated for the temple, but the Apollo *vs.* Hercules plaque was predicated on an earlier vase painting type. Significantly, it is not the popular "classical" vase painting composition – where Hercules has already shouldered the Delphic tripod which he is attempting to steal – that is chosen, but, instead, a rare "archaic" model

Fig. 2. Apollo versus Hercules, terra cotta Campana plaque from the Temple of Apollo on the Palatine, Rome.

which focuses on an earlier moment in the struggle, when Apollo and Hercules are ostensibly more evenly matched. Appearances, of course, can be deceiving, and, mythologically, the affirmation of Apollo's rightful possession of the tripod is a foregone conclusion, something that becomes the more important when it is recognized, as I first proposed in 1980, that what we are dealing with here is a thinly veiled allegory of the recent battle of Actium, cast in the form of a primordial contest between Apollo and Hercules, the divine progenitors of, respectively, Octavian and Antony.[6] The officially declared enemy, Cleopatra – pinioned between a male and a female sphinx, waving her sistrum as she does in Virgil's description of the battle of Actium[7] – appears here as the repeated sima decoration, literally enframing the whole.

The gendered discourse of the temple of Apollo on the Palatine extended to the porticus of the temple as well. Here, between columns of *giallo antico* marble – yellow marble spotched with blood red – statues of the fifty Danaids were on display.[8] These were not, *pace* Zanker, the Danaids as water carriers in the Underworld.[9] Rather, as both Propertius and Ovid make clear, this was the far rarer iconography of the wedding night itself, each Danaid with a dagger beneath her peplos – as is true of an example now in Basle – and Danaus, the *barbarus pater* standing with sword drawn.[10] Appropriately Greco-Egyptian, the Danaids were unequivocally linked to Cleopatra; yet, at the same time, the tale was undeniably one of cousins killing cousins, of fratricide and civil war. In the end, perhaps, it was the gender difference of the opponents that made the whole acceptable, an artful allusion to that which was ineffable – the undeclared civil war – and yet was to be avoided again at all costs.

For Romans who knew the statuary grouping at the Temple of Apollo on the Palatine and the scene engraved on the fatal *balteus* in the conclusion of the *Aeneid*,[11] the Danaids in each instance must have reinforced one another as both a justification and a warning. Whatever a viewer thought about the genuineness or the motivations for the behavior of the *princeps* in refusing Antony's request for a heroic single combat[12] or in offering *clementia* to those who asked forgiveness, that is, the *appearance* of difference, the civil wars were nonetheless at an end. Catching sight of the Danaids in their porticus or hearing how Aeneas' eyes fixed on the *balteus*, must have served as a perpetual reminder of the horrors of cousins killing cousins, thereby substantiating the need for an Augustus as well. Far from reflecting a wish to dissolve an episode of contemporary history into a universal Greek myth in order to forget the ambiguity of a victory over a Roman magistrate and a foreign sovereign,[13] the porticus of the Danaids at the Temple of Apollo on the Palatine was a monument that embodied this ambiguity and turned it to Augustan ends. This was meaning, however, that was implied and not inculcated.

The same significative play, in gendered terms, informs the other temple of Apollo in Augustan Rome, the Temple of Apollo Sosianus. Gaius Sosius, commander of the left wing of Antony's fleet at Actium, was a recipient of

---

[6] Kellum (1981):200; (1985); Zanker (1983).   [7] Virg. *Aen.* 8.696.   [8] Prop. 2.31.

[9] Zanker (1983):27–31.

[10] Prop. 2.31; Ovid *Trist.* 3.1.61–62; statue in Basle: E. Berger *AntK* 11 (1968), 65–7.

[11] Virg. *Aen.* 10. 496–9; 12.942ff.   [12] Plut. *Ant.* 75.1.   [13] Sauron (1981):286–94.

Fig. 3. Reconstruction of the Amazonomachy pedimental sculpture with youthful hero crowned by hovering Victory and Hercules, Temple of Apollo Sosianus, Rome.

Augustus' clemency and was even one of the *quindecimviri sacris faciundis* at the Secular Games of 17 BCE.[14] Surely Sosius' lavish restoration of the temple of Apollo was a factor here; it is a *tour de force* performance honoring both Sosius and the new emperor simultaneously. The temple, the very place where Atia, Octavian/Augustus' mother, declared her son had been engendered by Apollo,[15] now took its restorer's name, but had as its dedication day 23 September, the day of Augustus' birth.[16] Likewise, the pedimental sculptures representing an Amazonomachy may make reference to both (figure 3). On one level, it is a clear celebration of the victory at Actium over the feminine forces of the East and, of course, Cleopatra.[17] But, within this battle of the sexes, two male protagonists are juxtaposed: one is Hercules with his lion skin and the other is a young man, perhaps Theseus. It is visually apparent that it is the young man who is triumphant since it is he who wears the gilded crown bestowed by Victory. Hercules, like all gods and heroes, had his place in the Augustan dispensation; next door at the buildings of Octavia, for example, a spectator would have seen Androbius' painting of Hercules Ascending to Heaven, received there by Apollo,[18] but in the Actium-informed context of the temple pediment, it was surely Antony, who had prided himself on his physical resemblance to Hercules,[19] that would have come to the Augustan viewer's mind, just as at the Temple of Apollo on the Palatine. It was precisely this kind of identification, underscored by coinage imagery, that had wide currency in Rome, as the popular hue and cry surrounding Sextus Pompey and the statue of Neptune at the Circensian Games of 40 BCE attest.[20] If Hercules is associated with Antony, then the young victor is Antony's fellow Roman and yet rival Octavian/Augustus, and, at the same time, it is also Antony's lieutenant, Gaius Sosius, once triumphant himself over the forces of the East (*ex Iudaea* 34 BCE) and again in Augustan Rome as the dedicator of the Temple of Apollo Sosianus.

A ludic equivalent is to be found in a Pompeian wall-painting that has long been decorously ignored. Here the hovering Victory crowns an ithyphallic ass which mounts a male lion (figure 4). As Della Corte recognized, this is a parody of the battle of Actium: before the battle, Octavian/Augustus reportedly met an ass named Victor (Nicon) and his driver Prosper (Eutychus), both of whom he later honored with bronze statues, and the lion was synonymous with Antony's ancestor Hercules with whom Antony identified.[21] Since we now know that similar thinly veiled allegories of Augustus' victory over Antony adorned the temples built in Rome commemorating the battle, it becomes all the more

---

[14] Vell. 2.85.2, 2.86.2; *ILS* 5050, 1.150.   [15] *Epigrammata Borbiensia* 39; Dio 45.1.2–3.
[16] Plin. *NH* 13.53; 36.28; *Fast. Urb. Arv. ad ix kal. Oct.*; *CIL* 12. pp. 215, 252, 339.
[17] LaRocca (1985), *passim.*   [18] Plin. *NH* 35.139.   [19] Plut. *Ant.* 4.1–2.
[20] Dio 48.31.5–6.
[21] Della Corte (1951):25ff.; statues: Suet. *Aug.* 96.2; Antony: Plut. *Ant.* 4.1–2.

Fig. 4. Wall painting with hovering Victory crowning an ass which is vanquishing a lion. Pompeii Reg. II 6, 34–5.

likely that the Pompeian painting is a more bawdy equivalent, making the sexual dynamics of the situation clear.

That this multiple level of reference could occur, that, as at the porticus of the Danaids, an aspect of contemporary history could be artfully concealed and revealed at the same time, has everything to do with the fact that these monuments existed in a nexus of presuppositions about gender and power on the battlefield, in the bedroom, and in the law courts, that is historically specific and only tangentially related to our own. In order to explore this notion fully, I would like to focus now on a more detailed analysis of the Forum of Augustus with its Temple of Mars Ultor dedicated in 2 BCE (figure 5). Although usually presented as a staid monument of military history, filled

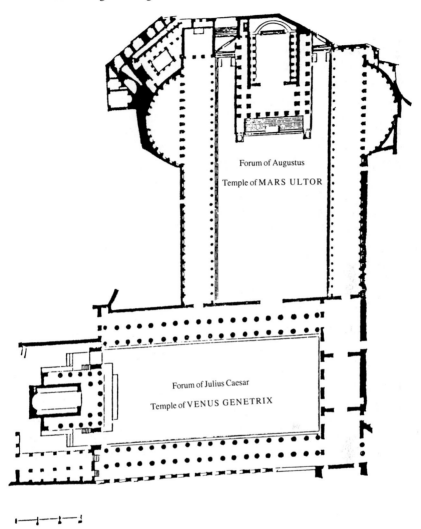

Fig. 5. Plan of the Forum of Augustus and the Forum of Julius Caesar, Rome.

with a didactic statuary program, and built by a leader who was by all accounts less than a virile super-hero, the Forum of Augustus was, I will argue, a sexually charged, gendered masculine environment.

The temple and the Forum functioned as the locus for the political and military rituals through which the masculine was defined.[22] Here young men

---

[22] Suet. *Aug.* 29.1–2.

came when they put aside the garb of childhood – the *toga praetexta* with its purple stripe and the *bulla*, a locket containing an apotropaic phallic amulet – to assume the all-white *toga virilis*, the garment of the Roman citizen.[23] A man would only have the right to wear the *toga praetexta* with its purple stripe again if he became a curule magistrate, and he would wear the *bulla* again only if he celebrated a triumph.[24] In both the civic and military spheres, it was once again in the Forum of Augustus that these roles would have been enacted. The "increase in the number of the people and of cases at law" was a primary impetus for the building of the Forum; here the *praetor urbanus* and the emperors themselves set up their tribunals and public prosecutions and jury selection were held.[25] Here governors on their way to military provinces were to take their leave of the city, here the Senate was to debate declarations of war and claims for triumph, and here, after ritually entering the city and processing through it in his quadriga, the triumphator – dressed in purple, wearing the *bulla*, his face painted red like that of the statue of Jupiter Capitolinus – would arrive to dedicate his scepter and crown to Mars.[26]

Present were not just the heroes of the moment, but those of the past. The walls of the forum were literally lined with a vast statuary program of *summi viri*, great military and civic heroes of the Roman past trooped around a statue of Aeneas carrying his father Anchises and leading his son Iulus by the hand in the central niche of the northern hemicycle, and one of Romulus carrying the *spolia opima* in the southern hemicycle.[27] Aeneas, the son of Venus, is shown as the model of filial piety saving his aged father and young son from the burning walls of Troy. He is en route to Italy and to siring the line that would lead to Romulus, the son of Mars and the founder of Rome, who had been the first to win the *spolia opima*, having slain an enemy leader in single combat. Set around them, ranged as if in a gigantic family atrium,[28] were all the leaders of the distant and more recent past, many of them familiar faces, copied from the statues that appeared on earlier familial monuments, gathered here as if by evocation. Former mortal enemies stood side-by-side in surrogate form, most – to judge by the statuary remains – wearing the civilian toga rather than military cuirass and each with an inscribed *elogium* beneath recording name and achievements.

Augustus himself is said to have had a hand in composing the *elogia*[29] and, not surprisingly, the patterns of multiple office-holding, triumphs, service in times of civil strife, concern for the gods and the embellishment of the city that can be traced in the inscriptions closely parallel the emperor's own

---

[23] Macrob. *Sat.* 1.6.7f.; Dio 55.10.2; *NSc* 1933 464–5, Nr. 85.   [24] Macrob. *Sat.* 1.6.9.
[25] Suet. *Aug.* 29.1–2; G. Pugliese-Carratelli *PP* 3 (1948), tablet XIV, p.2; Suet. *Claud.* 33.1.
[26] Serv. *Ecl.* 10.27; Serv. Dan. *Ecl.* 6.22; Suet. *Aug.* 29; Dio 55.10.1–5.
[27] Ovid *Fast.* 5.563ff.   [28] Cf. Plin. *NH* 35.6–7.   [29] Plin. *NH* 22.13.

career. In reconstruction the program hardly looks scintillating; to reclaim its visual excitement we must refashion in our mind's eye all the accoutrements that individualized these statues: the signet rings[30] and the spoils and prizes, like the Celtic bird helmet that the statue of M. Valerius Corvinus (the Raven) wore.[31] In actuality, the statues must have been as close to living presences as were the public funeral parades of ancestors personified by individuals wearing the death-masks and regalia of those long dead.[32] The statues must have been legible, probably even to the illiterate, since people were directed to tribunals according to which statue it was in front of.[33] Without question, the program set the standard by which all men were to be measured.[34]

Strategically, the viewer gained access to the statues of the *summi viri* by passing beneath an attic level frieze of repeated Caryatid figures. Like their counterparts from the so-called "porch of the maidens" at the Erechtheion on the Acropolis, which marked the grave of a hero and founder of Athens, these figures may have functioned on one level as designators of the Forum as a hero monument. However, within the masculine environment of the Forum of Augustus, the role of these repeated female figures was hardly a neutral one. Although our own Romantic notions of "the porch of the maidens" may obscure this for us, it is striking that Vitruvius, writing in the 20s BCE, read Caryatids in a very specific way. As an architect, he maintained that these "marble statues of robed women used as columns" had a history: after the Greeks destroyed Caryae, a city in the Peloponnese which had allied herself with the Persians, they led the matrons away into captivity, compelling them to retain their robes and matronly ornaments as permanent symbols of their shame.[35]

In the Forum of Augustus – the very performance space for the triumph – the Caryatids' significance as captive women and the time-worn analogies between the penetration of a woman's body and the breeching of enemy fortresses were certainly primary.[36] The extent of Rome's domination was mapped in turn by the repeated shield devices that appeared between each pair of Caryatids – Zeus Ammon for the East and a Gaul with torque for the West. Suetonius tells us that Augustus forced certain barbarian chiefs to come to the temple of Mars Ultor itself in the Forum of Augustus to take an oath to keep the peace and "in some cases, indeed, he tried exacting a new kind of hostages, namely women, realizing that the barbarians disregarded pledges secured by males."[37] The connection between the actual women hostages and

[30] Cf. Cic. *Att.* 6.1.17.   [31] Gell. *NA* 9.11.   [32] Cf. Polybius 6.53.

[33] *AEpigr.* 1969/70 no. 96,97; C. Giordano *RendAccNap* (n.s.) 41 (1966), 113–14; etc.

[34] Suet. *Aug.* 31.5.   [35] Vitr. 1.1.5.

[36] *Il.* 22.468–70, cf. *Il.* 16.100; *Od.* 13.388; Eur. *Hec.* 536–38, *Tr.* 308–13; Ovid *Am.* 1.9.15–20; Paul (1982) 144–55.

[37] Suet. *Aug.* 21.2.

the Caryatids, as well as the linkage between women and subdued barbarians, were likely not lost on a Roman audience.

In functional terms, then, the Forum of Augustus was a sexually fraught theater for the engendering of the masculine. This is also, I believe, fundamental to the very structuring of the building itself. Physically, the Forum of Augustus was considered one of the three most beautiful buildings the world had ever seen.[38] The precious marbles in its fabric underscored the scope of Rome's world supremacy: here *giallo antico* from Numidia was juxtaposed with black Lucullan marble, with *pavonazetto* from Phrygia and alabaster from Egypt. However, it is the framework in which these materials were arranged that is particularly revealing. Just as Vitruvius suggested that the members of a temple should take their harmony of proportion from the spatial potential of the outstretched limbs of the male human body traced in the geometric perfection of the circle and the square (figure 6),[39] so every element in the design was generated. Though cast on a gigantic scale, the entire complex was literally anthropocentric. In spatial terms, the relation of circle and square made this an arena in which both linear and circular time could be represented, in which present, past, and future were interchangeable. Fundamentally, the circle and the square are integral to everything from the flooring pattern to the outside envelope: the thirty-three-meter tall wall defined the Forum's unique shape, with its two symmetrical hemicycles and forecourt.

It is the addition of the hemicycles that distinguished the Forum of Augustus from all previous fora and they have been variously explained. I have argued elsewhere that the hemicycles with their statues of the *summi viri* should be compared to earlier semicircular *heroa* like those of the Argives flanking the Sacred Way at Delphi.[40] Others have suggested that the hemicycles were certainly the most spatially dynamic element, invisible to the visitor on entering the court, but opening to either side as the viewer approached the temple.[41] The hemicycles (or *exedrae*) are, however, very visible in plan and, as the recent discovery of a fragment of a new first-century CE marble plan of the city of Rome has confirmed, in all likelihood Augustan viewers could perceive their refurbished city in the form of a vast marble plan just as they could contemplate the map of the world displayed in Agrippa's Porticus Vipsania.[42] It is on this basis that I propose that the overall configuration of the Forum of Augustus had an extended anthropocentric significance.

---

[38] Plin. *NH* 36.102.   [39] Vitr. 3.1.3.

[40] Kellum *The City Adorned: The Visual Rhetoric of Augustan Rome* (forthcoming). See also Sauron (1981):294–307.

[41] Brown (1961):27.

[42] Plin. *NH* 3.17; Nicolet (1991):158–9; first-century plan: Conticello de'Spagnolis (1984), *passim*. It is our mapping convention to place North at the top. Like the famous third-century marble plan, the earlier version probably had South at the top. Thus, the trajectory was up, as it were.

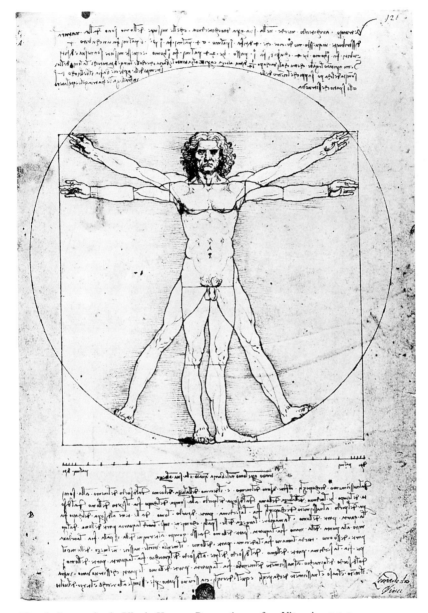

Fig. 6. Leonardo da Vinci. *Human Proportions after Vitruvius* 3.1.3.

Fig. 7. Phallus on paving stone from Pompeii.

In plan, with its two bulging *exedrae* and projecting forecourt, the forum resembles nothing so much as the schema for the phallus represented on buildings throughout the Roman world (figure 7). We do not, by the way, know the exact length of the forecourt or its point of termination since the Forum has never been completely excavated. There are, of course, later examples of phallic building plans like Ledoux's 1804 plan for the Oikema, an institutionalized brothel (figure 8).[43] Because to us, as to Ledoux's contemporaries, its form bespeaks its function, we recognize in it an example of *architecture parlante*. If the Forum of Augustus does not appear to speak to us in the same way, it is perhaps because our own concept of the phallus as signifier is as historically specific as that of ancient Rome.[44]

The sheer ubiquity of the phallus in that context, in scales ranging from the

[43] Vidler (1990):356–8; Marder (1979); Reutersvard (1971).   [44] Compare Lacan (1977).

gigantic to the minuscule, is difficult for us to imagine. The erect phallus certainly served as the shop sign of the *lupinar* (brothel), but equally appeared on house walls, on baker's ovens, on paving stones, at the baths, at fortress gateways, and on objects ranging from *ex votos* to suggestively flaming lamps.[45] Projected in at least three dimensions, and hung with bells, the polyphallus became a whimsical doorbell (*tintinnabulum*). In daily speech too, the male organ was everywhere; Augustus' nickname for one of his favorite poets, the short-of-stature Horace, was *purissimus penis* (most immaculate penis).[46]

Key to an assessment of this seemingly overweening plethora of display is an understanding of the primary function of the phallus as signifier in context. Like the phallic amulet in the child's *bulla* or the phallic harness ornament on the prized horse, representations of the phallus offered protection from the evil eye. By their *atopia* (singularity, absurdity) they attracted the harmful gaze of the envious.[47] It was not just children and race horses that were subject to the evil eye. As Carlin Barton has demonstrated, the competitive, status-conscious Roman world was predicated on a "physics of envy."[48] The more prominent one was, the more exposed to the evil eye of gods and mortals alike. Thus, the triumphator, dressed as a god and a king, wore his *bulla* and had an additional phallus (*fascinum*) hung beneath his chariot.[49] Within this system, the moment of being the most powerful was also the moment of being the most vulnerable, a fact which was both acknowledged and deflected by the scurrilous insults hurled by the troops at the triumphator during the triumph.[50] In so doing the community simultaneously protected, humiliated, and exalted the leader, and often in explicitly sexual terms. At his triumph in 46 BCE, for example, Julius Caesar was hailed as vanquisher of the Gauls and at the same time ridiculed for having been vanquished – for having lost his virginity – to Nicomedes the king of Bithynia.[51]

This allusion to Caesar's taking the passive role in a homoerotic relationship indicates another important aspect of the Roman concept of the phallus as signifier. In sexual, military, and judicial encounters, it was not the genitalia that mattered, but the role that one played. In fact, in anatomical terms, as the similarity of the schemata suggests, men and women were thought to have the same genitals, one on the outside of the body and one on the inside, with what we call the ovaries termed testicles.[52]

---

[45] On walls, the phallus could be vertically or laterally disposed: Ling (1990):51–55. In general, Johns (1982):61–75; Grant (1975).

[46] Suet. *Vit. Hor.* See Adams (1982):9ff.   [47] Plut. *Quaest. conv.* 5.7 *Mor.* 681f–682a.

[48] Barton (1993), *passim.*   [49] Plin. *NH* 28.39.

[50] Livy 3.29.5; Dion. Hal. *Ant. Rom.* 7.72.11.

[51] Suet. *Iul.* 49.3; cf. Cic. frg. inc. 5 Watt.

[52] Galen *On the Seed* 2.1–2 (citing Herophilus, third cent. BCE); *On the Use of the Parts* 14.6; on the crucial shift in the late eighteenth century, Thomas Laqueur (1986):2.

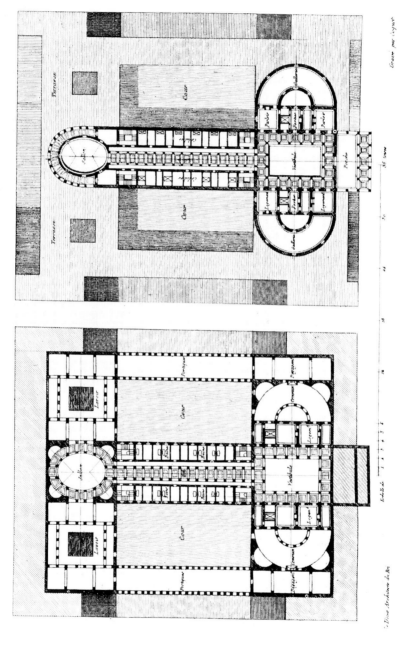

Fig. 8. Claude-Nicolas Ledoux. Plan of Oikema, Chaux, 1804.

There was, of course, still a presenting and a receiving role, and it was the aggressor who attempted to wield the phallus. The inscribed lead sling bullets, hurled by both sides at the siege of Perusia in 41/40 BCE illustrated this graphically. The technical name for sling bullet, *glans*, also meant tip of the penis, and not only did some bear representations of the phallus, but they were also aimed, by means of their inscriptions, at allocating their opponents the passive/receiving sexual role. Thus, a sling bullet intended for Antony's wife, Fulvia, was launched at her *landica* (clitoris), while another, decorated with a phallus and directed at her opponent, Octavian, targeted his anus.[53] Less explicit, but equally devastating examples occur in literature: in the final simile cluster of the *Aeneid*, Turnus' body is transformed into a city's walls ruptured by the spear of Aeneas.[54]

But if this is the nature of the phallus as signifier in the Roman sphere, what evidence do we have to indicate that it should be associated with the Forum of Augustus or its plan? Certainly the apotropaic significance of the phallus in the very ceremonies celebrated in the Forum, especially the triumph, have already been demonstrated, and the literary plays on the immense size of the Forum are suggestive,[55] but it is in the realm of the joke and of popular art that the most intriguing traces of this association are to be found.

First, it must be said that the Forum of Augustus – much like Virgil's great epic the *Aeneid*, to judge by the graffiti – seems to have captured the imaginations of Romans from many walks of life, as it is freely quoted in many contexts throughout the Roman world. Thus when Eumachia, a public priestess and patroness of the fullers in Pompeii, built the largest building on the forum, she modelled her benefaction on those of Augustus and Livia in Rome, including, in the statue niches on either side of the entry, copies of the statues of Aeneas and Romulus from the Forum of Augustus. Only the inscriptions remain, but around the corner and down the street, the fuller Fabius Ululutremulus (IX 13,5), seemingly emulating the patroness of his guild, replicated the statues of Aeneas and Romulus in the form of painted signs flanking the entry to his shop (figure 9). The interaction continued, for someone having just passed by the image of Aeneas we see on the right, scratched a graffito just inside the door parodying the first line of Virgil's *Aeneid*: "I sing of fullers and screech-owls, not of arms and the man."[56] The screech-owl was the mascot of the fullers and its name in Latin *ulula* plays not only on the name of the owner of the shop, Ululutremulus, but on the action of crying out, in pleasure or in pain. The serious and the amusing, the commemorative and the commercial, the military and the amatory, the high and the low: all were inextricably interlinked.

---

[53] Hallett (1977).   [54] Virg. *Aen.* 12.921–24; Schork (1986).   [55] Ovid *Fast.* 5.553.
[56] *NSc* 1913 141ff.

Fig. 9. Wall painting of Aeneas, Iulus, and Anchises, shop sign from the fuller of Ululutremulus. Pompeii IX 13,5.

This is equally the case for the one caricature that we know of the Forum of Augustus statue of *the* progenitors: Aeneas carrying his father Anchises and leading his son Iulus by the hand. In a painting from Pompeii, or possibly from Stabiae, Aeneas and little Iulus are tricked out with the universal lighting rod

Fig. 10. Wall painting with parody of Aeneas group. From Pompeii or Stabiae.

for the evil eye, the giant exposed phallus that formed a part of the costume of
the mime; Anchises carries not the household gods, but a dice box; and all the
figures have canine features (figure 10). It has been fashionable of late to dismiss
this as a simple example of anti-Augustanism, [57] but this is to miss both its wit
and its wisdom. Like the verbal appropriation of the first line of the *Aeneid* in
the graffito, this was exaggeration for effect. The image not only plays on the
weighty role of Aeneas – who is to sire the Alban kings leading to Romulus –
and of little Iulus – who is to found the line of Julius Caesar and Augustus –
but also by depicting the figures with the faces of dogs, generates a visual pun
on *canis*, which means both "dog" and "you sing."[58] For any Latin speaker, it
would have again been the first line of the *Aeneid* that would have come to
mind: "I sing of arms and the man" (*arma virumque cano*). Finally, aged
Anchises with his dice box is not just a slur on Augustus, who, like most
Romans, was addicted to the game,[59] but a play on the universal name for the
high roll, "the Venus,"[60] which the old man had certainly once thrown. Aeneas

---

[57] Zanker (1988a):209.   [58] Varro *L.L.* 5.99; Ahl (1988):41f.   [59] Suet. *Aug.* 71.2–4.

[60] Hor. *Carm.* 2.7.25; etc. The low roll was, of course the *canis*, so there is at least another level
of play here, as one member of the symposium audience noted.

Fig. 11. Venus, Cupid, Mars, cult statue grouping from the Temple of Mars Ultor as reflected on Algiers relief (Divus Iulius on right).

was, after all, the son of Venus and Anchises, as the inscription beneath his statue in the Forum of Augustus made clear and which the caricature both satirizes and affirms in terms of the phallus and the intermingling of the military and the amatory.

As Mikhail Bakhtin has said "The literary and artistic consciousness of the Romans could not imagine a serious form without its comic equivalent."[61] But this was operative both in official and in private spheres and brings us to the presence of Venus in the Forum of Augustus. Just as Aeneas, the son of Venus, and Romulus, the son of Mars, stood at the center of each of the Forum's *exedrae*, so Venus, with her son Amor, stood next to Mars Ultor both on the temple pediment and in the cult statue grouping. It is well known that Venus was the one deity capable of disarming Mars,[62] as we see Amor helping her to do here, but mythologically Mars and Venus were not husband and wife, but notorious lovers (figure 11). Since the reign of Augustus is often typified by the restrictive legislation on marriage and adultery it produced, this

[61] Bakhtin (1981):58.   [62] Lucr. 1.31f.

R O M A

O   M

M   O

A M O R

Fig. 12. Roma/Amor graffito, house wall, Reg. I, Pompeii.

coupling of Mars and Venus in the temple of Mars Ultor – even if dynastic-ally justified – has often been thought to be strangely contradictory. It was certainly played on by Ovid,[63] who like Propertius and Tibullus, developed the theme of love as a kind of warfare and every lover a soldier.[64] We tend to read these as personal criticisms of a strict moral regime rather than recognizing them as a part of the same system of ordering where the martial and the amat-ory were inherently a part of one another. It is perhaps the pairing of the aveng-ing Mars and the disarming Venus at the temple of Mars Ultor that affirmed the notion – played on in a Pompeian graffito – that the secret name of Rome, key to the possession and preservation of the city, was Amor (figure 12).[65]

Moreover, the relationship of Mars and Venus was inscribed on the city plan, since the phallic Forum of Augustus with its temple of Mars Ultor was juxtaposed with – perhaps literally wedded to – the Forum of Julius Caesar with its temple of Venus Genetrix (figure 5). The power dynamics here were the opposite of those that, according to rumor, obtained in Octavian's youth, when he played the bottom to Julius Caesar's top.[66] Here the Forum of Augustus is clearly dominant, much like the triumphant man bestriding his conquest in a graffito from a brothel in Pompeii.[67] It should not be forgotten, however, that this is the domain of the *double entendre*; in the Augustan era and thereafter even the characteristic epithets of Venus and Mars could be

[63] Ovid *Trist.* 2.295f. – see text below.   [64] *Ars Am.* 2.233; *Am.* 1.9.1–2; etc.
[65] *NSc* 1929, p. 465, n. 200; Plut. *Quaes. Rom.* 61; Plin. *NH* 28.18; on Aelius Aristides: Oliver (1953) 883.
[66] Suet. *Aug.* 68.   [67] Grant (1975), frontispiece.

used interchangeably for either deity in inscriptions.[68] Thus, Ovid, addressing
an audience that would have known the structures as well as the fact that
venus, in addition to being the name of the goddess, was also a common word
for intercourse and for penis,[69] could, in appearing to describe the cult statues
in the temple of Mars Ultor, shift the frame of reference to the topographical
and reverse their roles.[70]

> venerit in magni templum, tua munera, Martis,
> stat Venus Ultori iuncta, vir ante fores.

If she enters the temple of mighty Mars, thine own gift, Venus stands close to the
Avenger, in the guise of a man before the door. (*Trist.* 2.295–6).

As the architecture of the line indicates, Ovid sets up a parallel between
Venus standing next to Mars and a man (*vir*) standing before the door (*ante
fores*). The house door, possession of the husband, had long been synonymous with access to the wife/mistress, but in Augustan Rome, as Ovid points out,
it is Venus Genetrix in her Forum of Julius Caesar that literally stands before
the door of the Forum of Augustus with its temple of Mars Ultor.[71] What is
significant here, of course, is that Ovid's brilliant play is predicated on a
relationship that is built into the city plan itself (figure 5).

As difficult as these connections may be for us to grasp, they were seemingly not lost on contemporaries. The one graffito we have preserved from the
Forum of Augustus, scratched on the stylobate of the temple, depicts a violent
sexual encounter.[72] Although not an uncommon theme in graffiti, in this context
it might also be a comment on the multiply nuanced Forum and its maker.

Surrounded by Aeneas, Romulus and the *summi viri*, the Caryatids, and
the statues of Mars and Venus, the seminal point of the Forum of Augustus,
placed centrally within the projecting forecourt, was a statue of the emperor
himself in a triumphal quadriga and bearing for the first time the title *pater
patriae*.[73] Here, simultaneously risking envy and warding it off, Augustus
served as the formative point of mediation between his divine ancestors Mars
and Venus. Their divine child was Harmonia, Augustus was the creator of the
pax Augusta. Clearly the central role in the Forum belonged to Augustus.
Here he held sway over the heroes of the past, here there was no contradiction between the perpetually triumphant image of the emperor in his chariot
and the Augustus mocked by a delighted crowd in the theater when a line
directed at a Gallus (a castrated priest of Cybele) beating his orbital drum was

---

[68] *CIL* 11.5805, 5165; Galinsky (1969):233–4.   [69] Adams (1982):57, 188–9.
[70] Ovid *Tr.* 2.295–6.
[71] This is not the standard interpretation of the line, although I am not the first to suggest that
a topographical reading makes sense: K. Hiemer *RheinMus* 62 (1913):232.
[72] Kockel (1983):447, plate 20.   [73] *Res Gest.* 35.

taken to refer to the emperor – "do you not see that a *cinaedus* (a passive male homosexual) now rules the world with his (middle) finger?"[74] The chief Augustan victory celebrated here was a victory with a difference: within the temple of Mars Ultor were displayed the Roman military standards lost by the virile Antony (and Crassus) in Parthia and regained by Augustus in 20 BCE through diplomatic means.[75]

This bloodless victory[76] was paralleled in the courtroom drama that Augustus played on in the following witticism: "Since many of those accused by the prosecutor Cassius Severus were acquitted, but the architect of the Forum of Augustus kept putting off the completion of the work, . . . [the emperor quipped] . . . 'I could wish that Cassius would accuse my Forum too and get it off my hands.' "[77] If we do not get the joke, it is not, I think, just because the contemporary law case no longer lives for us, but because our entire frame of reference is different. In 9 BCE the emperor's close friend Nonius Asprenas had been accused by Cassius Severus of having poisoned to death 130 guests at a banquet.[78] Cassius Severus was a prosecutor who resembled a gladiator and was famed for his unrestrained acerbic oratory;[79] Augustus countered this hyper-masculine opponent by simply attending the court and sitting on the side witness benches in silence; his friend was acquitted.[80] Having exercised power without, as it were, having to lift a finger, Augustus problematized, modified and reinscribed the construction of the masculine in the courts, that other theatrical arena for the demonstration of the interrelatedness of gender and power, and an institution also housed in the Forum of Augustus.

The language of the courts was equally sexually laden. As every visitor to the Forum of Augustus would have known, *testis* was the word for witness as well as for testicle and was frequently punned on.[81] Rhetorical styles too were assessed in metaphors of sexual potency.[82] As is recognized in literary criticism, this was an atmosphere in which simultaneity of meaning thrived. It was an era in which the ingenious *purissimus penis* himself, Horace, could write *Satires* 2.1 and, in addition to making bows to Callimachus, Lucilius and others, have it read on one level as a serious discussion on the moral and legal issues involved in the writing of satire, and on another as a sustained discussion of states of erection, playing mercilessly on his own cognomen Flaccus (limp, hanging down).[83] This was the world of the Forum of Augustus, of the Temple of Apollo on the Palatine, and the Temple of Apollo Sosianus. What we see here depends on the interpretative lenses we use. If gender as a category of analysis has transformative value, it is precisely because in

---

[74] Suet. *Aug.* 68.   [75] *Res Gest.* 29; Ovid *Fast.* 5.580ff.
[76] Cf. Ovid *Am.* 2.12.5–6 for the amatory equivalent.   [77] Macrob. *Sat.* 2.4.9.
[78] Plin. *NH* 36.164; Dio 55.4.3.   [79] Plin. *NH* 7.55; Tac. *Dial.* 26; Quint. *Inst.* 11.1.57.
[80] Suet. *Aug.* 56.3.   [81] *Priapea* 15.7.   [82] Quint. *Inst.* 12.1.22; 12.10.12; Tac. *Dial.* 18.
[83] Freudenburg (1990).

destabilizing the perception of this one aspect of the past, it necessitates a re-examination of all the presuppositions which underlie the traditional political history of the period. Since the time of Edward Gibbon, it has been primarily Tacitus who has informed history's vision, and, for Gibbon, it was Augustus with his "mask of hypocrisy" that was to be seen, a specter made all the more real by the great Tacitus of the twentieth century, Sir Ronald Syme in his 1939 *The Roman Revolution*. In addition, although it is still too seldom mentioned, we in the latter-day twentieth century still perceive Augustus through the filters of the excavations, reconstructions, and image-making of Benito Mussolini.

The displays of Augustan Rome were not the simplistic equivalences of a Mussolini. What may, from without, look, as Paul Zanker has said, "unrelentingly didactic"[84] to us, was, from within Augustan Rome, both multiplex and mimetic. Visual programs were of a piece with the cultivated plain speech of Augustus and his spare phrases in the *Res Gestae*, which in their seeming artlessness demonstrated their art, and with the structuring of a social system which at once affirmed traditional class hierarchy (the *Lex Julia Theatralis* or the marriage laws) *and* opened paths to status and ritual participation in the state to a far wider spectrum of the population than ever before, as the burgeoning numbers and dedications of the Augustales and freedmen *apparitores* demonstrate.[85] It was often members of these newly privileged groups who erected monuments in the imperial mode, not as hollow generalized "internalizations" of official art,[86] but as active *appropriations* with individual meanings in local contexts. Thus on the funerary altar of two ambitious freedpeople, Annius Eros and Ofillia Romana,[87] the figures of Romulus and Remus being nursed by the she-wolf, along with other founding figure nursling groups on other sides of the altar, play not only on Ofillia's *cognomen* Romana, but also on the fact that these two are indeed founders of their own own freeborn family. So too, the ships' rostra, at the very foundation of the whole composition, are not haphazard choices. They parallel the rostra from Actium on display at the Forum Romanum. Actium marked the beginning of an era in more than a calendric sense, and it was much celebrated in the art produced for freedmen, no doubt as a celebration of the foundation legend of the new social dispensation that was the making of their lives and fortunes. Theirs was the the world of Numerius Popidius Celsinus, the first freeborn member of his family, who when he restored the Temple of Isis in Pompeii after the earthquake was made one of the *decuriones* even though he was only six years old, or of the two most famous freedmen in Pompeii, Aulus Vettius Restitutus and Aulus Vettius Conviva, Augustalis, who celebrated their freeborn

---

[84] Zanker (1988a):209.   [85] Ostrow (1990); Purcell (1983).   [86] Zanker (1988b):2, 8–12.
[87] Metropolitan Museum L 1984 119.1.

offspring in the traditional area for family display, the atrium. They also alluded to their connection to the imperial sphere through sea battle painting vignettes of a kind known from at least seven other freedmen contexts in Pompeii and which I believe should be associated with Actium. More blatant appropriations are also to be seen, as demonstrated by a Pompeian house façade, probably of an Augustalis, outdoing even the *princeps* by painting the foliage of his plaster version of the *corona civica* a perpetual green and by gaily gilding the acorns.[88]

This is not an ossified system, nor should we construe it as one. In order to understand the visual language of Augustan Rome, it is necessary to understand the many dimensions of signification it encompassed on all social levels. Here the clever allusion, the simultaneous concealing and revealing of art, the familiarity with figured speech were not simply the adversarial strategies of beleaguered writers,[89] but the cultural strategies of the entire population, emperor and freedperson alike.

The usefulness of gender as a category of analysis is in the potential it holds for questioning the fixity of binary absolutes, whether it is the supposed opposition between male and female, between official and private, between "high" and "low" art, or between the ribald and the serious. Viewing the monuments of Augustan Rome as culturally and historically specific constructions reveals the levels of play that can exist within gendered performance spaces.

---

[88] Pompeii II 2.4 (Casa della Corona civica). *Pompei. Pitture e mosaici* v.3 (1991):109–11.
[89] Ahl (1988):17f.

Questions of authority: the invention of
       tradition in Ovid *Metamorphoses* 15

Philip Hardie

Opening questions

Book 15 of the *Metamorphoses* opens with a question. The first word,
quaeritur, in fact introduces the first of a number of searches or questions
that are laid out in rapid sequence in the first eleven lines of the book: who is
to succeed the first king of Rome, what is the nature of the universe, who
founded the Greek city of Croton in Italy? The answers to these questions will
detain us until the end of the Speech of Pythagoras and the return of Numa to
Rome to take over the reins of power in succession to Romulus, at a point
well over halfway through the book (15.484). This initial set of questions has
a somewhat rag-bag appearance; what unites them, and the answers to them,
is their pertinence to what will emerge as the final topic of the book and the
poem, the designation and legitimation of the current ruler of Rome. To be
exact, that is not quite the final topic, for Ovid signs off with a nine-line
epilogue, seemingly detachable but in truth indissolubly bound up in the
representations of imperial power immediately preceding. And we shall see
that the questions at the beginning of the book touching the second king of
Rome at the very point of his succession to Romulus' throne are questions
which the poet himself is empowered to answer through *his* relationship to
his poetic predecessors. But it will be the relationship between poet and
princeps that constitutes the *envoi* of the *Metamorphoses*. Ovid's final triumph
is to reverse the expected dependence of poet on *princeps*, as chronicler and
panegyrist. In an ineluctable collusion between artist and ruler we finally see
the prince of poets foist on his master a poetics of principate.

   To return to the beginning. The first word *quaeritur* introduces a question
of practical politics, that of finding a successor to Romulus. The first line
already looks to the end of the book, for the Virgilian allusion in <u>tantae</u>
pondera <u>molis</u> "so weighty a burden"[1] hints that this is not a question relevant
only to the eighth century BCE: the phrase *tantae molis* may be appropriate for
the scale of the labours of Aeneas prior to the founding of a nation, but it is
scarcely exact for the burden of governing a city notoriously undersized in

---

[1] *Aen.* 1.33 *tantae molis erat Romanam condere gentem.*

its infancy.[2] It suggests rather the Rome of 44 BCE – or of the later years
of Augustus.[3] To this question an answer is immediately and ungainsayably
forthcoming (3–4) "rumour, foretelling the truth, (*praenuntia veri \ fama*)
designates renowned Numa for the throne". So it might seem; on the other
hand the relationship between *fama*, "rumour, fame", and truth is notoriously
slippery, especially when you end the line with another Virgilian tag that
tells only part of the story: *Aen.* 4.188 (*Fama*) *tam ficti pravique tenax quam
nuntia veri*, "as much attached to falsehood and distortion as she is a messenger of the truth".[4] *Fama* is also the preserve of the poet, above all the epic
poet constructing the fame of renowned men. Thus one criterion for judging,
or even fabricating, the "truth" is drawn to our attention, not for the last time
in the book.

The next two and a half lines, 4 to 6, present an opposition between two
types of knowledge, the sacral lore of the Sabines which Numa already knows
(*cognosse*), and the "greater" matter of *de rerum natura* "natural philosophy",
the object of Numa's own inquiring (6 *quae sit rerum natura requirit*).[5] The
opposition perhaps raises another question, that of the respective utility for
the designated king of Rome of the two expertises. What does a ruler need to
know?[6] There is another point: while the nature of the universe is arguably an

---

[2] Cf. *Fasti* 3.179–80 *parva fuit, si prima velis elementa referre,\ Roma*. The Virgilian *moles*
  becomes a theme in *Met.* 15: at 433 *mole sub ingenti rerum fundamina ponit*. Bömer (1986)
  takes *sub* of attendant circumstances, "amidst great labour". But are foundations not placed
  "under" a massive structure? The architectural image is perhaps already hinted at in *Aen.* 1.33
  tantae molis erat Romanam condere gentem. Cf. also 765–6 *quanta mihi mole parentur\ insidiae*;
  on 809 *molimine vasto* see p. 192 below.

[3] Tac. *Ann.* 1.11.1 *solam divi Augusti mentem tantae molis capacem. capax imperii* is "ein
  taciteischer Zentralbegriff" (Koestermann [1963], *ad loc.*, comparing *Ann.* 1.4.3 *tantae moli
  parem, Hist.* 1.49.4, 2.1.2, 2.77.1, and referring to Syme [1958], 58 n. 4). Numa's capacity for
  power is equalled by his capacity for knowledge, *Met.* 15.5 *animo . . . capaci*. On the relevance
  of the succession to Numa to the situation in Rome in the last years of Augustus see Soubiran
  (1989).

[4] The line is the model for *Met.* 12.54 *mixtaque cum veris passim commenta vagantur*, in the
  description of the House of Fame: on which see Feeney (1991:247–9), linking the passage with
  15.871–9. See also Zumwalt (1977). With the Ovidian line-ending cf. also *Aen.* 11.139 *Fama
  . . . tanti praenuntia luctus*, where the synecdoche in *luctus* (= "cause of grief, tragedy")
  suggests also how Rumour herself creates "grief". In *Met.* 15.3–4 one might equally read
  fama's preview as self-fulfilling. The role of *fama* in the processes of succession and imperial
  adoption is another Tacitean theme: *Hist.* 1.17, 2.1, 4.11; *Ann.* 4.11, 13.1; *Agric.* 3.18 *fama spe
  veneratione . . . omnes destinabantur imperio*; cf. *Agric.* 9.7 *haud semper errat fama; aliquando
  et eligit* (in a non-imperial context); cf. also *Ann.* 1.4.3.

[5] Is there a pun in *quae sit*? Cf. *Fasti* 1.115 *accipe, quaesitae quae causa sit altera formae*
  (pointed out to me by Julian Thompson); Varro *Ling. Lat.* 6.79 *ipsum quaerere ab eo quod
  quae res ut reciperetur datur opera*.

[6] In general on the history of the relationship between rulers and philosophers in Rome see the
  essays by M. Griffin and E. Rawson in Griffin and Barnes (1989).

absolute through the centuries, the status of religious learning is not. What for Numa are simply the contemporary institutions of his own people, from the perspective of Augustan poet and reader will have become the material of aetiological antiquarianism. To pursue his new scientific interests Numa leaves his fatherland (like so many other characters in this book), to travel to Croton. There we do indeed find him in the role of inquirer (10 *quaerenti*), but his scientific zeal has now been diverted on to a ktistic, aetiological track.[7] The Callimachean authority of the old man of Croton who plays Evander to Numa's Aeneas is sealed with another Virgilian tag, but one that grounds certainty in the past rather than in the future (as in the case of *fama* seven lines before), (11) *veteris non inscius aevi* "not ignorant of times past": compare the description of Vulcan at *Aen.* 8.627 *haud vatum ignarus venturique inscius aevi* "not ignorant of the prophets and of time to come."[8]

The juxtaposition of legendary-aetiological and scientific inquiry at the beginning of *Metamorphoses* 15 is haphazard only in appearance; Sara Myers in her recent book (1994) demonstrates that the conjunction is central not only to the *Metamorphoses*, but also to other areas of contemporary literary and ideological activity. For example, the conjunction is found in the first couplet of the *Fasti*, which announces as subject of that poem the union of the historical and aetiological (*tempora cum causis*) with the cosmological (*lapsaque sub terras ortaque signa*). The combination is appropriate in a dedication to the astronomically minded prince Germanicus, in this respect a worthy successor to the second king of Rome, Numa, who in adding the first two months to the calendar (*Fasti* 1.43–4) corrected the mistake of *his* predecessor Romulus, who (29) "had more knowledge of arms than of stars".[9] In the first sustained exercise in aetiological enquiry in the *Fasti*,[10] in conversation with Janus, Ovid receives instruction in matters both cosmological and antiquarian.[11] At the end of the Janus episode Ovid turns from the subject of Roman religious history to ask (295–6) "Who debars me from telling also of the stars", a move that is replicated in Numa's dissatisfaction at *Metamorphoses*

---

[7] *quaero* is of course a central term in aetiological poetry (as (ἀν)ειρεσθαι in Callimachus' *Aetia*); see Myers (1994), 81. For another example of an Ovidian book that opens with the word see *Fasti* 5.1 *quaeritis, unde putem Maio data nomina mensi?* on whose programmatic function see Barchiesi (1991), 1.

[8] Note (i) the substitution of *veteris* for *venturi* (but what for Vulcan is in the future is in the past for Virgil's reader); (ii) *haud vatum ignarus* is exactly true of Ovid as he quotes Virgil. On the textuality of Vulcan's Olympian certitudes see p. 189 below.

[9] Cf. *Fasti* 3.101 ff. *Romanae artes* in Romulus' time lead him to ignorance of stars; 119 *animi indociles et adhuc ratione carentes*. On 3.151 ff. see below.

[10] At the lexical level note *Fasti* 1.115 *quaesitae ... formae*; 145 *requirere*; 161 *quaesieram*; 219 *quaeris*; 278 *quaesiti ... causa*.

[11] See Hardie (1991).

15.4–6 with sacral knowledge alone, because of his capacious spirit's thirst for the "greater" matter of *rerum natura*.[12] The two types of knowledge that concern Numa also correspond to two of the headings of Andrew Wallace-Hadrill's discussion of cultural transformation, Time (the astronomical rationalization of the calendar) and Tradition.[13]

The Speech of Pythagoras

The *Fasti* grounds the Roman religious calendar both in the authority of the past history of Rome and in the invariability of the celestial motions. As Ovid in the *Metamorphoses* brings down the story of the world *ad mea tempora*, the general pertinence of the aetiological episodes, of which the story of Myscelos is the first in book 15, is clear enough. Augustus' political exploitation of Roman antiquarianism needs no discussion. (True, the ktisis of Croton seems obtrusively irrelevant in a context of *Roman* aetiology, but to this problem I shall return at the end of my discussion.) But how are we to accommodate Pythagoras' 40-line speech *de rerum natura* within the Roman themes of book 15? Numa, after listening patiently for 400 lines, returns home to accept the throne and unceremoniously dumps his scientific research interest as he looks to those previously contemned Sabine *ritus* for lessons in political education: 483–4 "he taught them sacrificial rituals and led a people used to cruel war to the arts of peace".[14] Is the Speech of Pythagoras then a gigantic red herring? This in effect is the conclusion of Peter Knox, for whom the whole passage does little more than "form a structural balance with the opening cosmogony [of book 1]".[15] Knox's very valuable discussion brings out the importance of questioning and inquiry in *Metamorphoses* 15 by focussing on the book's aetiological nature, but he blinds himself to the full extent of the theme of knowledge through an excessive concentration on the Callimachean antecedents, and by his insistence that what is at issue is only a "literary problem". The result is a total misprisal of the political meanings of the book that leads Knox to claim (p. 67) that "The figure of Numa is in itself insignificant; he serves only to connect." Only to connect? *Only* connect, rather.

---

[12] *Fasti* 1.295 ff. likewise aims at a loftier flight, under *duces* (309) who might be seen as alternative authorities to the *duces* (Roman statesmen) of 67. In *Fasti* 1, after three brief couplets of astronomical matter, Ovid turns in the next long section (317–456) to the origins of sacrifice, a passage closely related to Pythagoras' discussion of sacrifice at *Met.* 15.111–42.

[13] See pp. 12ff. above.

[14] In *sacrificos ritus* might be scented an ironic comment on Numa's obedience to Pythagoras' attack on blood-sacrifice (though these might as well be the bloodless sacrifices mentioned by Plut. *Numa* 8.8): for a subtle argument for Pythagoras as a failed didactic voice see Barchiesi (1989), 77–83.

[15] Knox (1986), 74.

The Speech of Pythagoras casts a retrospective shaft of light through the whole of the Latin hexameter tradition, illuminating and reanimating a line of culture heroes who offered the Romans insights into the grounding of their social and historical world in the mysteries of the natural world; at the same time the Speech comments on the place of the *Metamorphoses* itself within that hexameter epic tradition.[16] Validation of the Roman state is coterminous with legitimation of the epic poet. Knox is alert to the importance for the Speech of Pythagoras of the Dream of Homer at the beginning of Ennius' *Annals*, but his refusal to acknowledge the epic qualities of Ovid's hexameter poem leads him to focus exclusively on the Callimachean affiliations of the Ennian prologue. These matter, but I would stress rather the line of succession leading forward from the opening of the first Latin hexameter epic, the *Annals* of Ennius, through Lucretius and Virgil, and finally to Ovid. That finality is written into the structural position of the Speech of Pythagoras within the *Metamorphoses*. Ennius marks the beginning both of his epic and of the Latin hexameter epic tradition with the Dream of Homer. The Ennian Dream is evoked by Lucretius at the beginning of *his* hexameter poem, and subsequently becomes the model for Aeneas' interview with Anchises in *Aeneid* 6. Now, by staging an interview with Pythagoras Ovid in a sense stakes a claim to priority over the Ennian Dream, in which Ennius had used a device that depends on the authority of Pythagoras;[17] but at the same time Ovid marks the *end* of the line when the voice of his Pythagoras sweeps up fragments of Ennius, Lucretius, and Virgil, in the *last* book of a long hexameter poem, as the end-product of a kind of continental drift, during which the Ennian model, loosed from its moorings at the beginning of a poem, had reached a provisional halting-place at the centre of Virgil's epic, before coming finally to rest at the end of Ovid's.[18]

The Speech of Pythagoras comments on Latin epic's use of natural philosophy to validate Roman history, the great men of Roman history, and the poetic spokesmen of Rome. The Ennian Dream lends to the founder of the Latin hexameter tradition nothing less than the authority of Homer himself (precisely and fully himself in a sense, through his reincarnation in the body of Ennius). The disquisition by the *eidolon* of Homer on the nature of the world and of the soul seems also to have functioned as a prelude to the main historical matter of the *Annals*. That combination of natural philosophy and history is repeated in the two parts of the Speech of Anchises in *Aeneid* 6.[19] The *Heldenschau* recapitulates the main subject-matter of the *Annals* and then

---

[16] For a fuller version of this argument see Hardie (1995); on the Speech of Pythagoras Myers (1994), ch. 4, is now essential.

[17] Skutsch (1985:164): "The descent of Ennius' soul from Homer is clearly modelled on that of Pythagoras' soul from Euphorbus."

[18] On the line see Hardie (1993), 101–6.   [19] See Hardie (1986), 66–83.

completes it by designating Augustus as the historical *telos* of the combined natural-philosophical and Roman themes of Anchises. Ovid's Pythagoras also combines (albeit in very different proportions) the natural-philosophical and the historical, as his discourse on cosmic mutability reaches a climax with historical examples of the rise and fall of cities, ending with a prophecy of the greatness of Rome and, lastly, of Rome's great man Julius Caesar (15.431–49). "The sky will be his end" (449) prepares us for the skyward journeys with which the book will conclude; this posthumous cosmic legitimation of the Roman ruler has particular authority in the mouth of a man whose mental powers grant him the freedom of the skies: 62–4 "although far removed from the heavenly regions, in his mind he approached the gods, and with the eyes of the spirit he took in the things that nature denies to human sight." The implied connection between scientific expertise and imperial validation finds more explicit expression at *Fasti* 3.151–60:

Numa Pompilius, brought to Rome from the land of olive-groves, first realised that the year lacked two months, whether instructed by the Samian who believes that we are capable of rebirth, or by his own Egeria. But even after that the calendar was faulty, until Caesar attended to it among his other many concerns. That god, the founder of so great a line, did not think this an unworthy task; he wanted prior knowledge of the heavens promised to him so that he should not when a god come as a stranger to his new home.[20]

Of course in reality, as Andrew Wallace-Hadrill observes (p. 17), "It is not . . . Caesar or Augustus themselves who lay claim to this superior knowledge", but Ovid's panegyrical fiction neatly encapsulates the kind of "imperial privatization" involved in the relocation of authority that is Wallace-Hadrill's subject.

The Speech of Pythagoras suggests that both Rome (and its rulers) and the poet Ovid have their rightful place in a long succession. In the case of Rome, the perspective of universal change naturalizes the growth of Rome and the apotheosis of its great man as part of the inevitable cosmic process. In the case of the poet's authority, the Speech of Pythagoras fashions itself as the last in a series of scenes of esoteric initiation vouchsafed by the earlier masters of the Latin hexameter tradition. The line of imitations of the Ennian Dream is inherently self-referential, in that the subject of that originary episode is nothing less than poetic succession, Ennius' entrance into the inheritance of Homer through the claim that the true soul of Homer is reincarnated in the breast of Ennius; this is a literary device that claims an extra-literary authority, one based on the "real" autobiography of the poet. Ovid, as one might expect, exploits to the full the ambivalence between the fictional and the real. If Pythagoras' sermon on mutability lends to the expansionism of the Roman

---

[20] 157 *auctor* is loaded. Note the stress on knowledge in *praenoscere, ignotas*.

state the legitimacy of a natural process, it does so only as the last reflection of a series of texts.[21] By the end of the book we will have seen the impossibility for the characters (and their creator) of escaping from a textuality that reaches out to trap the *princeps* himself.

To authenticate his doctrine of metempsychosis the Ovidian Pythagoras appeals to "his own" experience, 160–2 "I myself, I remember (*ipse ego [nam memini]*), was Euphorbus, son of Panthus, at the time of the Trojan War, in whose breast was fixed the heavy spear of Menelaus." This is one of the many occasions in Latin epic when the word *ipse* is anything but itself:[22] Pythagoras asserts his identity by the claim that he was not always himself. Furthermore the appeal to personal memory is in reality an allusion to the *poetic* memory of a statement by the Ennian Homer (*Ann.* II Skutsch) *memini me fieri pavom* "I remember that I became a peacock". Rightly seen, it is the poet Ovid who "remembers" his Ennian model.[23] This prefatory equivocation in the Speech of Pythagoras between personal and poetic memory surfaces again at the climax as Pythagoras proclaims (much too loudly) the authority of his forecast of the rise of Rome, 15.431–51:[24]

Now too rumour has it (*fama est*) that Trojan Rome is rising up . . . (434) As she grows she changes shape, and in the future will be the capital of the huge globe. This, say the seers, is the fate sung of by the oracles (*sic dicere vates\faticinas ferunt sortes*); and as I remember (*recordor*), Priam's son Helenus, when Troy was tottering, had told a weeping and anxious Aeneas: "Son of the goddess, if you are sufficiently familar with what my mind foresees (*si nota satis praesagia nostrae\mentis habes*) . . . (449) the sky will be Caesar's end." From my own recollection I tell you that this was what Helenus prophesied to Aeneas, bearer of the Penates (*haec Helenum cecinisse penatigero Aeneae\mente memor refero*).

Here Pythagoras' memory of his incarnation as Euphorbus is to be read as Ovid's memory of the speech of Helenus in *Aeneid* 3, which begins (374) *nate dea* "son of the goddess", and ends with the injunction (462) "make Troy great through your deeds and raise her to the sky", reworked by the Ovidian Helenus into a prophecy of the personal celestial destiny of Caesar (*caelumque erit exitus illi*). Once again Pythagoras'/Ovid's memory of Virgil is inexact, for in the *Aeneid* Helenus delivers his prophecy in Buthrotum, not at Troy. Tradition, we are reminded and as Augustus knew well, is conveniently malleable.

---

[21] The meeting between Numa and Pythagoras itself was of course a notorious fiction.

[22] For the general point see Hardie (1993), 113.

[23] Pythagoras remembers his Ennius well, but he has become hazy about the more remote Homer, where we are told that Euphorbus was wounded not in the chest, but (*Il.* 17.47) "at the base of the throat". On Pythagoras' "intertextual memory" see Barchiesi (1989), 84–5. Pythagoras is as diligent a student of Ennius as Mors at *Met.* 14.813–14 (*nam memoro memorique animo pia uerba notavi*)\ "*unus erit, quem tu tolles in caerula caeli*".

[24] Note *nomina . . . nomen* in the previous two lines, alluding to *Aen.* 6.776 *haec tum nomina erunt*; for other plays on *nomen* see p. 193 below.

And in this passage the equivocation on memory is nested in a dense concentration of the vocabulary of verbal authority, that simultaneously authorizes Roman history and traps it in a web of words and texts: *fama, dicere, ferunt, dixerat, cecinisse, refero.* The pun on *vates* "prophet/bard" in 435 reminds us of the wide reading of the Virgilian Vulcan as he makes his very Ennian shield, not ignorant of the *vates (Aen.* 8.627).[25] The authority of a memory that claims a privileged personal continuity between past and present turns out to be a purely textual authority.

Who in the end is Pythagoras, or who speaks through him? One answer is the hexameter tradition of philosophico-political revelatory verse, which Ovid pushes to the centre of the Roman epic tradition by a selective and partial rewriting of that tradition. Another answer, or rather another embodiment of the same answer, is Empedocles. The fragments of the pre-Socratic hexameter poet reveal the same combination that is found in the Speech of Pythagoras of a vatic revelation of the doctrine of metempsychosis, with the consequent necessity of vegetarianism, and a natural-philosophical exposition of the cyclical processes of the cosmos. The general homology is reinforced by a number of verbal echoes of Empedocles, who is inscribed in the *Metamorphoses* as the founding father of the Roman hexameter tradition, the final (Greek) authority for the Roman epic vision that grounds history in *rerum natura.* But if Empedocles speaks through Pythagoras as the first voice in that tradition, then the latest re-embodiment of Pythagoras must be Ovid himself. As many readers have divined, Pythagoras is the last and grandest of the many characters within the *Metamorphoses* who figure, more or less obliquely, the poet himself.[26]

How to succeed

Both Pythagoras and Ovid are terrestrial exiles who find a new citizenship in the heavens. Becoming a god or like a god is also the achievement of Empedocles, who claimed (B112.4–5) "I come to you as an immortal god, no longer a mortal, honoured among all". In the less favourable biographical tradition Empedocles was notorious as a human being who fabricated his own divinity, staging the final apotheosis with his leap into Etna.[27] Apotheosis is

---

[25] There may be an etymological link between 431 *fama* and 436 *faticinas*. This kind of Virgilian prophecy-in-hindsight presents as (future) *fatum* what in reality is (past) *fama*.

[26] The doxography: Crahay and Hubaux (1958); Primmer (1983:24) on Ovid and old age at 15.228 ff.; Petersmann (1976:199) for parallels with Pythagoras' divine utterances and astral wanderings.

[27] Diog. Laert. 8.69 βουλόμενον τὴν περὶ αὐτοῦ φήμην βεβαιῶσαι ὅτι γεγόνοι θεός; Philostr. *Vita Apollon.* 8.7; Hor., *Ars Poet.* 464–6 *deus immortalis haberi | dum cupit Empedocles, ardentem frigidus Aetnam | insiluit.* Horace's placing of this incident at the end of his poem is perhaps an ironic comment on the practice of closing a poetic work with the claim to immortality, for example *Odes* 2.20.

a privilege that Empedocles himself granted generously: the final rung on the ladder of the soul's ascent to divinity is occupied by "prophets and composers of hymns and doctors and rulers . . . whence spring gods most highly honoured" (B146). This shared destiny of prophets and princes points us to the very end of the *Metamorphoses*, where the future journey of Augustus to the sky is immediately capped by the *vates* Ovid's confident prediction of his own celestial destination. The heavens certify the power of both *princeps* and poet. Or so it seems; in fact it turns out that both *princeps* and poet certify the authority of the heavens. In the case of Ovid, the language of the astral immortalization of the soul turns out to refer to nothing more substantial than – words. In this overbidding of Ennius' posthumous life on the wing[28] the "soul" of Ovid is nothing more or less than the *Metamorphoses*, a body of words that guarantees the indelibility of that other word, the *nomen* of the poet.[29] The sleight of hand conflates two *topoi*, that of the immortality of the soul, and that of the immortality of fame.[30]

At *Ex Ponto* 4.8.55–64 Ovid boldly claims that "gods, too, are created through poetry, if it is lawful to say it . . . Recently, Caesar Germanicus, poetry had a part in the consecration of your grandfather, whose virtue raised him to the stars." How much of a verbal construct is the astral immortality of Julius Caesar and Augustus as represented in *Metamorphoses* 15? In the last

---

[28] *volito vivos per ora virum*, Ennius *Epigr.* 10 Warmington. Note the (Lucretian) pun on Ennius' name in *perennis* at *Met.* 15.875.

[29] For the transformation of a body into *nomina* cf. 8.537–41 (Meleager).

[30] These are the two (partly exclusive) consolations for death of Cic., *Tusc.* 1. Both then enter the tradition on the death of Cicero himself: Sen. *Suas.* 6.5–6 (Arellius Fuscus, teacher of Ovid) *immortalis humanorum operum custos memoria, qua magnis viris vita perpetua est, in omnia te saecula sacratum dabit . . . nihil aliud intercidet quam corpus fragilitatis caducae . . . animus vero divina origine haustus . . . onerosi corporis vinculis exsolutus ad sedes suas et cognata sidera recurret.* Cf. Vell. Pat. 2.66.5 *vivit vivetque per omnem saeculorum memoriam, dumque hoc . . . rerum naturae corpus – quod ille paene solus Romanorum animo vidit, ingenio complexus est, eloquentia inluminauit – manebit incolume, comitem aevi sui laudem Ciceronis trahet* (fame guaranteed by the natural universe). The (auto)biographical tradition on Cicero is yet another source for Ovid's construction of his own biography, another example of a voice whose immortality frustrates the tyrant's violence. The comparison of the poet's exile to the experience of living through the sack of a city at *Tr.* 1.3 finds a parallel in Cic., *Dom.* 98; see further Nagle (1980:33–5), Fuchs (1969) on Ovid's diversion of Ciceronian topics on the consolatory powers of philosophy to an expression of thanks to the poetic Muse in *Tr.* 4.10.115–22. Other examples of the *topos* of posthumous life.: Cic., *Amic.* 102 *mihi quidem Scipio quamquam est subito ereptus, vivit tamen semperque vivet*; Plin., *Ep.* 2.1.11 (Verginius Rufus) *vivit enim vivetque semper atque etiam latius in memoria hominum et sermone versabitur postquam ab oculis recessit*; Tac., *Agr.* 46.4. Albrecht (1984:99), comments on the end of the *Metamorphoses*: "Ovid denkt hier offensichtlich an eine Unsterblichkeit in doppelter Gestalt: einmal als unsterbliche Seele . . . , zum anderen, . . . als rezeptionsgeschichtliches Phänomen."

episode of the poem (746–870) the two themes of apotheosis and succession are tightly woven together. The son Augustus honours his father Julius with deification, and the deified Julius in turn sheds lustre on his son. But both sons and gods can be made, and in ways that mimic the makings of an epic poet (and more especially of the epic poet of the *Metamorphoses*) (746–51):

It was not so much wars capped with triumphs, domestic achievements, and a swift career of glory that turned Caesar into a new star, the plumed comet (*in sidus vertere novum stellamque comantem*), as his own offspring. Among the acts of Caesar there is no greater work (*neque enim de Caesaris actis|ullum maius opus*) than that he was Augustus' father.

Bömer (1986:455) notes the unusual and repeated emphasis on the biological paternity of Julius (751 *pater*, 758 *genuisse*, 760 *semine cretus*, 819 *natusque suus* – the last in an address to Venus, another constructed ancestress). In fact it was Caesar's *acta* (literally "things done", but by extension the official record of those acts, a written construct)[31] that made the son, his "greatest work", with the allusion to the creative power of the epic poet in *maius opus*.[32] One good "turn" deserves another (760–1) "so that the son should not be born of mortal seed, the father had to be made a god (*ille deus faciendus erat*)." The suggestion of a "poetics of divinity" leads naturally into a large-scale use of divine machinery in the reworking (at the end of an epic) of the interview between Venus and Jupiter at the beginning of the *Aeneid*. Within this poetic fiction Jupiter again adverts to the "making" of the god at 818–21 "the apotheosis and worship of Caesar will be the work of yourself and his son (*tu facies natusque suus*), the heir to his name, who singly will bear the burden placed on him." But then it is no secret that one of the most important texts for the construction of the divine pretensions of the Julian house is the *Aeneid* itself. Other texts also play their part: Knox points to the allusion in the "hairy star" *stellam comantem* of line 749 to the *Coma Berenices*, suggesting a Callimachean model for the fiction of an astral apotheosis in the last book of a poem. But the *Aitia* is only one in a chain of texts that associate stars, hair, and apotheosis: at the end of book 14 after the apotheosis of Romulus a falling star sets fire to the hair of Hersilia who then herself is translated to the heavens; behind this glows the flaming hair of Lavinia in *Aeneid* 7, related in turn to the omen of the fire that plays over the hair of Ascanius in *Aeneid*

---

[31] Cf. *TLL* s.v. *acta* 1408.16 *vocabulum tum ad ipsas actiones pertinet tum per metonymiam transfertur ad scripta quibus, quae acta sunt, continentur.* At *Met.* 14.783–5 *sola Venus portae cecidisse repagula sensit|et clausura fuit, nisi quod rescindere numquam|dis licet acta deum*, Fate is reduced to the status of human decrees, or in poetic terms the "script" of the traditional story of the Sabine siege of Rome.

[32] Virgil uses *maius opus* to refer to the "greater", Iliadic, half of his epic at *Aen.* 7.45; Ovid also uses the phrase at *Met.* 8.328, where the narrator turns from a love-story to the properly epic business of the boar-hunt.

2, a passage related to other allusions to the *sidus Iulium* within the *Aeneid*, and to the story of Servius Tullius as reported in book 1 of Livy.[33] How are we to read this? As a succession of literary representations that authenticates the *sidus Iulium*, just as the literary history implicit in the Speech of Pythagoras authenticates Ovid's claim to succeed to a great line of hexameter *vates*, or as the emptying out of imperial self-representation into a bottomless pit of textuality?[34]

Knox states that "Augustus [is] . . . as much a literary motif as a political issue" (p. 79). These words are truer than Knox, I suspect, guesses. *Metamorphoses* 15 is not a literary game played in a demilitarized zone outside the "realities" of contemporary politics. Rather Ovid reveals the seamless continuity between the representations of imperial ideology – of all ideologies – and those of literary texts. Appropriately it is Jupiter, supreme god of the Roman state and ruler of the epic pantheon, whose words (*fata*) make some of the clearest connections between World and Text.[35] His speech at 15.807–42 owes its very existence to another text, the Speech of Jupiter in *Aeneid* 1. In his first words he alludes to another, non-poetic, text, when he converts his own *spoken* words, *fata*, into the written text of the celestial *tabularia* 'public records office', whose *molimen vastum* 'huge bulk' is perhaps, when all is said and done, the only *moles* that will still bulk large when Rome is dust and ashes. Allusion to the bronze and to the meteorological depredations of Horace *Odes* 3.30, closely imitated just a few lines later in Ovid's own Epilogue, reverses the comparison in those two passages of the work of poets to the work of kings. Towards the end of his speech at line 832 the Virgilian Jupiter starts to ventriloquize in words that come uncannily close to those of another author, the author of the *Res Gestae* (and other autobiographical statements) of Augustus.[36] The "deeds" of Augustus are just another kind of text to quote, nestling cosily within the retrospective prophecy of a Virgilian Jupiter. Is this

---

[33] The horns on Cipus' head also form part of this image-structure; Galinsky (1967) notes the parallels with *Aen.* 2.680 and 8.680. The whole complex also concerns myths of succession.

[34] Zumwalt (1977:218): "both legend and history . . . blend into a continuum inaccessible to such values as truth and objectivity. . . . there is no difference between immortality granted to an Ino or a Memnon and that secured by an Aeneas or a Caesar".

[35] In general see Feeney (1991:151–5) on the relativities of the Virgilian Jupiter.

[36] See Bömer (1986:477), referring to Binder (1971:94–5), "Man meint fast, Worte der Res Gestae in . . . Versen aus dem Schluß der Metamorphosen . . . zu lesen." With *Met.* 15.832–4 *pace data terris animum ad civilia vertet iura suum legesque feret iustissimus auctor/exemploque suo mores reget* cf. *RG* 8.5 *legibus novis me auctore inlatis multa exempla maiorum exolescentia iam ex nostro saeculo reduxi et ipse multarum rerum exempla imitanda posteris tradidi.* (The last words could equally apply to a poetic tradition!) For the possibility of Ovid's direct imitation of autobiographical works by the emperor himself see Fairweather (1987:193–5), speculating that parallels between *Tr.* 4.10 and *RG* 1 point to a common source in Augustus' *Commentarii de vita sua.*

disrepectful to the emperor? Or is the *Aeneid* any less worthy a textual model for imitation than imperial pronouncements of the kind exemplified in the *Res Gestae*? Can the emperor refuse the poet's offer of his talents in the service of the construction of the imperial image? *Metamorphoses* 15 works hard to construct a not unflattering analogy between the successor to the first king of Rome and the successor to Julius Caesar; the *princeps* might remember that Numa had set about his didactic and civilizing task *ducibus Camenis* "with the Muses as his guides" (or "leaders") (15.482). Ovid, like Virgil and Horace before him, offers himself as another poetic guide – even leader – in that continuing task.

The first question of *Metamorphoses* 15, the question of succession, remains the hardest to answer. As we have seen, it is also the issue that most tightly binds together the concerns of *princeps* and poet. The last books of the *Metamorphoses* offer a variety of models for succession. In this area it will emerge that in fact only the poet can be ultimately assured of success.

Julius Caesar's solution is to fabricate a "natural" son and give him a name which is also his own; this is the fiction of the ideal succession of the same by the same, as spelled out at 819 *nominis heres* ("heir to the name", of Augustus Caesar) and 837 *ferre simul nomenque suum curasque iubebit* ("he will bid him bear both his name and his responsibilities", looking forward to Tiberius Caesar), and also suggested by the narrative parallelism between the apotheoses of Julius and Augustus. Caesar = Caesar, the imperial fiction.[37] But we do not forget that continuity is achieved at the expense of a change of name (Octavian's). Furthermore the equivalence of "father" and "son" is also threatened by that wild card in the process of legitimation, *Fama*, an agent of orderly succession in the case of Numa at the beginning of the book (4), but now beyond the control of the ruler (852–4): "although he forbids that his acts be given precedence over those of his father, yet free report (*libera fama*), answerable to no command, gives him precedence against his will, and rebels in this one particular."[38] On one level this is a courtly compliment, testimony to the continuance of a Republican freedom of speech under the principate; on another level it hints at the ultimate instability of power structures founded on verbal representations. Verbal licence, *fama*, controls deeds, *acta*. Maybe this is the price that has to be paid if the ruler

---

[37] Barchiesi (1989:94): "Cesare viene plasmato da Augusto come suo 'doppio'. I due personaggi sono speculari." On the cult of Julius as a "maquette" for Augustus' own future apotheosis see White (1988), 355.

[38] Moulton (1973:7), sees here an "ironic colouring". Bömer dissents, yet notes that *nullis obnoxia iussis* uses the "Terminologie der Diktatur". Shades of *haud mollia iussa*? At 855, *sic magnus cedit titulis Agamemnonis Atreus ...* , *titulus* introduces another moment of textuality, followed by *exemplis ipsos aequantibus* of the – mythical – Saturn and Jupiter. For similar tricks see *Amores* 1.3.

changes his name yet again, choosing a title *Augustus* that already contains in its root *augeo* the notion of increase, a going beyond.

Ideally the imperial succession should replicate that of the (self-evidently fictional) phoenix, whose method of self-perpetuation, perhaps surprisingly, finds a place in Pythagoras' discourse on universal change at 392–407. (392) *una est, quae reparet seque ipsa reseminet ales* "there is one bird that recreates itself and provides its own seed" – as Julius would like to have done (760 *semine*). The phoenix is perhaps imperial in its longevity,[39] and in its costly funeral pyre? The burden to which it must grow to be equal is literally its parent, 403 "when maturity has given it strength and it is capable of bearing the burden" (cf. 15.1–2), a type of the Julian *gens* in its pious (405 *pius*) consecration of its father.

But the poet transcends even the ideal self-replication of the phoenix, finally exempt from the processes of change and decay as he remains true to (the better part of) himself and soars off into a perpetual immortality. 874 "my name will be indestructible": "Ovid" will always be "Ovid", unlike Caesar Augustus, or Romulus and Hersilia who both change their names on apotheosis (14.849–51); and also unlike Pythagoras, who in an earlier incarnation was "Euphorbus".[40] In the end it is the poet who controls *Fama*: 878–9 *perque omnia saecula fama, | siquid habent veri vatum praesagia, vivam* "and through all ages, if there is any truth in the bards' presentiments, I shall live in fame." This falsely modest reworking of the procedure that marked out Numa as successor at 3–4 ("*fama*, foretelling the truth, designates renowned Numa for the throne") conceals the truth that only within the circle of the poet and his readers can the relationship between *fama* and *verum* become unproblematical; in this poem the poet's voice defines what is true and what is not. Even that last self-fulfilling prophecy *vivam* is caught within the text. It is self-fulfilling because it is self-exemplifying, the word itself proves the point – but only as long as there are readers to read it. Ovid indeed beats the emperor at his own game of replicating his own order of things, but only because in that order of things the World has been completely reduced to Text. Augustus' problem, we may grant, is more difficult.

Appropriately Ovid's success is matched only by that of the ultimate epic hero, Achilles, the touchstone of *Fama*, at *Met.* 12.615–19:

Now he is ashes, and of the great Achilles there remains but a something that would not properly fill a small urn. Yet there lives on a glory to fill the whole earth; this is the measure that answers to the greatness of the man, and in this Peleus' son is equal to himself, and has not felt the emptiness of Hades.

---

[39] *Met.* 15.838 *nec nisi cum †senior similes† aequaverit annos*: the text may be beyond repair.

[40] The last sentence of the *Metamorphoses* alludes, among so much else, to *Geo.* 3.46–8 *mox tamen ardentis accingar dicere pugnas | Caesaris et nomen fama tot ferre per annos, | Tithoni prima quot abest ab origine Caesar*, where the text lays itself open to competing identifications of the *nomen*: "Caesar" or "Vergilius"?

Implicit here is the body/name contrast of 15.871–9; explicit is the claim for the perpetual life of one who remains equal to himself, exempted from mutability.[41] [*I*]*nania Tartara* "the emptiness of Hades" suggests the contrast between the "weight" and fullness of Achilles' fame and the insubstantiality of ghosts in the Underworld, but also recalls us to the nature of poetic fiction, "empty" because non-existent outside the poets. By a further twist the phrase also marks the purely textual nature of Achilles' posthumous glory; we all remember of course that the "real" Achilles "feels" the inanity of the Underworld all too keenly in *Odyssey* 11.[42]

The matchless poet at the very end, with no anxiety about *his* succession, stands in pointed contrast to the difficulties of finding an imperial successor. The contrast becomes sharper, barbed even, if the concealed agenda in the last 120 lines of the poem is not the heir to Julius Caesar, but the succession to Augustus in the 'teens of the first century CE, whence the interesting parallels with Tac. *Ann.* 1 (see above).[43]

Turning black into white

By the end of the book the pretensions of the Roman epic tradition to naturalize the power of Rome and her great men within the order of the cosmos, and the legitimation of a privileged line of succession, have been shown equally to have a purely textual, constructed authority. What of the other type of science offered to Numa at the beginning of the book as a vehicle for the validation of political structures, ktistic aetiology? The story of Myscelos, the founder of the Greek city of Croton, seems curiously out of place in what becomes an increasingly Roman book. But, with only a little nudging, it tells a tale that touches the Romans most nearly. It is in fact the Virgilian foundation story that we had *not* been told in book 14 where we might have expected the reworking. And if Croton is not Rome, in the past the Greek city had held a comparable primacy among the cities of Italy: Pythagoras might well have

---

[41] And also a "match" for himself, in death as he was in life (as *aristos*).

[42] Even within the *Metamorphoses* Achilles is seen in the form of a ghost, if appropriately a ghost undiminished in size from the form of the living man (13.441). The death of Achilles sparks another succession crisis at the beginning of book 13 (as the death of Romulus at the end of book 14 leaves a power vacuum to be filled at the beginning of book 15), 13.133 *quis magno melius succedit Achilli?* We will not be surprised to learn that the answer is the man of words rather than the man of action. By making the Shield of Achilles the centre of a succession crisis Ovid may comment obliquely on the function of the Virgilian Shield of Aeneas, that marks out its bearer as the successor to Achilles (as well as Atlas and Hercules), and which bears for device the succession in time from Aeneas, *Aen.* 8.731 *famamque et fata nepotum*. Other examples of *succedo* in Ovid: *Tr.* 2.467 *his ego successi* (a poetic succession); *P.* 2.5.75 *succedatque suis orbis moderator habenis.*

[43] There may also be a parallel with the anxiety about the succession at a much earlier date that is precipitated in the Marcellus episode at the end of *Aeneid* 6.

taken his own chosen city as another example of the alternating rise and fall of cities (15.420 ff.).[44]

The interview between Numa and the old man in "the city of Hercules' host" (8) replicates the meeting between Aeneas and Evander in the centrally Roman book 8 of the *Aeneid*. Hercules had stopped off at the site of Croton on the same swing through Italy that brought him to the site of Rome. His promise of the future foundation, 18 *hic locus urbis erit* "this will be the site of a city", is made in the words of the Virgilian Helenus, *Aen.* 3.393 *is locus urbis erit, requies ea certa laborum* "that will be the site of the city, a sure rest from your labours" (a prophecy whose migration from the lips of Helenus to those of Hercules is a miniature example of the migratory tendencies of the whole Myscelos episode).[45] The story that the old man tells is of a pious man (20 "most favoured by the gods of men of that time") impelled by a divine command received in a dream to flee from his native land to seek a new home in Italy.[46] The old man's story is also an example of the Virgilian pattern found in *Aeneid* 1, the tale of a city-founding exile addressed to one who is himself in transit from his homeland.[47]

From this point the Virgilian model will take us no further. Myscelos' native city is no Troy. It still stands, and its laws forbid its citizens to leave their city on pain of death, or as Ovid puts it (29) "death is the penalty fixed for him who wishes to change his fatherland" (*patriam mutare volenti*). In a work entitled *Metamorphoses* the word *mutare* is unlikely to be completely innocent. One person who "changed his fatherland" and suffered death as a

---

[44] Cf. Cic. *Inv.* 2.1.1 *Crotoniatae quondam cum florerent omnibus copiis et in Italia cum primis numerarentur.* The parallelism between Croton and Rome informs the whole of the Croton episode in Petronius' *Satyricon*, where the city is described as *urbem antiquissimam aliquando Italiae primam*; the episode is full of Ovidian allusion: see Zeitlin (1971:69) "Croton was once (*aliquando*) the first city of Italy. Now of course, Rome bears that distinction". *Met.* 15.9–10 *Graia quis Italicis <u>auctor</u> posuisset in oris | <u>moenia</u>* might also suggest the kind of poetic claim for the transmission of Greek cultural goods to Italian soil found in *Odes* 3.30 and Prop. 3.1, thus preparing the way for the thoroughgoing merging of political and poetic models of transmission at the end of the book.

[45] The words *requies ea certa laborum* seem to be echoed two lines before at *Met.* 15.16 *requie longum relevasse laborem*. Helenus' words in Virgil are also, scandalously, migratory within the *Aeneid*, returning in the mouth of Tiberinus at 8.43–5 (= 3.390–2). The next line, 8.46 *hic locus urbis erit, requies ea certa laborum* (= 3.393, with the alteration of *is* to *hic*) is customarily excised by editors; *hic locus erit* are however the precise words of the Ovidian Hercules. A witty comment on the "correct place" for the words and on the place where future cities stand? Hercules' prophecy avoids all the problems that beset interpreters of *Aeneid* 8.

[46] The initial dream at 22–4 may remind us of the dream-vision of Hector in *Aeneid* 2; the repetition in more urgent form of the apparition at 32–3 alludes to the second appearance of Mercury, in a dream, to Aeneas at *Aen.* 4.556–70.

[47] *Aen.* 1.335–68 (Venus to Aeneas).

result was Julius Caesar,[48] an event followed by convulsive changes in the natural order of things, according to Virgil at *Georgics* 1.466 ff., beginning with the sun hiding his head in eclipse: 467–8 "he covered his gleaming head (*caput nitidum*) in a dark gloom, and the wicked age feared eternal night".[49] In the case of Myscelos the threat of death as punishment for "changing one's fatherland" is immediately followed by a natural plunge into darkness described in language that echoes the Virgilian portent: *Met.* 15.30–1 "the brilliant Sun had hidden his gleaming head (*nitidum caput*) in Ocean, and the thickest Night had raised her starry head."[50] But Myscelos has not yet suffered the penalty. How then to avoid the fate of Julius Caesar? Augustus' way was to pretend that in *his* revolution nothing had really changed. This is also the solution of Hercules in the case of Myscelos. [*M*]*os erat antiquus* "there was an ancient tradition . . ." (41):[51] as readers of Ennius know, *moribus antiquis res stat Romana virisque* "the Roman state rests on its ancient traditions and men" (*Ann.* 156 Skutsch). Hercules will alter nothing in this ancient legal institution; he will change only the colour of the voting pebbles, which went in all black and came out all white – as naturally as the bright day follows the dark night, perhaps.[52] No universal convulsions here. Catullus may not have cared too much to know whether Julius Caesar was a white man or a black man (Cat. 93.2); Augustus certainly cared how he appeared to his subjects, and he also was a master at making black appear white, as cunning perhaps as Autolycus, "capable in inventing all kinds of trick, one used to making black into white and white into black" (*Met.* 11.313–15).[53]

[48] For *mutare* in a political sense cf. Sen. *Ep.* 71.12 *quidni ille* [Cato] *mutationem rei publicae forti et aequo pateretur animo*? (followed by a passage on the mutability of the cosmos).

[49] The passage is imitated at length at *Met.* 15.782–98 in an account of the omens *before* the death of Caesar.

[50] The hiding of the head is an addition to the Ennian models for these lines, on which see Knox (1986), 70. The closest parallel is *Ann.* 84–5 Skutsch, at a key moment in the narrative of the founding of Rome.

[51] Cf. *Aen.* 7.601 *mos erat*, introducing the aetion of the venerable custom of opening and closing the gates of Janus.

[52] One of the natural changes catalogued by Pythagoras at 15.187 *et iubar hoc nitidum nigrae succedere nocti* (also an example of succession!).

[53] For the proverbial expression see also Juv. 3.30 with Mayor, *ad loc.* Other Ovidian examples of changing (or not) black into white, white into black: *Met.* 4.51–2; *Pont.* 3.3.95–8. Particularly interesting is the account of the metamorphosis of the raven at *Met.* 2.540–1 *lingua fuit damno: lingua faciente loquaci, | qui color albus erat, nunc est contrarius albo*, referring to Apollo's punishment of the bird for its garrulity; but the two lines, taken out of context, could also mean that changing white into black is within the verbal power of the tongue. A pupil of the lexicographer James Murray during his time as a schoolteacher remembered ". . . the tricks he could play with words. Such was his skill and knowledge that many of us firmly believed that by Grimm's law he could prove that BLACK really was the same word as WHITE; at least that was how it seemed to our poor intelligences" (Murray [1977:113]).

The Hercules–Myscelos team is as skilful at dissimulation as Cipus will be later in the book, when he conceals the horns of power beneath the laurel of peace, and reinforces his pretensions to constitutionality with the traditional prayer to the ancestral gods (593 *priscosque deos e more precatus*).[54]

The story of Myscelos is an *aition* that explains the foundation of a city through translocation, a passage from east to west, a small-scale example of a kind of narrative expanded to the monumental in the *Aeneid*. The laborious journey of the Virgilian Aeneas is also a figure for an "official version" of the painful but virtuous passage achieved by Octavian/Augustus from the wreck of the Republic to the *respublica restituta*. Other versions were available: the Ovidian foundation of Croton is a tale of manipulation and dissimulation that makes it a suitable preface to the picture of statecraft offered in the final book of the *Metamorphoses*. In its own way the story of Myscelos comments on the status of a cultural revolution that pretends to be no revolution.[55]

[54] Cf. Galinsky (1967); Barchiesi (1997). The metamorphoses in the Ovidian stories of Myscelos and Cipus are both within the power of Autolycus, who concealed the cattle that he had stolen from Sisyphus by changing black animals to white, and hornless animals to horned (Hyg., *Fab.* 201).

[55] I am grateful for their comments to the participants in the Princeton conference "The Roman Cultural Revolution", to Alessandro Barchiesi, an anonymous referee, and the editors.

11   A preface to the history of declamation: whose speech? whose history?

W. Martin Bloomer

In the opening essay of this collection, Andrew Wallace-Hadrill differentiates between the social and cultural dimensions of the Roman revolution. While acknowledging the importance of social change as described and debated by Syme and his successors, Wallace-Hadrill places emphasis on the cultural transformations, especially in the areas of authority and morality, that characterize the transition from late Republic to early Empire. In the present paper I would like to reunite the social and cultural strands so capably and usefully disentangled by Wallace-Hadrill by focusing my attention on the institution of declamation, or set school pieces, and on the treatise of Seneca the Elder that promotes declamation as a status-enhancing cultural practice. My argument will concern both the practice of declamation and its practitioners and will complement Wallace-Hadrill's essay as well as that of Florence Dupont. If, as Dupont argues, literary recitation was an attempt by an imperial aristocracy to lay claim to a space for *libertas*, school declamation can be understood as the means through which those of less than aristocratic status, either as youths or adults, laid claim to the cultural prestige of old-time oratory and strove to turn themselves into true Romans.

This essay considers one text prescriptive of Roman culture and Roman speech. The elder Seneca's treatment of Roman declamation seeks to display a very Roman world, where proper Latinity and Roman nobles censure the upstart and the Greek. The various speakers in Seneca's book pose as the successors to Ciceronian Latin and Republican oratory; they compete to demonstrate proper speech, one which is neither craven Caesarian flattery nor Ciceronian pastiche but a reworking of traditional topics that, if properly handled, reveals those defining characteristics of a traditional male citizen: *ingenuitas* and *libertas*, free birth and free speech. At the same time declamatory oratory was *oratio* displaced. It was school speech, a ludic version of forensic conflict, performed under the eye and even punishing hand of a schoolmaster by those at a distant remove in time and even origin from Cicero and Antony or the Catos and Scipios of the Republic. Thus a sense of linguistic inferiority is overlaid with worries about political and social inferiority. Praise of the past is nothing new in Roman society, but this new

medium of school exercises burgeoning into literature engaged in a fundamental and contradictory fiction. The boy could be fashioned into a man, into
a Roman man, by this play-speaking on behalf of prostitute-priestesses, un-
grateful sons, villainous stepmothers, and harsh fathers. Cultural and social
categories are here being defined and contested within that peculiarly liminal
site, the school with its fantasies of adult speech and life. For the cultural
historian, declamation is most interesting as the site of these myth-making
processes.[1] In this quasi-Greek world, a schoolteacher, who might well be an
ex-slave, taught an originally Greek academic subject, still filled with pirates
and tyrants, to Roman boys. From this world Seneca the Elder fashioned his
history of contemporary speech.

Seneca himself had good reason to feel anxiety about his own status at
Rome. A provincial equestrian, he made a very dubious authority for an
account of Roman oratory – and the set school debates known as declamation
had an equally dubious claim to being Roman oratory. My argument is that
Seneca's work has been naïvely read as an objective snapshot of Roman
public speech under Augustus and Tiberius whereas in fact the work's intent
was to set Seneca's family on the road to social distinction and to elevate
what was a schoolroom practice to the status of old-time oratory. In addition,
declamation itself reveals a concern about becoming Roman. Declamation
examines categories and roles essential to the socialization of the new imperial governing classes.

My discussion starts from the observation that the subjects of Seneca's prefaces are a suspect lot (each book has a preface devoted to one or two model
declaimers, then follow Seneca's selections of the declaimers' divisions of
the case, their *sententiae*, and those twists of plot known as *colores*). In brief
we do not get real declaimers or the most prominent declaimers but instead
actual orators (lawyers) and most curiously a group of Spanish *amici*, a select
circle of Seneca's choosing, whose provincial and at best equestrian status
would not have impressed the traditional consumers of Roman oratory.

Seneca adopts the stance that his three sons have begged him for an
account of the leading declaimers. Literature need not purport to be serious,
but when written from the avowed stance of the *pater familias*, it makes itself
out to be so. The Roman father writes of what he participates in: most traditionally, war (history) and agriculture, or memoirs of a consulship when
there is not much war to write about.[2] Seneca's address to his sons mixes the
seriousness of paternal instruction with a suggestion of the unimportance,

---

[1] See Beard (1993) on declamation as a cultural negotiation of social and familial conflict.

[2] Cicero's publication of his speeches conforms; the letters do not. Or the letters offer a different
tone and persona, the *amicus* writing to his equals. When he writes to Marcus for all the world
to read, a different tone and topic are evident.

the novelty of his subject. In later periods of history, so-called "women's literature" offers a parallel: the author both dignifies and apologizes for his subject through notice of the audience. In the one case, the persona of *pater* maintains the text's serious stance while in the other the young women addressees enable the author to write on a new topic – a handbook of etiquette, for example. Like a literature of instruction in behavior addressed to girls, a collection of Roman pedagogic exercises frees the author to write of what had been parental and oral. The author communicates avowedly traditional material, ostensibly to a new audience, one without familial connection to the subject.

Seneca's volumes were a sort of handbook of the etiquette of the new speech; he is greatly concerned with proper and improper style, especially with avoiding the vulgarism or Grecism that vitiates the Romanness of declamation. Neither in Seneca's case nor in that of manuals for feminine improvement need we believe, however, that the addressee is the sole or indeed the real readership. But why has Seneca chosen to add this particular subject to the course of young men's reading? Why has what properly belongs to the schools and to oral instruction become literature?

The answer lies beneath Seneca's assertion that he writes so that his sons, who have not heard the early declaimers, may know the genuine and the approved from the spurious and spurned. Seneca and his approved circle of critics, including his schoolmate Latro, and Asinius Pollio and Valerius Messala, are much concerned with issues of taste, of what constitutes proper and improper Latin, of vulgarity, license, *copia*, and control. The declaimers served up a public Latin demonstrably alien from the forensic and legal speech of Cicero's day. This difference Seneca hopes to bridge by his history of declamation with its insistence on the proper Roman style of his favored practitioners. Only thus can declamation be a worthy subject of study, a pursuit allied in setting (the schools) and style and purpose to the now so venerated and academic model of Cicero. Seneca thus makes two crucial junctures. The first refutes the charge of impracticality: declamation is the proper training for law (public speech and public life), philosophy, history, the gentleman's life.[3] The second, allied aspect of his program connects this innovation in style and pedagogy to the canonical past. Latro emerges as a new Cicero while emulation of Cicero is carefully delineated: neither aping nor censuring the old orator will do.

Any history of public speech includes itself. Seneca had available an authoritative history of Roman speech: Cicero's *Brutus* presented a chronological series of Roman orators, each with a particular virtue, culminating in the unstated but obvious apex of Cicero himself, most versed in Greek culture

---

[3] Seneca, *Contr.* 2 pr. 3: *facilis ab hac [eloquentia] in omnes artes discursus est.*

and the most perfect Latin orator. To write a new history of Roman speech or to add an appendix, Seneca must inscribe himself, his circle, and declamation into this authoritative genealogy. The recurrent criticism of declamation reveals the difficulty and ambition of Seneca's program: impractical, perhaps vulgar, and suspected of being Greek, declamation may not belong to the Roman curriculum.

The ambitions of Seneca *pater*

The elder Seneca was misnamed by later scholars *rhetor* – an affront to the equestrian who uses this term only of teaching professionals. He was an ambitious man, and one who succeeded in his ambitions. We have simply to look to his sons. The eldest, Novatus, was adopted by Junius Gallio, Tiberius' senator and later victim, who was the leading practitioner of the new style. Novatus himself reached the consulship and judged St. Paul while proconsul of Achaea (*c.* 52 CE). The middle son, after adulterous intrigue resulting in exile, repaired his fortunes by tutoring Nero (or perhaps more accurately, Agrippina had the philosopher Seneca recalled and made praetor in 49, eight years after his affair with Caligula's sister Julia Livilla).[4] Tacitus should not be believed when he describes Mela, the youngest son and father of the poet Lucan, as a financier who eschewed the public life; he tried the route in his case more lucrative, and more closely tied to the emperor, of the equestrian governmental posts.[5] The success of father and sons was not simply the rewards due a literary family. The elder Seneca's grandson, the failed conspirator Lucan, similarly mixed politics and literature. The account of declamation and the lost histories of the elder Seneca did not in themselves launch this provincial family into Roman letters and public life, but the extant collection reveals this program: Seneca dedicates his work to the public and moralizes throughout the work in ways that associate questions of taste with the health of Roman society. The philosopher son seems to express the ambition of the father when he writes that his father's writings, if published, would have lifted him to social prominence,

---

[4] On Seneca and Agrippina and more generally on Seneca's attachment to the circle of Sejanus see Stewart (1953).

[5] Tacitus, *Annales*, 16.17: *petitione honorum abstinuerat per ambitionem praeposteram ut eques Romanus consularibus potentia aequaretur; simul adquirendae pecuniae brevius iter credebat per procurationes administrandis principis negotiis.* Tacitus resents Mela's means of acquiring wealth and fame: he did not undertake the traditional *cursus honorum*, so the historian has in all probability misrepresented Mela's motives in not seeking the consulship; two brothers had reached the consulship a third honor might make the family too conspicuous, perhaps even dynastic in its ambitions. If Mela was the emperor's procurator, he may have been following his father's lead: de Mirmont (1912:13) suggested that Seneca returned to Spain to discharge an imperial procuratorship and that Tacitus "forgets" that his father-in-law's grandfathers were of this station, imperial procurators in Cisalpine Gaul.

to clarity, and perhaps nobility.[6] Perhaps it took the highhanded recognition
of Nero (and the adoption of Novatus by Junius Gallio whereby, as the son
of a consular, Novatus could be a *nobilis*) and not simply the pen of the
philosopher to make the family noble.[7] The elder Seneca stretches the orbit
of the word noble by applying it on a number of occasions not to those of
a consular line but of literary merit.

The father has masked his ambitions as successfully as he has written
himself out of declamation. The reader hears of some of his judgments or of
his questions to Cassius Severus in a preface, but the extant account would
have us believe that this habitué of the schools said nothing. Whatever his
actual role in the training of his children and the attendance on his friends, the
father's devotion to schooling, like that of Horace's father, has a clear social
aim. Fortunately, Tacitus communicates a recognition of Seneca's ambition
from two points of view. The condemned freespoken aristocrat Publius Suillius
taunts Seneca *filius* with two charges (in addition to his hatred for the friends
of Claudius and his adultery): Seneca has preferred impractical, academic
speech to real oratory, and he is an *arriviste*.[8] In a second passage from the
Annals of Tacitus Seneca proposes his own retirement to Nero using the
words of his aristocratic critic. Significantly, the historical *exempla* he chooses
to mirror his state are the ambitious, high-climbers Marcus Agrippa, reviled
for his supposedly low origin, and Maecenas. Horace, the freedman's son who
purports to have no social ambitions, when playing Maecenas' encomiast,
made his patron's non-noble birth into the virtue of self-sufficiency: Maecenas
the *clarus eques* who aims no higher; the mythological Etruscan royal ancestry
is no substitute for *nobilitas*. Suillius and Tacitus seem to speak through
Seneca's confession: "Born from an equestrian provincial family, am I to be
counted among the chiefs of state? Has my recent arrival outshone the nobles
and their long records of distinction?" (14.53: *egone equestri et provinciali*

---

[6] Seneca, fr. 98: *si quaecumque composuit pater meus et edi voluit, iam in manus populi emisissem,
ad claritatem nominis sui satis sibi ipse prospexerat: nam nisi me decepit pietas, cuius honestus
etiam error est, inter eos haberetur, qui ingenio meruerunt ut puris titulis nobiles essent.*

Horace refers to Accius' trimeters as noble (*Ars Poetica* 259), but this word is infrequently
applied to artistic works. Propertius, punning on the meanings of this word, ironically warns
Cynthia not to become a *nobilis historia* (1.15.24). Elsewhere, Propertius stretches the usage
of the word by applying it to places (like the Forum, 4.9.20, which would have been filled with
nobiles, living and statuary). He refers to an ivory decoration of the Temple of Apollo as
Libyci nobile dentis opus (2.31.12), a phrase followed by Ovid.

[7] Helvia's aunt married C. Galerius, prefect of Egypt from 16 to 31. Perhaps Seneca the philosopher aimed above this equestrian pinnacle.

[8] Suillius refuses to submit his ancestral, familial rank and station to the *nouveau riche* Seneca
(*Ann.* 13.42: *simul studiis inertibus et iuuenum imperitiae suetum liuere iis qui uiuidam et
incorruptam eloquentiam tuendis ciuibus exercerent ... ueterem ac domi partam dignationem
subitae felicitati submitteret*).

loco ortus proceribus civitatis adnumeror? inter nobilis et longa decora praeferentis novitas mea enituit?).

The Senecas reveal a concern with engrafted nobility rather like Latro when he used this unfortunate phrase before Maecenas and Augustus and Agrippa just when Agrippa had succeeded in marrying into the imperial family.[9] Like the senatorial historians who were new men, the elder Seneca professes an ardent, upper-class Romanness by castigating vice as effeminate, vulgar, and Greek. The felicity, the great good fortune that elevated a *homo novus* to the consulship, the "luck" of the son may be of the father's making.[10] The inscription of the sons into a history of oratory recommends the three young men to the community as surely as did Cato's dedication of his encyclopedia to his first son or Cicero's instruction of young Marcus in the *De officiis*.[11] A conservative, moralizing pedagogy publicizes the promise of all these Romans sons and was but part of the fathers' promotional activities. The readership of these works includes the sons, their Roman peers who are to take the writers' sons as models, and the older men who are to recognize the fathers' virtues in the new generation. Like their polemic, the circles of Cato and Cicero are far better known than those of Seneca *pater*. In the case of the imperial Seneca, the characters and critics within the work present a model circle: Pollio, Gallio, Latro, Messala, and perhaps beyond them the emperor are the real critics whose judgment must be satisfied.[12]

Seneca's work has the simplest pretensions: an old man recollects so as to instruct his sons. In fact, the pretensions are much grander: a selective memory drops important names and recollects as a single phenomenon what

---

[9] Having mentioned the ever-senatorial Tacitus' condescension toward Seneca, I should point out the similarity of their stations. If, as Syme suggested, Tacitus was of provincial background, we may well imagine his grandfather to have been very like the elder Seneca: a Western provincial, wealthy landowner, interested in education and in sending Tacitus or his father to Rome to complete his education. The rise of the sons by marriage and public speaking would be a common route to distinction. Syme (1970:10) suggested that Tacitus' assumption of *nobilitas* has fooled posterity and that Asinius Pollio is a good parallel. If the elder Seneca was Pollio's client (dependent friend), Tacitus might have judged him and his family unequals, despite their similarities to modern eyes.

[10] Syme (1970: 8) pointed out that Tacitus uses *felicitas* only twice, at 13.42 and 14.53, the two passages (discussed above) that refer to criticism of the younger Seneca (and his philosophical "felicity").

[11] Lockyer (1970:195–9) catalogs the instances of Roman literary works in which the author addresses his son.

[12] Seneca shares the disdain of this circle for the professional teacher. Suetonius (*De gramm.*, 4) records the attitude of Messala: *Eosdem litteratores vocitatos Messala Corvinus in quadam epistula ostendit, non esse sibi dicens rem cum Furio Bibaculo, ne cum Ticida quidem aut litteratore Catone; significat enim haud dubie Valerium Catonem, poetam simul grammaticumque notissimum.*

was inherently composite. By uniting speakers of different occasions, ages, and places in a single declamation, he has produced a cultural, social, and generational reduction.[13] The old man's protestations of a failing memory help him to exclude the more recent declaimers; so he can focus on Latro and his own circle. So too perhaps he can skirt the written sources of Otho and Cestius.[14] Publicly performed speech at Rome cannot be subsumed under the rubric of declamation, especially if one means by that term the picture familiar from Quintilian and the modern handbooks. Seneca's text betrays the actual variety: Latro spoke, never gave instruction. Albucius spoke only five or six times a year in public.[15] In all probability, a number of the speakers never engaged in such declamation (Cassius Severus, Asinius Pollio, Votienus Montanus). Other passages indicate a contest of professionals.[16] What is most clear is the effect of Seneca's presentation: he has reduced all these forms of speech to the most academic type, the brand of declamation known from Quintilian's treatise and the declamations attributed to him, where the master offers preliminary analysis and model speech.[17] The various Latin declaimers have become Seneca's pupils, while the Greeks are relegated to the rear and given short shrift, at least in part since Seneca makes the Greeks and not provincial Romans the antitype for good Latin.[18]

The ambition of the prefaces

The prefaces are the most ambitious part of Seneca's work.[19] Here Seneca distances his project from the technical treatise; here he proclaims his amateur

---

[13] Suetonius, writing of late Republican times, indicates the variety of primary education available: *temporibus quibusdam super viginti celebres scolae fuisse in urbe tradantur* (*De gramm.*, 3).

[14] Cestius is my suggestion. See Lockyer (1970) for written sources.

[15] Seneca describes Albucius' sketchy private declamations, his form of instruction, in the preface to book seven. He writes that when Albucius declaimed in public *ter bucinavit* (*C.* 7 pr. 1), which seems to imply that he spoke at night when the night watch sounded a trumpet every three hours.

[16] As does Petronius (*Sat.* 6), who has Encolpius harangue Agamemnon who has just finished performing inside and has been succeeded by another declaimer.

[17] Seneca has drawn most of Pollio's speech from occasions which are clearly *recitationes*. Indeed, we see Pollio leaving the recitation of a Spanish poet. Seneca manages to weave in such different discourse as forensic speech and recitation and historiography in his digressions, those notices of criticism that serve to delineate proper declamation.

[18] At *S.* 4.5 Seneca says that Fuscus declaimed more often in Greek than in Latin, yet Seneca's text has no Greek *sententiae* from Fuscus (once at *C.* 1.7.14 the scribes have omitted Fuscus' quotation of *Iliad* 24, 478–9, but this is the only Greek he speaks). The *suasoriae* do have Greek *sententiae*, but Seneca seems unwilling to have Fuscus, the model of the *suasoriae*, speak Greek.

[19] Their importance has been recognized: see Leeman (1963: 224): "Of these prologues it can be said without exaggeration that they were indispensable for a right understanding of the whole literary production of Imperial Rome"

and superior status. The ten subjects of the original prefaces and perhaps the subjects of a lost preface to the *Suasoriae*[20] constitute a circle not of professional schoolmen but of upper-class Romans. A rhetorician could have written a technical treatise and addressed it to his socially superior patron, but the form chosen by Seneca, a paternal epistle recommending models to his sons, asserts the equality or potential equality of all addressed. The prefaces, then, constitute textual, generational, and social juncture. Disparate occasions and different speakers are subjoined while, in an anachronism fit for declamation, men long dead plead alongside the peers and teachers of Seneca's sons. As the prefaces elevate the subject to be narrated, and the particular *controversia*, and more generally the role and importance of declamation, they, like any rhetorical juncture, slip by distinctive differences, here especially those of time, place, and status.

The peculiar distortion that Seneca has worked on Roman literary history is indicated by Suetonius' collected biographies of the leading speakers. Even in its lacunose state Suetonius' work seems a more objective account, primarily because his net is wider. In his prefaces Seneca offers as models of emulation figures Suetonius for the most part would not have listed as practitioners of declamation. Suetonius distinguished between professional teachers of grammar, teachers of rhetoric, and then actual orators – those who spoke in the courts or in the Senate. Seneca banishes the Greek professionals to the very end of each *controversia* or *suasoria*. The speakers who do appear in the prefaces are an unusual collection, for significantly and strikingly present are non-declaimers or non-professionals.

To treat the subjects of the prefaces in order: Latro is a professional, but through a number of techniques that elevate his fellow Spaniard, Seneca succeeds in suggesting that Latro is a new Cicero. His friend is no teacher but a performer: he takes no students, offers no criticism, but like the advocate of old or the canonical text is at hand only to be heard, perused, imitated. Fabianus is not a declaimer but a philosopher. As with Latro, Seneca is concerned to elevate his topic of declamation; Fabianus offers the first connection of declamation to philosophy. The thematic and personal importance of this connection needs to be emphasized. To represent Fabianus, the friend and teacher of his son, as a declaimer requires quite a trick of memory: Seneca

---

[20] The ten books of *controversiae* were probably not followed by two of *suasoriae*, of which only one is extant. Winterbottom (1974: xxi, n. 1) had maintained that originally there were more than one book of *suasoriae* since "MSS. B, V, D end the book of *Suasoriae* thus: 'liber primus explicit, incipit liber secundus.'" The colophon is an unsteady guide to the contents of manuscripts. One especially suspects works could be tacked on to a canonical author, and, in Seneca's case, the tradition would come to confuse father and son. Declamatory works were added to Quintilian's corpus. School works invited such forgery.

must recall Fabianus' school performances. Fabianus was, from the report of Quintilian, no great speaker and may have been a Spaniard.[21]

Cassius Severus, subject of the third preface, likewise was no professional or frequent declaimer. Indeed, this embarrassing reality demands some apology, and so, in trying to connect the world of the forum with that of the school-room, Seneca represents himself asking the lawyer why he declaimed so poorly. Asinius Pollio, whom Syme believed to be the leading literary force at Rome, after Augustus and perhaps alongside Maecenas, was no declaimer. We cannot know what Seneca recalled of him in the lost book four (the extant, excerpted version of the text does not indicate speakers); elsewhere in Seneca's work he speaks in a declamation only three times. The case of Quintus Haterius is similar. Here too Seneca's subject is being elevated by association.[22] Haterius was a prominent orator. The subject of the seventh preface, C. Albucius Silus, is the exception, for he was a famous, professional teacher.

Votienus Montanus, the subject of the ninth preface, who published his first speech before the centumviral court and who left other writings (*C.* 9.5.15 and 9.6.18), like Cassius Severus was a lawyer–orator not a declaimer: Seneca says that he declaimed neither publicly nor privately: "Votienus Montanus so completely avoided performing show declamation that he never even declaimed for practice" (9 *pr.* 1: *Montanus Votienus adeo numquam ostentationis declamavit causa ut ne exercitationis quidem declamaverit*). Montanus shares another similarity with Cassius Severus: Seneca has Montanus explain in his preface why his declamation was inferior to his legal pleading. Montanus' answer stresses the unreality of declamation, its remove from the bar. Seneca maintains that his sons had suggested Montanus' name – clearly he is not a declaimer – and this difficulty with finding suitable (prominent equestrians, or better, of the capital) subjects for the prefaces resurfaces in the final book. Here in a developed *praeteritio* Seneca lists those who will not qualify for his prefaces; here too he ranks the declaimers: the first tetrad (Latro, Fuscus, Albucius, Gallio) and the second? He refuses to stoop: "Let those lesser known (noble) go their own way, Paternus and Moderatus, Fabius and anyone else of midway fame and oblivion" (10 *pr.* 13: *Hos minus nobiles sinite in partem abire, Paternum et Moderatum, Fabium et si quis est nec clari nominis nec ignoti*). The names proposed by his sons he has rejected.

---

[21] Griffin (1972:16) adds epigraphical support to Syme's notice of the "Spanish look" of Fabianus' name (*HSCP* 73 [1968], 222, quoted by Griffin). Griffin finds Fabianus' style fluent, but "by comparing what the two Senecas say, we can see that Fabianus' oral and written style was cold, flat, and lacking in point, brilliance and precision."

[22] Tacitus makes an unreliable guide – highly prejudiced against such equestrians as Haterius, Seneca, and Cassius Severus.

The "nobles" who are included come as a surprise; Seneca proposes his fellow Spaniards Clodius Turrinus and Gavius Silo (whose provincial name might have raised a hoot of laughter). Silo's sole claim to fame was that Augustus, on hearing him plead on several occasions in Tarraco, had called him the most eloquent *pater familias* he had ever heard (10 *pr.* 14). Seneca even allows that Silo lacked force and independence: he was a devotee of Apollodorus and invariably founded his declamation on Latro's *color* (10 *pr.* 15: *Numquam non de colore Latroni controversiam fecit*). Seneca tells one other salient feature: Clodius Turrinus' grandfather had entertained Julius Caesar (10 *pr.* 16). Membership in the provincial gentry and a connection, however tenuous, to the Caesars validate the Spaniards.

To recapitulate: of the nine subjects of the seven extant prefaces only two were declaimers: Latro who performed but did not teach and Albucius Silus, one of the professional declaimer–instructors of Seneca's day. Conspicuously absent from the prefaces and relegated to second position in the text,[23] the Greeks who seem to have constituted the majority of rhetorical teachers are further slighted, for Seneca makes them the target of much invective centering about the new style, its corruption, and degeneracy from the old Roman. In addition, the leading teacher of declamation, Cestius, is excluded from a preface though Seneca quotes him in the body of the text very frequently.

Allegiances of the declaimers

Amid the series of names the modern reader may miss the peculiar quality of the set of declaimers commemorated. To an ancient reader certain allegiances and patterns would have been far clearer. Seneca has given no snapshot of public declamation. He presents a number of non-declaimers so as to connect practical legal oratory (and perhaps *recitatio*, the pre-publication of written works practiced by Pollio and by *literati* before him[24]) with this public pedagogy and art form. The circle he has chosen to present is, however, even more intimate, for he purports to show his reader the private world, the domestic performances of leading nobles.[25] He represents Asinius Pollio educating his grandson Marcellus. His reference to Messala, who never declaims but simply judges, likewise offers a private vision. We see Messala at home, conversing

---

[23] Compare the similar treatment and position of the Greek *exempla* in Valerius Maximus' chapters: Bloomer (1992:17, 28).

[24] Seneca writes, somewhat misleadingly, of this practice: *[Pollio] primus omnium Romanorum advocatis hominibus scripta sua recitavit* (C. 4 *pr.* 2). Dalzell (1955: 26) concludes: "Pollio's innovation was the establishment of public recitations on a more formal basis."

[25] Compare the literary social gesture of Cicero saying he met Cato in the library of the young Lucullus' house (*De fin.* 3.7), a dialogic fiction not to be believed but a social fiction uniting the upper crust, the *boni omnes*.

with Seneca, Gallio, and Tiberius after a public performance of Nicetes (*C.* 5.3.6) and once hosting a recitation by a Spanish poet (whose opening praise of Cicero and implied criticism of the sterility of the age so displeased Pollio that he left [*S.* 6.7]).[26] Seneca says he knows that Cornelius Severus was there too, thus implying that he was an eye-witness. Seneca also presents himself as present when Pollio, three days after the death of his son, gave a private performance (*C.* 4 *pr.* 4). M. Lepidus the "tutor of Nero" (*C.* 2.3.23), whom Seneca heard in Scaurus' house (*C.* 10 *pr.* 3), may have been the Lepidus who was the consul of 11 CE. Like his mention of old-fashioned speakers and like his introductory history of declamation, the inclusion of noble patrons and critics connects what was a public, professional performance with both practical oratory and with Republican precedent. Asinius Pollio's criticisms of the various declaimers legitimize and Romanize, in the same fashion as allusion to Cicero or to Augustus' visiting the halls of declamation, what the critics called a Greek, scholastic exercise. Of course, just as declamation was far more Greek than Seneca would have us believe, it was also not traditionally Roman. I do not seek to argue that, for example, public performance emigrated from Spain but that Seneca in proffering his own circle as the proper declaimers, continuators of good prose (not Greek, Asiatic, or corrupt, "libertine" style) has promoted a group of Spanish *amici* to the most prominent position in Latin letters. Latro, Junius Gallio, Clodius Turrinus, Gavius Silo and perhaps Fabianus, all subjects of the prefaces, were born in Spain. Asinius Pollio commanded the Caesarian forces in Spain in 44. This republican – but friend of Caesar – was the best prospect for patron a citizen from the Pompeiian city of Cordoba could hope for.[27] Others of Seneca's preferred speakers came from the Italian peninsula: Vibius Gallus was born in Perugia; Albucius Silus at Novaria.[28] Votienus came from Narbonne; to nearby Marseilles to open a school went Volcacius Moschus, defended unsuccessfully on a charge of poisoning by Asinius Pollio and Torquatus (20 BCE). So far will geography lead. I do not mean to suggest that some Western land-owners were a tight-knit salon dependent on Pollio, but that lines of allegiance – of class, geography and hence perhaps language (one thinks of

---

[26] Even if the line *Deflendus Cicero est Latinaeque silentia linguae* drove Pollio out, Seneca takes pride in this Spanish poet Sextilius Ena. Seneca identifies him as his *municeps*, the same distinction he had for the playwright Statorius Victor (*S.* 2.18).

[27] Syme (1958: 136) points out that Pollio's grandfather, leader of the Marrucini, fought against Rome (Livy, *Per.* 73) and writes approvingly of Pollio's independence, 569: "The Italian *novus homo* had no cause for indulgence toward the Roman aristocracy."

[28] Votienus seems to have broken ties with his hometown: he was accused before Augustus by Vinicius on behalf of the citizens of Narbonne (*C.* 7.5.11). He also advertized his status as a Roman *patronus* when he published his defense of Galla Numisia before the centumviral court (*C.* 9.5.15).

the thick-sounding poets of Cordoba alluded to by Cicero at *Pro Archia* 26), and those ties familial and social that the Romans called *amicitia* – and not oratorical excellence alone, distinguish Seneca's preferred declaimers. Clearly there were other Spaniards who did not matter to Seneca: perhaps the Seneca nicknamed Grandio and Quintilian *senex*, who may have been the famous rhetorician's father, were Spaniards like Marullus whom Seneca chose not to promote.[29]

Seneca's particular allegiances are made clearer; he writes of "our Latro," "our Gallio," and "our Passienus" (who had his own school). He attends Pollio instructing his grandson and he reports the private comments and conversation of Pollio and his fellow noble Messala. Seneca's sons must have attended the lectures of Musa, a freed Greek to whom father Seneca refers as "yours."

Like the naming of individuals in Catullus' and especially in Horace's poems, the author is not simply parceling out favours to friends and slights to enemies. The literary work participates in the elaborate signalling of connections and status that was a Roman reality. Cultural *amicitia* is a complex phenomenon, of which Florence Dupont has treated one most significant development in her analysis of the Roman imperial *recitatio*.[30] Roman declamation and Seneca's particular fashioning of its addressees, participants, and contexts provide a complementary model of social, cultural, and institutional change. Especially in the imperial East declamation would come to recover the prestige of Republican oratory: Libanius and John Chrysostom are the most famous practitioners of this civic art. But the brilliant, anachronistic performances of the Second Sophistic are an altogether different development of the traditions of ancient oratory and liturgy. What did a school practice in the Rome of Augustus and Tiberius have to offer? I have argued that it shifted paradigms of identity, thus making Roman and traditional new governors, provincials like the family of Seneca. Seneca has given declamation its own history which depends not simply on the memory of the old man, as he maintains, but on his not remembering Cicero. He thus shares with his readership

[29] My general conclusions disagree with Griffin (1972: 12) who argues from Seneca's disapproval of some Spaniards that "Seneca does not allow his keen interest in the speakers of his province to cloud his judgment." In addition, the wrong question lies behind the conclusion that no sense of Spanish nationalism ("national consciousness," p. 15) animated Seneca. As Griffin noted, the Senecas returned to Spain, married Spanish ladies, and, I would argue, advanced their Spanish friends. All of which is consistently the action of a Roman *patronus*, if we understand the Senecas' attitudes and behavior from the perspective of Roman provincialism rather than provincial nationalism. To be nationalist besides the anachronism would require a stance as an outsider, recognizable in Tacitus' Arminius but not in a provincial landowner.

[30] See above pp. 44–60.

an exclusively textual knowledge of the Republic and feels compelled to bring in historians' accounts of the death of Cicero. Just as with his prefaces he can thereby introduce authorities who were not declaimers. This serves his purposes of elevating declamation, of having it subsume other genres such as historiography, oratory, philosophy, and poetry, but it also casts the dead Cicero as the telos of *oratio*, replacing the dead Hortensius who had played that role in Cicero's *Brutus*. Against these symbols of the death of speech, the text asserts the possibility of more speech, of a continuing tradition.

The declaimers found in declamation a peculiar form of pedagogy. Speech on ridiculous topics is a fun and even profitable pursuit. A panegyric on salt advertises a product: in the ancient world, the versatile flexibility and resources of its composer. Even in such an exercise the selection of topic may be significant. Especially in Roman declamation the point does not seem to be solely that public speech and hence public distinction can be achieved through this novel means, nor that, like the salt-praiser, another career waits for the virtuoso declaimer. Declamation was not simply displaced *oratio* or ludic anticipation of the law.

Nothing is more commonplace in ancient discussions of declamations, even within declamation itself, than complaint about the fatuity of declamation. The critics complained that declamation did not adequately prepare the student for the bar: it fell short of real, legal discourse in pertinence (a criterion that, although it simply replicates the general complaint, does point to the differences of permissible subject), degree of ornamentation (i.e. excess versus restraint, figured versus straight speech), relationship to audience (declamation allows the audience's interruption, indeed seeks applause, the positive form of interruption – no such relief is granted the lawyer, Votienus Montanus says [*C.* 9 *pr.* 1]; the Imperial lawyer had to move a judge). In ancient terms *copia* characterizes declamation whose abundance spills over to include the audience in its play. In fact there are far greater points of contact between the practices of declamatory and legal speech, but to play the apologist within these limits simply replays the ancient division. To step out of the ancient rhetorical trope at least for a moment, the critic must posit other purposes and contexts of declamation. Declamation did provide the future lawyer, bureaucrat or administrator with certain valuable tools. Bonner has shown, so as to close debate on the Romanness or Greekness of the laws within declamation, that frequently the law as it appears in a *controversia* never recurred in the students's professional experience.[31] Of course the laws of declamation are convenient fictions, for had they been real Roman laws the discourse about them would have been severely limited, and part of the pedagogic point of declamation is to get teenage boys to speak freely. Had the laws been mined

---

[31] Bonner (1949: 5–6).

from Greek experience, then history, questions of fact, precedent, outcome, even legal practice, or some historian's version of these, would similarly have delimited what could be said.

Even at its most fantastic Roman declamation sets themes that depict and examine a conflict of allegiances. Formally, this conflict depends from the *divisio* that splits the case in question into two headings. Law is not simply set against justice in some abstract consideration of the conflict of the spirit and the letter of the law. Nor is declamation reducible to a series of alternative lexical classifications: is the present case an instance of homicide or manslaughter? Repeatedly, the declaimers examine conflicts of social allegiance.

The subjects that have given critics the greatest difficulty, those cases of ingratitude and of *lèse-majesté* which correspond neither to Greek precedent nor to Roman reality, illustrate well the tendencies and preoccupations of declamation. In these features Roman declamation has far more in common with Roman comedy. The fantasy of declamation mirrors that of Roman comedy: freedman and slave are so promoted that they are or have advocates. The son speaks against the father. Generational and social strife may be said to be surfacing, but, more concretely, Roman schoolboys were performing a sort of role-playing that practiced category-making. Indeed, declamation reads like much of New Comedy as a confrontation with the harsh prescriptions of role and behavior dictated by paternal script.[32] With father off the stage, in temporary exile, at sea, or away from school, the son takes his liberty of speech and imagined action. Law, the embodiment of the *patres'* severity, does not rule adolescent speech but is instead elaborated, embellished, its unyielding verbal texture resisted. Thus arises a speech not bound by law, not answerable to the single judge, to the older judge or even exclusively to the freedman schoolmaster or servile pedagogue but, to a degree, to peers.

The role-playing of declamation must have trained the rather insulated upper-class adolescent in a sort of situational ethics, for the speakers of declamation appropriate voices. This sort of transgression is no doubt fun, and much humor, and not simply comedy, depends on the disjuncture of person and speech type (so the old man of the *Miles Gloriosus* who speaks as the young lover or those masters of all the different registers of Roman society, the parasite and the plotting slave). In declamation the greatest challenge, the greatest training and virtuosity lay with the adoption of the minor voices. To speak with paternal authority, to castigate, to act the *laudator temporis acti* had become trite; it took Fabianus' philosophical reflections to animate such tired work. The father's part that offers some challenge is the speech on behalf of the father who would marry his daughter to his freedman. Thus declamation trained its pupils intensively in the hard part of advocacy.

---

[32] Compare the plot of Plautus' *Rudens* with the example of an old-fashioned *controversia* in Suet., *De rhetoribus* 1.

More generally, declamation trained a young Roman in a sympathy of view-point, emotions, motivations, and speech that he would need in treating his future clients. The freeborn official would need to write to and for freedmen. Declamation versed the schoolboy in the appropriation of voices from below his station as well as in the appropriation of the grand voices of past Roman heroes, the training he received from speaking historical exempla and from addressing the famous *maiores* in his *suasoriae*. To recommend or deprecate a course of action to the mighty, to speak as a traditional *nobilis*, to appreci-ate the voices and desires of the slave, the freedman, the woman, constitute the trinity of training for the early Imperial schoolboy.

Even a brief tour of a few bizarre and unreal *controversiae* reveals some of the specific techniques useful for Roman social life and imperial admin-istration. Most fundamentally, once through rhetorical school, a boy would sound like a young Roman, knowing not only epigram, division, or *praeteritio*, but the cultural stock of historical *exempla* and the shared experience of anachronistic, imaginative involvement with "the past," with "history." What could a boy learn from the historically inaccurate and legally impossible case of Callias' prosecution of his son-in-law Cimon for ingratitude? No Roman in real life need speak for and against a prostitute's application for the posi-tion of priestess (1.2), and this declamation hardly explores the nature of the sacred. Yet in discerning the holy from the most profane, the advocate must recommend the candidacy of one whose publicly perceived station, whose dress and profession, disqualify the petition. The declaimers take up what might have been philosophical investigation into interiority and exteriority, reality and appearance, as a question of a virtuoso letter or speech of recom-mendation. The recreated narrative rivals Cicero's technique in the ability to imagine a set of circumstances altogether decent in the eyes of the public that entirely mitigates the present awkward status of the defendant. To speak the other part, to disqualify a candidate for an office or a position, though also of great serviceability, has not the same challenge; *vituperatio* and *delatio* seldom do.[33]

Themes of social and societal injury (e.g. Cimon, ransomed by Callias whose daughter he marries and would execute for adultery, is sued by his father-in-law for ingratitude) reflect the general interest of declamation in investigating *pietas*, in determining the stance to be taken towards father, paternal authority and speech. The speakers' division attempts to isolate social roles that in fact are not separate, since, for instance, the *filius* can also be *sui iuris*, the woman can be daughter and wife. The liminal quality of speakers and subject needs to be emphasized.[34] The defendant appears torn in a call between

[33] *Facile est accusare luxuriem*, Cicero, *Pro Caelio* 29.
[34] Kennedy (1972: 334) has pointed out "the recurring question of the relationship of children to adults" within declamation.

two roles or modes of behavior, but the theme and structure for debate cannot be isolated from its speakers. Those who took up the theme of *pater filium abdicans* or *uxorem repudians* were still *liberi*, a word likewise ambiguous: free and child, those still in the domestic domain of the women, slaves, and freedmen with whom so much declamation is concerned. The schoolboys in their confrontation with or appropriation of paternal severity and paternal speech speak as men. But declamation was a broader social phenomenon: fathers themselves, even senators, chose to perform, to speak as adolescents imitating the serious speech of men.

Although he writes his part out of the written record, Seneca is of course the arch-declaimer because it is he who makes the most significant and abiding *divisio*. Good and bad, Latin and Greek, original and fake, he distinguishes in an embracing rhetorical project of a scope not to be contained by oral medium, indeed which spills over into ten books and the *suasoriae*. In the end rhetorical *copia* is best attested in his mastery of theme, division, *sententiae*, and *colores*. Seneca stands as the final censor of vulgarity and champion of proper Latin just as it is he who connects the new generation with the old, his sons with Latro, Latro and declamation in general through his introduction of the poets, historians, and of Cicero to the old republicans.

In writing to his sons Seneca also champions manly taste. On a number of occasions and most importantly in the first preface, Seneca sets the approved virile style, to be learned from his collection, against the reigning effeminacy of the day.[35] This highly useful topos delivered by an old man helps to elevate Seneca's circle from the general opprobrium directed against declamation. Seneca also styles himself as a dedicating magistrate or Roman censor: today's young are no genuine men, he erupts in this preface: "a perverse addiction to song and dance captivates the effeminate ... Among your set who is a real, I don't dare say genius or scholar, but man? Who wins popular approval, I won't say by great, but by his own, talent and effort?" (*C.* 1 *pr.* 8–10: *cantandi saltandique obscena studia effeminatos tenent ... Quis aequalium vestrorum quid dicam satis ingeniosus, satis studiosus, immo quis satis vir est? ... Quis est qui non dico magnis virtutibus sed suis placeat?*). He repeatedly assumes this stance of restoring virtues to their proper men and of combating contemporary vulgarity.[36] Indeed, Seneca emerges as the champion of

---

[35] So once Seneca reattributes to Florus a *sententia* alleged to be Latro's because of its *mollem compositionem* (9.2.24).

[36] Indeed, he even engages in a sort of *aemulatio* with past censors. In *S.* 1.12 a certain Dorion spoke the "most corrupt thing." Maecenas censured Dorion by comparison with Virgil. Seneca trumps this: *Multo corruptiorem sententiam Menestrati cuiusdam, declamatoris non abiecti suis temporibus, nactus sum in hac ipsa suasoria* (*S.* 1.13). Seneca's *nactus sum* contrasts strongly with the usual *memini* with which he vouches for the authenticity of his material. The episode also contrasts with the consensus opinion that Dorion's was the most corrupt *sententia*. Seneca's research has found one worse.

taste in a text that so rambles that it might seem vulgar if its *copia* were not controlled and punctuated by the consummate orator. The style of his first preface borrows heavily from Roman satire; its speech of adulterous and effeminate youth, its denunciation of contemporary speech as effeminate adulterer make Seneca the Roman satirist, master of Roman *sermo*, displaying his own control and restraint, showing his allegiance to the *imperium* of *Latinitas.*

The elder Seneca has fashioned this empire of Roman speech by presenting the declamatory display of his fellow Spaniard Latro and the education of his full-grown sons as manifestations of Romanness allied to Republican oratory, to contemporary poetry recitations, to the leading orators' styles, and to the conversational criticism of noble literary patrons. Thus for Seneca "literature" was a social institution, one that negotiates questions of identity and allegiance.[37] Declamation itself allowed iterable representations of what proper speech was, of who was noble and who base, of how slave and master, wife and proper son should speak and act. In these representations where there was no final word but instead only memorable *color*, twist of plot or suggestion of motivation, and memorable reductive *sententia*, a literate elite displayed and redefined crucial social fictions about the value and power of speech, the arrangements of status and authority, and the authoritative mouthpieces for these. In some struggles for culture the trick is to maintain that there is nothing new, nothing effeminate, nothing suspect here.

---

[37] The philosopher learned from his father: Stewart (1953: 81–3) described the politically animated choice of subject of the *Consolatio ad Marciam* wherein the author seeks to distance himself from connection with the fallen *Sejaniani* (newly oppressed by Caligula after the conspiracy of Lepidus and Gaetulicus) by addressing Cremutius Cordus' daughter. In playing father to the bereaved Marcia, the philosopher assumes a noble status.

Works Cited

Adams, J. N. 1982. *The Latin Sexual Vocabulary*. Baltimore.

Ahl, F. 1988. "*Ars Est Caelare Artem* (Art in Puns and Anagrams Engraved)." In J. Culler, ed., *On Puns*. Oxford. 17–43.

Albrecht, M. von 1984. *Interpretationen und Unterrichtsvorschläge zu Ovids Metamorphosen*. Göttingen.

Alföldi, A. 1971. "Die Penaten, Aeneas und Latinus." *MDAI(R)* 78:1–58.

Anderson, W. S. 1964. "Hercules Exclusus." *AJP* 85:1–12.

———. 1982. *Essays on Roman Satire*. Princeton.

———. 1992. "The Limits of Genre." In G. K. Galinsky, ed., *The Interpretation of Roman Poetry: Empiricism or Hermeneutics*. Frankfurt and New York. 96–103.

Andreae, B. 1997. *The Art of Rome*. New York.

Arkins, B. 1982. *Sexuality in Catullus*. (Altertumswissenschaft Texte und Studien, 8.) Hildesheim-Zurich-New York.

Armstrong, D. 1986. "*Horatius Eques et Scriba: Satires* 1.6 and 2.7." *TAPA* 116: 255–88.

Badian, E. 1993. "Livy and Augustus." In W. Schuller, ed., *Livius: Aspekte seines Werkes*. (*Xenia* 31) Konstanz. 9–38.

Baker, R. J. 1988. "Maecenas and Horace *Satires* 2.8," *CJ* 83:212–31.

Bakhtin, M. M. 1981. *The Dialogic Imagination*. Trans. C. and M. Holquist. Austin.

Barchiesi, A. 1989. "Voci e istanze narrative nelle Metamorfosi di Ovidio", *MD* 23:55–97.

———. 1991. "Discordant Muses," *PCPhS* 37:1–21.

———. 1997. "Endgames: Ovid's *Metamorphoses* 15 and *Fasti* 6." In D. Roberts, F. M. Dunn, and D. Fowler, eds., *Classical Closure: Reading the End in Greek and Latin Literature*. Princeton. 181–208.

Barton, C. 1993. *The Sorrows of the Ancient Romans*. Princeton.

Barton, T. 1995. "Augustus and Capricorn: Astrological Polyvalency and Imperial Rhetoric," *JRS* 85:33–51.

Bauman, R. A. 1983. *Lawyers in Roman Republican Politics: a Study of the Roman Jurists in their political setting, 316–82 B.C.* Munich.

———. 1985. *Lawyers in Roman Transitional Politics: a Study of the Roman Jurists in their political setting in the Late Republic and Triumvirate*. Munich.

———. 1989. *Lawyers and Politics in the early Empire: a Study of relations between the Roman Jurists and the Emperors from Augustus to Hadrian*. Munich.

Beard, M. 1986. "Cicero and Divination." *JRS* 76:33–46.

———. 1993. "Looking (Harder) for Roman Myth: Dumézil, Declamation and the Problem of Definition." In F. Graf, ed., *Mythos in mythenloser Gesellschaft. Das Paradigma Roms*. Stuttgart and Leipzig. 44–64.

Bedon, R. 1988. "Sur les pas d'Horace dans la Rome proto-Augustéenne." In R. Chevalier, ed., *Présence d'Horace* (Collection Caesarodunum 23bis) Tours. 25–33.

Benveniste, E. 1969. *Vocabulaire des institutions indo-européennes*. Paris. 2 vols.

Bernstein, M. A. 1992. *Bitter Carnival. Ressentiment and the Abject Hero*. Princeton.

Bettini, M. 1991. *Anthropology and Roman Culture: Kinship, Time, Images of the Soul*. Baltimore.

Binder, G. 1971. *Aeneas und Augustus*. Meisenheim.

Bleicken, J. 1963. "*Coniuratio*. Die Schwurszene auf den Münzen und Gemmen der römischen Republik." *Jahrbuch für Numismatik und Geldgeschichte* 13:51–70.

Bloomer, W. M. 1992. *Valerius Maximus and the Rhetoric of the New Nobility*. Chapel Hill and London.

Bömer, F. 1986. *P. Ovidius Naso* Metamorphosen. *Buch XIV–XV*. Heidelberg.

Bonjour, M. 1975a. "Les personnages féminins et la terre natale dans l'épisode de Coriolan (Liv., 2.40)." *REL* 53:157–81.

1975b. *Terre natale*. Paris.

Bonner, S. F. 1949. *Roman Declamation in the Late Republic and Early Empire*. Liverpool.

Boon, J. A. 1982. *Other Tribes, Other Scribes*. Cambridge.

Boswell, J. 1990. "Concepts, Experience, and Sexuality." *differences* 2:67–87.

Bowersock, G. W. 1990. "The Pontificate of Augustus." In K. Raaflaub and M. Toher, eds., *Between Republic and Empire*. Berkeley. 380–94.

Bremmer, J. N. 1990. "Adolescents, Symposion, and Pederasty." In O. Murray, ed., *Sympotica: A Symposium on the* Symposion, Oxford. 135–48.

Brown, F. 1961. *Roman Architecture*. New York.

Brown, P. and Levinson, S. C. 1987. *Politeness: Some Universals in Language Usage*. Cambridge.

Brown, R. D. 1990. "The Structural Function of the Song of Iopas." *HSCP* 93:315–34.

Brunt, P. A. 1971. *Italian Manpower, 225 B.C.–A.D. 14*. Oxford.

1988. *The Fall of the Roman Republic and other Essays*. Oxford.

Buchheit, V. 1965. "Tibull 2.5." *Philologus* 109:184–200.

1993. "Numa-Pythagoras in der Deutung Ovids." *Hermes* 121:77–99.

Buchner, E. 1982. *Die Sonnenuhr des Augustus*. Mainz.

Burkert, W. 1983. *Homo Necans: The Anthropology of Ancient Greek Sacrificial Ritual and Myth*. Berkeley.

Cairns, F. 1992a. "Propertius 4.9." In G. K. Galinsky, ed., *The Interpretation of Roman Poetry: Empiricism or Hermeneutics*. Frankfurt and New York. 65–95.

1992b. "The Power of Implication: Horace's invitation to Maecenas (*Odes* 1.20)." In T. Woodman and J. Powell, eds., *Author and Audience in Latin Literature*. Cambridge. 84–109.

Cameron, A. 1986. "Redrawing the Map: early Christianity after Foucault." *JRS* 76: 266–71.

Cantarella, E. 1988. *Secondo natura: La bisessualità nel mondo antico*. (Nuova biblioteca di cultura 289.) Rome. Trans. as *Bisexuality in the Ancient World*. New Haven, 1992.

1991. "Homicides of Honor: The Development of Italian Adultery Law over Two Millennia." In D. I. Kertzer and R. P. Saller, eds., *The Family in Italy from Antiquity to the Present*. New Haven. 229–44.

Carettoni, G. 1973. "Nuova serie di grande lastre 'Campana.'" *BdA* ser. 5. 58:75–87.

Ceaucescu, P. 1976. "*Altera Roma*: histoire d'une folie politique," *Historia* 25:79–108.

Champlin, E. 1991. *Final Judgments: Duty and Emotion in Roman Wills, 200 B.C.–A.D. 250*. Berkeley.

Chartier, R. 1991. *The Cultural Origins of the French Revolution*. Trans. L. Cochrane. Durham and London.

Chauncey, G. 1994. *Gay New York: Gender, Urban Culture, and the Making of the Gay Male World*. New York.

Clarke, John R. 1991. "The Decor of the House of Jupiter and Ganymede at Ostia Antica: Private Residence Turned Gay Hotel?" 89–104. In Elaine Gazda, ed., *Roman Art in the Private Sphere*. Ann Arbor. 89–104.

Clifford, J. and Marcus, G., eds., 1986. *Writing Culture: the Poetics and Politics of Ethnography*. Berkeley.

Coarelli, F. 1980. *Guida archeologica di Roma*. Bari.

Cohen, D. 1991. "The Augustan Law on Adultery: The Social and Cultural Context." In D. I. Kertzer and R. P. Saller, eds., *The Family in Italy from Antiquity to the Present*. New Haven. 109–26.

Colin, J. 1952/3. "Juvenal, les baladins et les rétiaires d'après le manuscrit d'Oxford." *Atti della Accademia delle Scienze di Torino*, Classe di scienze morali, storiche e filologiche 87:315–85.

Commager, S. 1962. *The Odes of Horace*. New Haven.

Conticello de'Spagnolis, M. 1984. *Il tempio dei Dioscuri nel Circo Flaminio*. Rome.

Corbett, P. 1986. *The Scurra*. Edinburgh.

Courtney, E. 1980. *A Commentary on Juvenal*. London.

  1984. *Juvenal. The Satires*. Rome. = Instrumentum Litterarum 1.

Crahay, R. and Hubaux, J. 1958. "Sous le masque de Pythagore." In N. Herescu, ed., *Ovidiana*. Paris. 283–300.

Curran, L. C. 1964. "Ovid *Amores* 1.10." *Phoenix* 18:314–19.

Dalzell, A. 1955. "C. Asinius Pollio and the Early History of Public Recitation at Rome." *Hermathena* 86:20–28.

Daremberg, Ch. and Saglio, M. 1877–1919. *Dictionnaire des antiquités grecques et romaines d'après les textes et les monuments*. 5 vols. Paris.

D'Arms, J. H. 1990. "The Roman Convivium and Equality." In O. Murray, ed., *Sympotica*. Oxford. 308–20.

  1991. "Slaves at Roman Convivia." In W. J. Slater, ed., *Dining in a Classical Context*. Ann Arbor. 171–83.

Daube, D. 1956. "The Accuser under the *lex Iulia de adulteriis*." *Hellenika* 9:15–21.

  1972. "The *lex Iulia* concerning Adultery." *Irish Jurist* 7:373–80.

  1978. "Biblical Landmarks in the Struggle for Women's Rights." *Juridical Review* 90:177–97.

Davidson, A. I. 1987–88. "Sex and the Emergence of Sexuality," *Critical Inquiry* 14:16–48.

Davis, G. 1990. *Polyhymnia: The Rhetoric of Horatian Lyric Discourse*. Berkeley.

Dean-Jones, L. 1992. "The Politics of Pleasure: Female Sexual Appetite in the Hippocratic Corpus." *Helios* 19:72–91.

Deininger, J. 1985. "Livius und der Prinzipat." *Klio* 67:265–72.

Della Corte, M. 1951. *Cleopatra, M. Antonio e Ottaviano nelle allegorie storico-umoristiche delle argenterie del tesoro di Boscoreale*. Pompeii.

de Martino, F. 1989. "Il modello della città-stato." In E. Gabba and A. Schiavone, eds., *Storia di Roma*. 4:433–58.

Denyer, N. C. 1985. "The Case against Divination." *PCPhS* 211:1–10.

Dirks, N. B., Eley, G., and Ortner, S. B., eds. 1994. *Culture/Power/History. A Reader in Contemporary Social Theory.* Princeton.

Dougherty, C. and Kurke, L., eds. 1993. *Cultural Poetics in Archaic Greece.* Cambridge.

Dowden, K. 1989. *Death and the Maiden: Girls' Initiation Rites in Greek Mythology.* New York.

Dumézil, G. 1949. "*Pères* et *fils* dans la légende de Tarquin le Superbe." In *Hommages à Joseph Bidez et à Franz Cumont* (= Collection Latomus 2). Brussels. 77–84.

Dupont, F. 1985. *L'acteur-roi.* Paris.

DuQuesnay, I. M. Le M., 1984. "Horace and Maecenas: The Propaganda Value of *Sermones* 1." In A. J. Woodman and D. West, eds., *Poetry and Politics in the Age of Augustus.* Cambridge. 19–58.

Dyson, S., and Prior, R. 1995. "Horace, Martial and Rome: Two Poetic Outsiders Read the Ancient City." *Arethusa* 28:245–64.

Eagleton, T. 1986. *William Shakespeare.* Oxford.

Earl, D. C. 1967. *The Moral and Political Tradition of Rome.* London and Ithaca.

Edward, W. A. 1928. *The Suasoriae of Seneca the Elder.* Cambridge.

Edwards, C. 1993. *The Politics of Immorality in Ancient Rome.* Cambridge.

Elias, N. 1978. *The Civilizing Process, vol. 1. The History of Manners.* Oxford. Originally published as *Über den Prozess der Zivilisation.* 1939.

    1983. *The Court Society.* Oxford. Originally published as *Die höfische Gesellschaft.* Darmstadt. 1969.

Elsner, J. 1991. "Cult and Sculpture: Sacrifice in the Ara Pacis Augustae." *JRS* 81:50–61.

Fairweather, J. 1987. "Ovid's Autobiographical Poem, *Tristia* 4.10." *CQ* 37:181–96.

Farrell, J. 1991. *Vergil's* Georgics *and the Tradition of Ancient Epic.* New York and Oxford.

Feeney, D. C. 1991. *The Gods in Epic.* Oxford.

Fehling, D. 1974. *Ethologische Überlegungen auf dem Gebiet der Altertumskunde.* Munich. = Zetemata 61. pp. 7–38 reprinted under title "Phallische Demonstration" as pp. 282–323 of A. K. Siems, ed. *Sexualität und Erotik in der Antike.* (Wege der Forschung 605) Darmstadt. 1988.

Feldherr, A. 1998. *Spectacle and Society in Livy's History.* Berkeley.

Ferguson, J. 1979. *Juvenal The Satires.* New York.

Ferrary, J.-L. 1988. *Philhellénisme et imperialisme. Aspects idéologiques de la conquête romaine du monde hellénistique, de la seconde guerre de Macédoine à la guerre contre Mithridate.* Rome: BEFRA vol. 271.

Fitzgerald, W. 1995. *Lyric Poetry and the Drama of Position: Catullan Provocations.* Berkeley.

Flobert, P. 1981. "La *patavinitas* de Tite-Live d'après les moeurs littéraires du temps." *REL* 60:193–206.

Foucault, M. 1970. *The Order of Things. An Archaeology of the Human Sciences.* Originally published as *Les mots et les choses,* Paris 1966.

    1977. *Discipline and Punish. The Birth of the Prison.* Harmondsworth. Originally published as *Surveiller et punir: naissance de la prison.* Paris 1975.

    1978. *The History of Sexuality.* Originally published as *Histoire de la sexualité.* Paris 1976. New York.

Fowler, W. W. 1911. *The Religious Experience of the Roman People.* London.

Fraenkel, E. 1957. *Horace*. Oxford.

Freudenburg, K. 1990. "Horace's Satiric Program and the Language of Contemporary Theory in *Satires* 2.1." *AJPh* 111:187–203.

1993. *The Walking Muse: Horace on the Theory of Satire*. Princeton.

1995. "Canidia at the Feast of Nasidienus (Hor. *S.* 2.8.95)." *TAPA* 125:207–19.

Frier, B. W. 1985. *The Rise of the Roman Jurists: Studies in Cicero's* pro Caecina. Princeton.

Fuchs, H. 1969. "Ovid in der Besinnung auf Cicero." *Museum Helveticum* 26: 159–60.

Galinsky, G. K. 1967. "The Cipus episode in Ovid's *Metamorphoses* (15.565–621)." *TAPhA* 98:181–91.

1969. *Aeneas, Sicily and Rome*. Princeton.

1981. "Augustus' Legislation on Morals and Marriage." *Philologus* 125:126–44.

Gamel, M. 1989. "*Non sine caede*: Abortion Politics and Poetics in Ovid's *Amores*." *Helios* 16:183–206.

Gantz, T. 1975. "The Tarquin Dynasty." *Historia* 24:539–54.

Geertz, C. 1983. *Local Knowledge. Further Essays in Interpretative Anthropology*. New York.

1988. *Works and Lives: the Anthropologist as Author*. Stanford.

Gellner, E. 1983. *Nations and Nationalism*. Oxford.

Gentili, B. 1988. *Poetry and its Public in Ancient Greece from Homer to the Fifth Century*. Trans. T. Cole. Baltimore.

Giddens, A. 1992. *The Transformation of Intimacy: Sexuality, Love and Eroticism in Modern Societies*. Stanford.

Girard, R. 1977. *Violence and the Sacred*. Trans. P. Gregory. Baltimore.

Gladigow, B. 1976. "Römische Erotik im Rahmen sakraler and sozialer Institutionen." *Würzburger Jahrbücher für die Altertumswissenschaft*, N.F. 2:105–18. Reprinted as pp. 324–46 in A. K. Siems, ed., *Sexualität und Erotik in der Antike*. (Wege der Forschung 605) Darmstadt 1988.

Godbout, J. T. 1992. *L'esprit du don*. Paris and Montreal.

Goffman, E. 1959. *The Presentation of Self in Everyday Life*. New York.

Goldhill, S. 1995. *Foucault's Virginity: Ancient Erotic Fiction and the History of Sexuality*. Cambridge.

Gordon, R. 1990. "The Veil of Power: Emperors, Sacrificers and Benefactors." In M. Beard and J. North, eds., *Pagan Priests: Religion and Power in the Ancient World*. London. 201–31.

Gowers, E. 1993. *The Loaded Table: Representations of Food in Roman Literature*. Oxford.

Grant, M. 1975. *Erotic Art in Pompeii*. London.

Greenblatt, S. 1990. "Culture" in F. Lentricchia and T. McLaughlin, eds., *Critical Terms for Literary Study*. Chicago. 225–32.

Griffin, M. T. 1972. "The Elder Seneca and Spain." *JRS* 62:1–19.

Griffin, M. T. and Barnes, J. 1989. *Philosophia togata. Essays on Philosophy and Roman Society*. Oxford.

Grimal, P. 1952. "Les Intentions de Properce et la Composition du Livre IV des Elégies," *Latomus* 11:183–97.

Gruen, E. S. 1974. *The Last Generation of the Roman Republic*. Berkeley.

1992. *Culture and National Identity in Republican Rome*. Ithaca.

Guey, J. 1952. "Avec Properce au Palatin: légendes et promenades." *REL* 30:186–202.

Gurval, R. A. 1995. *Actium and Augustus: The Politics and Emotions of Civil War.* Ann Arbor.

Habinek, T. N. 1982. "Aspects of Intimacy in Greek and Roman Comic Poetry." *Themes in Drama* 7:23–34.

1990a. "Towards a History of Friendly Advice: The Politics of Candor in Cicero's *De Amicitia.*" *Apeiron* 23:165–85.

1990b. "Sacrifice, Society and Vergil's Ox-Born Bees." in M. Griffith and D. J. Mastronarde, eds., *Cabinet of the Muses, Essays on Classical and Comparative Literature in Honor of Thomas G. Rosenmeyer.* Atlanta. 209–23.

1992. "An Aristocracy of Virtue: Seneca on the Beginnings of Wisdom." *Yale Classical Studies* 29:187–203.

Hallett, J. P. 1977. "*Perusinae Glandes* and the Changing Image of Augustus." *AJAH* 2.2:151–71.

Halperin, D. M. 1990. *One Hundred Years of Homosexuality.* New York.

Halperin, D. M., Winkler J. J., and Zeitlin, F. I., eds. 1990. *Before Sexuality: The Construction of Erotic Experience in the Ancient Greek World.* Princeton.

Harder, R. 1952. "Das Prooemium von Ciceros Tusculanen (Die Antithese Rom-Griechenland)." In *EPMHNEIA. Festschrift Otto Regenbogen.* Heidelberg. 104–18.

Hardie, P. R. 1986. *Virgil's* Aeneid: *Cosmos and Imperium.* Oxford.

1991. "The Janus Episode in Ovid's *Fasti.*" *MD* 26:47–64.

1993. *The Epic Successors of Virgil: A Study in the Dynamics of a Tradition.* Cambridge.

1995. "The Speech of Pythagoras in Ovid *Metamorphoses* 15: Empedoclean *Epos.*" *CQ* 45:204–14.

Harris, W. V. 1986. "The Roman Father's Power of Life and Death." In R. S. Bagnall and W. V. Harris, eds., *Studies in Roman Law in Memory of A. Arthur Schiller.* Leiden. 81–95.

Heinze, R. 1930. *Die augusteische Kultur,* ed. A. Körte. Leipzig.

Hellegouarc'h, J. 1963. *Le vocabulaire des relations et des partis politiques sous la république.* Paris.

Henderson, J. 1993. "Be Alert (Your Country Needs Lerts): Horace, *Satires* 1.9." *PCPS* 39:67–93.

Herescu, N., ed. 1958. *Ovidiana.* Paris.

Herter, H. 1966. "Das Königsritual der Atlantis." *RhM* 109:236–59.

Heuss, A. 1956. "Der Untergang der Republik und das Problem der Revolution." *Historische Zeitschrift.* 182:1–28.

1973. "Das Revolutionsproblem im Spiegel der antiken Geschichte." *Historische Zeitschrift* 216:1–72.

Heuss, A., ed. 1982. *La rivoluzione romana: inchiesta tra gli antichisti.* Bibl. Labeo 6. Naples.

Hobsbawm, E. and Ranger, T. 1983. *The Invention of Tradition.* Cambridge.

Hoggart, R. 1957. *The Uses of Literacy.* London.

1970. "Contemporary Cultural Studies: An Approach to the Study of Literature and Society." in M. Bradbury and D. Palmer, eds. *Contemporary Criticism.* London.

Hollis, A. S. 1977. *Ovid Ars Amatoria Book I.* Oxford.

Hoelscher, T. 1990. "Römische Nobiles und hellenistische Herrscher." *Akten des XIII. internationalen Kongresses für klassische Archäologie Berlin 1988*. Mainz. 73–84.

Homo, L. 1951. *Rome impériale et l'urbanisme dans l'antiquité*. Paris.

Hopkins, K. 1978. *Conquerors and Slaves*. Cambridge.

Hudson, N. A. 1989. "Food in Roman Satire." In S. H. Braund, ed., *Satire and Society in Ancient Rome*. Exeter. 69–87.

Hunt, L. 1989. *The New Cultural History*. Berkeley and Los Angeles.

Hunt, L. ed. 1993. *The Invention of Pornography: Obscenity and the Origins of Modernity, 1500–1800*. New York.

Instinsky, H. U. 1964. "Schwurszene und *Coniuratio*." *Jahrbuch für Numismatik und Geldgeschichte*. 14:83–8.

Institut français de Naples, Centre Jean Bérard. 1983. *Les "bourgeoisies" municipales italiennes aux IIe et Ier siècles av. J.-C*. Colloques internationaux du Centre national de la recherche scientifique, 609. Naples.

Jacques, F. and Scheid, J. 1990. *Rome et l'intégration de l'Empire*. 2 vols. Paris.

Jameson, F. 1981. *The Political Unconscious: Narrative as a Socially Symbolic Act*. Ithaca.

Johns, C. 1982. *Sex or Symbol: Erotic Images of Greece and Rome*. Austin.

Johnson, W. R. 1982. *The Idea of Lyric: Lyric Modes in Ancient and Modern Poetry*. Berkeley.

Jones, A. R. 1991. "Reading City Women with Men." *Women's Studies* 19:239–49.

Jones, C. P. 1991. "Dinner Theater." In W. J. Slater, ed., *Dining in a Classical Context*. Ann Arbor. 185–98.

Kahn, B. M. 1987. *Cosmopolitan Culture: The Gilt-Edged Dream of a Tolerant City*. New York.

Kaster, R. A. 1988. *Guardians of Language. The Grammarian and Society in Late Antiquity*. Berkeley.

Katz, J. N. 1990. "The Invention of Heterosexuality." *Socialist Review* 20:17–33.
    1995. *The Invention of Heterosexuality*. New York.

Kellum, B. 1981. "Apollo vs. Hercules: The Temple of Apollo on the Palatine and the Battle of Actium." *AJA* 85:200.
    1985. "Sculptural Programs and Propaganda in Augustan Rome: The Temple of Apollo on the Palatine." In R. Winkes, ed., *The Age of Augustus*. Archeologia Transatlantica. 5:169–76.
    1990. "The City Adorned. Programmatic Display at the *Aedes Concordiae Augustae*." In K. Raaflaub and M. Toher, eds., *Between Republic and Empire*. Berkeley. 276–308.
    1994a. "The Construction of Landscape in Augustan Rome: The Garden Room at the Villa *ad Gallinas*." *The Art Bulletin*. 76.2:211–24.
    1994b. "What We See and What We Don't See. Narrative Structure and the Ara Pacis Augustae." *Art History* 17.1:26–45.
    1996. "The Phallus as Signifier: The Forum of Augustus and Rituals of Masculinity." In N. B. Kampen, ed., *Sexuality in Ancient Art*. New York. 170–83.

Kennedy, D. F. 1992. "'Augustan' and 'Anti-Augustan': Reflections on Terms of Reference." In A. Powell, ed., *Roman Poetry and Propaganda in the Age of Augustus*. Bristol. 26–57.
    1993. *The Arts of Love: Five Studies in the Discourse of Roman Love Elegy*. Cambridge.

Kennedy, G. 1972. *The Art of Rhetoric in the Roman World*. Princeton.

Keuls, E. 1993. *The Reign of the Phallus*. Berkeley. Reprint of New York 1985.

Knox, P. E. 1986. *Ovid's* Metamorphoses *and the Traditions of Augustan Poetry* (C. Phil. Soc. Supp. Vol. 11). Cambridge.

Kockel, V. 1983. "Beobachtungen zum Tempel des Mars Ultor und zum Forum des Augustus." *MDAI(R)* 90.2:421–48.

Koestermann, E. 1963. *Cornelius Tacitus. Annalen. Buch 1–3*. Heidelberg.

Konstan, D. 1986. "Narrative and Ideology in Livy: Book I." *CA* 5:198–216.

    1993. "Sexuality and Power in Juvenal's Second Satire." *LCM* 18:12–14.

    1994. *Sexual Symmetry: Love in the Ancient Novel and Related Genres*. Princeton.

Kraus, C. S. 1994. *Livy: Ab Urbe Condita, Book VI*. Cambridge.

Kunkel, W. 1952. *Herkunft und soziale Stellung der römischen Juristen*. Weimar.

Labate, M. 1981. *Quinto Orazio Flacco: Satire*. Milan.

    1984. *L'arte di farsi amare: Modelli culturali e progetto didascalico nell'elegia ovidiana*. Biblioteca di *MD* 2. Pisa.

Lacan, J. 1977. "The Signification of the Phallus." In *Ecrits*. Tr. A. Sheridan. New York. 281–91.

Laffi, V. 1967. "Le iscrizioni relative all'introduzione nel 9 A.C. del nuovo calendario della provincia d'Asia." *Studi Classici e Orientali* 16:5–98.

Lancaster, R. 1992. *Life is Hard: Machismo, Danger, and the Intimacy of Power in Nicaragua*. Berkeley.

La Penna, A. 1950, 1951. "Properzio e i poeti latini dell'età aurea." *Maia* 3:209–36; 4:43–69.

    1962. "Esiodo nella cultura e nella poesia di Virgilio." *Entretiens Hardt* 7:213–52.

    1977. *L'integrazione difficile*. Turin.

Laqueur, T. 1986. "Orgasm, Generation, and the Politics of Reproductive Biology." *Representations* 14:1–41.

    1990. *Making Sex: Body and Gender from the Greeks to Freud*. Cambridge, Mass.

La Rocca, E. 1985. *Amazzonomachia. Le sculture frontonali del tempio di Apollo Sosiano*. Rome.

Latte, K. 1960. *Römische Religionsgeschichte*. Munich.

Lauritsen, J. 1993. "Political–Economic Construction of Gay Male Clone Identity." *Journal of Homosexuality* 24:221–32.

Leach, E. W. 1971. "Horace's *Pater Optimus* and Terence's Demea: Autobiographical Fiction and Comedy in *Serm*. 1.4." *AJP* 92:616–32.

Leeman, A. D. 1961. "Are We Fair to Livy? Some Thoughts on Livy's Prologue." *Helikon* 1:28–39.

    1963. *Orationis Ratio*. Amsterdam.

Leopold, H. M. R. 1936. "Roma quale la vide Orazio." *Mnemosyne* 4:129–42.

Levi, M. 1986. *Augusto e il suo tempo*. Milan.

Ling, R. 1990. "Street Plaques in Pompeii." In *Architecture and Architectural Sculpture in the Roman Empire*. Oxford. Oxford University Committee for Archaeology, monograph 29:51–66.

Lintott, A. W. 1972. "Imperial Expansion and Moral Decline in the Roman Empire." *Historia* 31:626–38.

Lockyer, C. W. 1970. *The Fiction of Memory and the Use of Written Sources: Convention and Practice in Seneca the Elder and Other Authors*. Diss. Princeton.

Lonie, I. M. 1981. *The Hippocratic Treatises "On Generation" "On the Nature of the Child" "Diseases IV"*. Berlin.

Luce, T. J. 1990. "Livy, Augustus and the *Forum Augustum*." In K. Raaflaub and M. Toher, eds., *Between Republic and Empire*. Berkeley. 123–38.

Luisi, A. 1987. "Significato politico di 'confine' in Orazio e Virgilio." *Invigilata Lucernis* 9:89–102.

Lyne, R. O. A. M. 1995. *Horace: Behind the Public Poetry*. New Haven.

Malherbe, A. 1977. *The Cynic Epistles: A Study Edition*. Sources for Biblical Study 12. Missoula, Montana.

Marder, T. A. 1979. "Context for Claude-Nicholas Ledoux's Oikema." *Arts* 54.1: 174–6.

Marouzeau, J. 1962. *Traité de stylistique latine*. Fourth edition. Paris.

Martindale, C. A. 1993a. "Introduction," in C. A. Martindale and D. Hopkins, eds., *Horace Made New: Horatian Influences on British Writing from the Renaissance to the Twentieth Century*, Cambridge. 1–26.

  1993b. *Redeeming the Text: Latin poetry and the hermeneutics of reception.* Cambridge.

Mastrocinque, A. 1988. *"Lucio Giunio Bruto: Ricerche di storia, religione e diritto sulle origini della repubblica romana."* Trento.

Mauss, M. 1950. *Essai sur le don*. Paris.

McGushin, P. 1977. *Bellum Catilinum: A Commentary* (= *Mnemosyne Supplementum* 45). Leiden.

McKeown, J. C. 1987, 1989. *Ovid Amores. Text, Prolegomena and Commentary.* 2 vols. Leeds.

Meier, C. 1966. *Res Publica Amissa. Eine Studie zur Verfassung und Geschichte der späten römischen Republik.* Wiesbaden.

Michels, A. K. 1967. *The Calendar of the Roman Republic*. Princeton.

Mielsch, H. 1987. *Die römische Villa: Architektur und Lebensform*. Munich.

Miles, G. B. 1995. *Livy: Reconstructing Early Rome*. Ithaca.

Millar, F. and Segal, E. 1984. *Caesar Augustus: Seven Aspects*. Oxford.

Milligan, Don. 1993. *Sex-life*. London and Boulder, Colorado.

Mirmont, H. de la Ville de 1912. "Les déclamateurs espagnols au temps d'Auguste et de Tibère." *Bulletin Hispanique* 14:229–43.

Mommsen, T. 1887–88. *Römisches Staatsrecht*. 3 vols. Leipzig.

  1889. *Römisches Strafrecht*. Leipzig.

Moore, T. J. 1989. *Artistry and Ideology: Livy's Vocabulary of Virtue*. (Beiträge zur klassischen Philologie 192) Frankfurt am Main.

Moulton, C. 1973. "Ovid as Anti-Augustan: *Met*. 15.843–79." *CW* 67:4–7.

Murray, K. M. E. 1977. *Caught in the Web of Words. James A. H. Murray and the Oxford English Dictionary*. New Haven and London.

Murray, O. 1985. "Symposium and Genre in the Poetry of Horace," *JRS* 86:39–50.

Myerowitz, Molly. 1992. "Domestication of Desire: Ovid's *Parva Tabella* and the Theater of Love." In A. Richlin, ed., *Pornography and Representation in Greece and Rome*. New York. 131–57.

Myers, K. S. 1994. *Ovid's Causes. Cosmogony and Aetiology in the* Metamorphoses. Ann Arbor.

Mynors, R. A. B. 1990. *Virgil*, Georgics. Oxford.

Nagle, B. R. 1980. *The Poetics of Exile: Program and Polemic in the* Tristia *and* Epistulae ex Ponto *of Ovid*. Brussels.

Nagy, G. 1994. "Copies and Models in Horace *Odes* 4.1. and 4.2." *CW* 87:415–26.

Nicolet, C. 1988. *The World of the Citizen in Republican Rome*. Berkeley. Originally published as *Le métier de citoyen dans la Rome règublicaine*. Paris 1976.

1991. *Space, Geography, and Politics in the Early Roman Empire*. Ann Arbor. Originally published as *L'inventaire du monde: gèographie et politique aux origines de l'Empire romain*. Paris 1988. Ann Arbor.

Nippel, W. 1984. "Policing Rome." *JRS* 74:20–29.

Nisbet, R. M. G. and Hubbard, M. 1970. *A Commentary on Horace: Odes. Book One*. Oxford.

1978. *A Commentary on Horace: Odes. Book Two*. Oxford.

North, J. A. 1989. "The Roman Counter-Revolution." *JRS* 79:151–6.

O'Connor, J. F. 1990. "Horace's *Cena Nasidieni* and Poetry's Feast." *CJ* 86:23–34.

Ogilvie, R. M. 1965. *A Commentary on Livy, Books 1–5*. Oxford.

Oliensis, Ellen. 1995. "Life after Publication: Horace, *Epistles* 1.20." *Arethusa* 28: 209–24.

Oliver, J. H. 1953. *The Ruling Power. Trans. Amer. Philos. Soc*. n.s. 43.4. Philadelphia.

Ostrow, S. E. 1990. "The *Augustales* in the Augustan Scheme." In K. Raaflaub and M. Toher, eds., *Between Republic and Empire*. Berkeley. 364–79.

Parker, H. N. 1992. "Love's Body Anatomized: The Ancient Erotic Handbooks and the Rhetoric of Sexuality." In A. Richlin, ed., *Pornography and Representation in Greece and Rome*. New York. 90–111.

Palmer, L. R. 1954. *The Latin Language*. London.

Paul, G. M. 1982. "*Urbs Capta*: A Sketch of an Ancient Literary Motif." *Phoenix* 36:144–55.

Pease, A. S. 1920. *M. Tulli Ciceronis* De Divinatione liber primus. Urbana.

1923. *M. Tulli Ciceronis* De Divinatione liber secundus. Urbana.

Pennacini, A. 1989. "L'arte della parola." *Lo spazio letterario di Roma antica* 2: 254–67.

Perkell, C. 1989. *The Poet's Truth. A Study of the Poet in Virgil's* Georgics. Berkeley.

Petersmann, M. 1976. *Die Apotheosen in den Metamorphosen Ovids*. Diss. Graz.

Phillips, J. E. 1979. "Livy and the Beginning of a New Society." *CB* 55:87–92.

Pillinger, H. E. 1969. "Callimachean Influences on Propertius." *HSCP* 73:171–99.

Pitt-Rivers, Julian. 1966. "Honour and Social Status." In J. G. Peristiany, ed., *Honour and Shame: The Values of Mediterranean Society*. Chicago. 21–77.

Plumpe, J. C. 1932. *Wesen und Wirkung der Auctoritas Maiorum bei Cicero*. Munster.

Pokrowskij, M. 1907–1910. "Neue Beiträge zur Charakteristik Ovids." *Philologus* suppl. 11:353–404.

Pounds, N. 1994. *The Culture of the English People*. Cambridge.

Powell, A. 1992. "The Embarrassments of Augustus" in A. Powell, ed., *Roman Poetry and Propaganda in the Age of Augustus*. Bristol. 141–74.

Primmer, A. 1983. "Ovids Metamorphosen in neuer Sicht." *Wiener humanistische Blätter* 25:15–38.

Purcell, N. 1983. "The *Apparitores*: A Study in Social Mobility." *Papers of the British School at Rome* 51:125–73.

Quinn, K. 1980. *Horace: The Odes, edited with an Introduction and Commentary*. London.

1982. "The Poet and his Audience." *ANRW* II.30.1:155–58.

Radke, G. 1990. *Fasti romani: Betrachtungen zur Frühgeschichte des römischen Kalenders*. (Orbis antiquus 31). Munster.

Rawson, E. D. 1976. "The Ciceronian Aristocracy and its Properties." In M. I. Finley, ed., *Studies in Roman Property*. Cambridge. 85–102.

1985. *Intellectual Life in the Late Roman Republic*. London and Baltimore.

Rech, H. 1936. *Mos Maiorum. Wesen und Wirkung der Tradition in Rom*. Marburg.

Reutersvard, O. 1971. *The Neo-Classic Temple of Virility and the Buildings with a Phallic Shaped Ground-Plan*. Lund.

Richardson, L. P. 1992. *A New Topographical Dictionary of Ancient Rome*. Baltimore.

Richlin, A. 1981. "Approaches to the Sources on Adultery at Rome." In Helene Foley, ed., *Reflections of Women in Antiquity*. New York. 379–404.

1992. Introduction to re-issue of *The Garden of Priapus*. Oxford.

1993. "Not Before Homosexuality." *Journal of the History of Sexuality* 3:523–73.

Roloff, H. 1937. *Maiores bei Cicero*. Leipzig.

Ross, D. O. Jr. 1987. *Virgil's Elements. Physics and Poetry in the* Georgics. Princeton.

Rudd, N. 1976. *Lines of Enquiry: Studies in Latin Poetry*. Bristol.

1982. *The Satires of Horace*. Berkeley.

1986. *Themes in Roman Satire*. Norman.

Rudd, N., trans. 1979. *Horace: Satires and Epistles; Persius: Satires*. New York.

Saller, R. P. 1988. "*Pietas*, Obligation, and Authority in the Roman Family." In P. Kneissl and V. Losemann, eds., *Alte Geschichte und Wissenschaftsgeschichte: Festschrift für Karl Christ zum 65. Geburtstag*. Darmstadt. 393–410.

Samuel, A. E. 1972. *Greek and Roman Chronology*. Berlin.

Santirocco, M., 1987. *Unity and Design in Horace's Odes*. Chapel Hill.

Sauron, G. 1981. "Aspects du néo-atticisme à la fin du Ier siècle avant J.-C.: formes et symboles." In *L'Art décoratif à Rome à la fin de la république et au début du principat*. Collection de l'école française de Rome, 55. Rome.

Scafuro, A. 1989. "Livy's Comic Narrative of the Bacchanalia." *Helios* 16:119–42.

Schiesaro, A. 1993. "Il destinatario discreto. Funzioni didascaliche e progetto culturale nelle *Georgiche*." *MD* 31:129–47.

Schmitzer, U. 1990. *Zeitgeschichte in Ovids Metamorphosen. Mythologische Dichtung unter politischem Anspruch*. Stuttgart.

Schofield, M. 1986. "Cicero for and against Divination." *JRS* 76:47–65.

Schork, R. J. 1986. "The Final Simile in the *Aeneid*: Roman and Rutulian Ramparts." *AJPh*. 107:260–71.

Schrijvers, P. H. 1992. Response to H. P. Syndikus. In W. Ludwig, ed., *Horace*. Fondation Hardt: Entretiens 39: 254–5. Geneva.

Schulz, F. 1946. *History of Roman Legal Science*. Oxford.

Schutz, M. 1990. "Zur Sonnenuhr des Augustus auf dem Marsfeld." *Gymnasium* 97:432–57.

Scivoletto, N. 1981. "La città di Roma nella poesia di Properzio." *Colloquium Propertianum* (Acc. prop. del Subasio). Assisi. 27–38.

Scott, J. W. 1986. "Gender: A Useful Category of Historical Analysis." *AHR* 91.5: 1053–75.

Scullard, H. H. 1981. *Festivals and Ceremonies of the Roman Republic*. London.

Selden, D. 1942. "*Ceveat lector*: Catullus and the Rhetoric of Performance." In R. Hexter and D. Selden, eds., *Innovations of Antiquity*. New York. 461–512.

Serres, M. 1982. *The Parasite*. Trans. L. R. Schehr. Baltimore.

Setaioli, A. 1975. "Un influsso ciceroniano in Virgilio." *SIFC* n.s. 47:5–26.

Sherwin-White, A. N. 1973. *The Roman Citizenship*. 2nd edn. Oxford.

Skutsch, O. 1985. *The* Annals *of Q. Ennius.* Oxford.

Solmsen, F. 1961. "Propertius and his Literary Relations with Tibullus and Vergil." *Philol.* 105:273–89.

Solodow, J. B. 1977. "Ovid's *Ars Amatoria*: The Lover as Cultural Ideal." *Wiener Studien* n.f. 11:106–27.

Sommariva, G. 1980. "La parodia di Lucrezio nell'*Ars* e nei *Remedia* ovidiani." *Atene e Roma* 25:123–48.

Soubiran, J. 1989. "Autour de Numa (Ovide, Métamorphoses XV)." *Vita Latina* 113: 11–17.

Stewart, Z. 1953. "Sejanus, Gaetulicus, and Seneca." *AJP* 74:70–85.

Strazzulla, M. J. 1990. *Il principato di Apollo. Mito e propaganda nelle lastre 'Campana' dal tempio di Apollo Palatino.* Rome.

Stroh, W. 1979. "Ovids Liebeskunst und die Ehegesetze des Augustus." *Gymnasium* 86:323–52.

Svenbro, J. 1988. *Phrasikleia: Anthropologie de la lecture en Grèce ancienne.* Paris.

Syme, R. 1939. *The Roman Revolution.* Oxford.

1958. *Tacitus.* Oxford.

1959. "Livy and Augustus." *HSCP* 64:27–87.

1970. *Ten Studies in Tacitus.* Oxford.

1978. *History in Ovid.* Oxford.

1984. "The Crisis of 2 BC" In *Roman Papers,* vol. iii. 912–36. Oxford.

1986. *The Augustan Aristocracy.* Oxford.

Taylor, L. R. 1949. *Party Politics in the Age of Caesar.* Berkeley.

Thomas, R. F. 1988. *Virgil,* Georgics. Cambridge.

Thomas, Y. 1984a. "*Vitae necisque potestas*: Le père, la cité, la mort." In *Du châtiment dans la cité (Collection de l'école française de Rome* 79). Rome. 499–548.

1984b. "Se venger au forum: solidarité familiale et procès criminel à Rome." In R. Verdier and J.-P. Poly eds., *La vengeance: Vengeance, pouvoirs et idéologies dans quelques civilisations de l'antiquité.* Paris. 65–100.

Thompson, E. P. 1963. *The Making of the English Working Class.* London.

Timpanaro, S. 1988. Cicerone, *La Divinazione.* Milan.

Tränkle, H. 1965. "Der Anfang des römischen Freistaats in der Darstellung des Livius." *Hermes* 93:311–37.

Vallette-Cagnac, E. 1993. *Anthropologie de la lecture dans la Rome antique.* Diss., Paris.

Vasaly, A. 1993. *Representations: Images of the World in Ciceronian Oratory.* Berkeley.

Veyne, P. 1978. "La famille et l'amour sous le Haut-Empire romain." In *Annales E.S.C.* 35–63.

1979. "The Hellenization of Rome and the Question of Acculturations." *Diogenes* 106:1–27.

1982. "L'homosexualité à Rome." In *Sexualités occidentales.* Paris.

Vidler, A. 1990. *Claude-Nicolas Ledoux.* Cambridge, Mass.

Walbank, F. W. 1960. "History and Tragedy." *Historia* 9:216–34.

Wallace-Hadrill, A. 1981. "Family and Inheritance in the Augustan Marriage-Laws." *PCPhS* 207:58–80.

1987. "Time for Augustus: Ovid, Augustus and the Fasti." In M. Whitby, P. Hardie, and M. Whitby, eds., *Homo Viator. Classical Essays for John Bramble.* Bristol. 221–30.

1989. "Rome's Cultural Revolution." (Review article on P. Zanker, *The Power of Images in Augustan Rome*.) *JRS* 79:157–64.

Weeber, K. 1978. "Prop. 4.1.1–70 und das 8. Buch der Aeneis." *Latomus* 37:489–506.

Weeks, J. 1989. *Sex, Politics and Society: The Regulation of Sexuality Since 1800*. Revised edition. London.

White, K. 1993. *The First Sexual Revolution: The Emergence of Male Heterosexuality in Modern America*. New York.

White, P. 1988. "Julius Caesar in Augustan Rome." *Phoenix* 42:334–56.

1993. *Promised Verse: Poets in the Society of Augustan Rome*. Cambridge, Mass. and London.

Williams, G. 1995a. *"Libertino Patre Natus*: True or False?" In S. J. Harrison, ed., *Homage to Horace*. Oxford. 296–313.

1995b. "Postumus, Curtius Postumus, and Rabirius Postumus." *CP* 90:151–60.

Williams, R. 1958. *Culture and Society*. London.

1980. *The Sociology of Culture*. New York.

1982. *The Sociology of Culture*. New York.

1983. *Keywords: A Vocabulary of Culture and Society*. Revised edition. London.

Winterbottom, M. 1974. *The Elder Seneca. Declamations I and II*. Cambridge, Mass. and London.

Wirszubski, C. 1950. *Libertas as a Political Ideal at Rome During the Late Republic and Early Principate*. Cambridge.

Wiseman, T. P. 1978. "Flavians on the Capitol." *AJAH* 3:163–78.

1985. *Catullus and his World: A Reappraisal*. Cambridge.

Woodman, T. 1992. "Nero's Alien Capital." In T. Woodman and J. Powell, eds., *Author and Audience in Latin Literature*. Cambridge. 173–88.

Yavetz, Z. 1984. "The *Res Gestae* and Augustus' Public Image." In F. Millar and E. Segal, eds., *Caesar Augustus: Seven Aspects*. Oxford. 1–36.

Zanker, P. 1968. *Forum Augustum*. Tübingen.

1976. *Hellenismus im Mittelitalien: Kolloquium in Göttingen von 5. bis 9. Juni 1974*. 2 vols. Göttingen.

1983. "Der Apollontempel auf dem Palatin." in *Città e architettura nella Roma imperiale*. Analecta Romana Instituti Danici 10. Copenhagen. 21–40.

1988a. *The Power of Images in the Age of Augustus*. Trans. H. A. Shapiro. Ann Arbor.

1988b. "Bilderzwang: Augustan Political Symbolism in the Private Sphere." In P. Zanker, S. Walker, and R. Gordon eds., *Image and Mystery in the Roman World: Papers given in memory of Jocelyn Toynbee*. Gloucester. 1–13.

Zeitlin, F. 1971. "Romanus Petronius." *Latomus* 30:58–82.

Zetzel, J. E. G. 1980. "Horace's *Liber Sermonum*: The Structure of Ambiguity." *Arethusa* 13:59–77.

1982. "The Poetics of Patronage in the Late First Century B.C." In B. Gold, ed., *Literary and Artistic Patronage in Ancient Rome*. Austin. 87–102.

Zumwalt, N. 1977. *"Fama subversa*: Theme and Structure in Ovid *Metamorphoses* 12." *CSCA* 10:210–22.

Index of passages cited

Index of subjects and proper names

Achilles, 194–5
actio, 44
Actium, battle of (31 BCE), 107n, 122, 125,
    160–1, 163, 180; parody of, 163–4
adultery, 28–30; in declamation, 213; in
    poetry of Ovid, 40; *see also* Augustan
    moral legislation
Aeneas, 173, 176, 196; caricature of, 174–6
aestimatio, 39
aetiology, 184–5, 198
agricultural crisis, 116–17
Agrippa (Marcus Vipsanius Agrippa), consul
    37 BCE, 107, 203
Alexandria, 26, 122
amicitia, 52–3, 59, 98, 120, 200n, 210
analogy, 18, 86–7
anomaly, 18
antiquarianism, 13n, 14, 20, 185
Antony (Marcus Antonius), triumvir, 161,
    163, 179
Apollo Actius, 36n
Apollo Sosianus, 161–3
apotheosis, 189–91, 193n
Ara Pacis, 105, 156
Aristaeus, 65–8
Asianism, 10, 209
Atticism, 10
auctoritas, 11
Augustan moral legislation: aims of, 5, 9,
    176–7, 180; and Livy, 154; removes
    sexual behavior from familial context,
    28–30
Augustus (Gaius Iulius Caesar Octavianus),
    emperor: addicted to dice, 175; and
    antiquarianism, 185; architectural aims
    of, 134, 166–7; and barbarians, 167–8;
    as *cinaedus*, 178–9; as critic of
    literature, 204, 207–8; in Horace's
    poetry, 93, 121; military career of,
    120n, 163; in Ovid's poetry, 191–4; as
    patron, 96n; precarious health of, 110;
    purported republicanism of, 52; as

reformer of *mores*, 4–6, 9–12; as
    sacrificant, 156; in Virgil's poetry, 80,
    88; other mentions of, 16, 21, 188, 197
aurea mediocritas, 111
authority, xx, 7, 11–12, 190–3; moral, 91n;
    of the *nobiles*, 13, 19, 136; paternal,
    213; relocation of, xvii, 12–22, 110; of
    Roman history, 185

bankruptcy, 92
belief in gods, 71–6, 84–5
bougonia, 64n, 65
bourgeoisie, 4–6
Bucolics, public performance of, 46n
bulla, 39, 166, 171
bumbling, 96

Caesar (Gaius Iulius Caesar), dictator: adoptive
    father of Augustus, 193; death of, 197;
    and declaimers, 208–9; deification of,
    191–4; as grammarian, 18–19
calendar, reform of, 16–17
Campus Martius, 44, 105–9, 122
capitalism, 42
Capitoline (mons Capitolinus), 109, 130
caritas, 141, 144
carpe diem, 111
Caryatids, 167–8
Cassius Severus, orator, 179, 203, 205, 207
Catullus (Gaius Valerius Catullus), poet:
    alienation of, 28, 43; on homosociality,
    38; on sexual activity, 27–8, 38–40
causa, 81–2
Cicero (Marcus Tullius Cicero) orator,
    philosopher, consul 63 BCE: cultural
    theories of, 8; death of, 190n; on fall of
    republic, 21; on history of oratory,
    201–2; as model for declaimers, 201,
    209, 211; praise of Varro by, 13; as
    understood by Virgil, 78–80
Cicero, Quintus (Quintus Tullius Cicero),
    praetor 62 BCE, 73–4

235